John Bartlow Martin

John Bartlow Martin

A Voice for the Underdog

Ray E. Boomhower

INDIANA UNIVERSITY PRESS

Bloomington & Indianapolis

This book is a publication of

INDIANA UNIVERSITY PRESS
Office of Scholarly Publishing
Herman B Wells Library 350
1320 East 10th Street
Bloomington, Indiana 47405 USA

iupress.indiana.edu

The paper used in this publication
meets the minimum requirements of
the American National Standard for
Information Sciences – Permanence of
Paper for Printed Library Materials,
ANSI Z39.48–1992.

Manufactured in the
United States of America

*Library of Congress
Cataloging-in-Publication Data*

Boomhower, Ray E., [date]
 John Bartlow Martin : a voice for the
underdog / Ray E. Boomhower.
  pages cm
 Includes bibliographical references and
index.
  ISBN 978-0-253-01614-0 (cloth : alk.
paper) – ISBN 978-0-253-01618-8 (ebook)
1. Martin, John Bartlow, 1915–1987.
2. Authors, American – 20th century –
Biography. 3. Journalists – United States –
Biography 4. Speechwriters – United
States – Biography. 5. United States –
Politics and government – 1945–1989.
I. Title.
  PS3525.A7525Z59 2015
  818'.5409 – dc23
  [B]
                          2014036943

1 2 3 4 5   20 19 18 17 16 15

Dedicated to the memory of my father, Raymond Walter Boomhower, who always believed in me. He is missed.

A professional writer cannot, like a teacher, be dull and be protected in his dullness. He must recapture his audience with every new start. He must be fascinating, bright, or pontifical, he must impress, charm, amuse, inform.

WALLACE STEGNER

The freelance writer is a man who is paid per piece or per word or perhaps.

ROBERT BENCHLEY

Contents

Preface

COLONEL ROBERT R. MCCORMICK OF THE *CHICAGO TRIBUNE* AND
Eleanor "Cissy" Patterson of the *Washington Times-Herald* were not only
cousins, but publishers that held enormous sway as isolationists warning against American involvement in World War II. In 1979 their stories
were told in separate biographies, McCormick by Joseph Gies and Patterson by Ralph G. Martin. Considering the books, a reviewer in the
September 30, 1979, issue of the *Tribune* used the opportunity to muse
on the endless difficulties involved in writing a biography. "Too much
detail will bore the reader, too little will disappoint him. To what extent
should the author act as an advocate of his subject? To what extent a
critic?" the reviewer asked. "How is he to make his subject come alive,
to breathe? How can he answer the terrible question: What made him
the man he was? How much of his private life as well as his public life to
include? What, aside from the laws of libel and invasion of privacy, sets
limits? Taste? But whose taste? The biographer's obviously; but this is a
grave responsibility."

The reviewer, John Bartlow Martin, was no stranger to the field, as
just a few years before he had produced the definitive two-volume biography of former Illinois governor and two-time Democratic presidential
candidate Adlai E. Stevenson. To Martin, the authors of the McCormick
and Patterson biographies had failed to make their subjects come alive
for their readers. The works on the newspaper titans paled in comparison to writers he believed had admirably surmounted the difficulties he
had posed for crafting a biography – Arthur M. Schlesinger Jr. in *Robert
Kennedy and His Times* and William Manchester in his biography of

General Douglas MacArthur, *American Caesar* (both favorites of this author as well).

I came across Martin's questions for biographers early on in my research for the biography that follows, and kept them in mind as I wrote the book, realizing the "grave responsibility" any biographer has in detailing the life of his subject. My introduction to Martin happened early in my career at the Indiana Historical Society, where I have worked since 1987. His classic *Indiana: An Interpretation,* originally published in 1947 and republished in 1992 by Indiana University Press, greatly influenced my thinking about the state's past and future. As a former reporter turned historian, as Martin had been, I aspired to reach and inspire an audience as well as he had done during his heyday, and promised myself that one day I would write his biography. I took tentative steps at fulfilling this promise with an article on Martin in the spring 1997 issue of the IHS's popular history magazine *Traces of Indiana and Midwestern History,* and with detailing his prominent role in Robert F. Kennedy's run for the Democratic presidential nomination in my book *Robert F. Kennedy and the 1968 Indiana Primary,* published by Indiana University Press in 2008.

It has been quite a journey. Along the way I received helpful guidance from such dedicated professionals as the staff at the Manuscripts Division of the Library of Congress in Washington, D.C.; Janet C. Olson at the Northwestern University Archives in Evanston, Illinois; Marcus Robyns and and Glenda Ward at the Central Upper Michigan Peninsula and Northern Michigan University Archives, Marquette, Michigan; and Susan L. S. Sutton at the Indiana Historical Society William Henry Smith Memorial Library in Indianapolis, Indiana. In addition, Jasminn Winters at the Library of Congress proved invaluable when it came to obtaining reproductions of images from Martin's papers for use in the book.

Dan Carpenter, former columnist for the *Indianapolis Star,* provided helpful suggestions for improving the book both early on and late in the process. At Indiana University Press, Linda Oblack, Sarah Jacobi, and Michelle Sybert provided patience and understanding, both sorely needed whenever a book is shepherded into print.

Although not an authorized biography, this book would not have been possible without the support and encouragement of Martin's three children – Cindy, Dan, and Fred. They were tireless in answering questions I had about their parents' lives, and they corrected errors without interfering with my interpretations of what happened. Cindy served as an indefatigable tour guide of Martin's haunts in Michigan's Upper Peninsula, taking me to her family's former cabin at Three Lakes and allowing me to visit the camp at Smith Lake. She also shared family photographs and made sure I saw Martin's portable Remington Rand typewriter as well as the rubber stamps he had made for use in commenting on his student's papers while teaching at Northwestern University's Medill School of Journalism.

In talking with Cindy, Dan, and Fred, I was delighted to learn how much of a role their mother, Fran, played in Martin's writing career. It was another connection between subject and author, as my wife, Megan McKee, has been a part of every book I have written, offering wise counsel and invaluable editing. She has always been, to borrow a statement Martin made about Fran, "just wonderful."

Acknowledgments

PORTIONS OF THIS BOOK PREVIOUSLY APPEARED IN THE SPRING 1997 issue of the Indiana Historical Society publication *Traces of Indiana and Midwestern History* and in my book *Robert F. Kennedy and the 1968 Indiana Primary* (IUP, 2008).

John Bartlow Martin

ONE

The Responsible Reporter

THE BODIES BEGAN COMING UP FROM DEEP WITHIN THE BOWELS of the earth days after the first explosion at the Centralia coal mine on March 25, 1947. Members of the Illinois prairie community of Centralia began hearing about how an explosive charge meant to dislodge coal had ignited the unstable coal dust permeating the air more than five hundred feet below ground at the mine south of town in Wamac. The wives of the miners whose fate was not yet known gathered at the washhouse – the place where during the workweek their husbands changed out of their grimy, coal-streaked clothes at the end of their shifts. Avoiding the rescue teams wearing their oxygen tanks and "other awkward paraphernalia of disaster," the women gravitated toward sitting beneath their loved ones' clothing, settling in for the long wait to learn about their men's fate.[1]

Friends and relatives of the trapped men gathered outside in the cold near the mouth of the mine hoping to hear any news. One was a young Illinois college student named Bill Niepoetter, who worried about his father, Henry, and three other relatives. "One rescue worker would come up and say, 'It's bad, there are not going to be any survivors,'" Niepoetter said. "The next one would come up and say, 'It's not going to be as bad.' We had no notion." Helplessness set in as Niepoetter viewed rescue workers emerging from the mine without any survivors. "They'd come up and you could see from their faces that this was not going to be a good week," he said. Those miners not killed outright by the blast were poisoned by the carbon monoxide and carbon dioxide left behind in the atmosphere. Ambulances from Centralia and nearby towns idled their engines in the cold night air in an attempt by the men inside to keep warm as they waited to be called upon to transport the deceased to the local Greyhound bus station, which officials had converted into a temporary morgue. As a shiny limousine drove away from the mine, taking with it one of the 111 men killed in the disaster, a friend of the deceased, standing with others in the crowd, remarked, "I bet it's the only time he ever rode in a Cadillac." Four days after the blast, Niepoetter, who had gone to his grandmother's house, learned that his father had been one of the victims. He had already made arrangements for a funeral. "Good thing I did – they sold a lot of caskets," he said, recalling that for several days funeral processions made their solemn way down the road leading to the cemetery.[2]

A year after the blast at Centralia, *Harper's* magazine offered its readers the usual literate blend of fact and fiction. The March 1948 issue included a poem from John Ciardi titled "Hawk," a feature from William Harlan Hale on former vice president Henry Wallace's independent presidential campaign, and a report by Eric Bentley on the previous year's theatrical offerings. The bulk of the issue, however, twenty-eight pages, was reserved for a lengthy examination of the Centralia tragedy. The story, written by freelance writer John Bartlow Martin and titled "The Blast in Centralia No. 5: A Mine Disaster No One Stopped," was written in spite of threats of violence against him made by mining officials and was praised by the *Harper's* editors as a "top-notch reporting job, to be compared . . . with John Hersey's 'Hiroshima.'" It shocked the nation. Illustrated with twenty-four drawings by social-realist artist Ben Shahn, the story, the longest ever printed in *Harper's* in its approximately hundred-year history, told about the helpless miners and their struggle to save their lives, only to come face to face with an uncaring government bureaucracy, lackadaisical union officials, and greedy mine owners more concerned about profits than their workers' lives. When Driscoll O. Scanlan, a state mine safety inspector, warned his supervisor, Robert M. Medill, that conditions were so bad at the Centralia mine that an explosion might sweep through it and kill everyone underground, Medill, according to Scanlan, had replied, "We will just have to take that chance." Later reprinted in condensed form in *Reader's Digest,* a magazine with the largest paid circulation in the world, the article played a major role in bringing about the downfall of Illinois's Republican governor Dwight Green and electing Democrat Adlai E. Stevenson. The federal government also stepped in and enacted a stricter safety code for mines. Martin, however, offered his readers scant hope that a similar disaster might not befall another mining community in the future. He remembered the somber words of a young miner he met sipping a beer at a saloon in a neighboring town:

> "I got a wife and one kid. It takes a lot of money to raise kids. Where else could I make thirteen-o-five a day? The railroads pay eight, nine dollars. And that's all there is around here." At a table in a corner a couple of old miners are arguing quietly, and behind the bar the lady bartender is listening sympathetically to a lady customer whose husband is always crabbing about what she cooks. The young miner says, "Sometimes I'd like to leave for good. But where'd I go? I don't know anything else. I don't know what hell you would call it. Well, it is life, in a way too. I just wish my life away, when I go below I just wish it was tomorrow. Wish my life away. And I guess the others are the same way, too."[3]

Only dimly aware of the disaster at first, Martin began his work on the Centralia explosion following a suggestion from Paul Palmer, a *Reader's Digest* editor he had previously worked with, who promised him a large fee ($2,500) and offered to pay his expenses (the *Digest* often planted stories in other magazines with small budgets, making their own arrangements with writers and then reprinting the article). Martin then broached the idea to an editor at *Harper's*, who agreed to read the article when it was finished. "I set forth . . . thinking, 'I've got a hell of a nerve, starting out single-handed, with nothing but my typewriter, to overthrow the political machine of the governor of Illinois,'" Martin recalled. To uncover what had happened at the mine, Martin, a former newspaper reporter, began his research in Saint Louis, Missouri. The *Saint Louis Post-Dispatch* had done yeoman work in exposing Green's failure to prevent the tragedy in spite of numerous warnings that dangerous conditions existed at the mine, including a large accumulation of volatile coal dust. For its efforts, the newspaper won the 1948 Pulitzer Prize for public service. "The *Post-Dispatch* editors gave me access to their files," Martin said. "They were proud of what they had done and well they should have been; they helped me, for they wanted the story told."[4]

From Saint Louis, Martin traveled the approximately sixty miles east to Centralia. The town of sixteen thousand looked nothing like Martin had expected it to be. Instead of a "dismal [coal] company town" like ones in West Virginia, Centralia had the look of a typical midwestern farming community: "wide main street lined with low flat-faced stores, sprawling railroad shops and the ungainly black coal-mine tipple on the edge of town." Martin began his work here by obtaining background information on the town itself, talking to farmers, local businessmen, and housewives. Only then did he begin interviewing those involved in the disaster, beginning with the miners and the miners' widows, because, as Martin noted, "they were the victims, the aggrieved, and would want the world to know. I did not want the story to turn into a debate among the powerful – Governor Green, and John L. Lewis of the UMWA [United Mine Workers of America], and the coal company. I wanted it to be the miners' story, the story of helpless ordinary people."[5]

One of the first miners Martin talked to was William Rowekamp, who as recording secretary of Local 52 of the UMWA had sent a two-page letter to the governor, typed while sitting at a cluttered oak desk in his living room, pleading for his help. While the letter praised Scanlan, calling him the "best inspector that ever came to our mine," it castigated his superiors at the Illinois Department of Mines and Minerals for their inaction. "In fact, Governor Green," the letter stated, "this is a plea to you, to please save our lives, to please make the department of mines and minerals enforce the laws at the No. 5 mine of the Centralia Coal Co.... before we have an explosion like just happened in Kentucky and West Virginia." In addition to Rowekamp, the three other men who signed the letter included Jake Schmidt, Local 52 president, and Thomas Bush and Elmer Moss of the union's mine committee; only Rowekamp survived the massive Centralia underground explosion, described by one expert as being like "a huge shotgun blast down a long corridor."[6]

Although taciturn by nature, Rowekamp soon began talking freely to Martin, telling him that some miners were worried enough to even tell their wives their fears about their safety. When he finished the interview, Martin asked the miner, as he always did at the end of an interview, if he knew of anyone else he should talk to, and Rowekamp gave him the names of other miners. "For the next few days," said Martin, "I went from one to another and I took to hanging around the bare upstairs union hall and they became so used to seeing me that they paid little heed, always what a reporter wants." He soon learned that the miners considered themselves a breed apart, superior to those who worked on farms or factories. "The danger they were always in was part of the fascination," noted Martin. "They were fierce fighters for their rights. They had a strong sense of being the underdog." Martin, who grew up during the Great Depression and saw his father lose his successful business, shared their underdog mentality, and that mind-set "remained a powerful force in my life and my writing."[7]

To bring the disaster home to his readers even more, Martin talked to the widow of one of the miners who died in the explosion, Mrs. Joe Bryant, a big, forty-four-year-old woman who had borne eleven children; two had died in infancy. Martin asked her to tell him everything about the day of the explosion, and while she did, several small children played around her legs, pulling on her dress in an effort to distract her. She shared with him a note her husband had scrawled on a page torn from a time book while he was trapped in a tunnel, waiting to die as the breathable air ran out. Bryant had written, "Dear Wife fro Give [forgive] me Please all love you Be shure and don't sign any Paper see Vic Ostero [a warning against signing away her compensation rights] My Dear wife good By." Funeral expenses had taken most of the compensation the widow had received from the union and other sources, and she could only expect payments of $44 a week for the next five years from the state's industrial compensation fund and Social Security. When Martin asked her who she blamed for the loss of her husband, she said, "I don't know nothin' about the mine, I wouldn't blame no one, accidents happen, seems like it just has to be."[8]

Driving away from the Bryant home on a dusty road, Martin turned his car for Springfield, the state capital, where he uncovered the second half of his story: politics and government bureaucracy. Martin got a lucky break. When he visited the offices of the Illinois Department of Mines and Minerals, he expected some foot dragging from its staff, but an employee on duty that day said Martin could go through all the files, as they had already been published during the various investigations into the Centralia explosion. "But it turned out they hadn't," Martin noted. "I found a mountain of paper accumulated over five years. Piled up, the evidence was devastating." He traced, almost hour by hour, the reports issued by Scanlan finding that the mine was dangerously dusty and warning that such conditions could lead to an explosion. Medill, the department's director, had not seen Scanlan's first thirteen reports; they were handled by his deputy, who read some but not all of the scathing reports. Form letters indicating the department agreed with Scanlan's findings were mailed to the Centralia mine company's Chicago office. "Not only did the company not comply with Scanlan's recommendations, it did not even bother to reply," said Martin. When federal mine inspections started in 1942, they found the same violations and made the same recommendations as had Scanlan. "The company ignored them too," said Martin, who spent days in the department's office making notes on "scores of federal and state inspection reports, correspondence, transcripts of the six hearings and investigations into the Centralia disaster." After interviewing Medill, whom he described as "a large jovial man with a loud blustery voice," at his home in Lake Springfield, Martin returned to the Illinois capital, where he talked to legislators, union officials, lobbyists, and coal operators. He tried, and failed, to interview Governor Green and Lewis.[9]

Martin was now ready to start writing his story, but he resisted the temptation to start. He had never forgotten the advice of a writer friend, W. Adolphe Roberts, the author of numerous historical novels, who Martin said had told him, "'We always send our stories in too soon,' before we've made them the best we can." Also, the story had become so "big and complex, jumbled up in my head, all disorganized and out of order," said Martin, that he had to take a few days off to fish in Upper Michigan, "trying not to think about Centralia, letting it marinate." It worked; driving back to his home in suburban Chicago he began to see the story unfold before him. "The principal elements were the town of Centralia, the miners, their union, the mine operators, and state and federal authorities," he said. "The story's impact would depend upon two things: bringing the characters alive, and piling up the evidence of the history of the disaster."[10]

Because he had such an abundance of research for his Centralia article, Martin abandoned his old system of organizing his material on three-by-five notecards. Instead, he went through his notes and documents, gave each a code number, and then numbered the pages. When he came across an item he wanted to use in the article, he typed it out, triple spaced, and keyed it to code and page numbers. "I then cut up the typing line by line into slips of paper," said Martin. "I moved the slips around, arranging and rearranging them." When he had all the slips arranged to his satisfaction, he pasted them together, resulting in a long scroll that he rolled up, placed on his typing table, and consulted as he began writing, letting the scroll fall to the floor as he worked. When he came to the end of the scroll, he had his rough draft finished. Martin eventually abandoned this system when, years later, one of his scrolls measured more than 150 feet long, "running out of my room and out the front door and across the lawn." He went back to organizing his research on note cards, this time using five-by-eight cards.[11]

A friend, reading a rough draft of Martin's story, told him, "If *Harper's* publishes this in anything like its present form, it'll make your reputation." At 18,500 words in rough-draft form, the article was the longest Martin had ever written. "What made it so long and what made it so powerful was the relentless documentation – I kept piling it up and piling it up and piling it up – showing that for years everybody had known the mine was going to blow up but nobody had stopped it," Martin recalled. When *Harper's* chief editor Frederick Lewis Allen read the story, he wrote Martin a long letter praising the writer's work and ended by saying, "The whole office is rocking with cheers." (Upon its publication Allen tried to have the story nominated for a Pulitzer Prize, but he discovered the journalism award had no magazine category.) After he had read Martin's manuscript, Shahn had called Russell Lynes, the editor at *Harper's* who had asked him to provide drawings for the article, at home to tell him he thought the article was "wonderful." Lynes added that when "Shahn says 'wonderful' it sounds as though he means it. The first syllable takes three times as long as the other two." The artist was so inspired by the tragedy that he produced sixty-four drawings, saying that once he started he felt compelled to keep on drawing. John D. Voelker, a bestselling author known best today for his novel *Anatomy of a Murder,* had met and became friends with Martin during his frequent vacations in the Upper Peninsula, where Voelker lived. Voelker called the Centralia story "a glorious piece of plain writing and of social detection and exposure." He expressed his amazement at how fair Martin could appear to be, and maybe was, in the article, but at the same time how he was able to "expose the wound in all its rawness. You can hit low so fast that even the victim doesn't know it."[12]

The Centralia story that cemented Martin's reputation as one of the country's finest freelance writers was just one in a score of serious non-fiction (Martin liked to use the term "heavy-fact") stories on national issues that he created on his busy Underwood typewriter over the years. With his ubiquitous horn-rimmed glasses, bow tie, and mild manner, Martin looked more like a schoolteacher or a laboratory technician than a nationally known writer. He believed more in hard work more than in talent, once commenting, "Hell, I'm just a reporter." The Indiana-raised writer had honed his observational skills as a gritty police, city hall, and rewrite reporter on the *Indianapolis Times* in the late 1930s and as a regular freelance contributor to such true-crime periodicals as *Official Detective Stories* and *Actual Detective Stories for Women in Crime*. In the 1940s and 1950s he progressed to having his work appear frequently in the "big slicks," the mass-circulation magazines printed on glossy paper with such famous names as the *Saturday Evening Post, Life, Look, Collier's, Esquire,* and *Harper's.* In the 1950s, before television decimated their ranks, these magazines were turning away from depending upon fiction to draw subscribers and instead were relying on nonfiction. They turned to freelancers such as Martin, and they quickly became, as *Collier's* editor Roger Dakin noted, "the backbone of the magazine industry." Martin transcended the conventions of the fact-detective magazine genre in his true-crime articles for national magazines and attempted to place the subject in its social context. He avoided "the artifices, the false suspense and phony emotion" of typical reporting about crime and tried to preserve "the narrative value of the stories rather than transforming them into dry case histories." What remained were powerful stories that eschewed any contrived suspense for "the suspense of fine inevitability," the type of suspense felt by those attending prizefights. "To me, waiting for this to happen is stronger than any contrived suspense could possibly be," said Martin. Crime became for him a way to write about "human beings and our society, a matrix, a prism through which one viewed life."[13]

Martin became one of but a select few freelancers in the country able to support his family, which included his wife, Fran, and three children, Cindy, Dan, and John Frederick (called Fred by his family) through his writing. A 1955 *Time* magazine article on the "ruggedly individualistic breed" of freelance writer estimated that out of the thousands who attempted to make a career in freelancing for magazines, only seventy or eighty managed a yearly salary of $10,000. "His idea of heaven was reaching a mass audience with a serious piece of writing or rhetoric," Fred said of his father. When the senior Martin hit his stride in his early freelance days writing stories for true-crime detective magazines, he churned out a million words a year, selling a third of them at two cents a word. By 1957 *Newsweek* magazine cited Martin as one of the highest paid freelance magazine writers in the country, estimating his income at $32,000 in a good year. "I like everything about free-lancing," said Martin, "with the exception of the lack of security. Sometimes it's four to six months between checks, and that creates problems for my grocer and everybody else." He made ends meet by juggling advances from publishers, securing loans from his bank, and borrowing money from his parents. Fred reflected that his father possessed "a bookkeeper's precision with money, was neither profligate nor cheap, denied himself nothing he wanted, saved well, and always worried about money." Martin also turned his lengthy magazine stories into books, publishing seventeen during his lifetime, but he seldom expected to achieve high sales figures. "I don't depend on books for my income," he once told a reporter, showing him a recent royalty check from an English book distributor for forty-nine cents. "If I did, I'd starve to death. Books are a luxury I can afford."[14]

In his writing for the big-slick magazines, Martin produced long, detailed drafts of his articles in a large downstairs bedroom he converted into his workroom at his Victorian home in the Chicago suburb of Highland Park, Illinois, and a cabin retreat he owned on Smith Lake in the Upper Peninsula of Michigan. When asked where he was from, however, Martin always responded, "I'm from Chicago," a city that often exasperated him, but for which he never lost his affection. Although invited several times to join the East Coast staffs of *Life* and the *Post* on a full-time basis, Martin preferred to remain in the place he knew best, the Midwest. As a freelance writer (a profession he once described as "champagne today, crackers and milk tomorrow"), staying in the area he knew so well gave him a tremendous advantage. "The Midwest was where things happened, it was, almost, the locomotive of America," Martin said. "And I as a writer almost had it all to myself, while in New York little happened and writers were scrambling all over each other." He treated his freelance career as though it was a regular job, working from nine in the morning until five in the evening, with a half-hour break for lunch, from Monday through Friday; he took Saturdays off and spent his time on Sundays dealing with correspondence and "other accumulated afflictions," as well as planning his work schedule for the upcoming week. Although during his teenage years Fred recalled lively talk in the house about politics, foreign affairs, social justice, and public policy matters, especially around the dinner table, his father seldom, if ever, discussed what writing project he might next tackle. "Like any writer," said Fred, "he was loath to talk about his writing as the piece was being formed."[15]

Pitching ideas to editors, and receiving suggestions from them, Martin did not cover breaking news, preferring instead to bide his time. "I won't touch a story when it first breaks because all the reporters are there, all asking questions trying to outdo each other," Martin explained. "After that's all over, I feel that I can get closer to it." Whenever he began his research, or "legwork" as he called it, Martin feared that the people he would be interviewing "knew so much" while he still knew so little about his assignment. Also, when he worked for a newspaper, he reasoned that he had the right to ask questions because a newspaper "had an inherent right to keep the public record," but as a magazine writer, he did not believe he had that same privilege. "The only way to cure my hesitancy was to master the facts – to study the public record until I knew more about the case than anybody directly involved," Martin said. One of his close friends described Martin as "fact obsessed." Spending anywhere from a few weeks to more than six months pursuing a story, he kept digging until he had all the facts he could gather, especially the human details that "made the bald facts real." Writing and editing were important to a story, he later said, but "in the end everything depends on reporting." A particular favorite reading material for Martin became the questions and answers taken down by court reporters, a profession he praised as having "the most competent, least appreciated, of men." Reflecting on those days, Martin expressed astonishment at his "energy and single-minded, almost relentless, devotion" to his work. "I was out of town more than I was home," he noted. There were times when he returned from a trip on a Saturday, repacked his suitcase, and left the next day on another assignment. Such commitment to his craft was necessary because a lot of bad reporting, he noted, stemmed from a writer's reliance on only a single source. A journalist writing about Martin during these busy freelance days described him as a "tall, thin man with glasses and a collegiate crew cut," and noticed that his pockets bulged with pencils and his briefcase was crammed full of railroad timetables, "the requisite of the roving writer."[16]

Digging for the facts necessary to construct his stories, Martin developed a few tricks of the trade for interviews. Whenever possible, he tried to talk to his subject at the subject's home, because the person would be "at ease there and the objects that surround him will suggest questions to you and remind him of details." Although he always used a notebook and spurned tape recorders, he usually kept the notebook out of sight when beginning an interview. To get it out of his pocket and start taking notes, Martin asked his subject a question requiring a number for an answer, such as, "when were you born?" "You should always try to establish an understanding, a sympathy even, with everyone you interview, even the villains; they're not totally evil, only human, and what you want to discover is why they behaved the way they did," he said. If a subject proved reluctant to talk, Martin often began relating his own experiences. "Tell him your story," he said, "pretty soon he'll likely tell you his." He preferred doing interviews face to face, not over the telephone, and always aimed at doing so for at least two hours "because you'll waste the first 45 minutes, you'll get your best stuff between then and 1½ hours, and you'll waste the last half hour." Martin realized he could not possibly collect all the facts on a subject, and even if it were possible nobody would publish the resulting story, as it would be too long. "A writer has to be selective," he said. "Complete objectivity is impossible. He'll pick the facts as he sees them and write them in the light of his own experience. That's really all he can do." Fred remembered his father's writing as being "lavish with facts, stingy with opinions," and filled with details.[17]

Despite often feeling apprehensive about flying, Martin usually went to his assignment via airplane, renting an automobile upon his arrival. He depended, however, upon hitting the pavement to get the material he needed. "If I'm doing a story on slums," he told one reporter, "the best thing to do is walk around. . . . Any story is made on the street." He pounded out rough drafts of his stories on a typewriter in his office, or "workshop" as he referred to it, at his home, never by longhand or by dictation. Usually starting his work at about 8:45 A M, Martin took a cup of tea with him into his office, closed the door, and worked until lunch, which often consisted of a bowl of consommé or consommé madrilène and a tuna fish sandwich. Martin wrote quickly, an average of fifty pages a day, sometimes finishing a story in the morning and starting another one that same afternoon. The room was often littered with notebooks, reference books, and memorandums dealing with the subject he was writing about. Dedicated to his craft, Martin barred his first child, his daughter Cindy, from entering his room when he was writing. That dictate relaxed in later years when his second child, Dan, was allowed to crawl in the room and remain if he stayed quiet, while Martin's youngest son, Fred, was "allowed to climb up on my lap and pretend to help" him write. Martin worked until nearly 5:00 P M. He never ended a day "written out, with nothing more to say." Instead, he made sure to finish by typing out a quarter or half page of notes about exactly what was coming next so the next morning he could take up where he had left off. Martin discovered that getting started on a story or a day's work was the hardest part of his job. In the evenings Fran read her husband's writing and offered her comments. "She was not reticent about making criticisms," Fred remembered. She also read aloud the near-final drafts (typed on goldenrod paper and called "the golden rod") of what Martin had written to catch "mistakes or infelicitous phrasing or something wrong with the structure that he caught more easily hearing than reading," noted Fred. "I believe that nearly every major thing he wrote was read out loud by her with him listening and holding a second copy which he marked up as she read."[18]

Writing in the days before computers, word processing, and the easy storage of information, Martin made sure to make a carbon copy of everything he wrote, especially his rough draft. He did not keep the copy in his house, but secured it elsewhere, always worried about what might happen if a fire – the ultimate "nightmare" for a writer – ever broke out. Martin knew of a writer who had worked on a novel for two years in a cabin in the Minnesota woods; the cabin burned down and with it the only copy of the novel. Tackling a rough draft of a story, Martin did what he called "heavy rewrite," moving sentences and paragraphs around until few if any sentences from his rough draft survived until the final draft. He tried to cut lines he was "especially pleased with, doing the real polished writing on rewrite, not rough – in spite of all this the basic organization remains the same." It took him as long to rewrite as it did to write the rough draft. Martin's system worked for him, but he realized other writers might have preferred a different way. "There is no 'right' way to write; there is only *your* way," he said.[19]

In constructing his stories, Martin concentrated on using what he called the "three C's" – conflict, characters tightly related to conflict, and the controlling idea. "I sometimes made a conscious effort to get a fictional effect out of a fact story, inventing nothing, simply handling the material as a novelist might," Martin said, adding he probably had always been "a frustrated novelist." Most of his stories went through as many as six rewrites. Writing, to Martin, was "more like carpentry than art." He also considered writing to be a solitary profession, one reason it was "both so hard and so rewarding." When he wrote his stories he imagined someone reading over his shoulder, an editor who, if Martin was tempted to "overwrite a sentence, or leave one loose, or collapse upon a cliché, or otherwise write something idiotic, the imaginary reader would frown; I would fix it." Early on in his career that editor was Allen of *Harper's* or illustrious book publisher Alfred Knopf, while during his heyday writing for the "big slicks" it was Stuart Rose of the *Post*.[20]

Odd and sometimes dangerous things happened to Martin as he conducted the legwork necessary for his stories. Attending an inquest into the killing of a young wife, he was startled when a key witness, asked to identify the man accused of the woman's murder, her husband, instead pointed to Martin, who sat in the courtroom taking notes. It gave him, he said, "a funny feeling." When Fran tried to call him while he was on another assignment, a six-part series for the *Post* about the life of the mentally ill at an Ohio psychiatric hospital, a switchboard operator there told her she could not connect her with her husband, noting, "He's on a locked ward." While staying overnight on that ward Martin learned that one patient had killed another patient. For a series of articles in the *Post* on Illinois's state legislature, he arranged a night meeting with Republican state representative Clem Graver, who allegedly had ties to the mob, at his twenty-first ward headquarters at Eighteenth and Halsted streets in Chicago. Something came up and Martin could not keep his appointment. That night three men kidnapped Graver and he was never seen again.[21]

Martin realized he ran risks with the stories he covered and tried to take precautions. Walking on a dark street in a tough part of a strange city, he always avoided walking near buildings and stayed close to the curb. "You never pick up hitch-hikers," said Martin, "you tell your wife not to let strangers into the house when she's alone, and you tell your daughter not to go for a ride with strangers or accept candy from them." Whenever he interviewed a criminal, he made sure to keep his friend, Emil Smicklas, a veteran Chicago police detective, informed about the meeting. Martin also had an unlisted telephone number and kept his home address off of his work stationery. "I always tried to keep myself professionally apart from the people I interviewed and wrote about," said Martin, "but sometimes, I suppose inevitably, it proved impossible: I did a story and book about a professional criminal and I had him in my home for two weeks, and later he occasionally came to dinner with my family and me."[22]

The results of all of Martin's efforts were exceptional. His peers considered him "the best living reporter" and "the ablest crime reporter in America," with his stories several times winning the magazine industry's highest honor at the time, the Benjamin Franklin Award, sponsored by the University of Illinois's School of Journalism and the Society of Magazine Writers. His nonfiction focus on criminals and their effect on society predated the literary nonfiction work of such famous authors as Truman Capote and Norman Mailer. "I am basically a serious person," Martin told a reporter in 1960. "I don't like to do frivolous stories." He had a fierce belief in a writer's responsibility to interest the public at large in serious subjects that might threaten to weaken the country's democratic system. Martin's work impressed other writers, including poet and literary critic Robert Penn Warren, who waxed lyrical about his stories in a conversation with editors at *Harper's*. "Your ears should have been on fire!" exclaimed Russell Lynes, managing editor at *Harper's* in a letter to Martin. "He [Warren] said he thinks you and John Hersey are the best in your business and he gives you the edge by a large margin." A Chicago newspaper reporter said he had to be careful because if a writer read enough of Martin's work he would soon find himself "unconsciously writing like him." Journalist and Martin friend Herman Kogan said that the range of subjects Martin tackled during his writing career made "the rest of us look like bums," adding that when a reader finished one of Martin's pieces he "knew everything there was to know about that subject. He never bored you." Another colleague, Robert Sherrod, a World War II correspondent and later editor at the *Post*, described Martin as "possibly the best reporter I've ever known." Fran, whom Martin married in 1940, believed there were three reasons why her husband became a success in his profession: "He is terribly intelligent, he has much more compassion than most of us, and he is scrupulously honest." Something else, however, set Martin apart from his contemporaries, including such renowned journalists as Theodore H. White and James "Scotty" Reston, and that was a deep and abiding concern for the lot of individual human beings in a society grown increasingly complex, dysfunctional, and unforgiving. "Most journalists," he noted, including Reston and White, "make a living by interviewing the great. I made mine by interviewing the humble – what the Spaniards call *los de abajo*, those from below."[23]

During his long career writing stories for national magazines and many books, Martin took his readers into the worlds of such forgotten people as the victims of a gruesome highway crash in Michigan, the mother of a teenage boy who wondered why her son and two others killed a nurse for no apparent reason, a convict from Jackson Prison talking about the hell of life behind bars, a crusading journalist gunned down in cold blood for daring to expose corruption in his town, a dedicated psychiatrist trying to save damaged lives at an Ohio mental institution, and an illiterate black steelworker bringing to life the real meaning of segregated housing in a northern city. As the writer of heavy-fact stories, Martin said it was his fate to "thrive on other people's troubles." Once a person involved in the Hollywood film industry asked him,

"Don't you ever write any happy stories?" Martin told him, "No, I don't. I don't think the human lot is a very happy one. Maybe an analyst could figure that out . . . but I do take my work seriously and feel dedicated to it." In Martin's mind there was a gulf between the matter-of-fact newspaperman who saw little difference between covering a football game and a hanging, and the serious journalist he aspired to be, one who writes significant articles "about serious subjects and takes them seriously and so becomes himself engaged – engaged in his society, in his times, in the human condition."[24]

Martin also produced revealing insights into such nationally known personalities as a young congressional investigator named Robert F. Kennedy, Teamsters union leader Jimmy Hoffa, and notorious murderer Nathan Leopold, who had spent thirty years in prison after conspiring with Richard Loeb to kill fourteen-year-old Robert "Bobby" Franks in 1924. "The individual man, the woman, the child – that was what mattered to a storyteller," said Martin. Writing did not provide him a medium for self-expression or self-indulgence. Instead he believed: "The basic idea of writing is to communicate. If a man has nothing to say, he has no business writing. This is just as true in non-fiction as fiction. There are levels of experience fiction can reach that non-fiction can never reach. Fiction is a higher art than non-fiction. Nevertheless, the basic purpose of the two forms is identical: to communicate clearly from writer to reader." Martin's stories showed that he possessed what he claimed to be the one indispensable characteristic needed by a writer: an inquiring mind. He added that a writer's chief responsibility was always to tell the truth. "I make a distinction between a story and an article," he once told a reporter. "I write stories. Stories have people in them . . . and they bleed." As a magazine writer, Martin believed he had the advantage over a newspaper reporter working on a daily deadline, because he was able "to put a story in perspective, conceptualize it." Martin said that only rarely, if ever, did he pursue a story as an investigative reporter might, producing evidence of a crime before authorities knew anything was wrong. His stories, however, evoked powerful emotions from readers, and Martin, trying to avoid exploiting the tragedy and misery in people's lives, attempted to achieve a literary effect in his heavy-fact writing. He noted that the French army's retreat from Moscow under Napoleon

Bonaparte existed as a historical fact, but became an epic event only after being written about by Leo Tolstoy in *War and Peace*. "Nor, if I may say so," Martin said, "did the Centralia mine disaster exist in that sense until I conceived and wrote my piece." Throughout his career, Martin wrote almost instinctively about individuals who had suffered failure during their lives. "Only the humble and lowly will talk to you honestly," he said. "They usually have nothing to lose. This is not to say they are better people. They merely don't have the motive to lie or deceive."[25]

What fueled Martin's concern for America's forgotten class – its underdogs – were his memories of an often dark childhood spent in Indianapolis. A bookish, small child who often disappointed his contractor father, Martin endured the tragic loss of his two brothers to illness and saw his father's once-thriving business fail in the late 1930s with the onslaught of the Great Depression. The Martin family survived through the assistance of New Deal programs from the administration of President Franklin D. Roosevelt, programs that saved their home from being foreclosed upon and offered Martin's father a job with the Works Progress Administration. "Roosevelt saved us all," said Martin. His experiences during the Great Depression, combined with his intellectual awakening in high school, spurred by reading such authors as Ernest Hemingway, John Dos Passos, Sinclair Lewis, and Theodore Dreiser, helped to form his viewpoint as a classic New Deal liberal who believed in the America of Frank Capra and John Steinbeck, the promise of "what the people could make of themselves." He maintained that belief for the rest of his life, recalling that one of the best things he ever wrote was for a talk given by Democratic politician Adlai E. Stevenson to the Princeton University senior class banquet in 1954. "The highest condition of man in this mysterious universe is the freedom of the spirit," Martin wrote. "And it is only truth that can set the spirit free."[26]

Martin's life changed in the 1950s when he was asked by an attorney friend to edit a book of speeches by Stevenson, then the governor of Illinois, who had used the Centralia disaster as an effective tool to strike at and defeat his Republican opponent, incumbent Dwight Green. Martin turned the book of speeches into a short biography of Stevenson that was released in time to take advantage of Stevenson's surprise capture of the 1952 Democratic Party presidential nomination. Martin went to work for the governor, turning away from his first assignment helping the candidate's press secretary with the national media and instead joining a group of noteworthy speechwriters dubbed the Elks Club, so named because the Stevenson campaign had rented space for them in an Elks Club building in Springfield, Illinois. Members of this group, who called themselves "speech researchers" to outsiders to help assuage Stevenson's ego at having others produce his speeches, included among others such notable figures as Pulitzer Prize–winning historian Arthur M. Schlesinger Jr., Harvard University economist John Kenneth Galbraith, and former Harry S. Truman administration official David Bell.

At first, Martin felt uneasy about his changing circumstances from being a reporter observing and then writing about events, to being on the inside and having an effect on events. Eventually, Martin took to his new role with relish and became particularly adept at crafting whistle-stop speeches in the days when candidates traveled by rail, stopping at small hamlets throughout the country to woo voters to their cause. "No one then, and I think none since, could make a point more succinctly, support it more sharply with evidence and then, of all things, stop," Galbraith said of Martin. Newton Minow, a key Stevenson aide who became good friends with Martin during the campaign, noted that he appeared to be a "natural at writing anything," turned out to be particularly good at writing political speeches, and, thanks to his days as an "extraordinary" reporter, possessed skills as a "great human observer." Another speechwriting veteran of the Elks Club, John S. Fischer, marveled that Martin worked under extreme pressure "better than any writer" he had ever known, adding that his friend had "the ulcers to prove it." The ulcers were a natural byproduct of his involvement in one of America's favorite and dysfunctional pastimes: electing a president. "Few things anywhere," he later noted, "contain the frenzy, the drama, the unbelievable tensions and pressures of a presidential campaign. . . . It is a bloody and bloodthirsty spectacle. But there is a fascination and exhilaration in it too."[27]

Stevenson's defeat by Republican Dwight D. Eisenhower in 1952 failed to dampen Martin's enthusiasm for politics. For the next twenty years he was part of the campaign staffs of every Democratic presidential nominee from Stevenson again in 1956 through George McGovern, who ran and lost in a landslide to incumbent GOP president Richard Nixon in

1972. In Stevenson's 1956 effort to once again win the Democratic presidential nomination, and in John F. Kennedy's 1960 run for the White House, Martin devised a niche for himself as what he termed an editorial advance man, attempting to bring together two vital aspects of any campaign – scheduling and speechwriting. "I'd go into a state in advance of the candidate to interview people, trying to find out what the local issues were," he recalled. "I would talk to the local Democratic leaders, businessmen, newsmen, taxi drivers, waitresses, bartenders, anybody I could find." Once he had ferreted out enough information, he produced a report and rejoined the campaign party as it traveled through the area he had just visited. The candidate could take the briefing sheets Martin produced and use them to speak extemporaneously and expertly about the issues facing a community, and he never had to arrive at a speech without "knowing what to expect and what was expected of him," said Martin. Editorial advance, noted Schlesinger, "sharpened the impact of speeches and also influenced political strategy."[28]

Martin also used his gift for words to craft an enduring phrase describing America's burgeoning television culture. His friend Newton Minow, the new chairman of the Federal Communications Commission, was set to give a speech in May 1961 before the National Association of Broadcasters, a group the FCC chairman wanted to inform about his intentions to reform television on behalf of the public interest. Martin, who had been researching and writing a series about television for the *Saturday Evening Post,* had sat down and watched twenty straight hours of programs. With this in mind, he suggested that Minow say to the broadcasters: "I invite you to sit down in front of your television set when your station goes on the air and stay there . . . and keep your eyes glued to that set until the station goes off. I can assure you that you will observe a vast wasteland of junk." Martin noted that Minow, in editing and honing his final speech, had the good sense to cut from the text the words "of junk," but kept the phrase "vast wasteland," which captured the attention of the press and the public and continues to be used today whenever the quality of television programming is debated. Minow noted that of all the speeches Martin produced for political candidates, from Stevenson to John and Robert Kennedy, the "vast wasteland" address is the one that received the most attention.[29]

Working for politicians, Martin discovered something about his former profession. "No reporter can ever know what's really going on; he is on the outside looking in," he said. "As JFK used to say, the only man who knows what it's really like is the man that fights the bull. Having been a reporter, I wanted to get on the inside, to make things happen in politics and government." Martin received his chance to see how the other half lived during the Kennedy administration, when he was selected to serve as the U.S. ambassador to the Dominican Republic, an island nation he had visited early on during his days as a freelance writer when its people had been under the brutal rule of dictator Rafael Trujillo. "I used to say, during those years as Ambassador, that I was really just doing what I'd always done – reporting and writing – but now I was doing it for a smaller audience: Instead of several million *Saturday Evening Post* readers, my readers were the President and the Secretary of State and a few of their staffers," said Martin.[30]

The following years were busy and often tragic ones for Martin. As ambassador, he worked tirelessly, often sixteen hours a day, to support the Dominican Republic's first democratically elected government, but he saw his hopes dashed by a military coup. Just two months after Martin returned to the United States to discuss with the administration what to do next, a gunman assassinated Kennedy in Dallas, Texas. A heartbroken Martin resigned his ambassadorship. "Ours was a house in mourning for several years after 1963," said Fred. Although the senior Martin admitted he "had no heart for government service" after Kennedy's death, he believed that his government experience contributed to making him, in the long run, a better reporter. It also gave him a new appreciation of the difficulties involved in conducting public affairs. He became much "less zealous about attacking the failings of our public officials and arrogating all virtue to the vigilant press. I found out just how hard it [governing] really is."[31]

Robert F. Kennedy's surprise run for the Democratic nomination for the presidency in 1968 revived Martin's hunger for politics. He served as a key adviser to the Kennedy campaign in its first primary race in Martin's old home state of Indiana. Because of his knowledge of the state, honed in part by his extensive research for his 1947 book *Indiana: An Interpretation*, Martin played an influential role in Kennedy's primary

win against governor Roger D. Branigin and U.S. senator Eugene Mc-
Carthy of Minnesota. After a successful effort in Indiana, Martin went
on to work for the Kennedy campaign in subsequent primary battles in
Nebraska, Oregon, and California. Kennedy's assassination just moments after celebrating with his supporters his close primary victory
in California "broke the back of my father's spirit," Fred noted. Martin
went on to work on behalf of the eventual Democratic presidential nominee, Hubert Humphrey, and finished his political speechwriting career
in 1972 with McGovern's campaign.[32]

The routine Martin developed of speechwriting for a candidate every four years and his own writing in between made him realize just how
much his creative energy as a writer had been "burned up in speechwriting." He saw the task of a speechwriter as not just developing lofty
rhetoric, dealing with the issues of the day, or matching a style to a particular candidate, but the more creative act of conceptualizing a speech.
Archibald MacLeish had done this for Stevenson in 1952 when he wrote
a speech to deliver before a hostile audience, the American Legion, on
the nature of patriotism, and Martin had done it for Humphrey in 1968
by conceiving an address to be given in the South attacking George Wallace, the segregationist former governor of Alabama. Martin wondered
what great novels he might have written (or might not have) if he had not
expended his creative energy on politicians. "But then I would not have
been an ambassador nor would I have learned to care so deeply about
certain public issues nor come to understand so fully the importance
of serious politics to the life of our democracy," he said. "No regrets."[33]

In his later years Martin did find himself spending more and more
time on the one thing that had always been his salvation: writing. It always seemed to be on his mind, even when he was engaged in his favorite
pastimes of hunting and fishing. In the long hours of silence waiting for
fish or game to appear, Martin wrote, "Almost automatically, in my mind
I form sentences, an idea or a snatch of description; then rearrange the
words, then revise them inside my head again and again," he noted. With
big-slick magazines losing out on the entertainment field to television,
instead of heavy-fact stories, Martin produced a number of books, including an account of his days as ambassador in the Dominican Republic; an examination of the U.S. government's policies in the Caribbean;

a mammoth two-volume biography of Stevenson, a project that took ten years of his life; a novel that he based on his extensive background as part of numerous political campaigns; and finally his memoirs.[34]

For a decade Martin also taught courses in advanced writing at Northwestern University's Medill School of Journalism. He offered extensive, helpful comments on his students' rough drafts and completed stories, tried to find financial help for promising writers to pursue further research on their articles, and even invited some of his students to his home for one-on-one critiques of their writing. Although his comments on his students' work could run several pages in length, he could also be brief. On one final draft he offered just two words: "Damn good." Peter Jacobi, a colleague of Martin's at Medill and today professor emeritus of journalism at Indiana University, noted that Martin's reputation as a gifted journalist preceded him. "One sensed always that he cared about his subject," said Jacobi, "that he considered it – at the moment of writing – the most important subject in the world, one he wanted his reader also to care deeply about. There was total commitment in what he produced. . . . There was passion behind every choice of word and content." Martin's contributions to the university won the respect of students and faculty alike, and in 1988 Medill honored his memory by establishing the John Bartlow Martin Award for Public Interest Magazine Journalism to encourage journalists to do as Martin had done in his writing, "to make a difference with their words."[35]

Whatever disappointments and tragedies life threw at him, Martin coped by retreating to the solitude of a region he had first discovered on his honeymoon in 1940 with Fran: Michigan's Upper Peninsula, selected because they "thought northern Wisconsin too civilized, too crowded with tourists, too organized," noted Martin. Over the years, the region's remote, wild country in whose woods he once spotted a timberwolf, became for Martin "the most healing place on earth." For relaxation and rejuvenation, Martin could retreat to the approximately 180-acre camp he had purchased in January 1964 on Smith Lake near Herman, Michigan. "He liked the solitude, the absence of people, the forest, the fishing, the wild animals, and also the surrounding Scandinavian communities of loggers and miners," noted Fred. The family's land on Smith Lake, said Dan, "is a place that does not change, where the wind in the pine is constant and where what is important is whether or not one sees a deer at the meadow." Dan noted his father did not believe in cutting down trees or even their branches on his land. "Every building at Smith Lake was built around trees," he said, "so roofs were cut out to accommodate living trees." In front of the camp were hemlocks, cedars, and birches that obscured the view of the lake from the cabin's screened porch. "My mother would complain, as I did," said Dan, "and my father said, 'If you want to see the lake, go get in the boat and see it.'"[36]

The Martins spent the summers at Smith Lake in a thirty-by-thirty cabin with a living room, kitchen, and bedroom, without the usual amenities of the twentieth century – telephone, radio, television – driving the nearly hour and a half to L'Anse, Michigan, every two weeks to pick up their mail, groceries, and gin. "We need go no farther; we have everything we want at Smith Lake," Martin noted. During those summer months Martin fished, tried his hand at carpentry, did some writing, and relaxed in a sauna decorated with the front page of the *New York Times*'s issue announcing the resignation from the presidency of his longtime foil Richard Nixon. Martin, Fran, and his children went for long Jeep rides in the uninhabited wilderness to the north of their camp, exploring old logging roads and figuring out the best spots for the fall partridge hunting season. The evenings could feature reading Robert W. Service poems aloud or singing favorite songs. "One night we sang 'America the Beautiful,' and the coyotes across the lake sang back – very patriotic coyotes up here," Martin recalled. In the 1980s Martin stopped fishing a new lake or stream every year, preferring to catch his limit close by at Smith Lake – the fish he told other people he had been saving for his old age. "What a pleasant way to date the aging of man," he said. "If you have to do it at all."[37]

At the end of his life, Martin displayed the same candid attitude about death as he had employed in his writing. "I never knew anyone more matter-of-fact than he: more direct, straightforward, and capable of telling (or bearing) the most awful news without drama," said Fred. Martin had a more sentimental side, admitting that music and good writing moved him deeply, and listening to certain passages of Beethoven could set him to weeping. His death from throat cancer in 1987 finally silenced a man that his fellow journalist John L. Perry, who met Martin while covering the Dominican Republic's civil war in 1965, described as possessing the essential qualities required by any good reporter – talent, guts, idealism mixed with realism, durability, independence, accuracy, and effectiveness. Perry said in the years to come he would remember Martin as a "remarkable man with the endless energy, insatiable curiosity and unfettered love for people who have little else going for them but someone such as he."[38]

TWO

A Mean Street in
a Mean City

FOR MORE THAN A DECADE, AS THEY STRODE ALONG THE sidewalks on the Circle, the center of Indianapolis's original Mile Square plat, people craned their necks to peer over a high wooden fence plastered with posters advertising theater offerings, hoping to catch a glimpse of a structure destined to dominate the city's skyline for years to come. On May 15, 1902, the city's citizens, along with visitors from all over the state and nation, crammed downtown streets for the formal dedication of the Soldiers and Sailors Monument. Built of gray oolitic limestone from Owen County, Indiana, at a cost of approximately $600,000 and standing 284 feet tall, the edifice honored "Indiana's Silent Victors," the average Hoosier soldiers who had given their lives in the Mexican-American War, the Civil War, and the Spanish-American War. "They are my best beloved," intoned Civil War veteran Lew Wallace, presiding officer for the dedication ceremonies, "who, in every instance of danger to the nation, discover a glorious chance to serve their fellow-men and dare the chance, though in so doing they suffer and sometimes die."[1]

Twenty-some years after the survivors of those who wore blue fighting for the Union cause in the Civil War had marched proudly in a street parade for the opening to the public of what was reputed to be the second highest monument in the United States, a different group stood ready to rally around Indianapolis's Monument Circle. Instead of wearing ribbons touting their loyalty to the Grand Army of the Republic, these men wore the stark white robes and pointed hoods signifying their membership in the Ku Klux Klan – the white supremacist, anti-Catholic, anti-Jewish, and anti–African American organization that dominated Indianapolis's and the state's politics for much of the 1920s. The Klansmen, who marched "in dead silence" in seemingly endless numbers around the Circle, made a tremendous impression on a young man from Indianapolis, John Bartlow Martin, who noted, "The grand dragon of Indiana proclaimed, 'I am the law in Indiana,' and he was." Martin, who later described the Klan as "Indiana's experiment in homegrown dictatorship," witnessed the parade with his father, John Williamson Martin, called J. W. by his friends. The senior Martin was a well-to-do general contractor born in southern Ohio near the Indiana state line and a lifelong Democrat who disliked the Republican-dominated Klan in the state and refused to join its ranks. "There was a lot of talk about the Klan, and I've seen the fiery crosses burn, while traveling through Indiana with my father on his business trips," Martin recalled. "I remember rumors about which of our neighbors were and which weren't Klansmen." Although Martin's father resisted the Klan's blandishments, the group's views permeated the Hoosier psyche during those years. Martin's mother, Laura, a devout Christian Scientist from Liberty, Indiana, confided to her eldest son her belief that Catholics always built "their churches on the top of hills; she had been taught they were preparing to take over the country and the churches would be their military strongpoints."[2]

Perhaps it was those dark memories of the Klan that influenced Martin's grim view of his youth in Indianapolis. In writing his memoir, published in 1986, Martin reflected that most people who write such books seemed to have enjoyed happy, carefree childhoods. "I hated mine," he wrote. "Many seem to regard the years of their youth as the easiest years of their lives. Mine were the hardest." Martin described the street he lived on in Indianapolis, Brookside Avenue, in harsh, stark terms – a "mean street in a mean city."[3]

Martin was born on August 4, 1915, in a small cottage on Franklin Street in Hamilton, the county seat of Butler County, Ohio, just north of Cincinnati. Before his grim days in Indianapolis, he lived what many would call a bucolic existence as a typical midwestern youth. Given the middle name Bartlow for his maternal grandmother, Nancy Bartlow, the young Martin had been raised with the help of his Aunt Lulu, who had recently returned to the country after serving as a nurse on the Austrian front during the war then raging in Europe. "It was a time of great turmoil, anxiety and excitement," Martin observed in an autobiography he prepared for an eighth-grade class assignment (the future writer received an "A+" for his report), "but I, with my laughing eyes and fiery red hair, knew nothing of it." He did have an early memory of a narrow escape from a tornado, a "big b'ack toud," as he called it. His mother hurriedly carried him to the "warm cellar" of a neighbor, Mrs. Brown, for safety during the storm. During quieter summer days, Martin loved to pick grapes from Mrs. Brown's yard, filling his apron with them and taking them to his house's back porch to feast upon. Martin's habit of wandering the neighborhood almost ended in disaster one day. Chasing a kitten through his family's small garden, he was stopped in his play by a sudden cry of horror from his mother, who scooped him up in her arms, took him inside, and bolted the door behind them. "At first I did not understand and started to demand an explanation when I happened to glance out to where I had been playing a few moments before," Martin recalled. "There sunning himself, lay a great blacksnake. Even as we watched, he rose and glided silently away, leaving a trail thru the grass. Then it was my turn to scream and hers to shudder."[4]

The Martin family lived for a short time in Lima, Ohio, before moving in 1918 to Nashville, Tennessee, where J. W. worked at the Old Hickory Powder Plant, the world's largest smokeless powder operation, eighteen miles from Nashville at Hadleys Bend on the Cumberland River. Built and operated for the U.S. government by the Du Pont Engineering Company, the factory produced 35.9 million pounds of material (sulfuric acid, nitric acid, and nitrocellulose [guncotton]) for the Allied effort in World War I. Overhearing discussions at the dinner table about the fighting in Europe, Martin figured out that the United States had entered the war with France and England against Germany and Austria-Hungary. "I played soldier every day," Martin said, "called myself 'One of Uncle Sammie's Soldiers,' and saluted everyone I saw." With the signing of the Armistice on November 11, 1918, Martin's father participated in a grand parade in Nashville celebrating the war's end. After the parade was over, Martin received from his father a drum carried in the celebration. "After I got the drum," said Martin, "I had a 'parade' every day down the street, beating the drum and shouting myself hoarse until I nearly drove the neighbors mad."[5]

With the war's end, the Martin family moved from Tennessee to the east-central Indiana community of Anderson, where they lived for a year with Laura's mother, Nancy. Before the Bartlow family made their home in Anderson, for many years the clan had lived on small farms along the southern Indiana border near the Ohio River. Martin said that his grandmother told him about the summer of 1863, when Confederate general John Hunt Morgan's men conducted their raid into Indiana from Kentucky. She remembered that the rebels, who ransacked homes and held communities for thousands of dollars in ransom, stole her family's best horses. Martin recalled reacting badly to the move to Anderson, so badly, in fact, that his mother was sometimes so desperate for some peace and quiet that she tied her son to a water pipe in the cellar until he calmed down, usually in an hour or so. That kind of parental behavior today would bring a visit from child protective services. When he could not stop his screaming and it proved too much for his mother to bear, in desperation, she turned him loose and sent him outdoors to track down neighborhood rabbits (often he merely followed dog tracks) or had him construct "sleds," which were nothing but a shingle with a piece of string tied through a hole. He also recalled calmer times when his mother read books to him.[6]

In 1919 the Martin family moved to Indiana's capital, Indianapolis, eventually living at 2215 Brookside Avenue on the city's northeast side. "The buzz of insects, the whir of the lawnmower, the swish of the garden hose in the long summer evening – this was my Indiana boyhood," said Martin. On Brookside Avenue he became best friends with an older boy, Harry Mayer. Because Mayer had to go to school each day, Martin found another friend, Frank Noffke, to spend time with from eight in the morning until three in the afternoon. Both Martin and Noffke owned tricycles, so they pedaled for hours on long "trips" around the neighborhood that actually lasted for only five blocks. They also amused themselves by digging "caves" in their backyards. To help with the construction, Martin used a hatchet. "One day when I was standing in the bottom of the partly-completed cave," he said, "hacking away at the dirt with all my might, of course barefooted. . . . The hatchet stroke fell short and the blade fell with increased impetus on my toe. I hobbled home, but soon returned undaunted, a few minutes later, with a big rag around my toe."

Martin also recalled days spent throwing apples at pedestrians from the roof of the family's shed, building snow tunnels with his mother during the winter, and knocking out two of his front teeth when he fell on the ice. The family also vacationed on the East Coast, visiting Mount Vernon, George Washington's home; the historic sites in Washington, D.C.; and the navy yard at Wilmington, Delaware, where they took a boat ride down Delaware Bay and gazed at the warships safely nestled in their dry docks. On the way home, Martin also visited the Gettysburg battlefield and toured one of Washington's Revolutionary War headquarters.[7]

Martin remembered Brookside Avenue as a "wide brick street with street car tracks and trolley wires, the houses small and wooden, a tumbledown wreck of a stucco apartment building, scattered neighborhood stores." His neighbors included a bricklayer, a railroad conductor, a minor league baseball umpire, and a painter. For a time a doctor lived next door to the Martins, but he quickly moved to the more prestigious north side of town, something Martin's parents also dreamed of doing and later achieved, moving to a stone ranch house on Kessler Boulevard. An African American family also lived across the street from the Martins, but because of the racial prejudice that existed in the neighborhood, they seldom showed themselves. "They knew they were not welcome there," Martin remembered. Also because of segregation in Indianapolis, few black children went to the grade school that Martin attended. As a boy, he feared the few African American youths who did share his classroom, keeping his distance because "they could fight too well."[8]

Born in Beavis, Ohio, J. W., who quit school at age thirteen to help support his family when his father died, worked as a carpenter, then as a carpenter contractor, and finally as a general contractor, first in business with his brother, William C., then as head of the Indiana Gunite and Construction Company (gunite is a building material that includes a mixture of cement, sand, and water). His contracts in Indianapolis included repairs to the Soldiers and Sailors Monument, building the sidewalks around the Indiana War Memorial, and constructing the Fountain Square Theatre building. As the owner of a prosperous business, J. W. owned two Buicks and employed a maid to help his wife around the house. "Since he was a contractor and did public work there was always a lot of talk of politics and of 'deals,'" Martin said. He described his father as "a tall angular man just over six feet, a willful stubborn man, a bluff loud man in a noisy and rough industry from which I shrank." J. W. wanted his son to attend an engineering school when he was old enough and follow in his footsteps when it came to a career, but Martin, who "read all the time," had other ideas. He hoped to become a writer – a profession that his father doubted could provide him with a livelihood.[9]

Although his father sometimes derisively referred to his son as "the bookworm" and himself read nothing but the *Engineering News-Record,* he nonetheless bought Martin books for Christmas. Perhaps Martin shied away from life as a contractor as a result of memories of accompanying J. W. on Saturday evenings as he drove his Buick touring car to Indiana Avenue, the heart of Indianapolis's African American district, to find workers for his various construction projects. J. W. would pull up to a crowd of black men, Martin recalled, and after using a racial epithet, asked if any of them wanted to go to work on Monday. "There was no malice in it; it was his way of hiring labor," Martin said. Upon J. W.'s death in 1960, his obituary said that anyone in his employ knew "they could expect a square deal from him." Anything J. W. did, he did with "great, even boisterous enthusiasm," said Martin. Martin worked for his father once, but J. W. fired him when he saw a photograph of his son "sitting on a gravel pit reading a book when I should have been discharging my duties as a timekeeper." Burning his hand on a red hot dolly bar used by riveters on one of his father's bridge construction projects also discouraged him from pursuing a career in construction. One of the few times Martin saw his rowdy father humbled occurred one afternoon when J. W. returned home early with signs that he had been in a fight. "I got whupped," he told his wife and son. An official for an ironworkers union had come to one of his job sites to organize the workers. J. W. had tried to run him off, the union man had refused, they fought, and "the union boss had knocked my father down and beaten him up and stomped him," Martin said.[10]

Some of Martin's memories of his father were happier, including rabbit hunting trips with him and his friends, some of whom were local public officials, and learning woodworking skills he used later in life. J. W. also took his son fishing in the spring and summer, as well as on treks to the countryside to gather walnuts and hickory nuts in the fall. There were also one- or two-week vacations to Winona Lake in Kosciusko County, where evangelist and former professional baseball player Billy Sunday had an impressive home. On fishing trips, J. W. would invariably put one finger to his lips and whisper loudly, "Shh – don't say anything – you'll scare the fish," all the time stomping noisily on the bottom of the boat. A "quintessential consumer," J. W. switched from using live bait in the 1920s to casting artificial bait for bass. "His method of casting was to stand up in the boat," Martin said, "to draw back his arm full-length, and then, spinning his whole body half-around, to heave the bait . . . toward shore not overhead but sidearm, which is not only inaccurate but downright dangerous to anyone else in the boat – I always had to duck." For relaxation, J. W. also listened to records of Enrico Caruso, playing them on an old Victor Victrola phonograph. "Why my father, uneducated, a carpenter and contractor in a rough business, the son of a rural man, loved music I have never known; but he did," he recalled. Laura was the polar opposite of her brusque husband; her son remembered her as "small, quiet, soft, sweet, and always sad." Although romantic about her children, life, and God, she did not display the same attitude toward her husband. The few times Martin witnessed his father attempting "to demonstrate affection toward her, she fended him off."[11]

For the first nine years of his life, Martin had been an only child. As the family grew, tragedy and difficulties followed with the birth of a brother, Billy. Not long after his birth, a third child, Dickie, joined the family. One Sunday morning, when Dickie was just six months old, Martin went into his room, looked into the crib, and found that his brother had died. "My mother dressed his body in his best white dress and a lacy bonnet and brought it downstairs to the front porch," said Martin, "where I was sitting in the wicker swing shaded by the awning, and put his body in my lap and told me to hold it." Life also turned out to be difficult for Billy. "My father doted on my brother," said Martin, "perhaps because there was something wrong with him." Billy was late in learning how to walk, could hardly talk at the age of six, and entered school long after most children of his age had started. Later in life Martin believed his brother suffered from a mental deficiency due to an Rh factor incompatibility. He said his family rarely, if ever, talked about his brother's condition, except when Billy learned something new, such as when Martin taught him how to clean his hands by wiping them on his overalls. "See, he's getting better. He's healing," Martin quoted his mother as saying after he had proudly shown her what he had taught his brother. The family never knew exactly what was wrong with Billy, because Laura, faithful to her Christian Science faith, depended upon prayer, not doctors, when sickness struck, and refused to have her son examined by a physician. "He's God's child," said Laura. "God is love."[12]

Financial and medical disasters struck the family a double blow in the early 1930s. In the booming economy of the 1920s, J. W. had taken the earnings he had received from his successful business and invested them in common stocks. When the stock market crashed in October 1929, inaugurating a worldwide financial catastrophe that became the Great Depression, Martin noted that his father "lost everything . . . and ultimately he had to put his business through receivership." A proud man, J. W. refused to declare bankruptcy, considering such a move "dishonorable," and spent several years working to pay off his creditors in full. In 1931, when Martin was fifteen and in his third year at Indianapolis's Arsenal Technical High School, the family suffered another crisis when he became ill with scarlet fever, a serious, infectious illness in the days before the widespread use of antibiotics. Although Martin became "deathly sick," his mother turned for help not from a doctor, but from her Christian Science practitioner, who offered prayers but not medical assistance. Martin recovered, but before he did Billy also came down with the illness. "He became even sicker than I, delirious, his body burning red," said Martin. Once again, Laura depended upon prayer rather than a doctor's care, taking a streetcar downtown to consult her practitioner. Late one evening, with Billy deathly ill, J. W., unable to take it anymore, ignored his wife's protests and left the house to secure medicine to treat his younger son's sickness. "When he returned," said Martin, who was huddled in his bed, "my mother met him at the top of the stairs and said to him, 'He's gone, John.' I always thought she spoke almost in triumph but surely I was wrong." For the first time in his life, Martin saw his big, strong father break down and cry. Martin shared his father's agony, believing he was to blame for Billy's death.[13]

When his business had been profitable in the 1920s, J. W. had taken several construction jobs in Cincinnati, Ohio, where he met and became involved with another woman. The two of them attended the opera, bet on the horses at the Latonia Racetrack in Covington, Kentucky, and danced and drank bootleg whiskey at the Hotel Gibson's roof garden. Martin did not believe it was this affair that led to the breakdown of his parents' marriage, but instead he blamed the breakup on Billy's death and his father's business failure. "He had to get away – away from my brother's death, away from Christian Science and my mother, away from failure and no job, away from Brookside Avenue," said Martin. Although his father wanted a divorce, he could not afford to keep two households going, so the three of them stayed together for the next year and a half, with the only dialogue going on between mother and son. Laura tried to convince her remaining son it was his father's fault. "They quarreled often, 'fighting,' they called it, and seemed to enjoy it, sometimes she tried to hit him with her fists, and I have memories of violent scenes," said Martin. He realized later in life that he could not be sure about the accuracy of his memories of this time and the effect of Billy's death on his father and on himself.[14]

Although adversity plagued his home life, Martin had the good fortune to attend a high school that nurtured his academic achievement and advanced his dream of becoming a writer. The third high school opened in Indianapolis, Arsenal Tech, or Tech as its students referred to it, began its life as the seventy-five-acre home of the state and federal arsenal on Michigan Avenue before opening as a manual and technical training school in 1912. Tech soon earned a reputation as not only a place to learn a trade, but also as a top-notch college preparatory institution. The school's 350 faculty members offered a wide array of classes that ranged, as one historian of Tech noted, "from dry cleaning to Shakespearean drama, from cosmetology to analytic chemistry." By 1930 Tech's student population had grown to approximately eight thousand, making it one of the largest high schools in the country. "When I first got there I must say I was overwhelmed," remembered Alfred Kuerst, who graduated from Tech in 1933. "I hadn't expected anything so huge, anything with a campus so sprawled out and so many students. But it was a very, very friendly school."[15]

Mary Johnson Brown, a 1935 Tech graduate, had vivid memories of her teachers and their inspirational instructional methods. One day she was sitting with her fellow students in her English literature class waiting for their teacher, Bjorn Winger, to appear. Suddenly, the door burst open and in stepped Winger clad in a cape "flowing over his shoulder [and] quoting poetry." Martin was an excellent student (for the January to June 1932 school term he earned A+ grades in all his classes), and he later said he learned more during his last two years in high school than he had in his entire time in college. He had a new world opened to him by another Tech English teacher, a woman who introduced him to modern literature. He could not recall her name, but he remembered sitting in the front row of her classroom, dodging her spittle as she read poetry out loud to her students. Inspired by his teacher, Martin put away his western novels by Zane Grey and adventure yarns by James Oliver Curwood and began reading works by the leading writers of the 1920s and 1930s – Ernest Hemingway, John Dos Passos, Theodore Dreiser, William Faulkner, Sherwood Anderson, Sinclair Lewis, and H. L. Mencken. "I read them all, some several times, especially Dos Passos's *The 42nd Parallel* and Thomas Wolfe's *Look Homeward, Angel*," said Martin, "for in the first I found a world I aspired to know and in the second I thought I could see myself." Particular favorites of Martin's included Hemingway's *The Sun Also Rises* and *A Farewell to Arms*. Every month Martin eagerly read his new issue of *The American Mercury,* the influential literary magazine created by Mencken and George Jean Nathan, and studied issues of *Writer's Digest* to learn all he could about writing. "Throughout high school, and even in grade school, I wanted to write," he said. He began producing short stories, a novel, and even a play, "all imitative of those authors, no doubt, all unpublished and forgotten." Martin also tried to write poetry, jotting down some verse and sending it to his aunt Verl Garrison in Anderson, who he wrongly imagined knew more about the subject than his parents did.[16]

Martin achieved his first literary success while a Tech student, working for a couple of years on *The Arsenal Cannon,* the school's yearbook/magazine published twice a year and featuring news on student activities as well as the literature they created. In addition to serving as the *Cannon's* sports editor, writing articles on the triumphs and failures of the football, basketball, track, golf, and tennis squads, Martin also created poetry and prose for its pages. Martin compared freshmen and senior students in the January 1931 *Cannon* issue in his poem, "The Difference," ending with the stanza, "And so it goes from first to last / Freshies happy 'cause they're leavin' / Seniors walkin', heads bowed down, / Grievin' 'cause they'll soon be leavin'." In the January 1932 issue his poem "Contentment" won second place in a contest sponsored by the *Cannon* for his senior English class. The poem contrasted the garden planted by his neighbor, with its flowers swaying in the breeze, with the garden that existed in his own mind, "Which I made by myself, / There is no goldfish pond in it, / No images of elves; / Although hers is more beautiful, / More gaudily built, and fine, / I would not trade its grandeur / For the simplicity of mine."[17]

Another major influence on Martin came through his friendship with a young man he met at Tech, the son of an immigrant ironworker who lived in an Indianapolis working-class neighborhood. Called Wolfgang by Martin in his memoir, the boy introduced him to "Marx and Spengler, Kant and Nietzsche and Schopenhauer. I could not manage the *Critique of Pure Reason* or *Das Kapital,* but I read the others." He also spent a lot of time discussing modern American writers with another Tech friend, Francis S. Nipp, who also worked on the *Cannon* and with whom Martin often consulted about his writing in later years. Under such heady influences, Martin could not control himself and got kicked out of his Sunday school class for quoting Schopenhauer and for swiping a copy of Oswald Spengler's *The Decline of the West* from an Indianapolis bookstore (he did not have the money to buy a copy). Late on many nights Martin could be found at Wolfgang's house drinking the home brew made by his father and talking about the Great Depression, the union movement, and the Communist Party. Martin listened as Wolfgang, who could roll his own cigarettes with one hand while ambling down a railroad track, recited the life histories of such labor heroes as William Dudley "Big Bill" Haywood and Joe Hill. The two young men also walked together through the slums of Indianapolis, filled as they were with men unable to find work, and talked about the coming revolution that would come if the economy failed to improve.[18]

By the spring of 1933 the city's unemployment rate had reached an unprecedented 37 percent – a figure that had not been dented by Indianapolis mayor Reginald H. Sullivan's "Made Work Program," which had those out of a job going door to door throughout the city to solicit odd jobs. Private charities struggled to help those in need, with Indianapolis's Sunshine Mission unable to keep up with the demand in spite of providing meals to three hundred people a day and parceling out six thousand items of clothing. "I had always heard my father talking politics, but Democratic-Republican politics," said Martin. "This was a new political awakening." As a member of the Young Communists' League, Wolfgang tried to convert Martin to communism and invited him to be part of a demonstration at a small Indiana town. Martin intended to participate in the march but did not make it; those who participated were beaten and jailed. "I used to say that I didn't go because I had a date with a girl," said Martin, "but to be honest I don't remember why."[19]

In 1932, at the age of sixteen, Martin, who had skipped two grades while in elementary school, was one of approximately 960 students to graduate from Tech. Such a large senior class necessitated Tech hosting two commencements, one on June 7 for students whose last names were from A to K, and one on June 9 for students with last names from L to Z. With money tight in the Martin household, J. W. could not fulfill his dream of having his eldest son attend an engineering school such as Purdue University in West Lafayette, Indiana. "It was not really his decision – he could not afford to send me to college at all," said Martin. Instead, he had to depend upon financial help from his grandmother in Anderson. Martin first applied to Indiana University in Bloomington, but shortly before school started Tom Ochiltree, an older brother of one of his friends from high school and an upperclassman at DePauw University in Greencastle, Indiana, told him that if he went to DePauw he could get him a place in his fraternity, Delta Chi; Martin changed his plans and enrolled at DePauw. So far as he knew, no member of his family on either side had ever graduated from college.[20]

Founded in 1837 by the Methodist Church under its original name, Indiana Asbury University, DePauw had as its goal education "forever to be conducted on the most liberal principles, accessible to all religious denominations, and designed for the benefit of our citizens in general." Instead of a liberal intellectual climate, however, Martin viewed the university as possessing "a hidebound moral climate; so I didn't do very well, either morally or intellectually." During high school Martin had experienced more freedom from parental oversight than most teenagers of those days, sneaking out of his house to patronize "black-and-tans," dance halls that were predominantly African American but welcomed white patrons to listen to musicians such as Louis Armstrong and Fletcher Henderson. Late at night at his fraternity, Martin and other like-minded music fans gathered around the radio to listen to big-name bands from New York and Chicago. Martin admitted he "behaved like a fool" while a freshman at DePauw. Instead of studying and attending classes, he spent time on weekends "drinking and whoring" in nearby Terre Haute, while during the week he drank and played poker at the Delta Chi house on Locust Street. His late-night revelries made it hard for him to wake up for his morning classes, and he took to wearing his clothes over his pajamas to cut down on the time it took him to dress.[21]

Owen R. Davison, a Delta Chi fraternity brother from Hershey, Pennsylvania, said that during the time he knew Martin the Indianapolis native enjoyed a reputation as "a bit of a 'rounder,' especially for the conservative and traditional climate of Greencastle in the mid-1930s." He added that those who knew Martin could see he was a student with "great talent and creativity who would undoubtedly make a name for himself, at least if he did not get caught up in too many of the forbidden pleasures of life." Reflecting on his early days at DePauw, Martin said that although he had come of age intellectually during his last two years in high school, he "simply couldn't handle being away from home, happy as I was to escape Brookside Avenue." It all came to a head one day near the end of his freshman year when he got drunk alone in his room in the morning, went down to lunch, and threw food around the dining room. A fraternity brother studying to be a minister reported Martin's bad behavior to the university's dean of men, who allowed him to finish out the year but forbade him from returning to the campus the following fall. "I could not have anyway – I was flunking German, which I had taken at my father's insistence, and my grandmother was short of money because she had been loaning my father money to try and save his business," Martin recalled. The ministry student also attempted to have Martin kicked out of Delta Chi, and the fraternity held a trial. Fortunately for Martin, his friend Tom Ochiltree offered an inspired defense on his behalf and he was acquitted. Martin could remain in the fraternity if he returned to DePauw.[22]

Once he got back to Indianapolis, Martin was greeted by stony silence from his father and a plea from his mother not to let his grandmother know about his expulsion, fearing the bad news might kill her. With the collapse of his contracting business, J. W. spent most of his time in the summer of 1933 looking for a job, any job. "Sometimes he took me with him – they might hire a young fellow where they wouldn't an older man," Martin said. One day the two of them awoke at dawn to be the first to stand in line at the employment gate at the Real Silk Hosiery Company, which manufactured women's lingerie and undergarments and was not far from their Brookside Avenue home. When the factory opened, Martin and his father were greeted by a foreman placing a sign on the entrance gate that read, "No Help Wanted." Although Martin began to feel sorry for himself, J. W. had hopes that things were going to get better under the administration of the new president, Democrat Franklin D. Roosevelt, who had defeated Republican incumbent Herbert Hoover in the 1932 election. During his first hundred days in office, Roosevelt instituted a host of federal programs to offer relief to a beleaguered nation, such as the Civilian Conservation Corps to put young people to work, the Public Works Administration to construct major public buildings, the Federal Deposit Insurance Corporation to protect bank depositors, the Securities and Exchange Commission to shield investors from Wall Street's shenanigans, and the Agricultural Adjustment Act to aid beleaguered farmers. Martin remembered that every time Roosevelt gave one of his "fireside chats," radio broadcasts explaining to the American people in plain language what the federal government was doing to stem the financial crisis, "my father sat in front of the old Atwater-Kent radio, listening to every word, agreeing vehemently."[23]

Times were hard for the Martin family and their neighbors in the 1930s, but compassion showed through the cracks of despair. "When we saw a hitchhiker," Martin recalled, "we picked him up; for we knew it was not his fault he lacked train fare. If a hobo came to the door and we had food, we gave it. We outdid each other in remembering the forgotten man." During that summer of want, Martin said a miracle happened – he found a job. Sam Ochiltree, the father of his school friends, worked as head of the Associated Press's Indianapolis bureau and hired Martin as a stock gummer. "My task was to take stock market quotations off a ticker tape and gum, or paste, them onto sheets of paper containing the names of stocks," Martin said. He received nine dollars a week and for several months it was the only money coming into the Martin household. Slowly, Roosevelt's New Deal relief programs began to make a difference for the Martins. Thanks to the government's Home Owner's Loan Corporation, J. W. fended off a banker threatening to foreclose on his house. He also became one of the millions of workers in the United States employed by the Works Progress Administration, serving as foreman for a small crew making a topographical map of Marion County. Martin wondered how someone could make such a map of anything as flat as central Indiana, but he noted the WPA worked many miracles during the 1930s. "Roosevelt – *there* was a leader!" said Martin, who, because of the National Recovery Act's setting of a national minimum wage of $14.50 a week, had his pay increased. "The New Deal touched our lives directly," said Martin. "It gave us many things. What it gave us above all else was hope."[24]

After six months on the job with the AP, Martin received a promotion to night copyboy, working from 3:00 PM to 11:00 PM in a sparse office filled with chattering Teletype machines. During his shift Martin had to tear copy from the machines and distribute it to the *Indianapolis Star*'s telegraph editor, the head of AP's night office for distribution to the Indiana wire, and to the "pony editor" responsible for editing copy for distribution to smaller state newspapers. "If the story was hot," he said, "I delivered it on the dead run. I loved it." Martin became enamored of newspaper work and learned how to operate a Teletype machine, edited copy for the pony editor, rewrote copy, covered some stories, assisted an AP photographer sent from New York to open a photo bureau in Indianapolis, and attended the state political convention with the AP's political reporter. His responsibilities might have only consisted of running the reporter's copy back to the office, he said, but the experience of sitting at a press table in front of the immense meeting hall made him feel as though he was covering the convention himself and heightened his interest in working in journalism. He aspired to join a boisterous profession. Reporters in Indianapolis after World War I and during Prohibition were "a wild and wooly bunch," noted John L. Niblack, who worked on the *Indianapolis Times* and later became a Marion County judge. Reporters were by nature cynical, he added, and they firmly "believed that eighty-five percent of public officials were crooked, or would be if properly tempted. There was no hero worship." Working with these kind of men on a daily basis rubbed off on Martin, who took to wearing his hat indoors on the back of his head like the Hildy Johnson reporter character in the Ben Hecht and Charlie MacArthur hit play *The Front Page.* "I have seldom been happier than at this time," said Martin. "I hoped it would last forever." He asked Ochiltree for a job as a reporter or editor, but the older man turned him down, saying he would not do so until Martin returned to college and earned his degree. Although disappointed, Martin, who was back at DePauw at the start of 1935, was relieved to be away once again from the turmoil of his Brookside Avenue home. His mother and father were still living together, but they slept in separate bedrooms and seldom spoke to each other, eating their dinner together in silence as J. W. waited to earn enough money to afford a divorce, which he finally managed to do a few years later (the couple later remarried).[25]

Martin was not the same reckless youth he had been when he first entered DePauw. Because of his year and a half working for the AP, he felt different from his fellow students at DePauw and "bore down hard" on his studies, majoring in political science and taking history and economics courses. Martin also "put a good deal of energy" into working for the student newspaper, *The DePauw,* a four-page broadsheet published every Monday, Wednesday, and Friday during the school year. Those who attended the Greencastle institution had been able to read a newspaper on campus since 1852, when the *Asbury Notes* became the first printed newspaper on what was then known as Indiana Asbury University. In 1935 the newspaper, along with the yearbook, *The Mirage,* found a permanent home with the opening of the Publications Building, next to Asbury Hall and funded by profits from the publications and loans from the Central National Bank of Greencastle. Students printed copies of *The DePauw* on presses using handset type at the downtown offices of the *Greencastle Banner.* "The type had ink on it, and it was a dirty, dirty job," said Mary Elizabeth Dye Walker, a proofreader for *The DePauw*. "The hard-working, always cheerful typesetters made the corrections by hand, removing each small metal type to add in the correct one. It was time consuming, but fast, capable hands made quick work of the job."[26]

During his time on *The DePauw*, Martin worked as its feature editor, city editor, and editor during the fall term in 1936. "Every night in the Delta Chi house the sound of Martin's typewriter could be heard after midnight," said James S. Sweet, a young fraternity brother. "He was always writing." Paul Van Riper, who worked as a reporter under Martin's editorship and later became a professor and chairman of the political science department at Texas A&M University, remembered it was under Martin's guidance that he first truly learned "how to combine facts and human interest with brevity." Van Riper added that as a brilliant writer, the best he ever knew personally, Martin was a hard taskmaster. "But you only learn to write by writing," said Van Riper, "and the experience worked for me."[27]

In addition to his other responsibilities for the newspaper, for two years Martin, called Johnny or John by his newspaper colleagues and college friends, wrote a regular column on the editorial page under the title "The Dog Watch," a perfect outlet for his fertile and creative mind. He possessed a knack for taking an idea and quickly turning it into a piece of writing. Davison noted that during his days at DePauw one of the popular songs was the mournful tune "Gloomy Sunday," originally composed by Hungarian pianist Rezső Seress and later recorded by Paul Robeson and Billie Holiday. One night Martin said to Davison, "I have an idea for a good short story on 'Gloomy Sunday.'" In the next instant, Davison said Martin sat down at his typewriter and in about an hour had produced a story. "I doubt if John ever submitted it for publication, but it was a good example of John's mind, ever running on a fast track," Davison recalled.[28]

Martin used whatever sprung to mind as subjects for his column, the name of which came from his experience with the AP in Indianapolis. As he noted in his first column, which appeared on May 17, 1935, if anyone happened to wander into the city room of a morning newspaper at around 2:00 AM he or she would not find a drunken brawl or gambling in progress. Instead he or she would find a young copy boy studying his algebra lessons and a middle-aged man ensconced on the copy desk's rim, holding down the dog watch, or lobster trick, while other staff members were home in bed. "He will be reading the previous edition, or watching the clock or just holding down the chair," wrote Martin. "Once in a while the boy will bring him a piece of copy, and usually he will glance at it and throw it away. Once in a while – about once a month, maybe – he will go to work and make over the front page just as it begins to roll." Martin related a story about a sportswriter on a Louisville newspaper assigned to the dog watch at a time when the pope, who had been ill, had recovered and the crisis appeared to be over. The presses were about to roll when a copy boy ran up with a bulletin with the news: "Pope Sinking." Thinking fast, the sportswriter wrote a new banner headline for the morning edition that read, "Pope Leads Death by a Nose."[29]

On Wednesdays Martin was obligated to report on campus gossip, which proved to be a must-read item that students eagerly scanned to see if they might have been mentioned. On other days Martin had the freedom to write about what he wanted. He often offered a jaundiced view on the news of the day, including the opening of Congress, the controversial love affair between Wallis Simpson and King Edward VIII of England, First Lady Eleanor Roosevelt's six-day-a-week newspaper column "My Day," the high salary of Saint Louis Cardinals pitcher Dizzy Dean, the gossip journalism employed by national columnist Walter Winchell, and the annual fuss made each fall over big-time college football. Martin also had the temerity to lampoon one of the most sacred events in Indiana, the Indianapolis 500 race held each Memorial Day. Two days before drivers started their engines for the race, he wrote, people from all over the country had lined up outside the gates of the Indianapolis Motor Speedway in an attempt to have their photographs in newspapers as the first person in line. "They come from all parts of the country," he noted, "and these early birds drive old automobiles and are frequently pretty terrible people." On race day those in attendance at the speedway included an army of ice cream and bond salesmen, banana peddlers, and "tens of thousands of guys named Joe. . . . It's just like a county fair, only the bearded lady and the Streets of Paris and the Ferris wheel are missing. It's the greatest county fair of them all." Martin also compared the action on the brick track to the gladiatorial combat of the Roman Empire, with drivers in their tiny automobiles crashing into walls at a hundred miles an hour, steering their flaming vehicles away from others in the race while others cut in and cause cars to crash. "It is the Roman Holiday of the great unwashed," Martin wrote. As a show, however, it could not be beat, and he planned on probably being a face in the crowd when the race started.[30]

Although his writing could be flippant and condescending at times, there were occasions when in his column Martin produced work reminiscent of his later long-form magazine journalism that dealt with the underdogs of American society. Approximately a year after the July 22, 1934, death of Hoosier gangster John Dillinger, Martin reflected on how Dillinger went from a "two bit hood from a hick town in the heart of the corn belt" to a legend not only in his home state of Indiana, but throughout the Midwest. "He captured the public fancy as no one has since the days of Jesse James, and he took the breaks as they came and went out quiet," wrote Martin. In their imaginations, people began to see Dillinger everywhere at night, "flitting before a full moon over some darkened road, hunched over the wheel of a fast car, roaring through the night." But even legends come to inglorious ends, as Martin pointed out that when he prepared to bury his son, Dillinger's father learned the suit Johnny would wear for eternity was too big. Martin also produced a quieter character study of a boxer he met at a bar who boasted that he had been the welterweight champion of the world in 1910. The man, who said his name was Tommy Burns, came in to the tavern and began to tell his stories of gambling and fast living all around the world, talking "well, if somewhat profanely, and all who listened to his ramblings laughed continuously," Martin observed. "But once in a while, you felt you were laughing at him and not with him." Nonplused by his audience's tone, the boxer told of the time when one of the bartenders had beaten up a man cheating in a card game, bragged about his ability to pick winners in horse races, and reminisced about his time as an infantry captain in World War I. Finishing his stories by noting he had friends everywhere – New York, San Francisco, Chicago, London – the fighter finally made his exit. When Martin asked the bartender about the veracity of the man's stories, the bartender responded:

"He's been around. It's a little mixed up to him. But it's all true."

"But how old is he? He doesn't look over 30."

"He's 49 now. Does look young, doesn't he?

"Sure does. Married?"

"No. Just wandering around. A funny guy."

"Yes. A funny guy."[31]

Rooming alone at the Delta Chi house, Martin often worked late into the night on his writing, making it difficult for him to wake up for his morning classes. "I can assure you that Martin did not appreciate being awakened in the morning, as I had the task once in a while," said Sweet, responsible for this unwanted duty as a Delta Chi pledge. Sweet also had to pick Martin's dirty clothes off the floor and place them in a corrugated paper and canvas laundry bag to mail home for cleaning, something, Sweet said, practically every student at DePauw did with their own laundry. When he worked in Indianapolis during the summer of 1935, Davison said Martin introduced him to a number of new experiences, including soft-shoe dancing at a café on North Meridian Street and a visit to a large public dance hall to hear Louis Armstrong and his band perform. "John and I, as the only Caucasian faces in the hall, sat in the balcony, looking down on a sea of couples weaving to the rhythms and soaking up the Satchmo's crackly singing and pure hot jazz of the Armstrong trumpet," Davison said.[32]

During his junior year at DePauw, Martin began a romantic relationship with a freshman student and Delta Delta Delta sorority member, Barbara Bruce, who came from a wealthy family in the Chicago suburb of Evanston, Illinois. When he first met her, Barbara, whom Martin described as "a gorgeous lascivious blonde," reminded him of Lady Brett Ashley, the seductive siren in Hemingway's novel *The Sun Also Rises*. Her manufacturer father, Alexander Douglas Bruce, a Canadian immigrant who had begun life as a factory worker in Chicago, was rich enough to drive a large Packard and pay for another daughter to have her debut at the Stevens, a posh Chicago hotel, with music provided by swing legend Benny Goodman. To Martin, Barbara's mother seemed "formal and distant"; neither of her parents drank alcohol. He remembered trips to Chicago with Barbara, dining at the Blackhawk Restaurant and over- hearing the waiters speak with Italian and East European accents that he "had never heard in Indiana; an exotic place." Although her experi- ence with Chicago had been limited to nightclubs and the expensive stores on Michigan Avenue, Barbara, Martin believed, had introduced him to a new, exciting wonderland, and he "fell in love with Chicago, a love affair that never ended." The city stood as a Mecca for young men in the Midwest like himself, he noted, who may have not known what they were seeking, but believing, as they heard train whistles blare, that "somewhere there must be more than the town they lived in." Martin fell "wildly in love" with Barbara in spite of their differences – she came from polite society, while he was the son of a workingman. Martin could not imagine how they both knew they were in love at such a young age and realized she possessed faults as well as beauty. "She was vulnerable, easily hurt, and she had an almost childlike manner," he said.[33]

After only a year at DePauw, Barbara dropped out and returned to Evanston. Fearing that her father might try to end her relationship with Martin by setting private detectives on her trail, she returned to the university to tell her beloved she wanted to get married immediately. Martin acquiesced to her wishes, and on a bitter winter night on January 23, 1937, in the shabby quarters of a justice of the peace on the square in downtown Greencastle, they were wed. "I met him on the street when he had just gotten married," Sweet said of Martin, "and he showed me a bottle of gin he had bought to celebrate." Martin went to Chicago to break the news to Barbara's father, who dispassionately responded, "You married her, now support her." With his small earnings as editor of the DePauw student newspaper and as string correspondent for the *India- napolis Times,* Martin rented a small, furnished room for the two of them off campus. He had worked as the *Times's* Putnam County correspon- dent for at least a year before his marriage, dealing with Robert Baker, the newspaper's state editor, who often encouraged the young writer in his correspondence. Baker commiserated with Martin over lost letters, lack of space in the *Times* for his work, and slow payment for his pub- lished articles. In early 1936 Baker urged Martin not to "get discouraged and don't feel I am letting you down. It's always a little awkward getting a correspondence started, but once we hit the stride everything will be jake." Martin responded by peppering Baker with story ideas, including a revision of the student government's constitution, results and news from DePauw's various sports teams, and arrests made by the county sheriff's office. By the time the 1936 elections rolled around in November, Baker trusted Martin to come through when it mattered, writing him that the newspaper knew it could "depend on you to do the usual good job."[34]

Editors at the *Times* must have been pleased with Martin's work because in the spring of 1937 they offered him a full-time job at a weekly salary of $22.50. Martin accepted their offer and arranged with university officials to finish his coursework in absentia while working in Indianapolis. "They were insistent that I come at once," Martin said of his editors, "and I was afraid not to, remembering 1933." The April 26, 1937, issue of *The DePauw* included an editor's note announcing the end of "the lively two-year career of Johnny Martin's column, 'The Dog Watch.'" The note added that Martin had resigned to devote his full time to "winding up his college work in time to graduate by May 10, when he will take a position on the INDIANAPOLIS TIMES."[35]

The newlyweds moved into a one-room apartment in Indianapolis and were able to furnish it thanks to a loan from Barbara's father, who might have relented because Martin had found a job on an established newspaper. First published as the *Indianapolis Sun* in 1888, the newspaper became the *Times* in 1923 after its purchase the year before by Scripps-Howard Newspapers, headed by Roy Howard, who had grown up in Indianapolis and worked for both the *Indianapolis Star* and *Indianapolis News*. The *Times* enjoyed a reputation as a vigorous and crusading newspaper, winning the Pulitzer Prize for public service in 1928 for its coverage the year before exposing the oppressive influence of the Ku Klux Klan in the state. In comparison to the other newspapers in the city, which Martin described as supporting the Republican Party and filled with dull, uninspired reporting, the *Times* was "lively, aggressive, liberal, and leaning Democratic, more fun to read and to work on. The *Times* hired you young, paid you little, and promoted you fast." On Martin's first day of work at the newspaper he received a curt assignment from the city editor, who told him, "Report to Heze Clark at 4 A M tomorrow. He'll tell you what to do."[36]

Clark, whose full name was Hezlep Williamson Clark, had been the police reporter at the *Times* since July 1, 1928, and remained in the same position until his death in 1956, earning a distinction as the oldest working police reporter in the country. Although born in Michigan, Clark had come as a youth to Bluffton, Indiana, where his father and uncle operated a newspaper that staunchly supported Prohibition. Later in life Clark still had vivid memories of falling into a batch of printer's ink at the age of five. He also enjoyed reminiscing about the time in 1891 when his father, also the son of a newspaperman, brought him for the first time to Indianapolis. After a fire engine raced by the duo, Clark's father took him by the hand and said, "you might as well cover your first fire." A star football player at Shortridge High School in Indianapolis, Clark went on to earn All-American honors as a halfback during his junior year at Indiana University, graduating in 1907. He started his newspaper career as an assistant sports editor with the *Star,* covered the police beat on the *Terre Haute Tribune,* and returned to Indianapolis to cover the federal courthouse for the *Sun.* He left journalism in 1923 to coach athletics at Rose Polytechnic Institute (today Rose-Hulman Institute of Technology) in Terre Haute, leaving five years later to join the *Times* as its police reporter. Over his many years on the job, Clark, a chunky, balding figure, became known for his tenacious recording of facts on cases, his loyalty to the newspaper, his unrelenting work ethic, and his detailed memory. Once asked the secret to his longevity, the respected newsman responded, "Come to work a little earlier, work a little harder and work a little longer and you'll always be on top."[37]

Martin had the unenviable task of replacing the then sixty-year-old Clark on the 4:00 AM to noon police reporter shift (Clark switched to the afternoon shift). For a week Martin followed the veteran newsman as he prowled around the corridors of police headquarters, raced to the scene of crimes and fires, collected all the facts he could, and phoned them in to the rewrite men on the *Times* news desk. Martin discovered that although Clark could not write a proper English sentence, he was the "most thorough collector of facts on police cases I ever knew." The neophyte reporter learned from Clark whom to talk to, whom he should avoid, and what questions he should ask. "They didn't call it 'on the job training' or 'internship;' they called it 'breaking the kid in,'" Martin re-

membered. "That's what it was. After a week I was there alone. That's how
I became a reporter." Many years later, while teaching at Northwestern
University's Medill School of Journalism, Martin wondered how a student could manage to spend thousands of dollars and a full year "learning less than Heze Clark taught me in a few days [for] free." Martin must
have learned well from Clark, because he graduated from covering the
police beat to doing rewrite on the city desk, taking telephone calls from
reporters, jotting down notes on what they had discovered, and writing
the stories for the next afternoon's edition. "I wrote fast and apparently
satisfactorily," said Martin, "and Norman Isaacs, the managing editor,
later a well-known editor and educator, told me I should be writing magazine, not newspaper pieces." By the time he had turned twenty-three in
August 1938 Martin had been promoted to covering the Indianapolis
City Hall, one of the most coveted beats at the newspaper.[38]

Even before Isaacs's suggestion, Martin had itched to escape the
grind of daily newspaper work. Although he loved his job as a reporter,
he had begun to realize it was a profession that "didn't pay anybody any
money." He had also begun to realize that the profession was a trap he
was caught in, with little chance of ever escaping to publish articles with
national magazines or try his hand at writing a novel. "Because it is pretty
near impossible to pound a typewriter for eight hours a day then come
home at night and pound one some more," said Martin. "You are writing
your guts out on the paper each day and you haven't got anything left at
night to put into a book because it is all spilled out on newsprint that
ladies will use to wrap the garbage in or paper the pantry shelves with
tomorrow." Barbara had seemed happy enough to come and live in Indianapolis, but after a year of marriage Martin sensed some discontent had
developed between the two of them. "We both knew vaguely it wasn't
exactly what we wanted," he noted.[39]

In the fall of 1937 Martin had contracted pneumonia and his doctor
had recommended a warmer climate for the winter, perhaps a cruise in
the tropics, a laughable suggestion for the cash-strapped Martin. Fortunately, Martin's father-in-law gave him and his wife the money for
the trip, the *Times* approved a leave of absence, and Barbara's uncle, a
travel agent, booked them on a thirty-day Caribbean cruise on a 1,600-
ton freighter, the *Stella Lykes*, equipped to carry only eight passengers.

"I was feeling so expansive that I bought a copy of *Harper's* magazine, at fifty cents; a luxury I could not ordinarily afford, and we took a train to Louisiana," said Martin. "I had never been so far from home." The freighter made several port calls in Puerto Rico before heading back to the United States. Unwilling to face the frigid Indianapolis weather, the couple decided, by chance, to disembark when the ship docked at Santo Domingo (then called Ciudad Trujillo), the capital of the Dominican Republic. "We knew nothing whatever about the Dominican Republic; we picked it only because the other passengers on the boat were Texans getting off there to drill for oil," Martin said.[40]

On the island of Hispaniola, the Dominican Republic, about the size of the combined states of Vermont and New Hampshire, dominates the eastern two-thirds of the island, while Haiti occupies the western third. Martin, who stayed in the Dominican Republic for several months with Barbara, became enchanted by the country's beauty, especially its high mountains, jungles, rushing streams and rivers, glittering, nearly empty beaches, as well as its affordable cost of living. "In those days nearly all travelers arrived by boat," said Martin, "their baggage hauled to hotels by horsedrawn carts. Men sipped rum in Parque Colón, affianced couples promenaded there on a Sunday evening, the streets were clean and the people well-dressed, and a room cost a dollar a day at a little thick-walled waterfront hotel." Most of the time Martin and Barbara preferred to stay in native villages away from the places tourists usually congregated because, as he noted, it "was cheaper and more fun." Beyond this "idyllic façade," however, lurked a totalitarian state run since 1930 by its president, Generalissimo Rafael Trujillo, who imprisoned, tortured, and killed those who dared oppose his rule. "Everyone whispered. Everyone feared. No one trusted anyone," said Martin. Informers and spies for the government recruited from every level of society honeycombed the country, while soldiers and members of the secret police buttressed Trujillo's dictatorial rule with their ruthless behavior. Trujillo made the military into a privileged class, and its officers grew rich thanks to his beneficence. "When I traveled, I was stopped frequently by troops at checkpoints," Martin recalled. "My mail was opened. When I shopped in the capital, clerks, no doubt informers for the secret police, knew my name, perhaps because upon arriving I had listed my profession as journalist.

The foreign press was censored. The local press was servile. Everybody feared Trujillo." In spite of all the country's problems, Martin developed a deep affection for the Dominican Republic. The Dominicans seemed wonderful to him, he said, "perhaps because they had suffered so much." In subsequent years he often pondered on what a splendid place the Dominican Republic could be if only its people could win their freedom from Trujillo's tyrannical government. "That doomed beautiful island republic played a crucial role for me lifelong," he said.[41]

Martin's experiences in the Dominican Republic, and another chance occurrence, started what became a long career as a magazine writer. Leaving for home, Martin and Barbara traveled on a luxury ship of the French Line shipping company to Santiago de Cuba on the southeast coast of Cuba. From there, the couple took a bus to Havana, where they booked passage on a ship to Miami, Florida. Martin said they had just enough money to buy steerage tickets (the cheapest class) for the trip to the United States, but he convinced the ship's steward to upgrade their accommodations to a first-class cabin. Once in Miami, Martin and Barbara received an infusion of cash, probably from her father, and spent the next six weeks enjoying the white-sand beaches of Fort Myers Beach, Florida. One warm morning the two of them were relaxing on a deserted beach when another couple, older than they were, appeared and sat down to talk. The man introduced himself to Martin as Jack DeWitt and said that he earned a living as a writer. "All my life I had wanted to be a writer, but I had never met one," said Martin.[42]

DeWitt told Martin he wrote stories for fact-detective magazines, including *American Detective Magazine* and *Inside Detective Magazine,* a genre of writing the young reporter had never before heard of or read. These periodicals published supposedly true accounts of criminal cases, and DeWitt gave Martin the name of a man in Chicago, Harry Keller, editor of *Official Detective Stories* and *Actual Detective Stories of Women in Crime,* who might be open to submissions from an unknown writer. As DeWitt later wrote Martin, Keller could give him "more real help than anyone I know. Besides that he'll be glad to do it. He has a hell of a lot of background experience and can shortcut you to writing better copy." During their meeting on the beach, Martin told DeWitt of his encounters with the Trujillo dictatorship and its seemingly all-powerful soldiers, and DeWitt responded by saying that an article on Trujillo might interest the editors at *Ken: The Insider's World,* a liberal-leaning, biweekly magazine published by *Esquire* that often printed exposés. Martin related to DeWitt how one night at a dance in a small town in the country's interior he had seen a soldier take a teenage girl by the hand and lead her outside, where they disappeared together into the darkness. Although Martin was uncertain whether the girl had been afraid of, or just enamored with, the soldier, DeWitt said he could embellish the tale as an example of the military's power. "He went on to tell me how to organize the piece – start with the Haitian massacre or the girl episode," Martin said, "give a few paragraphs on the republic's history, relate Trujillo's origins and how he came to power, describe his regime, and end by explaining the United States' policy toward him."[43]

Upon his return to Indianapolis in the spring of 1938, Martin attempted to write freelance articles for magazines, a difficult task with a full-time job. He failed to convince editors at *The New Republic* and *The Nation* to accept his articles on such topics as the National Greenback Party, which had its headquarters in Indianapolis, as well as what was happening with Doctor Francis Townsend's old-age pension scheme, known as the Townsend Plan. He labored over his typewriter at night and on weekends trying to break free from newspaper work. Martin finished a travelogue he had begun while in the Dominican Republic, writing most of it while in the mayor's office covering the Indianapolis City Hall beat, but could find no publisher for it. Using DeWitt's name, Martin wrote Keller, and the editor invited him to submit outlines of criminal cases he might write about for his magazines. Martin also received encouragement when he wrote to Arnold Gingrich, the founder of *Esquire* and editor of *Ken,* about his idea for an article on Trujillo, a subject Gingrich had been interested in for some time. "I did the piece fast and sent it in," said Martin. "He sent it back for rewrite." For his next attempt, Martin took his time, getting help from Vern Boxell, city editor at the *Times,* who helped him tighten the piece. "I did as DeWitt had suggested: invented a girl who was raped by a soldier," Martin said. "I never again invented an episode in a serious magazine piece, for it is a shabby trick, a counterfeit substitute for solid reporting." It worked; Gingrich accepted the article and paid Martin $150. For years until it finally wore out, Martin carried in his wallet the voucher from the first check he ever received for a freelance story.[44]

Misfortune intruded on Martin in the summer of 1938 when Barbara's mother in Evanston fell ill and died. Her father, the self-made Republican businessman who liked to remind his university-educated son-in-law that "I went to the college of hard knocks," asked the young couple to leave Indianapolis and move in with him; they agreed, which Martin later admitted was a mistake. This time the management at the *Times* refused to grant Martin a leave of absence, so he resigned and decided to find out if he could make a living freelancing. "I was trying to write but found it hard going in that house," he said. Living near Chicago, at that time the fourth largest city in the world and a place he called the capital of the Midwest, excited Martin. "The horizons in Indiana seemed suffocatingly close," he said, "the ceiling in Chicago unlimited." It had been that way when he had made his first trip to Chicago as a boy when his parents took him to visit a distant cousin. For the rest of his life he remembered the view from his cousin's apartment overlooking "unbelievable Lake Michigan"; how his cousin made gin in his bathtub; how he lived not far from Wrigley Field, the home of the Chicago Cubs; his cousin's breezy "side-of-the-mouth accents"; and one unbelievable night when his cousin drove to a movie with his wife and his car broke down and he traded it on the spot for a new one, "a magnificent gesture" that Martin long believed had something to do with the Chicago spirit.[45]

Attempting to take advantage of the "bright lights and excitement and boundless opportunity" Chicago offered, Martin visited the editors of *Ken* at their impressive offices in the thirty-seven-story Palmolive Building on the lakefront at the head of Michigan Avenue to share ideas he had for articles. "They were not enthusiastic – the ideas were not really worked out, were only glimmering of ideas," he said. Keller, a tall, bald man in his forties with offices in Chicago's warehouse district, proved to be more welcoming. "He encouraged me to write for him – at present he had no reliable contributor in the Chicago area," Martin recalled. "I told him about an old murder case in Indianapolis, and he thought it sounded promising." Keller also introduced Martin to his associate editors, Wiley S. "Mickey" Maloney and Phil Weck, both of whom secretly wanted to be writers. After the workday had finished, Martin joined the three men for drinks at a dark and dingy saloon across the street.[46]

As Martin struggled to make a start with his freelance career, his marriage suddenly fell apart. One morning he awoke to discover that Barbara had left sometime in the night. After dressing, he went downstairs to breakfast and, after the maid had brought his coffee, asked Barbara's father where she had gone. The older man said his daughter had taken his Packard and driven to Columbus, Ohio, the hometown of the man she had intended to marry before she met Martin. Barbara returned to Evanston after a couple of days and told her husband she no longer loved him, had intended to reconnect with her old boyfriend, discovered he had married somebody else, and now did not know what she wanted to do. Still, she believed Martin should leave her father's house and they should get a divorce. "That night in our bedroom I pleaded with her to change her mind," Martin said. "She would not. Then she laughed at me and said I was being silly, she didn't love me anymore. I did not understand but accepted it as though I did." The next day Martin packed up his few belongings and Barbara drove him to Keller's office. "We said goodbye, she in the car, I standing in the cobblestone gutter, and she drove off," Martin recalled. Although the couple's divorce became final on October 16, 1939, for some time he "could not shake the memory of her lying naked with me in an apartment fold-down bed in the hot Indianapolis summer night."[47]

After Barbara drove away, Martin picked up his bags and went to meet with Keller. He told the editor that his marriage had ended and he wanted to return to Indianapolis (Martin had five dollars, enough for a one-way coach railroad ticket) to do the necessary legwork on the old murder case they had previously discussed, and then come back to Chicago to freelance. By this time, after studying Keller's magazines and talking to Maloney and Weck, Martin had learned much about how to tailor his writing for the true-crime market. Keller could see that Martin had taken his personal troubles hard, and he magnanimously gave Maloney the afternoon off so he could sit and drink beer with Martin at the bar across the street until it was time for Martin's train to leave. "I never forgave Barbara's defection," said Martin, "but never ceased being

grateful to her for introducing me to a wider world than Indianapolis."
He returned to Indianapolis, stayed with his mother at the family's house
on Brookside Avenue, did the necessary research on the murder case,
wrote the article, and sent it to Keller. While in town, Martin also conducted preliminary legwork on two story ideas he had in mind for *Ken*
magazine, one on the political fortunes of Paul McNutt, former Indiana
governor and high commissioner to the Philippines, and the other an
exposé about the Indianapolis 500. Martin's father lived in an apartment
on the north side of town on West Twenty-Eighth Street with his new
wife, Mae, whom Martin liked, as she was "so much jollier than my poor
sad mother." During a visit there, J. W. expressed his doubts about his
son beginning a freelance career in Chicago. Mae, however, as Martin
recalled, told his father, "Let him go, John." Martin eventually learned
that his father had taken a copy of the issue of *Ken* that featured his article on Trujillo to proudly show it off to "his lawyer and his banker and
the construction cronies with whom he ate lunch." When his father died,
Martin discovered among J. W.'s papers a copy of the magazine with the
page number of his article written on the cover in his father's handwriting. "He did not like me much in my teens and my early twenties, nor I
him," said Martin, "but long before he died I realized he'd been right at
that time, I'd been a fool, and I regained my love and even my respect
for my father."[48]

Keller bought Martin's Indianapolis murder story for $175, about
twenty-five dollars over the usual rate the editor paid freelancers. With
the money from that sale, and equipped with a typewriter his grandmother had bought for him while he was in high school, Martin returned
to Chicago for a career in the haphazard world of freelance writing. "It
worked out," Martin said. At the time he thought he decided to go to
Chicago because he wished to escape from Indianapolis. Upon reflec-
tion, though, Martin believed he returned because he wished to "show
my divorcing wife that I could succeed in the big town at my chosen
work and without her – as though she'd care – and perhaps too because
for a time I wanted to be near her and hoped she would change her mind
about having fallen out of love." Barbara, however, never returned and
Martin never saw her again. He was on his own in a city that had nurtured writers as diverse as Edgar Lee Masters, Carl Sandburg, Vachel

Lindsey, Theodore Dreiser, and James T. Farrell and that had lionized such Progressive-era icons as Jane Addams of Hull House and attorney Clarence Darrow, who fought for lost causes because they "were the only ones worth fighting for." Martin had finally shaken off the mental shackles imposed by Indianapolis's Brookside Avenue and had made it to a place "where the action was."[49]

THREE

Two Cents a Word

AT THE NORTHWEST CORNER OF RUSH STREET AND GRAND Avenue in Chicago, the 217-room Milner Hotel, part of the coast-to-coast empire of 130 units in twenty-six states owned by company founder Earle Milner, offered the tired traveling businessman and tourist basic lodging at a reasonable price – "A Room and a Bath for a Dollar-and-a-Half," boasted the chain's motto. It was at the Milner that John Bartlow Martin resided when he returned to Chicago from Indianapolis in the fall of 1938. In addition to the Milner's inexpensive rates (five dollars a week on a monthly basis), its management paid the cab fare from the railroad station for guests and also provided them free laundry service. "It suited me fine," said Martin. "I had nothing but one suitcase and a portable typewriter. I had a room with a bed and through the dirty window a view of the fire escape."[1]

After escaping from his depressing Indianapolis childhood, Martin was thrilled to be in a vibrant and colorful city and delighted in its "free-wheeling, go-getting" spirit. While a high school student, he had wandered with a friend though Indianapolis's scanty slums, disappointed they were so small, while in Chicago "there were acres and acres of them, all mine." Martin even enjoyed the noisy traffic on Outer Drive and Western Avenue, the sound of the elevated trains as they "roared by overhead on the wondrous El, reared against the sky," and the bright lights of Randolph Street's theater district. "There was nothing like this in Indiana," he said. As he had while a young student at DePauw University, Martin, suddenly single, behaved foolishly for a time, sleeping most of the day, writing at night, and drinking beer while he worked. He soon discovered, however, that he could not keep up such a lifestyle and make a living, and he fell into a regular routine he followed for years to come, writing from nine in the morning to five in the evening and avoiding alcohol during those hours.[2]

The near north side neighborhood in which the Milner stood, and its sometimes shifty clientele, offered their own distractions for the budding freelancer. A scattering of garrets, apartment houses, French restaurants, and nightclubs filled with artists, writers, performers, and hoodlums dotted the neighborhood. "In the expensive nightclubs," Martin remembered, "you could see not only well-to-do suburbanites, but big shot Syndicate men with their show girls. Ever since [Al] Capone's time, Chicagoans have enjoyed gangster watching." A disappointed Martin soon discovered that many who inhabited the area were, like himself, "kids out of college drinking beer by a fireplace at the Pub [a bar across the street from the Milner], and most went into the advertising business and moved to the suburbs or to New York." Gambling – roulette, craps, blackjack – was widespread, with dice games running twenty-four hours a day in saloons along Rush Street. Upon entering a tavern, patrons could flirt with the "26" girls who ran a dice game, for which the prize was often coupons for free drinks. Jazz singer Anita O'Day, who got her start as a "26" girl at Kitty Davis's University Bar and Cocktail Lounge, noted that a "bunch of pretty girls in low-cut, slit-skirt gowns were a big attraction for any guy who wandered in."[3]

Everyone Martin met in Chicago seemed to have paid a bribe to a policeman or expected to do so. Bar patrons nervously eyed one another, "each wondering," he observed, "if all the others were gangsters, and it seemed to be part of the code not to talk to strangers, but to stand at a bar hour after hour almost shoulder to shoulder, never speaking, never quite touching one another, lest a false move, as in a Grade-B Western, trigger bloodshed." Martin took to carrying his money loose in his pocket instead of in a wallet. "It was all rather innocent foolishness," he said of those days. While living at the Milner, Martin befriended a man who claimed he worked as a newspaper police reporter, but he never seemed to be at his job, carried a large roll of cash, and drove a flashy Cadillac. The man delighted in driving close to traffic policemen on rainy nights, splashing them, and shouting curses at them as he drove away at top speed. "When I discovered he carried a gun," said Martin, "I stopped seeing him."[4]

Martin had enjoyed some freelance success with a couple of articles for *Ken,* including one on Paul McNutt, the former Indiana governor and U.S. High Commissioner to the Philippines, and his chances for securing the 1940 Democratic presidential nomination, which ran in the magazine's May 18, 1939, issue under the title "The Return from Manila," and a piece on the Black Hand, a precursor of the Mafia, which had been published by *Esquire.* His meal ticket, however, proved to be writing articles for editor Harry Keller's true-crime magazines *Official Detective Stories* and *Actual Detective Stories for Women in Crime,* known in the trade respectively as OD and AD. During its heyday from 1935 to 1945, the true-crime genre attracted millions of readers across the country, with consumers having their pick of as many as seventy-five different periodicals on the average corner newsstand. A host of notable names in American literature wrote for these magazines, including Dashiell Hammett, Erle Stanley Gardner, Jim Thompson, Harlan Ellison, Ellery Queen, and Nunnally Johnson. Because he felt uneasy interacting with Chicago's intimidating police, Martin at first depended upon writing about older cases, doing his research at the public library to obtain the necessary information for the 7,500-word stories Keller sought. Martin gradually developed the nerve to interact with beat cops and detectives. Because detectives were under orders from the police commissioner not to speak to reporters without his authorization (they talked to newspaper reporters anyway, but not to Martin), he sidestepped this regulation by visiting outlying district police stations, and cops soon became used to his presence. "Sometimes I took a bottle of good brandy to a detective or promised to 'buy you a hat' – give him a twenty dollar bill," said Martin. He also established a small network of sources, including court clerks, the superintendent at the Cook County jail, assistant state's attorneys, and the coroner. The last two, often neglected by newspaper reporters, became his best sources, as the assistant state's attorneys allowed him to access official police reports when detectives refused, and the coroner, in his questioning of detectives, extracted information they would have otherwise reserved for trial proceedings.[5]

In each of his articles for the true-crime trade, Martin included every single fact he had space for, letting, he noted, "the facts speak for themselves." He tried to be meticulous when checking details about each case, making sure the dates and names of those involved were correct. Each story of his had to be accompanied by an affidavit stipulating that he could produce documentary evidence of the facts in each story. "In my stories documentation must be like plumbing: It must be there but it must not be visible," he explained. Unlike some fact-detective writers, Martin visited the scenes of the crimes to make his descriptive passages even more convincing. "I tried to get some of the flavor of Chicago itself into the stories," he said, "sometimes using Chicago dialect in the dialogue and the grim Chicago humor." Martin also had to try and meet Keller's high expectations. "He took his work very seriously and demanded that we do too," said Martin. The two great nightmares in this type of writing – libel and the threat that postal officials might find the material obscene and deny the magazine's publishing firm its second-class mailing privilege – guided Martin. "The trick," he said, "was to write right up to the edge of the obscene and stop." Beyond the few basic facts in a criminal case, the stories published in OD and AD included invented dialogue, embellished episodes, and fabricated clues. "To sell these stories must be sensationalized," he noted, pointing out that police reports or trial transcripts by themselves would not interest a layman. This did not make the writing any easier. "I worked as hard at this writing as at any I ever did and, given the constrictions of the genre, made it as good as I could," he said.[6]

In his work for Keller, Martin learned the uses of such techniques as "description, dialogue, characterization, and perhaps above all narrative pull – that mysterious invisible force that pulls the reader onward." The stories served as perfect training for his later career writing serious fact pieces for national magazines, teaching him how to conduct research and how to interview people. It also introduced him to the real Chicago, not the luxurious shops and restaurants his former wife had taken him to, but its vast political wards, where millions of working men, the people who built the city, lived in two-family dwellings, and its numerous slums that bred the thousands of criminals who gave Chicago its unsavory national reputation. Visitors yearned to believe that Chicago was wicked, said Martin, as a way to make themselves feel virtuous in comparison. "Chicago is everybody's whipping boy," he said.[7]

Doing stories for magazines such as AD, freelancers ghostwrote articles on behalf of victims or criminals. The subjects of the stories received a byline credit and $50 for their troubles, while the writer pocketed $150. Many of the women Martin wrote about in AD needed the money to help pay for a lawyer, while others were just thrilled at seeing their names and life stories in print. "I always sat with the woman and waited while she read her story, so she wouldn't change her mind or show it to someone else who might persuade her not to do it," he recalled. Martin could be quite persuasive with these women, setting out his qualifications and playing to their morality, vanity, greed, and hopes for aid with their legal problems. A potential article on a young Italian girl's troubles typified the difficulties Martin sometimes encountered trying to write about real-life tragedies. One day Martin went to a tenement in Chicago's Little Italy and persuaded the girl, the victim of incest or rape (he could not remember which), to permit him to write a story under her name; she agreed. "I interviewed her, went home and wrote the story," said Martin, "then took the story back for her approval. She asked me to read it to her, explaining to me she couldn't read." He was surprised to see other family members, and even a few neighbors, gathered around in a bare kitchen to hear the story. "Never did confession magazine sentences sound so peculiar, the stock sentences, that is, which were a convention of byliners," he recalled. Both the girl and her family, however, had a positive reaction to Martin's work, believing it to be an excellent story. "Actually, it wasn't," said Martin, "and the editor turned it down; rightly, I'm sure." Not only did Martin not get paid, neither did the girl, which convinced her angry brothers that the writer had cheated them. They started to hang around the magazine's office, waiting to confront Martin, before the editor there finally had enough and telephoned the police to come and remove the trespassers.[8]

Although edited by Keller, OD and AD were part of a publishing empire owned by Moses Annenberg, a veteran of the Chicago newspaper circulation wars whose control of the *Daily Racing Form* and the Nationwide News Services provided horse-racing information and allied him with gambling and criminal interests throughout the country. Annenberg's expansion of his publishing enterprise – starting a new crime magazine, *Intimate Detective,* and a true-confession magazine, *Living Romance* – offered Martin additional outlets for his writing. The divorced Martin even produced a monthly advice-to-the-lovelorn column for *Living Romance,* writing letters to himself and publishing his answers under the pen name Kathleen Stanhope. Annenberg's interest in the Molly Maguires, a secret society of Irish coal miners in Pennsylvania supposedly responsible for a variety of criminal activities after the Civil War, led him to suggest that Keller send a writer to do a series on the Mollies for OD, and the editor picked Martin for the job. "Keller and I had intended perhaps three pieces," said Martin. "But Annenberg became so engrossed in them that he could not get enough, and I believe I strung it out for eleven months." Martin remembered Annenberg coming in person to Keller's office to read advanced galley proofs, unable to wait for the published version. Annenberg's own legal troubles failed to dim his enthusiasm for the series. Pleading guilty to tax evasion charges, Annenberg received a three-year jail term, and before he went off to jail, Martin noted, he asked Keller for advance galleys of OD to learn how the story on the Mollies ended.[9]

At the peak of his true-crime and confessional writing career, Martin pounded out on his typewriter a million words a year, at first selling about a third of them, and later about half, at two cents a word. "The two-cents-a-word market, as we called it," he said, "wasn't bad." Martin often used pseudonyms (H. L. Spade was one favorite) and had three or four stories in one issue of Keller's magazines. "Toward the end Keller was taking just about everything I could write. . . . None of this seemed extraordinary to me," said Martin. "I had set out to be a freelance writer and I was one." If one of his stories failed to pass muster, he could talk about its deficiencies with associate editors Phil Weck, "a natural writer with a creative bent," Martin noted, and Wiley S. "Mickey" Maloney, who had worked several years for United Press, during one of their frequent meetings to drink a few beers and discuss writing. On Saturday nights he often went to their homes in the suburbs to eat dinner, play nickel-and-dime poker, and continue to talk about their work. When Maloney took his family to a rented cottage on a lake in northern Wisconsin, Martin visited them, relaxing from his busy writing schedule by fishing, an activity he had enjoyed since childhood. Keller and his wife sometimes joined them at the dinners. Keller proved to be a "difficult man," said Martin, adding that he was moody and drank far too much and even asked his employees to call him "Papa," perhaps imitating the famed writer of the time, Ernest Hemingway. "Imperious, highly opinionated, he ran his employee's lives to the extent he could," said Martin.[10]

Because of his newfound status as a regular contributor, Martin no longer had to closely read OD and AD for style tips, but could read whatever he pleased, and he became a fixture at Ben Abramson's Argus Book Shop at 333 South Dearborn Street in Chicago. Martin remembered Abramson as a "red-haired gnome-like little man with a mottled complexion who not only sold books but also read them – and loved them. He liked to encourage young writers." Abramson introduced Martin to Henry Watson Fowler's timeless 1926 stylebook *A Dictionary of Modern English Usage* and recommended that he read the section on rhythm. "I had never read anything about writing so exciting," Martin recalled. "I bought a copy and I use it yet. I was beginning to take writing seriously." He also pored over new works by John Steinbeck and Hemingway and old books by E. M. Forster and Aldous Huxley, studying them to try and adapt their fictional devices to his own crime writing. "I was reading *Harper's* and *Life* and dreaming of the day when they would lie on my desk not because I enjoyed them but because I was working for them," said Martin. He did not, however, have much time to pursue such possibilities, as he could not "afford to take time off from the stuff that was almost sure to sell." Years later, he still remembered taking the streetcar to the criminal courts building and Cook County jail on the city's southwest side. While the streetcar clattered its way to its destination, passing along the way the city's Jewish and Italian neighborhoods, Greek coffee shops, and gypsy encampments, Martin sat inside, absorbed in reading Marcel Proust's *Remembrance of Things Past*.[11]

As he prospered as a freelancer, Martin changed hotels every few months, residing at such establishments as the Hotel Maryland at 900 Rush Street and the Hotel Berkshire at 15 East Ohio Street. Each time he moved he traveled a few blocks north to better living arrangements, but he never left the city's north side, which had attractions that suited his tastes. A devotee of jazz while a young man in Indianapolis, Martin frequented Chicago's numerous musical venues, especially night-clubs along State Street, black-and-tan joints on the south side, and the Stevens and Congress Hotels. Usually alone, he often patronized the Three Deuces, a speakeasy during the days of Prohibition, at 222 North State Street. The club featured such fine musicians as cornetists Jimmy McPartland and Muggsy Spanier and trumpeter Wingy Manone. Martin's favorite singer, Chicago's own O'Day, also appeared at the Three Deuces with the Max Miller Combo. "She was the only girl vocalist I ever saw who sang more to the band than to the audience," said Martin. Alone late at night, Martin often walked up Michigan Avenue across the Chicago River and past the Wrigley Building and Tribune Tower. As he looked up at the black skyline and heard the throb of the traffic, he thought to himself, "There's a lot of power and money here, a lot going on." He wished he could write about what he felt about Chicago for serious magazines and vowed to do so "someday, somehow."

On another night out, this time at the Pub, with its sawdust floors and roaring fireplace, Martin sat drinking Scotch with a college friend, Grant Robbins, who had introduced him to his first wife while at De-Pauw University. Robbins had gone over to talk to some couples at the bar, and when he returned he asked Martin if he remembered the Ernest Dowson poem, "Cynara," as the people he met knew the first few lines but wanted to know the rest. "It happened that I did," said Martin, "and he and I joined the others." Robbins then introduced Martin to the woman who became his second wife, a "pretty little girl" named Frances Rose Smethurst, then twenty-one years old and a former student at Lawrence College in Appleton, Wisconsin. Martin recited the poem and managed to pry Fran, as he later came to call her, away from her date long enough to obtain her telephone number. (Perhaps cautious about this stranger, Fran gave Martin her work telephone number, not her home number.) The next day he asked her out on a date and took her to dinner at a north side restaurant. "She was slight," Martin said, "not quite five feet tall and one hundred pounds, with brown hair and brown eyes and a strong jaw which, on occasion, she set."[12]

The two dated regularly that winter and Martin met her parents, with whom she lived in a tumbledown house in Elmhurst, a middle-class suburb west of Chicago. Neither of her parents, including her father, a veteran of the Spanish-American War, drank, and they were shocked to learn that Martin's parents, his aunt, and of course Martin, had all gone through divorces. Eventually, Fran moved from her parents' Elmhurst house to an apartment on the near north side that she shared with two of her friends from her college days. "This pleased me greatly," said Martin, as he owned a 1937 Ford convertible with a torn top and no heater. In the winter months, the hour's drive from his Chicago apartment to Elmhurst "was enough to break up any romance." Martin's bad experience with marriage – he had been determined to never fall in love again – caused him to hold himself in reserve in this new relationship, which he said "seemed strange to Fran, though she said little about it, just looked knowing." She taught him how to sing and dance, while he introduced her to the beauties of jazz, how to play poker, and how to fish. Out of the blue one night in August 1940 while taking her home, Martin asked, "Why don't we get married?" Seeking to protect himself from too deep a commitment because of his first wife's betrayal, he warned Fran not to "expect a little white house in the suburbs with a picket fence." He added that if she agreed to his proposal, they would have to marry soon, as he wanted to go north to fish yet that week. Fran accepted and they were wed on Saturday, August 17, 1940, during a ceremony at the Congregational Church in Elmhurst.[13]

The couple's choice for a honeymoon spot occurred by chance. Martin did not want to return to northern Wisconsin, where he had fished with Maloney, as the area had grown "too civilized, too crowded with tourists, too organized." He and Fran decided on a trip to Michigan's Upper Peninsula, the land that runs horizontally across the top of Wisconsin. One writer described the region as "a wild and comparative Scandinavian tract – 20,000 square miles of howling wilderness on the shores of Lake Superior." The newlyweds took out a road map and came upon the name of a town they liked, Michigamme, which appeared remote because only one road, U.S. 41, ran nearby. Like many tourists, they were drawn to the Upper Peninsula by its "magnificent waterfalls, great forests, high rough hills, long stretches of uninhabited country, abundant fish and game," said Martin. It was the first of many such trips to the area in the years to come for the Martins. On their way north they passed through Wisconsin's rolling dairy region with its neat farms that were "small, tightly fenced, carefully tended," with German names emblazoned on the sides of enormous barns, noted Martin. Covered with a topcoat, Fran fell asleep in the car with Martin driving. Passing over a bridge near Pembine, Wisconsin, the car skidded. "I righted it, nothing happened," Martin remembered. "I looked at Fran. She was sleeping peacefully. Suddenly I felt a terrifying sense of responsibility. Now I really *was* responsible for her." He never had such a feeling for his first wife. "It took me a long time to grow up," Martin admitted.[14]

The newlyweds rented a camp, as cottages and cabins were called in that part of the country in memory of the days when lumber crews lived throughout the winter in logging camps, at Three Lakes, home to Ruth, George, and Beaufort Lakes. Conditions were primitive. "The camp was not much – a tarpaper shack with an attic bedroom, a big wood cookstove, a hand pump, an outhouse, and kerosene lanterns – but it was on the shore of beautiful Ruth Lake, and it shared the shore with a few other camps," said Martin. The region, he soon discovered, did not bend over backwards to welcome visitors. "You will have to do nearly everything for yourself," he warned other travelers. "The region is not geared to make your visit painless." Although the lack of modern conveniences and the clannishness of the locals could be maddening, if an outsider adjusted his thinking and fit into the system, he could find, said Martin, "no better vacation spot." A great spot, that is, if a visitor could accept another difficulty: mosquitoes, which in the Upper Peninsula were no joke, as they seemed to Martin to be as large as ducks and were equipped with stingers "like pneumatic drills." That first summer in the Upper Peninsula Martin worked every day on a half-dozen crime stories he had done legwork on in Chicago, relaxing by fishing in the evening. The fishing proved to be so good that he could tell Fran to select what she wanted for dinner – bass, walleyed pike, or northern pike – and he stood a good chance of getting "exactly what she ordered." Fran prepared meals for them on the woodstove and did their laundry on a scrubboard. "Some honeymoon," Martin reflected.[15]

The town of Three Lakes consisted at that time of just one country store, Numi's Service Station, operated by Earl Numinen, the son of a Finnish immigrant. As the social center for the tiny community, the store offered local residents and tourists gasoline from its two pumps (only one actually worked), fresh fruits and vegetables (once a week), beans, cigarettes, socks, Finnish boot grease, slabs of bacon, and a mosquito repellent known as Lollacapop. On Friday evenings Numinen's father fired up the sauna, or Finnish steam bath, and those who braved its overwhelming heat included miners attempting to sweat the hematite out of their pores and a few poor souls looking for relief from their hangovers. "A day lived at the store is like a year lived elsewhere," Martin said. He returned again and again to the area for summer vacations and began to believe he should write a book about this wild country. "These people are among the finest, friendliest on earth," he later observed, "and when they know and like you, there is absolutely nothing they will not do for you. But this takes time, you must not push, they have to find out about you."[16]

Two months after the December 7 Japanese attack on the American fleet at Pearl Harbor, and with the birth of their first child, Cindy, on February 5, 1942, the Martins moved from an apartment at 20 East Delaware Place in Chicago to a rented house at 1086 Crescent Lane on a quiet street in the Hubbard Woods neighborhood of Winnetka, Illinois. The move to a leafy suburb had been something Fran had been seeking ever since she had learned she was pregnant. In a July 1941 letter to Martin, vacationing alone in the Upper Peninsula, Fran said she could not stand the thought of living in "that one-and-a-half room job up on a top floor of some god-damn city building that I don't give a hang about! I want to be somewhere where I can see a blade of grass or a tree once in a while." She reminded her husband that she had been raised mainly outdoors in a big yard in Elmhurst, often vacationed in the wide open spaces of Colorado, and was not "made to look at nothing but buildings and sidewalks and stores and nightclubs." There were more practical reasons for the move, as in the coming months the pregnant Fran would be "rather ungainly looking and pretty awkward about getting around," particularly negotiating tricky El train platforms. She refused to "sit on her duff" for four or five months in a one-room apartment, wanting a place where she could go for a walk during the daytime and be closer to friends and family in Elmhurst. "Being a pregnant woman," she concluded, "I'd feel pretty out of place among the showgirls and prostitutes on Delaware Place." Fran got what she wanted, and Martin, though he doubted Winnetka itself had anything to do with it, noted that he and his young family "were happier there than before."[17]

Although he had at first held himself partially emotionally aloof because of the breakup of his first marriage, Martin had begun to realize just how important Fran had become to him, particularly in how he viewed his writing career. Musing in a letter to Fran while on a fishing trip to the Upper Peninsula, he noted that during his days as a bachelor in Chicago, writing meant to him "enough money to sit in bars all night talking about writing good," and he had a hunch that if it were not for her, he would still be stuck doing the same old thing, "wandering through swinging doors, the hero of a thousand drunks." Martin added that he thought of her "in everything I do or want to do," and sometimes it seemed "almost as if you are the reason I want to do the wonderful things, while it's mainly for me I want to do the wrong things." He believed he might be at his worst after spending time at his parents' house in Indianapolis, at his second worst alone, "but at my best with you, because you're something to live up to, because you're just wonderful." Later, Martin mused that Fran may have been the key to his coming of age as a writer and a man, as she gave him "an emotional base" on which to build a stable private life, and, by "attending to my writing, she set free something in me that had been till then locked up."[18]

While living in the Hubbard Woods neighborhood, Martin made an important reconnection with a friend from his days as a student at Arsenal Technical High School in Indianapolis. Francis S. Nipp, whom Martin called a "natural editor," was an English teacher earning his doctorate at the University of Chicago, and he and his wife, Mary Ellen, became frequent weekend guests at the Martins' home. The couples listened to music – Bix Beiderbecke, Benny Goodman, Fletcher Henderson, Jelly Roll Morton, and especially Louis Armstrong – and the two old high school friends talked obsessively about writing. Martin had begun to grow tired of the true-crime genre, which he once referred to as "monsters and ogres and fiends in human form." In addition to introducing him to serious classical music, Nipp convinced Martin to become a regular reader of *The New Yorker* and encouraged him to start thinking about submitting "serious nonfiction" to one of the country's most prestigious magazines, *Harper's*. Although it had a small circulation

(109,787 in 1940) and offered its contributors paltry fees (usually $250 for articles) in comparison to other magazines, *Harper's* reached a vital audience, what one of its editors described as "the intelligent minority" of opinion makers in the United States, "the thinking, cultured reader who seeks both entertainment and an enlarged and broadened point of view." By the late 1930s the magazine's subscribers could look forward to contributions from such noted writers as Elmer Davis and John Gunther, as well as monthly columns from historian Bernard DeVoto, "The Easy Chair," and E. B. White, "One Man's Meat." Frederick Lewis Allen, himself a bestselling author who took over as *Harper's* editor in October 1941, said the magazine under his watch intended to print "the exciting, the creative, the lustily energetic, the freshly amusing, the newly beautiful, the illuminating, the profound."[19]

Martin's entry into this world came about as the result of a bungled espionage operation in the United States by Nazi Germany's military intelligence organization, the Abwehr. On the pitch-black night of June 13, 1942, four men left a German U-boat and paddled their rubber dinghy to land on a beach near Amagansett, Long Island, south of New York City. The men were saboteurs sent by the German high command to infiltrate American society and, using high explosives and incendiary devices, wreck havoc on vital war-related installations on the East Coast. Known as Operation Pastorius in honor of the first German immigrant to the United States, Franz Pastorius, the bold plan also included a landing by another four-man team on June 17 at Ponte Vedra Beach south of Jacksonville, Florida. The daring venture disintegrated in rapid fashion; by June 27 the Federal Bureau of Investigation, tipped off by one of the saboteurs, George John Dasch, had arrested the members of each team and had recovered $174,588 of the $175,200 in U.S. currency given them to finance the operation. President Franklin D. Roosevelt insisted that the Germans were to be tried before a military commission. They were all found guilty and sentenced to death, but Roosevelt commuted Dasch's sentence to thirty years and gave another conspirator who had cooperated with authorities, Ernest Burger, a life sentence.[20]

Two of the eight doomed German agents were American citizens, including twenty-two-year-old Herbert Haupt, a worker at the Simpson Optical Company who had lived in Chicago with his parents on Fremont Street and had attended Lane Technical High School. During his youth his parents, especially his father, Hans Max, who had served in the German army during World War I, taught him to love Germany more than the United States. Haupt had been considered a bit of a playboy by his fellow saboteurs and after landing in Florida had gone on a shopping spree, buying a three-piece suit, a Bulova watch, silk handkerchiefs, and several pairs of shoes. He made his way to Chicago with thousands of dollars entrusted to him by his team members and tried to resume his old life there, only to be apprehended by the F B I.[21]

Writing a query letter to the editors of *Harper's* in early December 1942 about doing an article on Haupt and what happened to his parents and other relatives who helped him (they were tried and convicted of treason), Martin said the story could be seen as a tribute to the F B I's excellent work and that he had access to transcripts of the court's records. "This really is a fantastic story of how treason is nurtured," Martin wrote. He called it an "unbelievable true story of a youngster who grew up in a middle-class family on Chicago's North Side, was taken from a factory job and hauled by chartered plane and blockade runner more than halfway around the world to the Reich, was trained, with typical German thoroughness, in the methods of the saboteur, and returned to betray his country, and, failing, brought death to himself and his family and his friends." Eight days after sending his letter, Martin received an answer from Allen, who said the Haupt article seemed to be a "very promising possibility and we hope you give us a chance at it." Allen went on to warn Martin not to make too much of the story's moral or play up the dramatic and "fictionizable" aspects of Haupt's youth and background. "Simply and clearly told," Allen wrote, "with considerable sharp detail, it ought to be continuously interesting and impressive in its total effect. Of course you can do *some* pointing of the significance of the story; the great danger, I should think, would be of doing too much."[22]

At this point in his career, Martin did not yet really know how to write a serious fact piece for a national audience. His story on Haupt relied mainly on newspaper clippings, trial transcripts, and a certain amount of atmospheric writing that resulted from legwork he had done for his true-crime articles in German neighborhoods on Chicago's North Side, where Haupt grew up. "I plead ignorance," he said. "Later I became almost obsessed by being thorough in my research, and I always piled up high mountains of notes from interviews and documents and legwork on atmosphere that I could not use. But at that time I knew nothing of this and, I fear, wrote several pieces for *Harper's* mainly from clippings." He admitted he probably did less legwork on the Haupt article than he had done on many of his pieces for Keller's true-crime magazines. Considering the speed at which newspapers operated and the frequent inaccuracies they contained from being written by inexperienced reporters, Martin said it was a "miracle" he never had to answer a charge of libel or had any of his facts successfully challenged in his early work for *Harper's,* which also included a piece on the young members of Chicago's Polkadot Gang that robbed several taverns and killed an off-duty policeman.[23]

Martin had the good fortune to have as his editor Allen, who spent considerable time offering him suggestions for improving his Haupt manuscript before its publication in the magazine's April 1943 issue. Allen told Martin to alter his beginning, adding a reference to the initial landing of the saboteurs, "something everybody remembers and which will arouse sharp interest," and asked him to cut some of Haupt's pro-German sentiments, as they were repetitive. There were a few other queries and revisions he wanted Martin to review, but overall Allen said he did not believe there was anything that needed extensive revision. After seeking approval from the Office of Censorship, which Allen believed would not be a problem since the trial was public, he said the magazine would send Martin a check for $250. Martin wrote Allen back approving the new lead, saying it "sharpens the story and hammers home its significance." He ended his letter by noting his appreciation for the publication of his article and expressing the hope they "could click on another one before too long."[24]

Harper's became so interested in Martin and his work that he eventually traveled to New York to meet with Allen and his associate editors – Russell Lynes, George Leighton, John Kouwenhoven, Jack Fischer, and Eric Larrabee. Martin was impressed by this group, particularly Allen, whom he described as "a slight man, so slight he looked almost frail, with sparkling eyes and a ready laugh, a wise man with an endlessly inquiring mind." Back in high school or college Martin had read Allen's

classic book on America in the 1920s, *Only Yesterday,* and he eagerly
learned about how to write from the way Allen edited his stories, "cutting, tightening, endlessly tightening, and pointing up." Martin never
forgot one of Allen's pronouncements: "Never be afraid to address the
reader directly, to write, 'As we shall see,' or 'Let us first study the slum
itself,'" something Martin often did in his later multipart articles for the
Saturday Evening Post. Impressed by the work Martin had done on the
Polkadot Gang article, Leighton proposed that he begin writing articles
about what the editor called "crime in its social context," taking one
of his fact-detective cases, expanding the piece with additional facts,
getting rid of the fake detective work, and developing "the lives and
social backgrounds of the criminals and their victims." Subsequently,
crime became for Martin a way to write about his fellow human beings
and their place in society. He also learned that East Coast editors felt out
of touch with the rest of the country and often asked Martin about what
people cared and thought about in the Midwest. "Just as farm boys yearn
to go to New York, so do New York editors yearn to know what's on the
farm boy's mind," he said. "Sometimes they sounded almost anxious."
As he talked to them, some of the parochial concerns he had began to
fall away and Martin developed a different view of the country's problems and politics. "From editors I got something more valuable than
editing – insight and perspective," he noted.[25]

The leisurely, often luxurious trips Martin made from Chicago to
New York by railroad in the 1940s remained firmly etched in his mind
for years to come. For the sixteen-hour trip, he had his choice of two
trains – the Twentieth Century Limited, operated by the New York Central Railroad, or the Broadway Limited, run by the Pennsylvania Railroad. "You went down to the railroad station and waited at the gate with
the crowd and, when the gate opened, walked through clouds of steam
alongside the long train, all Pullman cars, and found your numbered
car," Martin remembered, "and the Negro Pullman porter in white uni-
form asked your space and, hearing it, called you by name and took your
bag and led the way to your roomette, the tiny antiseptic room with its
grey steel walls, its gleaming chrome washbowl that popped out of the
wall, the heavy windows with their rounded corners, the spongy uphol-
stery, the rust-colored blankets lettered PULLMAN, the little shoebox

with a door in the aisle so the porter could get your shoes and shine them during the night and replace them gleaming in the morning." Once he had stowed his bags, Martin retreated to the bar car so he could sit with a drink and watch through the window as the heavy industrial sights of northwestern Indiana faded into the flat plains of the northern part of the state. By the time dinner was served, the train had made its way to Ohio, the state where he had been born. After dinner, served on tables draped in white tablecloths and decorated with shining silverware and a bud vase with a single rose, he retired to his room to work for a time on his portable Remington Rand typewriter, usually preparing a memorandum or an outline for a story to share with an editor. "I would go to the bar car for a nightcap then back to my room," said Martin, "pull the bed down feeling it brush my pajamas, then squeeze into bed and snap off the lights and lie in bed watching the night, listening to the soft clickety-clack of the steel wheels on the steel rails in the night, sleeping."[26]

When Martin arrived in New York, he headed for 59 West Forty-fourth Street, the location of the Algonquin Hotel, where he always stayed, at first because of its writers' tradition (the hotel hosted the famed Algonquin Round Table that included Dorothy Parker, Robert Benchley, Heywood Broun, Ruth Hale, and George S. Kaufman), but later because he loved its "Edwardian elegance and [because he] came to know its staff and its owner and manager." Martin also preferred the Algonquin because of its location: the hotel was within walking distance of almost anywhere he needed to go to pursue his writing career. "Virtually the whole United States communication system was crammed into a postage-stamp-sized patch of midtown Manhattan," he noted, including *Harper's* offices on Thirty-third Street.[27]

Martin hit his stride in conducting true heavy-fact legwork for a story he did for *Harper's* on the wartime mood in Muncie, Indiana, which had a reputation, thanks to studies done in the community by sociologists Robert Stoughton Lynd and Helen Merrell Lynd in 1924 and 1935, as being the quintessential midwestern city. For his article "Is Muncie Still Middletown?" Martin traveled to the smoky factory town and interviewed at length union leaders, factory workers, businessmen, farmers, politicians, soldiers, college professors, and average people eating in cafeterias. "From several I drew their life stories. And repeatedly

I asked: 'What do you hear people talking about these days?' This was the heart of my story – what Midwesterners were thinking about in wartime," he said. Martin also believed a writer could get a more accurate sampling of public opinion through personal, lengthy interviewing than by "so-called scientific public-opinion polling." Through his interviews, Martin uncovered local prejudice not only against African American workers – the Ku Klux Klan still had its sympathizers in the city – but also against the influx of factory workers from Kentucky and Tennessee, called "hillbillies" by homegrown Muncie residents. At a local restaurant, a Muncie newspaperman related to Martin his newest favorite joke: "Haven't you heard that there are only forty-five states left in the Union? Kentucky and Tennessee have gone to Indiana, and Indiana has gone to hell." Although times had improved thanks to a booming job market because of the war, many in Muncie were anxious about the future, refusing to believe the good times could last and fearing another Great Depression.[28]

In spite of his growing connection with *Harper's* and freelance work with such magazines as *Outdoor Life* and *Esquire,* the bulk of Martin's income – and he was spending more money than ever before living in Hubbard Woods – depended upon his true-crime writing for Keller's publications. While visiting Martin one night at his home, Keller announced he and his editorial staff planned on moving to Philadelphia and asked Martin to come along. "I believed we should go," said Martin. "I couldn't make a living in other magazines – *Harper's* was paying either $250 or $350 for a full-length piece, as I recall it, and while that was more per story than Keller paid, it took far longer to do a *Harper's* piece than a crime story." His other freelance outlets could not make up the difference, as *Outdoor Life* paid only $100 to $150 per piece, while *Esquire* offered $150 per article. Fran opposed the move; she had never liked nor trusted Keller and longed for her husband to be free of his influence. "She had confidence that I could make a living by writing, either writing for him at long distance or not writing for him at all, which is what she really preferred," Martin recalled. Fran's tenaciousness won the argument, and Martin reluctantly told Keller he planned on staying in the Midwest. "Keller didn't like it," said Martin. "I wondered if I had made the mistake of my life." In spite of his anger, Keller still continued to buy stories from

Martin in the years to come, and they regularly exchanged letters. Keller bragged in a January 1944 letter to Martin that OD had grown to become the *Life* magazine of the fact-detective field, with an even half-million copies ready to be printed for the March issue, an all-time high.[29]

Fran's belief in her husband's talent paid off, and in a way that Martin never could have imagined. Ben Abramson, Martin's friend and book-store owner, had been in touch with one of the most influential figures in publishing – Alfred A. Knopf Sr., the man referred to by H. L. Mencken as "a perfect publisher" and someone Martin had idolized since his days in high school. Knopf founded his own publishing firm in 1915 and over the years had brought to print the works of such notable writers and thinkers as Thomas Mann, Sigmund Freud, E. M. Forster, Willa Cather, W. Somerset Maugham, Kahlil Gibran, and Langston Hughes. "Never had I dreamed I might write for him," Martin said of Knopf, "might even meet him." Abramson wrote to Knopf in February 1943 to introduce Martin as a successful magazine writer who had traveled in and studied the Lake Superior country and wanted to do a book on either the Upper Peninsula or the entire state of Michigan that might fit in with the publisher's series of books on Americana. Knopf expressed interest in the idea to Abramson, and in March Martin outlined his project to the publisher, noting:

> The book might be written about the entire Lake Superior Country, embracing parts of Wisconsin, Michigan, Minnesota and Ontario. But there is such a great wealth of material about the Upper Peninsula alone that I think it might be best to confine the book to the Upper Peninsula. There are other considerations, too. The U.P. is, really, the essence of the whole Lake Superior Country. I think it is better to do a really solid book about a small area than a more superficial book about a larger one....
>
> I would like to get hold of old letters and unpublished diaries kept by early settlers of the country, to study the early newspapers, to recount certain stories I have picked up in personal conversations about the early days. Then, after thus building up the historical background, I would like to write the latter part of the book from personal observation, perhaps including several sketches of characteristic Upper Peninsula men and women, either living or recently dead, together with personal experiences, anecdotes, etc. Thus I believe you could get at the flavor and the way of life of the Upper Peninsula in a way that has not yet been touched. Above all, I would like to put the emphasis of the entire book on people, with the politics, geology, geography, etc., covered thoroughly but handled as background.

Knopf was quick to respond to Martin's plans, writing him back that it was his firm's belief that he should confine his book to the Upper Peninsula alone. "I am sure we would be definitely interested in publishing such a book," wrote Knopf, who gave Martin a $1,000 advance for the project.[30]

During the summer of 1943, Martin and Fran drove to the Upper Peninsula to conduct research. He visited the Marquette County Historical Society, consulted newspaper clipping files, read books, and interviewed a number of people in the region's logging and mining communities – miners, lumberjacks, trappers, newspapermen, saloonkeepers, local historians, police officers, shop owners, retired prostitutes, game wardens, and older residents with long memories about the area's pioneer days. Martin realized that his work on the Upper Peninsula could be what is today known as social history, as it portrayed "how the American people talked, worked, and behaved." The stories he garnered from the people he interviewed were important because nearly everybody whose recollections of the old days were "entombed" in the book were themselves entombed not long afterwards. "It wasn't a bad idea to get them down on paper for our children," Martin said. There were times in the book, however, when he resorted to what those in television called a "docudrama" method. Some of the scenes in the book were not based upon written documents or eyewitness accounts, but were occurrences "that simply *ought to* have happened or *must* have happened." (He never again wrote a book in this manner.) In their research, Martin and Fran concentrated on the Marquette Iron Range, the Copper Range, and the wilderness in between. Two people were especially helpful: John D. Voelker, a liberal Democrat and Marquette County district attorney, who was also a budding author and remained a close friend for the rest of Martin's life, and Cal Olson, born eight years after President Abraham Lincoln's assassination and the caretaker at the camp where the Martins stayed at Three Lakes. "It was he," Martin said of Olson, "who took me around and introduced me to the people who had in their heads and in their characters the essence of the Upper Peninsula." In August Martin wrote Keller describing his work for Knopf, noting that he had "driven a couple thousand miles, covering the whole UP [Upper Peninsula]. . . . I've got a cardboard box completely filled with notes, another box of art, and something like 50 books (in addition to probably another 100 books etc. I've consulted in historical societies). So there isn't any question of having enough material; it's a question of what to throw away." Martin estimated that he had gathered enough information to produce three books.[31]

Organizing his research material and turning it into a cohesive narrative structure plagued Martin for a time. He shared his early struggles with Nipp, who expressed his sympathy and offered some guidance. He advised against dividing the book by subject or sections, preferring a "straight chronological division with related threads." When finished with his manuscript, Martin sent it off to Knopf. The publisher, he remembered, responded promptly and succinctly, telling him his work "was satisfactory and he was putting it into production." The writer expressed some disappointment at Knopf's tepid response, saying to Nipp he had hoped his publisher might be "enthusiastic" about the book, which Knopf had decided should be titled *Call It North Country* and released in early 1944. Nipp reminded Martin: "He's published books before." Martin did receive a piece of advice from an editor at Knopf's firm about writing that he never forgot: "Remember, one beaver trapper is like a hundred." Both Martin and Fran spent hours reviewing proofs sent to them by Knopf. "Proofreading," Martin wrote Keller, "is a job unfit for human consumption. I had no idea it was a big a job as it is." Although he was getting "pretty sick of Michigan," he was surprised to find only a few places where his writing had failed to deliver as promised, and he believed the book stood "up pretty well." And in spite of all the hard work, including preparation of an index, Martin said that an author seeing his first book in type "probably is a kick never repeated. You sign a contract then go out and do a lot of legwork then type page after page of copy and send it in – and then nothing happens, and you begin to wonder if maybe you weren't just sort of making it up. Then along come the proofs and bang – it's really going to be a book after all." The book also marked the first time Martin decided to use his full name, John Bartlow Martin, for his byline, as there were others who wrote under the name John Martin. He later had second thoughts, believing the name was too long to print or pronounce, "but once I did it I was stuck with it."[32]

Olson, to whom Martin dedicated *Call It North Country,* served as its backbone, as his life touched upon the region's essential tough character – a place where natives described its climate as "ten months of winter and two months of poor sledding." For most of his life, except for a brief time as a gold miner, Olson's father worked underground in the iron mines near Ishpeming, finally dying of "miner's consumption," most likely silicosis, a lung disease caused by inhaling crystalline silica dust. Too sick to work underground, Olson's father tried to work on the surface, but missed his old life and returned to the job he knew. "He was a miner, not a laborer; a miner he had lived and a miner he died," Martin wrote. The year after Olson was born, Ishpeming's 1,500 residents battled and contained a major fire that threatened to consume the community, and he remembered the tension between him and his Swedish comrades and the tough Irish kids they often fought in territorial battles. Olson had an eclectic career, working as a printer's devil, a teamster, a bartender, and a diamond driller. For a short time he tried working in an iron mine, but, as Martin wrote, he could not take "the weird dark world underground" and quit after working just two shifts. Olson knew many of the spirited men who attempted to tame the wilderness – Pete Moore, Neil Steffens, Dan Spencer – and shared "their independence and their feel for this hard lonely country, this Upper Michigan," Martin noted. "He belonged to it, and it to him."[33]

Call It North Country sold well for a regional book, approximately ten thousand copies, Martin estimated, and it received solid reviews from major newspapers, including the *New York Times.* James Gray, the *Times*'s reviewer, described the book as offering a "detailed, vigorous, and understanding interpretation" of the people who lived in the Upper Peninsula, and he praised Martin as a "young and hearty observer." A reviewer in the *Chicago Sun* indicated that the book's writer possessed an eye for "telling details," and because Martin told his story in a succinct manner, his account of Upper Michigan and its people proved to be "entertaining, informative reading, revealing in a corner of our great country how Americans got that way." Martin was most pleased, however, by the book's longevity and its acceptance by the people it described. Voelker had written him in June 1944 offering his opinion on the book, and said he felt "envious as hell" because it was the book

he should have written if he were not "so goddamn lazy." Perhaps, however, Voelker said, Martin should have been the one to do the task, as
nobody who lived in the Upper Peninsula "could bring to the story the
perspective you have. Yours is not the love of a mother for a besotted
son, but of a son for a roaring, aging and pathetic old man. Your book
is simply grand and you should feel proud as hell." On his many trips
to the Upper Peninsula, Martin came across old copies of his book in
other people's houses or camps that were "almost read literally to pieces,
their spines cracked, pages loose, pages pencil-marked and with coffee
spilled on them, books that have really been read. That is the readership
an author appreciates."[34]

Although Martin, who had as yet heard nothing from his draft board,
had discussed doing a book about advertising as his next project, he came
up with another idea that the publisher accepted – a book on Indiana. In
August 1944 Martin wrote Knopf that with his midwestern background
and his book on the Upper Peninsula, he wondered if he "ought not to
continue to mine the same vein, which I know pretty well." Indiana,
Martin said of the place he grew up, stood as an "excellent cross-section
of the whole Midwest, with its northern industrial area, its middle farm
belt, its southern rural slums bordering on the South, its few large cities
and numerous Main Street towns, and, of course, its shrewd bigoted
hard-headed friendly people." Knopf wrote back saying he had discussed
the idea with his staff and the "best bet by far" would be for Martin to
do a book on Indiana.[35]

Excited by the go-ahead from his publisher, Martin, who wanted
to start with Indiana as a first step to possibly producing a study of the
entire Midwest, set out to gather research material. He asked Nipp, who
was coming up to join him for a vacation in the Upper Peninsula, to bring
with him if possible the Works Progress Administration's classic guide to
the Hoosier State and a few of the books mentioned in its bibliography.
"Those of course are secondary ... sources; but by going through them I
probably can get the general outlines together," he wrote Nipp, "then can,
by independent digging, get the stuff I want. I want to read all I can at the
outset, especially in secondary sources, so I won't flounder too badly in
disorganized original sources." Martin's timetable for the book included
doing preliminary reading while in the Upper Peninsula, traveling to

Indianapolis for more detailed reading of sources at the Indiana State Library, sending a complete outline to Knopf by mid-October, a trip to New York in early November to sign a contract, conducting legwork in Indiana in November and December, beginning to write the book at the first of the year, and finishing it in April. "If things go well, it's a good schedule, just about right," wrote Martin.[36]

Unfortunately, things did not go as planned for Martin. On October 26, 1944, he received the famed "Greetings" letter from his local draft board, Number 142, formally ordering him to report at 7:00 AM on November 16 for induction into the armed forces. In March, Martin had passed his preinduction physical, but it marked an inauspicious start to his army career as the draft board's stenographer became, as Martin wrote Knopf, "infatuated with the sound of one of her own words, March, and so she used it not only as a date but also as a last name for me, and indeed, neglected to put my name anywhere on the induction notice. I regard this as an ill omen." It was; Martin had hoped that after he completed basic training, he would join the foreign staff of *Yank: The Army Weekly,* an illustrated magazine produced by and for enlisted men in the service that had bureaus in every theater of war in which the United States had troops. In New York during the fall of 1943 he had met *Yank*'s managing editor, who told him he would put in a requisition for Martin when he entered basic training and, if he got him, would send him overseas, which is what Martin wanted. "If I'm going to be in a damned war," he wrote Keller, "I want to see some of it; I don't want to get stuck in some camp in the States for the next couple of years."[37]

The staff position with *Yank* never materialized, and perhaps this colored Martin's view of his army service. At the time, the army seemed to him to be "a total waste of time." Although he later wished he had given a little more of himself to the army, at the time he could only see it as the force that had torn him away from his wife and daughter and was halting his "writing career just as it seemed to be getting started. (Too bad about me!)" As he wrote Fran from Fort Sheridan, Illinois, one of the four recruit reception centers in the country, nothing the army could do to him would be as bad as what it had already done "in separating me from you and Cindy." Because he had been so concerned, almost obsessively, with making a living as a freelance writer, Martin had not been concerned with the serious political issues of those times, even the war. "I was aware that I was living through great events but even though I was in the Army, I was not really engaged with those great events – was intent on getting out of the Army and getting on with my writing and my private life," he noted. Martin only became fully engaged in politics and public life when he joined Adlai Stevenson's 1952 presidential campaign as a speechwriter.[38]

Martin, army serial number 36-924-872, quickly became indoctrinated into the army way of life for recruits, as he was assigned "cleaning the latrine, cleaning the floor, cleaning the mail room, cleaning my bed, cleaning the trash can and every other damn thing in sight. So far as I can figure out the labors of a soldier consist chiefly in getting things dirty then cleaning them up." He also became used to standing in line and taking extra time to do everyday chores. As he wrote Fran, if it took five minutes to mail a package in civilian life, the same task took an hour in the army. "The ratio about holds all down the line, far as I can see," he added. Most of his fellow soldiers were younger than he was (twenty-nine at that time), but many had children, displayed photographs of their families, and "felt sorry for themselves." He impressed everyone in his barracks when they saw him taking a typing test. "That sets me apart and makes me a man of learning," Martin wrote. The recruits shared the same attitude about the army, treating it seriously and trying to be good soldiers while serving their country. "What the hell else can you do," he said. "All they want is to go home and, pending that, to avoid getting pushed around too much; and about the easiest way to avoid getting pushed around is to keep your mouth shut and try to look like soldiers." Martin did feel like a "human again" when he underwent classification, as a couple of the sergeants on duty had read his story in *Harper's* October 1944 issue about Colonel Robert McCormick, the non-interventionist and anti–New Deal owner and publisher of the *Chicago Tribune*. Martin did begin to realize the toll the war was taking on his fellow soldiers, as Fort Sheridan also served as a separation center for returning servicemen released from the army. He saw a sergeant wearing the Congressional Medal of Honor for his service on Bataan, and many other veterans of the conflict, in tears, emotional at being so close to finally seeing their families after many years away from home. "So there it is," he wrote to Fran. "It doesn't make it any more fun, but it does help you understand it."[39]

From Fort Sheridan, Martin went for basic training in early December 1944 to Camp Joseph T. Robinson, a huge army base about seven miles from Little Rock, Arkansas, and a place he later remembered as "nothing but an ocean of freezing mud" during the winter months. "You have the feeling that Robinson is a lot closer to the front lines than Sheridan," Martin wrote his wife as a member of Company D of the 116th Infantry Training Battalion, 78th Regiment. "There they are interested in what you did in civilian life and what you might do in the Army. Here they are interested in turning out, rapidly, a lot of expert infantrymen. This war, we were told, is a war of specialists. We will be, in 17 weeks, specialists in rifle fire. Scarcely seems possible." With American troops in Europe in a desperate struggle with German soldiers in the Battle of the Bulge, a group just ahead of Martin's had its training cycle cut short and was sent directly into the fighting in Belgium. "We expected the same," said Martin. In spite of the dangers facing the average enlisted infantryman in the European theater, and they were many, Martin turned down an opportunity to apply for Officer Candidate School. He had the romantic notion, or an underdog's instinct, that he preferred to remain with his fellow soldiers, and he nursed an enlisted man's inherent grudge against officers.[40]

Near the end of his time at Camp Robinson, Martin received a plush assignment, working in the orderly room as a company clerk. By mid-January 1945 Fran and Cindy had joined him, living in a rooming house in Little Rock run by a woman who regularly drank paregoric, a tincture containing opium, and who late at night turned down their gas heater when she thought they were asleep. Southerners, Martin noted, resented the invasion of soldiers from the North and saw them only as a way to make a profit for themselves. Working as a company clerk provided Martin with a "nice rest" after completing basic training, and he also found time to continue his writing career, finishing a story on a local mass murder case for Keller and rewriting a story for another true-detective magazine. "I'm glad for the chance to keep my hand in; and if I can make some money we can use it: We're going broke fast," he wrote his mother and father.[41]

Completing his prescribed course of basic training on March 16, 1945, Martin got a reprieve; he would not be shipped out as a replacement infantryman to slog through the final days of the war in Europe. Instead the army sent him first to a tent camp, then to Fort Sam Houston in San Antonio, Texas, to become part of the 246th Military Police Criminal Investigation Platoon in the army's new Criminal Investigation Division, which dealt with infractions committed by military personnel (the platoon eventually made its home at Camp Bullis, northwest of San Antonio). Members of Martin's platoon were mostly men of his age who in civilian life had worked as FBI agents, attorneys, or police detectives. "I had more in common with them than with the eighteen-year-olds in basic training," said Martin. "Every one of us was made a noncommissioned officer." The lieutenant in command proved to be sympathetic to Martin, who needed the extra income from his freelance writing to help support his family, which had followed him to Texas. Although the state "seemed like paradise" compared to the winter mud of Arkansas, Fran and Cindy had to live in a tourist cabin because private homes refused to accept couples with children. "Tourists cabins are all right," Martin noted, "but they charge nearly $100 a month for one room and a tin shower." The officer gave Martin the lowest noncommissioned rank possible – T-5, technician fifth grade, often addressed as "tech corporal" – because he knew Martin was still writing pieces for Keller and *Harper's* to supplement his army pay. If he did not have "heavy duties, as a staff sergeant would," Martin recalled, "I would have more time to write. It was fine with me."[42]

While walking in downtown San Antonio in early May 1945 trying to find a place to live, Martin and Fran, with Cindy in tow, learned about the end of the war in Europe. They spotted a crowd gathering around a newsboy on Houston Street, bought one of his newspapers, and saw the headline (premature, it turned out) that Germany had surrendered. "We wept, and a Mexican girl cried and patted our baby and said that now maybe her baby's daddy could come home; he had been in the Bulge," Martin recalled. Finally, on May 7, at Allied headquarters in Reims in northwestern France, General Alfred Jodl signed the unconditional surrender of all German forces, to take effect the next day. May 8 became Victory-in-Europe, or V-E, Day. In July Martin and his platoon received transfer orders to Houston, where he and his mates worked with the local police department for three weeks. Martin spent time with the burglary and theft division, and later spent about eight hours a day with homicide detectives. During his time off Martin collected additional information on local crimes and turned them into two articles for fact-detective magazines, "a fair amount of work even in civilian life," he wrote his parents.[43]

The army ordered Martin's platoon to prepare to leave Texas for Camp Edward Beale near Marysville, California, for duty in the Pacific theater. Before leaving for California, Martin received a furlough, part of which he spent in New York with Fran, staying at the Algonquin Hotel and attending the theater. The two of them were having lunch with Allen and his wife when they heard the announcement on August 6 from President Harry S. Truman that the United States had harnessed "the basic power of the universe" and had dropped an atomic bomb on the Japanese city of Hiroshima. The bomb caused widespread devastation and immediately killed eighty thousand Japanese. At the lunch in New York Fran had mentioned her belief that the United States, to secure the peace, should share the secret of the atomic bomb with the Soviet Union, and Allen, said Martin, had "looked at her as though he thought she'd lost her mind." Three days later, a second atomic bomb, this one dropped on Nagasaki, finally forced Japanese emperor Hirohito to announce in an August 15 radio address Japan's unconditional surrender to the Allies; a formal surrender ceremony took place on September 12 on board the battleship USS *Missouri* in Tokyo Bay. Martin and Fran had been listening intently to radio broadcasts about the possible peace, and when news finally came that the war had really ended, with Victory-in-Japan (v-j) Day declared on August 14, it had seemed "wonderful, of itself; unquestionable," said Martin. Friends in New York, however, had questioned the advisability of a peace that kept Emperor Hirohito in place, with one friend saying an atomic bomb should be dropped on the emperor's palace. Their doubts rankled Martin, who wondered, "Did they know about the mud and the cold, about how you march 15 miles with full field pack, starting hours before dawn, and arrive dripping with sweat, then shiver, chilled through your body, all the rest of the day in the drizzle? This is an unfair basis to put it on; they did not know, how could they? And it shouldn't make any difference, anyway. But it did."[44]

While Martin waited with the rest of his platoon at Camp Beale for their deployment to Japan, in November 1945 *Harper's* published an article by him, the only piece of "pure rhetoric" he ever wrote, that gave voice to all the enlisted man's complaints about the army and civilians – the ones they could not openly state, fearful their comrades would answer with the standard sarcastic rejoinder, "Your story is very touching. Would you like to see the chaplain?" Titled "Anything Bothering You, Soldier?" the piece expressed Martin's anger about the war, about how civilians at home had never learned much about the conflict, including the enormous indignities suffered by not only those who served in combat, but also by those who never saw action (he did note the paltriness of noncombatants' sacrifices compared to those of veterans who risked life and limb while overseas). Even advertisements in magazines had no shame. He noted seeing one in *Life* with pictures of tanks in the jungle and touting how it was the roughest, toughest test that brand of oil had ever faced, but saying nothing about the real dangers faced by the crews sitting inside the tanks. Martin pointed out that black soldiers were good enough to be buried side by side with white soldiers killed in Italy, but they were somehow not good enough to sit side by side with white passengers on a bus in Texas, and he mentioned a Jewish veteran whose friends and relatives were murdered by the Nazis in Germany, but in America could not gain entrance to a seaside hotel because the establishment was "restricted" and did not permit Jewish guests. "We were all in this together, so none of us should ever forget it," Martin wrote. "So somebody has got to talk about it. Yet this is futile, for the gap between soldiers and civilians is unbridgeable. What little the civilians knew about the war they have forgotten."[45]

How Corporal Martin escaped disciplinary action from the army for his frank article is unknown, but perhaps his superiors knew he would soon be on a transport sailing the Pacific Ocean to become part of America's occupation of Japan. His father, J. W., had even written him not to worry about his family, as he and Martin's mother would see to it that Fran and Cindy were taken care of while he was away. "It would be better for them if you were here," wrote J. W., "but under the circumstances, we will do our best." Martin received a stroke of good luck when, as the rest of his platoon packed their bags for the journey to

Japan and prepared to depart on December 8, 1945, he received orders to stay behind. "No reason," he wrote Fran, "they [the army] just did it." By mid-January 1946 his application for discharge had been approved. "What do you need from the PX [post exchange]? Kleenex? Soap chips? Old Golds [cigarettes]?" Martin asked Fran in a letter about his good fortune. "Have you taken up the straps of your nightdress? Where is my blue pinstripe suit? Is my typewriter repaired? Have my felt hat blocked. I have returned. Or at least I shall very soon." Earlier he had written his wife about his plans after he left the service, and they included making a break from his dependence upon fact-detective articles for his living. "I don't ever want to write them again," he confided to Fran, wishing for a fresh start for both of them. "When I get out I'll be well past 31, and I don't want to spend any more years writing garbage; the next few years have got to count, because if I don't get it made damn fast after I get out I'm not going to get it made. . . . I honestly think I can make a living without writing fact tec [detective]." Martin eventually made good on his promise, but it would take many years and the help of a notable New York literary agent, Harold Ober, and a mutually beneficial relationship with one of the country's most popular magazines, the *Saturday Evening Post*, to achieve his ambitious goals.[46]

FOUR

The Big Slicks

FOR MILLIONS OF VETERANS FOLLOWING THE END OF WORLD War II, their return home resembled what they had gone through upon their induction into military service: long waits in long lines. On Friday, February 16, 1946, after filling out the necessary paperwork at an army separation center at Camp Ulysses S. Grant near Rockford, Illinois, John Bartlow Martin achieved what he had been seeking for many months: discharge from the U.S. Army status as a civilian. He took a train to Chicago and by 8:00 PM was back home in Winnetka with his wife, Fran, and daughter, Cindy. Upon walking through the front door, Martin hugged his wife and turned to hug his daughter, and then the three of them embraced one another.[1]

Before returning home, Martin had written to Fran outlining his plans for the future. Someone had asked him what he wanted to do with the rest of his life, and Martin had responded, "I told him – and meant it and rather surprised him and perhaps myself – I wanted to be happy with you, then wanted to write well, then wanted to make a lot of money. In that order. (The order of the last two isn't quite as simple as it appears; it just means that I think I can make a very comfortable living AND write well, and if so I'd rather do it than write lousy and make a whole lot of money)." Martin added that he would take care of the final two items, but they were meaningless unless "you make me happy. And the best way to ensure that is for me to work a bit on making *you* happy. So that's what I'm going to [do]."[2]

The plans Martin had outlined for his future, however, proved difficult to achieve, as he had trouble readjusting to being a civilian. Harried by the army and its regimented ways, he had longed for "the old comfortable things" of his former life, but he discovered that they began to weigh on him after a time. He also had trouble reconnecting with his wife. "I don't feel as if I've seen Fran . . . this is no love affair reunion," Martin said. In addition, he had difficulty getting back in the rhythm of his old profession, writing. He admitted to his friend Francis Nipp that it was going to take him several months to recover his bearings. Doing a story for *Harper's* about a private detective, William V. Pennington of San Francisco, Martin found that he was "a lot less facile and more awkward than I used to be – and facility was never a strong point of mine, writing always did come hard. It comes like molasses now." He had also lost a bit of his confidence, telling Nipp it would be some time before he could say to an editor, "The legwork will take 6 days, 3 days to write, 2 days to revise, two in the mail – you can have the [manu]script in 13 days from now." Martin confided to Nipp that the next few years could be critical when it came to his writing career.[3]

Trying to readjust to life in peacetime, Martin set out to finish what had been interrupted by his wartime service, his book on Indiana for Alfred A. Knopf Sr. In March 1946 he wrote to his publisher reminding him that two years ago he had approved an outline of the Indiana book. Since he had been home, Martin told Knopf, *Life* magazine, impressed by his work in *Harper's,* had asked him to travel the Midwest for an article on the postwar mood in the region. He spent six weeks traveling between Columbus, Ohio, and Smith Center, Kansas, and between Louisville, Kentucky, and Bismarck, North Dakota, collecting hundreds of pages of notes on such issues as race relations in Louisville and Indianapolis, farmers' cooperatives in Minnesota, life on an assembly line in Kansas City, the conversion from tank manufacturing to building automobiles for the civilian market in Michigan, and labor strife in Ohio and Indiana. "Everywhere I asked 'What are people talking about?' and 'Who runs this town?' and 'How'd it change during the war – will it go back to the way it was?'" Eventually *Life* "simply did not know what to do with these facts" and decided to pay Martin for his time and effort but not publish his manuscript. "But I never considered the work wasted," he said. "I learned a lot about the Midwest." Martin told Knopf he believed there could be a "good book" based on his research, "a profile view of the Midwest today," which he described as a cross between Julian Street's "Abroad at Home" magazine serial done in the 1910s and John Dos Passos's 1944 book *State of the Nation*.[4]

Knopf responded by thanking Martin for the notes he provided, but said he and his editors believed it was best that he first do the book he had previously discussed about Indiana. "We think this would be much better for you and for us," Knopf wrote, "and that a book on a single state would have a better sale. There is a widespread feeling that books dealing with a whole *section* of the country taken at a given point in time never go over very well." Martin asked for, and received from Knopf, a slightly larger advance than what he had received for *Call It North Country*, from $1,000 to $1,200, but Knopf also, on his own, raised the royalty rate for the Indiana book, which had as its tentative title "Moonlight's Fair Tonight."[5]

By the middle of July Martin was in Indiana doing research and interviewing newspapermen, labor organizers, businessmen, workingmen, policemen, politicians, local historians, realtors, taxicab drivers, veterans, farmers, hotel doormen, waitresses, editors, and publishers. In gathering information, he discovered that his Indiana book would be quite different from the one he had written about Michigan's Upper Peninsula. "Instead of the earlier book's picturesque explorers and lumberjacks and miners," he noted, the characters for his new book were "politicians, union leaders, industrialists, writers." Instead of the vast wilderness of the Upper Peninsula, the atmosphere "was that of farm revolt, strikes, violence, industrialization, and bored farm-town life."[6]

As he contemplated the material he had collected, Martin realized that one man, poet James Whitcomb Riley, had played a major role in shaping how Hoosiers saw themselves and their state. As he talked to his sources about Indiana and what he should write about, they instead told him what did not belong in his book – the Calumet region in the northwest part of the state, socialist and labor leader Eugene Debs, novelist and journalist Theodore Dreiser, and sophisticated songwriter Cole Porter – because they did not really represent the state. "And finally you realize," Martin wrote a friend, "that they are chopping off chunks of Indiana to try to get Indiana to conform to what Riley said it was: A hayseed from Brown County." After Riley's death in 1916, people in Indiana demanded more of his sentimental style of work – poems praising "the homely, the simple, the rustic, the Hoosier." A host of other Indiana writers came along to supply the demand created by Riley, according to Martin, including William Herschell, *Indianapolis News* reporter and author of the poem "Ain't God Good to Indiana?"; George Ade, newspaperman and columnist known for his "Fables in Slang"; and Frank McKinney "Kin" Hubbard, creator of Brown County cracker barrel philosopher Abe Martin. The fact remained, however, that people such as Dreiser and Porter did come from Indiana, and someone like Debs could not have come from anywhere else, Martin noted. There existed a different type of nostalgia from the one Martin had initially believed permeated the state. This was nostalgia for the days when automobiles such as Marmon and National were made in Indianapolis and when "nobody accused George A. Ball the old bastard of ducking income tax but just thought he was a smart man who gave his money away to help those less fortunate." The real reason Indiana was so hard to get a hold on and write about was because it stood as the United States in microcosm, he continued, and the country was changing, "but nobody seems to know just how or why. I do think this: if this keeps up the book is going to surprise people who look for another book about Hoosiers. And if you hammer hard enough at that idea of infinite variety you can confound those who carp at it because it 'is just the faults one man finds with Indiana.'"[7]

Martin's analysis of the state raised some eyebrows. After reading the book, Ben H. Riker, the buyer for the book department at L. S. Ayres and Company, Indianapolis's leading department store, wrote Knopf that in his opinion Martin had "allowed his own political, social, and economic prejudices to color what ought to be an objective piece of reporting with unbiased interpretation. It is interesting enough, but it does not do what it purports to do – or at least what I was expecting it to do." In an ominous note for any publisher, Riker indicated that most literate Hoosiers, at least the ones who buy books, would not accept the book "as a true picture of Indiana, and a good many of them, I am afraid, will object to the constant damning by innuendo of the conservative elements in the State, which are pretty large and may even be in the majority."[8]

The manuscript on Indiana elicited two quite different reactions from his publishing firm, with the senior Knopf expressing disappointment, saying the book lacked "genuine integration" and lamenting that Martin seemed unable to describe the book "in more attractive and understandable language." Knopf's son, Alfred A. Knopf Jr., disagreed with his father's assessment, telling Martin that he had done "a perfectly swell job. The book is full of atmosphere and moods, and in a great many places it is completely 'un-put-downable.'" Although the book read more like a series of "first-rate magazine articles than like a continuous drama," the junior Knopf said he had told his father Martin's book was "what I expected, and more." Another Knopf employee, Irving P. Hotchkiss, called the book "one of the finest regional interpretations that I've read for a long time and I happen to have read quite a number. With its emphasis on interpretation of social forces, rather than on the usual recital of picturesque local detail, I believe it will have a general interest and sale beyond the usual expectations for such a book." Hotchkiss believed there would be a national audience for the book and advised Martin to ignore Riker's complaints, saying he would attempt to "talk him [Riker] out of his . . . attitude" when he next met with him.[9]

Published in 1947 with the title *Indiana: An Interpretation,* Martin's book set out from the start to confound the expectations of readers looking for another romantic paean to the state's steady rise to greatness. Convention had it that regional writing should be "rhapsodic, not critical," Martin wrote in the book's preface. His was not a book designed to "advertise or praise (or, for that matter, to condemn) Indiana." Instead, it was one man's interpretation of the state – the Hoosier character, thought, and way of life – and was not intended to be a comprehensive chronicle of Indiana's past. "This book is not history; it is journalism," said Martin, adding that it focused on people rather than events. He set out to examine the idea of Indiana and Hoosiers held by the rest of the nation, a conception, a good deal of which was myth, of "Indiana as a pleasant, rather rural place inhabited by people who are confident, prosperous, neighborly, easygoing, tolerant, shrewd." Martin viewed the 1880s and 1890s as the state's golden age, when Hoosiers were "confident of the future." After the 1900s, the state had suffered from a "hardening of the arteries" and had lost its way. Between World War I and World

War II the magic and wonder of Indiana's past – Riley's poetry and El-
wood Haynes's inventiveness, for example – had disappeared from the
scene, replaced by robed figures from the Ku Klux Klan. "A suspicion
had arisen that bigotry, ignorance, and hysteria were as much a part
of the Hoosier character as were conservatism and steadfastness and
common sense," Martin wrote. "One of Indiana's chief exports had long
been ideas, but so many of these had turned out to be wrong-headed,
wicked, or useless." The most likely suspects for this vein of bigotry and
intolerance could be seen in the careers of Klan leader D. C. Stephenson and homegrown bigot and isolationist Court Asher, but other possibilities included small-town capitalists who, fearful of labor unions,
discouraged outside manufacturers from moving to their communities;
labor union leaders more worried about jurisdictional disputes than
the interests of their members; and politicians obsessed with the day-
to-day business of garnering votes rather than the social and economic
ends of politics, which Martin labeled as "the little trickeries that make
Presidents and ward heelers alike."[10]

In addition to a skeptical view of the Indiana idea, the book featured vignettes of figures outside the Indiana mainstream. Some of the
book's best writing is featured in the "Voices of Protest" section, which
covers the careers of Debs, workplace democracy pioneer William Powers Hapgood, and his son, labor organizer Powers Hapgood. Debs is
given the longest chapter, and Martin later said that the man from Terre
Haute, Indiana, "almost ran away with the book," another reason why
"conservative booksellers from Indianapolis did little to sell the book."
They may have also been upset by how honestly Martin treated Terre
Haute's bawdy early twentieth century, when gambling and prostitution
ran rampant in the District, the area north of Second and Third Streets,
with establishments such as Madame Brown's whorehouse. Born near
the District, Debs stayed away from its wickedness (but not its drink,
calling temperance "this mean and narrow fanaticism"), and through
his work organizing railroad workers and representing workingmen as
five-time Socialist Party candidate for president, he stood in the van-
guard of Indiana protest, what Martin called "the ceaseless quest for
the better life begun by Robert Owen [of New Harmony], the uprising
against authority begun in William Henry Harrison's time. . . . They left

an impress and a heritage – Debs most of all. He was the greatest of Indiana protestants, the most effective."[11]

In writing *Indiana: An Interpretation*, Martin believed that because he had hated his childhood in Indianapolis, he assumed he would also hate the state. He had been surprised, however, to find "a certain affection suffusing parts of the book." Some Indiana critics of the book, however, failed to find in its pages the affection Martin had seen. "It is not a lovely book," noted an anonymous reviewer in the *Indiana Magazine of History,* a quarterly periodical published by Indiana University's history department. The reviewer accused Martin of administering a "shock treatment," comparing the author to a Jove hurling bolts of lightning at the state's citizens. "His work is not a 'sound' interpretation of Indiana as the publishers claim. Lacking is an evaluation of the good features of the state," noted the reviewer. Writing in the *Indianapolis Star,* Gene Pulliam Jr., the son of the newspaper's publisher, had grudging respect for Martin's efforts, calling the work "interesting and different as books about Indiana go." Henry Butler, writing in the *Indianapolis Times,* offered an accurate assessment of the view many people in the state would have of the book when he noted that true believers seldom liked to have their "articles of faith described as myth. And though the Indiana myth is no more fantastic than many phases of the greater American myth, of which it is a part, such a description of Hoosierism may strike some as offensive."[12]

The farther away one got from Indiana, the better the reviews were for the book. The *New York Times* credited Martin for his "rare adventure into the field of self-criticism" when it came to regional writing, praising him for presenting a "challenging indictment of what one might call 'grass-rootism.'" Martin's "interesting and well-written story" captured not only the salt-of-the-earth Hoosiers lionized by Riley, said the *Times* reviewer, but also covered in depth the tale of "grassroots mediocrity, of intolerance, of political myopia, or crass materialism, of political corruption." Writing in the *New York Herald-Tribune's* weekly book review, Elrick B. Davis said that Martin had finally presented a regional book "that makes sense," as it stripped Indiana from its costume and integrated the state into the social history of the United States. Calling the book a "regional psychograph," Davis praised the author for a work that was "amiably critical, interested but objective, warm with neighborly concern, sufficiently historical, pleasantly colorful – never gaudy – and without a single statistic to snag its biographic flow." Such praise continued in later years, with Harvard University historian Arthur M. Schlesinger Jr., who became a close friend of Martin's, referring to him on one occasion as "the author of the best book on Indiana," and longtime Indiana University professor of history James H. Madison noting that although *Indiana: An Interpretation* has its faults (it excludes, for the most part, discussions of the roles of women and African Americans), it remains "a modern and compelling piece of writing."[13]

Although Martin said *Indiana: An Interpretation* suffered from poor sales, he did not feel he had wasted his time writing the book, as it prepared him for his future nonfiction writing projects and for politics. Any possible disappointment he might have felt about the book's lack of success may have been tempered by some positive developments in his private life, especially the purchase of a new home at 60 Sunset Road in the Chicago suburb of Highland Park. Sunset Road proved to be a good place to live, as it was the "first home Fran and I had had for our marriage," noted Martin. "Always before it had been a string of hotels and apartments, motels and parents' houses, one rented house, all temporary, transient. Now we had a solid base." Martin and his family's previous residence had been in Winnetka, which he described as Republican, well-to-do, and filled with white Anglo-Saxon Protestants. Highland Park, too, was an affluent Republican community, but one that had been casting more and more votes for the Democratic Party in recent elections, was "far more heterogeneous than Winnetka, and had a large Jewish population," said Martin. He often shopped at a Highland Park bookstore owned by the wives of some Jewish businessmen and attorneys, and he became friends with their families. "All these people and many more whom we met were readers; all were better educated and better traveled than I; all were thoughtful people interested in ideas," said Martin. He found their influence on his life "liberating." From the bookstore he purchased and read books by such writers as Albert Camus, Jean-Paul Sartre, Franz Kafka, Louis-Ferdinand Céline, André Malraux, Mark Twain, Ring Lardner, and Arthur Koestler, and he became engrossed by such classic literature as Herman Melville's *Moby-*

Dick, Nathaniel Hawthorne's *The Scarlet Letter,* and Gustave Flaubert's *Madame Bovary.* "Why I had not read them sooner I do not know," Martin said. "They seemed to speak to me directly, especially Camus and Kafka." Because he was so preoccupied with getting his private life and career in order, he could not, however, "integrate all this closely into my work and life," especially due to his almost obsessive concern with the "precarious existence of a freelance writer."[14]

In addition to a stable life in Highland Park, Martin enjoyed a solid relationship with Frederick Lewis Allen and other editors at *Harper's* magazine. Martin's post–World War II work for the magazine continued to examine crime and the social context that produced it. Martin said he never consciously set out to specialize in crime, but criminal cases did offer "an opportunity to write about people in crisis, and their problems." His pieces in *Harper's* included an examination of the killing of Don Mellett, a crusading newspaper editor in Canton, Ohio, who had been uncovering corruption among the city's police and politicians ("Murder of a Journalist"), and the killing of Toledo, Peoria, and Western Railroad president George P. McNear, whose armed strikebreakers had shot dead a union member on the picket lines during a strike ("The McNear Murder"). Martin's *Harper's* story on McNear's still unsolved murder had been reprinted in *Reader's Digest,* and the editor who handled it for the magazine, Paul Palmer, had been intrigued enough by it to suggest that Martin should explore a recent mine disaster in Centralia, Illinois. The resulting *Harper's* article in March 1948, "The Blast in Centralia No. 5," made Martin's reputation. Writer Marc Rose, in a 1952 issue of *The Quill,* the magazine of the Society of Professional Journalists, called the Centralia story "one of the most magnificent examples of magazine journalism" he had ever seen.[15]

The story of the miners' plight moved many people over the years, including John Houseman, a theater and film producer best known for his acting in the 1973 movie *The Paper Chase.* Houseman had expressed interest in turning Martin's Centralia story into a movie, but instead had to settle for a television production. In 1957 Houseman signed a two-year contract to produce an anthology program for CBS Television called *The Seven Lively Arts.* Houseman described the show, which aired on Sunday afternoons, as a "project about which everyone was enthusiastic but no one had any clear or definite ideas – beyond the feeling that it must be original, entertaining, instructive, prestigious and, of course, popular." During its eleven-episode run from November 1957 to January 1958, the program featured a film essay based on E. B. White's "Here is New York," an adaptation of five Nick Adams stories by Ernest Hemingway, top jazz musicians of the day (Billie Holiday, Count Basie, Lionel Hampton, Thelonious Monk, and Coleman Hawkins) performing live, and an examination of American folk music. *The Seven Lively Arts* left the air "prematurely but with honor," said Houseman, with a dramatization of Martin's Centralia story. Directed by George Roy Hill, later famous for directing the film *Butch Cassidy and the Sundance Kid,* the production also featured a script by Loring Mandel, starred Maureen Stapleton as the widow of miner Joe Bryant, and included narration provided by Jason Robards as a journalist, representing Martin. "I had never before worked on a dramatic script, and thought it fascinating," Martin recalled. "The script was extremely faithful to my original story. One particularly effective sequence showed the bureaucracy endlessly shuffling and stamping and filing and ignoring the mine inspectors' reports warning that the mine was dangerous."[16]

Although *The Seven Lively Arts* had been a ratings failure and CBS had canceled it, Houseman considered the program on Centralia as "one of the most moving dramatic broadcasts I have ever been associated with." Martin attended the rehearsals for the show and offered some suggestions to Hill, including having the newspaper reporters attempting to interview Illinois governor Dwight H. Green in one scene not to behave as they were "a bunch of raucous characters out of *The Front Page* but that, rather, they be serious and subdued – after all, 111 men had just died." One bit of the script, taken directly from Martin's writing, ran afoul of the network, his observation that the system that runs our lives does not always work well. According to Martin, a CBS executive thought the word "system" "sounded vaguely 'communistic'; it would have to go." Houseman asked Martin to find substitute wording, and he came up with "the machinery that runs our lives," a phrase he considered to be an improvement; the change also satisfied the network. Hill allowed Martin to be a part of the episode, giving him a role as himself interviewing Stapleton, the miner's widow. Stapleton told Martin she was afraid she might forget her lines, so he dutifully copied them onto his reporter's notebook in a spot where she could read them if needed. When the program aired live on January 26, 1958, however, Stapleton did her scene flawlessly and did not have to depend on any cues from Martin and his notebook.[17]

Critics raved about the Centralia program, with the *New York Times* lauding it as a "brilliant dramatization" and praising Stapleton's "convincingly restrained style" in her role. "In its hour on the television screen," the *Times* reported, "the documentary covered the events preceding the tragedy with remarkable attention to detail." The review went on to compliment Mandel's script, Hill's direction, and Robert Markell's set direction for capturing "the somber quality of the story magnificently." Other newspapers were equally fulsome in their praise, and Houseman noted it seemed ironic "that these tributes were also our obituaries." Martin and Fran had a fine time at a party after the program hosted at the home of actress Viveca Lindfors, congratulating those involved in the production and receiving congratulations in return. The Martins flew home to Chicago later that night to be greeted by a blizzard, but Martin hardly noticed the bad weather. As he drove their Jeep from the airport to their Highland Park home through the snowstorm, he remembered shouting to his wife that it had been the greatest day of his life. "Not publishing a book, not publishing a magazine piece, not winning a prize is nearly so exciting as seeing something you wrote come alive on a screen," he said, adding that he cherished the experience for the rest of his life.[18]

A piece Martin did for *Harper's* just five months after his Centralia investigation proved to be just as powerful and moving as his exploration of the mine disaster, and it opened the nation's eyes to racial segregation in a northern city years before the civil rights movement and the U.S. Supreme Court's 1954 *Brown vs. Board of Education* decision striking down separate public schools for white and African American schoolchildren. "I wanted to do not an article, crammed with demographers' statistics," said Martin, "but, rather, a story about a man." As he explained, Martin tried to avoid doing what he called "articles," preferring instead to think of them as "stories." The difference to him was that an article was "about a subject while a story is about a person." He tried to find a broad subject area to write about and then find a specific person "to whom something has happened, so that the piece will have a narrative story line. There has to be drama." Although such a piece might never have the same penetrating quality as truly great fiction, Martin said it could have "more penetration . . . than any 'article' or second-rate fiction."[19]

The person he found for his *Harper's* story was James Hickman, an African American who had moved from the Deep South to Chicago in 1945 seeking a better life for himself and his family. Instead, Hickman ran headlong into tragedy with a fellow African American, his landlord, David Coleman, whom he shot and killed after a suspicious fire burned to death four of Hickman's children in their tiny apartment at 1733 West Washburne Avenue. To prepare for his *Harper's* story, Martin read Swedish economist Gunnar Myrdal's classic 1944 study of race relations, *An American Dilemma: The Negro Problem and Modern Democracy,* which Myrdal described as "not a *study* of the Negroes but of the American society from the viewpoint of the most disadvantaged group." Martin conducted extensive interviews with Hickman and his wife, as well as with Coleman's relatives. "I simply told the story of Hickman's and the landlord's lives," said Martin, "and their world – the world below." Martin visited the slum neighborhood where the Hickman family lived, making notes and gathering atmosphere for his story by walking the same streets they had walked.[20]

Hickman had been born on January 19, 1907, "in the country," as he put it, near Louisville, Mississippi, the son of sharecroppers raising corn and cotton. At the age of sixteen he married a neighbor girl, Annie Davis, and when their first child, Arlen, was born, Hickman, a deeply religious man, had vowed to God, "I was the head of this family and had to make a support for them. I was guardian to see for them as long as the days I should live on the land." Trying to raise a family that eventually included nine children on the paltry wages sharecropping afforded, Hickman looked to the North for the opportunities, including education, denied to African Americans in the South. Staying with an older daughter who had married and lived in Chicago, Hickman found a job with International Harvester's Wisconsin Steel plant near the Indiana border, receiving $1.25 an hour for guiding the burning steel as it rolled off the hotbed. "On the farm I'd be charged for a lot of things, I couldn't see what it was for," he said of his experiences as a sharecropper. "In the factory work it [his wages] come to my hand." He marveled at the size of the country's second largest city, as well as seeing whites and blacks riding together in buses and his fellow African Americans working in banks and post offices.[21]

Life in a northern city provided its own hardships for Hickman, particularly when it came to finding decent and affordable housing for his family. By the mid-1940s approximately 80 percent of Chicago's residential housing was covered by racially restrictive covenants that excluded blacks from buying or renting property in white neighborhoods. The city's African American population of 400,000 squeezed into a seven-square-mile area, called the "Black Belt" by Martin in his article, on the south side from Twenty-second Street (Cermak Road today) to Sixty-second Street between Wentworth and Cottage Grove Avenues. European immigrants who prospered in their new homeland could scatter throughout the city, noted Martin, disappearing and blending into the general population. "'Disappearing' – how can a black man disappear?" he asked. "He is not wanted. He is condemned to inhabit the areas nobody else wants." Landlords in the black ghetto, African American and white alike, did all they could to maximize their profits as the demand for already scarce housing rose during and after World War II. They divided apartments into smaller and smaller units, often called "kitchenettes," and charged outlandish rents for the tiny spaces they provided their tenants. "In this artificially restricted market, people of means bid high for hovels; rentals skyrocket; landlords gouge," Martin said. Hickman also had trouble finding a place to live because many landlords did not want to rent to someone with children.[22]

Unfamiliar with Chicago, Hickman sometimes wandered into white neighborhoods seeking a place to rent. He experienced little trouble, as people guided him to areas where African Americans were allowed to live. "I was born in a country where there's nothin' but white folks," Hickman told Martin, "and I knowed how to talk and carry myself and they treated me mighty fine." After a year of painstaking effort, Hickman finally found a home for his family at a four-story brick tenement owned by Coleman, who had also come to Chicago from Mississippi, worked hard to improve his station in life, and thought of himself as a businessman. Hickman, his wife, and six of their children huddled together in a small room in the building's attic that measured about fourteen feet by twenty-one feet in size. "There was no electricity; they used a kerosene lamp," wrote Martin. "There was no gas; they used a stove and heater burning kerosene. There was one window. There was no water; they had to go down to the third floor to use the toilet or to get water for washing and cooking." Hickman later told people he had never lived so poorly in Mississippi as he and his family had to live while in Chicago. Coleman had hinted to Hickman that a larger apartment might soon open up for his family on the second floor, but it never materialized, and Hickman, tired of the runaround and wanting back the $100 down payment he had paid Coleman, tried but failed to have his landlord arrested. To increase his rental income from the property, which he needed in order to meet his own late payments on the building, Coleman had sent a contractor to 1733 Washburne to divide the existing apartments into the more lucrative kitchenettes, but the tenants had resisted, saying it would take a court order to evict them. A defiant Coleman had threatened, "I am the owner, I don't have to go to Court to do that, I will get everybody out of here when I want to if it takes fire."[23]

Coleman's dire threat came true on the evening of January 16, 1947. Hickman had gone to his job at the steel mill at 9:00 PM, leaving his wife to help their children with their homework. The family went to bed at about 10:00 PM; an hour and a half later Annie woke up after hearing the "paper popping" on the ceiling – a fire. As flames raged throughout the attic space, Charles, the Hickman's nineteen-year-old son, escaped down the stairs, and Willis, the oldest son, and Annie barely managed to escape the fire by going out the window and falling to the ground below, escaping with only minor injuries. Unfortunately, four Hickman children – Leslie, fourteen; Elzena, nine; Sylvester, seven; and Velvena, four – were killed in what a Chicago fire chief called a "holocaust" of flames. Told at work that there had been trouble at home, Hickman returned at about 7:30 AM the following morning, only to be greeted by another tenant, who told him, "Mr. Hickman, I hate to tell you this, four of your children is burnt to death." The news devastated Hickman, who fell to the ground and had to be carried into the building's basement. "Mr. Hickman looked pretty bad, like he was losing his mind," a neighbor said to Martin. Hickman kept thinking about the threat Coleman had made to burn down the building if the tenants failed to clear out. A coroner's jury, however, failed to deliver any indictments for arson.[24]

Convinced that Coleman had been responsible for the fire and that justice had failed him, Hickman became bitter, sitting alone and having conversations with his dead children. "Paper was made to burn, coal and rags," he said again and again. "Not people. People wasn't made to burn." Taking a .32-caliber pistol he owned with him, he took a streetcar and bus to Coleman's residence, found the landlord reading a newspaper while sitting in a Buick taxicab owned by Coleman's half-brother, engaged in a brief conversation with him, and shot Coleman several times. "I had put a heavy load down and a big weight fell off of me and I felt light," recalled Hickman, who took a streetcar home and confessed what he had done to his wife. The Homicide Squad arrested him that afternoon and he confessed his crime to them. After Coleman died three days later, authorities indicted Hickman for the landlord's first-degree murder. Interviews of Hickman by two local newspapers, the *Chicago Daily Defender,* the city's leading African American newspaper, and the *Chicago Daily Tribune,* caught the attention of Mike Bartell, an organizer for the Socialist Workers Party. Bartell found a lawyer, M. J. Myer, a local labor and civil rights attorney, to defend Hickman. Two other attorneys – Leon Despres and William H. Temple – joined Myer in the case and they formed a Hickman defense committee to raise money to defend him in court and to educate the public about the horrible conditions in which African Americans lived in Chicago. Groups involved included the American Federation of Labor, the Independent Voters of Illinois, and the Committee on Racial Equality. "Many such groups degenerate into luncheons and resolutions," Martin observed. "Hickman's defenders worked hard, effectively, fast, and according to plan." The committee held rallies, collected donations from jars set out in African American businesses, and sought help from other like-minded organizations.[25]

During his trial, Hickman spoke eloquently and almost biblically, noted Martin, about what had happened to his children. When asked by his lawyer to describe his feelings between the fire and the shooting, Hickman responded, "I had two sons and two daughters who would some day be great men and women, some day they would have been married, some day they would have been fathers or mothers of children; these children would have children and then these children would have children and another generation of Hickmans could raise up and enjoy peace." The defendant's first trial resulted in a hung jury, with six men and one woman voting for acquittal and five women for conviction. Thanks to pressure brought on Chicago's political establishment by the defense committee and people from all over the country, however, an agreement was reached with assistant state attorney Samuel L. Freedman, and on December 16, 1947, a judge found Hickman guilty of manslaughter and placed him on probation for two years; he was home in plenty of time to celebrate Christmas with the surviving members of his family. "We really felt good when it was over," Willoughby Abner, an African American labor leader who had been involved in organizing assistance for Hickman, told Martin. "It shows everything isn't in vain, isn't all injustice, people will rally, it shows what can be done." The Hickman family found new accommodations in a housing project near the airport and intended to stay in Chicago. "I like Chicago," said Annie Hickman. "I used to like it very much when I had my children."[26]

Martin did not share Abner's optimism, pointing out that both Hickman and Coleman had been victims of Chicago's segregated system of housing, a system that showed no signs of changing. "The North has failed the Negro no less than the South, there is no place in this country for a black man to go," Martin wrote, calling Chicago's postwar housing record a total failure. "The housing problem is bad everywhere in America, in no major city is it worse than in Chicago, and Negroes are at the bottom of the heap because we put them there and keep them there." The more African Americans who moved to the city for a supposedly better life, the more they would be met with fierce white resistance: new restrictive covenants, Molotov cocktails and rocks thrown at their homes in white areas, and political speeches promising "racial purity." A year after the fire, Martin returned to 1733 West Washburne Avenue and found the building where the Hickman children had died deserted, its windows boarded up and charred, black timbers poking up to the sky. Martin came across an elderly black man tending a fire behind the abandoned building. The old man told him he had heard rumors of the building's owner fixing it up and offering it for sale. Asked by Martin if anyone would ever again live in such a place, the man laughed and said people would "be lined up here putting in their application. People got no place to go."[27]

The powerful indictment of Chicago's segregated housing had been aided immeasurably by sixteen drawings provided by Ben Shahn, the artist who had also illustrated Martin's Centralia article; he did the haunting drawings for the Hickman piece in just three weeks and for only $250 from *Harper's*. Shahn's illustrations included the shack the Hickman family lived in while sharecroppers, four-year-old Velvena pretending to study with her siblings, flames leaping from the brick building's upper windows, and the four dead Hickman children huddled together with their eyes closed in death. Martin and Shahn had discussed the story while in the paneled library at *Harper's* New York office. "He was a big burly man with the kindest eyes I ever saw," said Martin. "We became friends and collaborators." They spent weekends at each other's homes, and when Martin visited New York the artist took him on walking tours of the Lower East Side slums where Shahn had grown up, and Martin reciprocated by taking Shahn on tours of Chicago's African American and white criminal slums "where dwelt the people I wrote about," said Martin.[28]

In preparing his drawings for Martin's story Shahn at first had assembled visual material, then discarded it, said Martin, "for he felt the universal implications of the event transcended the immediate crime." The artist also abandoned an abstract approach and finally decided to concentrate on "the small family contacts, to the familiar experiences of all of us, to the furniture, the clothes, the look of ordinary people," an approach Martin also followed in his writing (during an interview he always made notes on the items in a person's home or apartment). Shahn, who had survived a tenement fire as a child, could not get the Hickman saga out of his mind after he had finished his drawings. The tongues of flame rising from the burning Chicago tenement building figured in one of his most powerful paintings, *Allegory*, with the figure of a great red beast – part lion and part wolf – standing over its victims, children huddled together. Shahn later said that he had developed a "curious sense of responsibility" about the Hickman fire and believed he owed "something more to the victim himself." Shahn gave Martin and Fran a copy of the painting and under it wrote, in Aramaic, "Where there is a pen there is no sword; where there is a sword there is no pen."[29]

Even before his triumphs with his stories on the Centralia disaster and Hickman's sad plight, Martin had reached the pinnacle at *Harper's*, something his editor, Allen, had also realized (in one year Martin had articles in eight of the magazine's twelve issues). Writing to Martin in July 1946, Allen had praised him as "an extraordinarily able journalist and a practically ideal contributor" to the magazine. His only fault, said Allen, involved a tendency to "over-write and leave a good deal of the process of selection to us. But this is certainly a good fault." Allen provided these details so Martin would not be upset when he presented his opinion that Martin was relying too much on *Harper's* as an outlet for his work and should branch out and do some writing for the "big slick" magazines of the time such as the *Saturday Evening Post, Collier's,* and *The American Magazine.* "This would be very handy financially and would not disturb us in the least if we could get, say, four or five articles a year from you," wrote Allen. He offered to help Martin connect with a reputable literary agent such as Harold Ober or Carl Brandt.[30]

Martin responded kindly to Allen's suggestion, noting that the editor had "grasped the problem firmly." In his letter to Allen, Martin set out what he had tried to do with his writing career after the army, including trying to break away from his dependence for income on true-crime articles, as he was "writing too many words for not enough money and wasn't having much fun (it was just blood, blood, blood). I haven't anything against fact tec pieces, certainly don't consider them beneath me or anything silly like that; but you just work too hard and the rewards are too small, both as to money and what some people call psychic income; and there just isn't any future in the field: It's too much like working on a newspaper copy desk all your life." Martin added that he had approached Brandt to represent him, but after sending him some queries on six articles had not heard back from the agent. Martin agreed with Allen that he needed an agent, as he had found editors at the "big slicks" difficult to deal with. "I think that in my present position I need an agent who is definitely interested in me and will supply guidance, suggestions, ideas, and so on, as well as a mailing service," he said. "I have always thought that an agent ought to accomplish at least one thing: He ought to be able to get faster action on a query simply because he could phone around New York, while I would have to mail an outline to one editor after another."[31]

Allen was true to his word and spoke to Ober on Martin's behalf. Graduating from Harvard University in 1905 with a degree in literature, Ober had started his career as a literary agent two years later with the firm of Paul R. Reynolds and Sons. In 1929 Ober started his own agency, Harold Ober and Associates, and over the years it represented such distinguished clients as William Faulkner, Pearl Buck, F. Scott Fitzgerald, Catherine Drinker Bowen, Philip Wylie, James M. Cain, John Gunther, Paul Gallico, Langston Hughes, J. D. Salinger, and Agatha Christie. "The literary business in New York is a small, tightly knit world," Martin recalled. "No figure in it commanded more respect than Harold Ober." By the time Martin had become a client, Ober also had working with him Ivan von Auw, who handled books, and Dorothy Olding, who with Ober handled the magazine market at the firm's offices in New York on Forty-ninth Street just off Madison Avenue. Ober, from New Hampshire and with white hair, looked to Martin more like a banker than an agent, with a "dour manner" but with sparkling blue eyes and courteous "almost to the point of seeming deferential – but not quite. He said little but listened to everything." Relations between a writer and editor are sometimes difficult, said Martin, and Ober "had a way of cutting through the difficulties, or, smoothing the way. I never heard an editor say anything of Harold except, 'He's wonderful.' They knew they could trust him completely. So could writers." Through the years Martin learned to lean on Ober not just in connection with his manuscripts, but also in helping make the major decisions that affected a writer's work and his life. "If Harold advised against taking up a subject," Martin noted, "I wouldn't take it up. If he thought a move, any move, unwise, I wouldn't make it. Harold was a rock, someone to turn to, to count on, when it mattered." With Ober running interference, including negotiating with editors about fees for articles, which Martin had never been good at, doors were opened for him that had been closed before. "Soon I was going to New York about five times a year to have lunch with editors or visit them in their offices, discussing story ideas; Harold arranged it," Martin remembered.[32]

In addition to Ober's influence in New York literary circles, Martin had attracted attention to himself with his fine work in *Harper's*, which he noted was one of the country's "high-quality, low-circulation (and low-pay) magazines that the editors of big slicks read seeking new writers." Editors from other journals sought him out, and Martin produced stories for such national women's magazines as *McCall's* (earning $2,500 for an article about Millard Gillards, the woman known as "Axis Sally," convicted of treason by the U.S. government for delivering Nazi radio broadcasts during World War II), *Redbook,* and *Cosmopolitan.* He also continued his close relationship with *Harper's,* confiding to Ober that he did so out of "loyalty, for the good of my reputation, for the good of my soul, and because they'll take some things [stories] no one else would and which I want to write."[33]

One popular national magazine, however, became Martin's favorite repository for his writing: the *Post,* owned and operated by the Curtis Publishing Company in Philadelphia, Pennsylvania. With a legacy stretching back to the days of Benjamin Franklin, the weekly *Post* had become a mainstay in middle-class American homes through the steady hand of its longtime editor, George Horace Lorimer, the son of a Boston minister. Lorimer set out, according to staff member Wesley Stout, to "interpret America to itself, always readably, but constructively." He succeeded; from 1899 to 1936 the magazine's yearly circulation increased from two thousand to more than three million. Lorimer discovered artist Norman Rockwell, whose idealized drawings of American family life were featured on more than three hundred of the magazine's covers. The *Post* also published fiction from such notable writers as Fitzgerald, Sinclair Lewis, Ring Lardner, C. S. Forester, John P. Marquand, William Saroyan, and John Steinbeck. "The *Post* was, in a few words, not unlike the network television that took away its audience – both frothy and serious," said Martin.[34]

By the 1940s, with Lorimer gone, the *Post* had begun to depend less on fiction and more on nonfiction to satisfy it readers – a perfect situation for a writer such as Martin; the magazine's audience, as he described it, included "people that enjoyed westerns, mysteries, love stories, humor, sports, heavy fact, and everything else." He broke through in the *Post*'s January 15, 1949, issue with "What the Miners Say about John L. Lewis," an article that examined the opinions of coal miners from Saint Michael, Pennsylvania, about the United Mine Workers of America president. Other stories for the *Post* followed in the early 1950s: a report on the rush to uncover uranium deposits in the Upper Peninsula, the causes behind a tragic fatal traffic accident on a lonely Michigan highway, and the hard life behind bars for inmates at the Illinois State Prison in Joliet, Illinois. Martin's work on these stories, and his previous ones on the Centralia disaster and the Hickman tragedy, had led him to believe "our society does not always work as well as it ought," and that what really mattered to a storyteller was the "individual man, the woman, the child."[35]

Crime, and its effect on American society, remained a mainstay of Martin's writing, and he also began branching out into the "mysteries of human behavior" with a story he did for the *Post* on the senseless slaying of a nurse, Pauline Campbell, in Ann Arbor, Michigan, on January 15, 1951. An unknown assailant had crept up behind the thirty-four-year old woman while she walked home from work and viciously smashed her in the skull with a heavy rubber mallet. The murder sent shock waves through the quiet college town (home to the University of Michigan campus), with police believing the crime had been committed by "a maniac." Residents were stunned when a few days after the murder, police were tipped off that three young men from the nearby town of Ypsilanti – Bill Morey Jr., Max Pell, and Dave Royal – had committed the crime, with Morey doing the actual killing. A jury found Morey and Pell guilty of first-degree murder and sentenced them to life in prison (Michigan did not have the death penalty at that time) without the chance for parole, while Royal was convicted of second-degree murder and received a twenty-two-years-to-life jail sentence. "They had no felony records," Martin noted. "They came from good families. They were nice-looking boys, well-spoken, neat, mannerly. They confessed." Morey's father's reaction to the news, "I can't believe it – I just can't believe it," reflected what many parents thought at the time. As Martin said, many parents in the community thought to themselves, "There but for the grace of God goes my own son."[36]

For a long time Martin had wanted to do a careful study of a murder involving a teenage suspect. He checked into several of these apparently senseless cases of slayings over a period of years, and in each one it did not take him long to discover "that the thing wasn't really senseless at all, that there was some clear reason assignable if one took the trouble to look – but the reason was so unusual, so special, that it deprived the story of what it ought to have above all else: Wide applicability." For example, he noted that sometimes a newspaper reported that the youth came from an average, respectable home, but in digging further the mother turned out to be an alcoholic, the father a criminal, or the home was in a slum neighborhood. It was the not the fault of the newspapers, said Martin, as they had to work fast and print what information they could find. "It is for this very reason that I think a magazine or book writer in the fact field can perform a useful service: by coming along after the event has occurred, he gains perspective and can see the event whole," he said. Martin checked into and dropped several cases, looking for one that involved young men "in whom any one of us might recognize our own children; parents in whom we could recognize ourselves." Only then could a single case have a wider application, he added, getting at some of the "fundamental problems and weaknesses of our world as a whole, and more especially of the way our world rears its children."[37]

When he heard about the Morey case, Martin traveled to Ann Arbor, as it "seemed to be what I was looking for – a crime readily explained by none of the standard 'causes' of 'juvenile delinquency,' a crime that by all the rules should not have happened but did happen." This was a few years before actor James Dean put the issue of teenage angst on the nation's consciousness with his performance as troubled youth Jim Stark in the 1955 film *Rebel Without a Cause*. It turned out to be one of the most difficult stories Martin ever covered, not in a technical sense, but personally. By April 17, 1951, the Martin family had grown to include a second child, a boy, Daniel, and a second son, John Frederick (called Fred by the family), came along on February 24, 1953. "I have children of my own," noted Martin. "I know a lot of other kids not very different from Bill Morey. I know a lot of parents not very different from his parents." When he was the same age as Morey, Martin and his friends had also done some of the stupid and dangerous things Morey had done: drink alcohol before they legally could, drive around recklessly in cars looking for excitement, and base their actions on the opinions of others in their age group. "The story rather frightened me," Martin said. Ann Arbor and Ypsilanti were by no means unique towns, and the teenagers who lived in those communities were not different from thousands of others in cities across the country. "We all think it can't happen here, not in my town; but it sure can, it happened in Ann Arbor," he noted.[38]

Ordinarily, in conducting his legwork for such a story, Martin would have chosen to interview the boys' parents last, but he realized that if they, especially Bill Morey's parents, refused to talk to him freely, he had no story. He decided to approach the Moreys first, so he traveled to Ypsilanti by bus and from there on foot to the Moreys' home on a quiet and shady street. Both parents were reluctant to talk to Martin. By then the trial had concluded, their son was in prison, and they did not want to relive what they had endured. As Martin noted, however, they were actually reliving what had happened every day, as they "dated everything in their lives as 'before *this* happened' or 'after *this* happened,' this terrible event, the murder." He explained to them that he was not trying to write a sensational story, but instead "a thoroughgoing study for a serious magazine [the *Post*] that would try to discover *why* it had happened." As he noted in his four-part series in the magazine, although no final answer might be found for the question "Why did they kill?" perhaps an understanding could be reached by getting at the facts of the case. "All is not," he added, "cannot be, darkness and mystification." In addition, Martin shared his own experiences as a sometimes wayward youth and his and Fran's lives as parents of a young daughter. After a time, the Moreys began to respond to Martin's gentle nudging, with Mrs. Morey nodding her head to what he was saying and volunteering information about her son. For an hour and a half they talked about Bill, as they still called him, and Martin decided not to press them on anything. Upon leaving, he asked if he could return the next day; they agreed and the three of them talked for two hours, "and the day after that for four hours, and the following week for more," Martin recalled.[39]

Subsequently, Martin spent weeks talking to the Moreys, to the families of the other two boys jailed for the crime, their schoolteachers, friends, the lawyers defending the boys, a psychiatrist (Doctor O. R. Yoder) who believed Bill had a "psychopathic personality," and the boys themselves while they were in prison. Martin's articles also examined the differences between Ann Arbor, the quiet college town, and Ypsilanti, where the boys had lived, which he described as "a blue-collar town turned upside down by the war." The war had drawn thousands of "hillbilly" workers from Kentucky and Tennessee to Ford Motor Company's massive Willow Run bomber plant, and after the war they had gone on "relief and turned Willow Run into a slum," wrote Martin, with their children running wild, smoking marijuana and drinking. "Ypsilanti and the automobile with its roaring exhaust became characters in the story," he said.[40]

In his concluding piece in the *Post,* Martin pointed out how hard the case had been to understand, especially given the grief and guilt felt by the boys' parents and the difficulty in obtaining reliable information from the teenagers involved, as they seemed to inhabit "a world of their own" and were exceedingly loyal to one another. "I never really answered the question of why – why they had killed. Why? – to a reporter, it is the only question that matters and it is the only question he can never really answer," said Martin. Although bitter about the way their son had been treated by local newspapers, by police, and by the prosecution during his trial, Mr. and Mrs. Morey, too, had no final answers for what their son had done. When Martin had asked him why his son had killed the nurse, Bill Morey Sr. had quietly responded, "I couldn't tell you. It is a mystery." Civic leaders in Ypsilanti and Ann Arbor agreed there existed no more juvenile delinquency in their towns than in most communities, Martin reported. "If this is true, then adult Americans have little notion of what their children are up to – and this is by no means unlikely," he noted.[41]

The series about the case in the *Post* prompted numerous letters to Martin, and worried parents in suburban communities across America made stronger efforts, he reported, to cooperate with school officials, civic leaders, and police "in the hope they can find out what is wrong with their own towns and thus, possibly, prevent the same thing from happening again." Martin expanded what he wrote into a book, published by Ballantine Books in 1953 as *Why Did They Kill?* The book received strong reviews upon its release. Croswell Bowen, a crime writer for *The New Yorker,* described Martin in his critique for the *New York Times* as "probably the ablest crime reporter in America" and said the book was "as smooth and gripping as a first-rate novel." *Why Did They Kill?* continued to receive praise from critics in the years to come, especially with the release in 1966 of Truman Capote's bestselling book *In Cold Blood*, which examined the vicious murder of Herbert Clutter, his wife, and two of their children in Holcomb, Kansas, by Richard Hickock and Perry Smith, who were found guilty and hanged for the killings. First serialized in *The New Yorker*, the book received strong support for its literary achievement. "It seemed to me," Capote said in an interview with the *New York Times*, "that journalism, reportage, could be forced to yield a serious new art form: the 'non-fiction novel,' as I thought of it." He went on to say that very few "first-class creative writers" had ever bothered with journalism, except as a sideline, "something to be done when the creative spirit is lacking, or as a means of making money quickly," and dismissed journalism as "unbecoming to the serious writer's artistic dignity."[42]

Over the years questions have arisen about Capote's veracity and his claims that the book was "immaculately factual." Although *The New Yorker* ran Capote's articles, its editor, William Shawn, had been concerned about how Capote could be so certain of what had been said in private conversations he had no part in. Shawn later expressed regrets at having published the articles in his magazine. At the time of *In Cold Blood*'s publication as a book, some writers, including Kenneth Tynan and Ned Rorem, criticized Capote for profiting off the death of two people and not doing enough to save Hickock and Smith from their fate. Stanley Kauffmann in *The New Republic* denigrated Capote's work, saying it was "ridiculous in judgment and debasing of all of us to call this book literature." He spoke for many of the anti-Capote critics by instead recommending Martin's book as a cut above *In Cold Blood*. "His 131-page book," Kauffmann said of Martin's *Why Did They Kill?* "is superior to Capote's in almost every way, makes some attempt to answer the question in its title, and is devoid of any suspicion of conscious self-gratifying aggrandizement into Literature." Other critics, however, preferred Capote's work, with Joseph Haas writing in the *Chicago Daily News* that he read Martin's book "with respect and pleasure" and that it displayed all the virtues of the best modern news writing – accuracy, responsibility, thoroughness, and interpretation. But, Haas added, *Why Did They Kill?* suffered from a host of limitations. "It tends to pedestrian prose, pat pop-sociological conclusions, uninspired organization and a shortage of perceptive insight. It lacks the substance of art: rich in facts, it is poor in truth," he wrote. Haas and other Capote supporters may have faulted Martin's literary skills, but few people ever disputed his facts.[43]

A focus on crime's effect on American society led inevitably to Martin exploring in his writing the place where most criminals ended up: prison. In writing for the *Post* about inmates at the Illinois State Penitentiary, Joliet Branch (called Stateville) at Joliet, Illinois, and a riot at Jackson Prison in Michigan, Martin studied the roots of criminality and became convinced that prisons in America were being run according to a myth – the "myth of rehabilitation," which he believed was impossible inside a maximum-security prison. "The truth is that the usual prison 'program' is really designed not to rehabilitate the inmate," Martin said, "but rather to prevent trouble in prison." He called for such reforms as separating hardened criminals from the general prison population; razing old, out-of-date institutions such as Jackson; building new prison camps and farms, medium-security prisons, and institutions for the criminally insane; releasing about half of all inmates to these prison farms and camps, plus parole; putting the dangerous ones into small maximum-security institutions; revising what had become an inequitable criminal code; and abolishing the death penalty. The reforms were needed, he added, not out of kindness for those incarcerated, but for "our own safety. Ex-convicts walk among us," Martin noted. Still, he realized his pleas for change would probably fall on deaf ears. "You can't tell people, exhort them, to pay more attention to the administration of criminal justice," he said. They would respond by telling the reformer to "drop dead" and say they preferred to watch a popular show such as *Gunsmoke* on television. For a time in the 1950s, however, Martin's name did become synonymous with the subject of penology. Once Fran, who served on the Illinois board of the American Civil Liberties Union, wrote to Washington, D.C., for research material on prison management and criminal rehabilitation. She received back a letter suggesting a book on prison reform, *Break Down the Walls*, the book by her husband based on the series he had done in the *Post* on Jackson Prison.[44]

Although he never had any illusions about being "a Sir Galahad of the downtrodden" and did not consider himself to be an investigative

reporter, Martin nevertheless sometimes found himself personally involved in a story. In one case the friendships he had developed while
living in Highland Park placed him squarely in the middle of a crime
that had been one of the biggest news stories of the 1920s, the "thrill murder" in 1924 in Chicago of fourteen-year-old Robert "Bobby" Franks by
Richard Loeb and Nathan Leopold, two young Jewish men from wealthy
families. Both men confessed to the crime and received ninety-nine-year
sentences for kidnapping and life sentences for the murder, and they
were incarcerated at the Joliet Prison (later transferred to the nearby
Stateville facility). In 1936 Loeb was killed by a fellow inmate at Stateville, but Leopold, nineteen when incarcerated, survived and continued
doing his time and attempting to win parole. In 1955, two years after a
parole board had denied Leopold's request for release, Martin wrote a
four-part series on Leopold's thirty years behind bars for the *Post* titled
"Murder on His Conscience." Martin said he had been inspired to write
about Leopold because he wanted answers to such questions as: "What
happens to an intelligent man during thirty years in prison? How has
Leopold spent his time? What has prison done to him? And what are his
chances of ever leaving prison alive?"[45]

To seek answers, Martin drove to Joliet, Illinois, in late April 1954
to visit Leopold. As Martin outlined what he planned to do, Leopold
listened to him without expression. "Then in his precise pedantic voice,
he said he wanted to consult his lawyers, his brother, other advisers,"
Martin recalled. On about May 10, Martin received a telephone call from
Ralph Newman, the proprietor of the Abraham Lincoln Bookshop in
Chicago and a close friend of Leopold's brother, Mike, who had died
in 1953. Newman said he represented Leopold and asked for a meeting.
They met on May 13 and Newman told Martin that publishers had expressed interest in having Leopold write his autobiography, and novelist
Meyer Levin wanted to do a fictionalized version of the notorious crime.
Newman asked Martin if he intended to do a third-person article (and
perhaps a book) under his byline, or whether he might want to do a
first-person story under Leopold's name. In either case, Leopold wanted
compensation. "I said that as to money," Martin wrote in a memo to the
Post, "I would not give him [Leopold] any because I cannot afford to split
story checks; therefore any money would have to come from the Post;

and I said I didn't know whether you'd want this badly enough to pay him anything or not. Newman asked me to find out and I said I'd prefer to talk first with either a member of the Leopold family or the family lawyer."[46]

On May 21 Newman arranged a meeting with Martin and two other men, William Friedman, the Leopold's family lawyer, and A. G. Ballenger, Morris Paper Mills vice president and trustee of a fund established for Leopold by his father. The men discussed the possibilities before them, and Friedman, Ballenger, and Newman said they preferred a third-person story, which would leave Newman free to try and find a publisher for Leopold's autobiography (released in 1958 as *Life Plus 99 Years*). "As for money, they repeated that Leopold wanted money," Martin recalled. "They said he had none except his trust fund, which he can't touch while in prison." When asked by Martin why Leopold wanted to be paid, as he did not need money while incarcerated, Newman said that as "much as the money itself Leopold wanted the satisfaction of having earned some money." Martin informed them that if any funds went to Leopold, the money had to come from the *Post* and the advisers should negotiate directly with the magazine on such matters, not with him. Later, Martin also met with Levin, who had been working on his novel since the previous fall, and the two men reached an understanding, with Martin indicating he saw no conflict between what they were doing. "In effect, we divided Leopold up," Levin recalled. "He [Martin] was going to write mostly about Leopold in prison, and I planned to write about what happened before he got there." Levin published his book, *Compulsion*, to critical and popular acclaim in 1956, selling more than a hundred thousand copies.[47]

Leopold finally agreed to cooperate with Martin without direct compensation from the sale of the story to the *Post*, but the inmate would get half of the sale of any subsidiary rights and had "absolute veto over factual errors," Martin noted, as well as the ability to object to matters of interpretation. "He and his advisers concluded that he would cooperate with me because they thought I knew something about prisons and crime," said Martin. Leopold's advisers, in addition to being men of substance in Chicago, presented special problems for Martin when he began his work on the story, as some of them were "friends of ours who belonged to the Jewish community of Highland Park. We saw them at dinner parties, some were involved in Fran's ACLU or in liberal Democratic affairs . . . some had grown up with Leopold himself, and their parents had been friends of his parents." Memories of the 1924 crime were still painful ones in the Jewish community, but Martin received full cooperation from Leopold's friends and family and "had full access to all information available to them." He was the first person ever granted such access.[48]

Martin started to work full-time on the subject on June 18, 1954, spending two weeks at Stateville interviewing Leopold alone with no guards in a compact room where the parole board usually held its hearings. "There is a window in a room, barred," Martin noted. "The room is small and bare. There is a desk and a couple of chairs. Just through the window you can see the inside of the prison wall." The writer and the inmate met two times a day, once in the morning and again in the afternoon. At lunchtime Leopold ate in the regular inmate dining room, while Martin dined with Warden Joseph E. Ragen. Martin had worked with Ragen on a previous story for the *Post* about the Illinois prison, which might have smoothed away any problems about access to Leopold and the ability to interview him away from the usual visiting room and without the presence of any guards. In his talks with Leopold, Martin found him to possess "insight and perspective on himself to a degree unusual in people generally, and extraordinary in somebody who has been imprisoned for so long."[49]

Martin had to contend with a variety of issues with his series on Leopold, including the inmate's fears that a recapitulation of his crime might endanger his chance at eventual parole, worries from Leopold's family about how the homosexual relationship between Leopold and Loeb would be handled, and the *Post*'s unwillingness to include in Martin's final installment an outright plea for the inmate's parole. Leopold even wrote Martin from prison expressing his fears that the article "would do me incalculable harm. It will also make living under my present circumstances very difficult. You do not, I know, want to hurt me, especially since you realize what an enormous stake I have in the matter. Knowing that you are a good guy, I'm sure you wouldn't want that on your conscience." All parties were able to iron out any difficulties, however, and after the entire series had been published, an elderly neighbor of the Martins who had known Leopold's parents, now both deceased, told the writer his effort had been "the first fair and understanding story she had ever read about him."[50]

In the first part of the series, Martin explored Leopold's early life, his friendship with Loeb, and how they came to commit their infamous crime. The other articles concentrated on Leopold's life in prison and his attempts to deal with the crushing monotony of prison life by studying semantics, helping rebuild the prison's library after a riot, establishing a correspondence course for inmates, volunteering as a test subject during World War II for a U.S. Army study of potential new drugs to combat malaria, working as an X-ray technician in the prison hospital, and trying to win parole. Inmates who knew Leopold well thought highly of him, but to those who did not his personality seemed forbidding, Martin reported. "He [Leopold] is inclined to be opinionated, stubborn, literal-minded, humorless, tactless," said Martin. "He seems to need, for reasons of his inner security, to assert himself, to win his arguments. He is formal, detached, correct, precise, legalistic." Martin presented an even-handed evaluation of the pros and cons on whether or not to parole Leopold, pointing out his crime resulted from a situation that would never occur again. "Leopold thinks he has been rehabilitated in spite of prison, not because of it," Martin wrote. "Leopold's prison career is surely one of the most unusual on record. Few men have lived lives at all like Leopold's."[51]

The state of Illinois granted Leopold a rehearing on his parole in 1958, and Martin, upon the request of one of Leopold's attorney, Varian B. Adams, wrote a letter to Governor William G. Stratton outlining the reasons why the inmate should be paroled. Martin wrote the governor, "In my opinion, Leopold is a good parole risk. He has a good record in prison. He will not be cut adrift without resources if paroled. And so on – judged by these and other standards set up in the parole predictability tables ordinarily used by parole boards, including, I believe, yours, he rates as a good risk." Martin also appeared at the parole board hearing to testify on Leopold's behalf. He told members of the parole board that neither the coroner nor the judge at the original trial had, in spite of tabloid newspaper reports to the contrary, found any evidence that

Franks, the murdered boy, had been sexually assaulted, and that during all his time in prison, Leopold had never been cited by a guard for any homosexual activity. The board paroled Leopold, and a newspaperman later told Martin it had been his testimony that had spurred the board's action, as it took its members "off the hook for paroling a 'sex criminal.'" After being freed from prison on March 13, 1958, Leopold spent the rest of his life working as a medical technician at a Church of the Brethren hospital in Puerto Rico. He died on August 29, 1971.[52]

Over the years, Martin's work became a fixture in the *Post*, and the magazine trumpeted his work with advertisements in newspapers across the country as "One of America's Great Reporters." It was, he said, "heady stuff." Martin developed particularly close relationships with two of the magazine's staff members, Ben Hibbs, the magazine's editor in chief, and Stuart Rose, the *Post*'s senior editor. Martin often dealt directly with the two men without any assistance from Ober. "But I always kept him informed, I always submitted the completed manuscript first to him and asked him to pass it along to the editor if it seemed alright," said Martin, "and I always paid his 10 percent commission." In working with other editors, sometimes Martin came up with the idea for a story, while other times the editor did. The *Post*'s editors seldom, if ever, made an assignment, but if they liked Martin's proposal, he said they were "almost certain to buy the final manuscript unless you blew it, for the *Post* editors, unlike many, knew what they wanted. And they not only bought pieces; they also published them – and the point of anybody's writing is, of course, to publish." He added that during his career he would rather have an expression of interest in one of his story ideas from the *Post* than a "firm assignment from several other magazines," noting that *Life* offered him a number of assignments but did not pay him full price or publish one of his articles until 1965. The *Post* paid between $1,500 and $2,500 for a story, plus travel expenses, and as Martin wrote more and more for the magazine, Ober secured him a pay raise plus a "generous bonus" on almost every published article; for a March 24, 1951, story about a police informant, John Kuesis, who worked with the Chicago police, Martin received $5,000. "Moreover, the *Post* would give you a decision in a week and pay you in another, important to a freelance," said Martin.[53]

When he traveled to New York, Martin met with Rose, who normally handled fiction for the magazine, during the editor's regular Tuesday trip from the *Post's* offices in Philadelphia in search of manuscripts. The two men were unlikely collaborators. Martin described Rose as looking like "the classic man-about-town," and he supported the Republican Party. "Stuart Rose and I had little in common except a love of writing and a confidence that, as he put it, a good reporter could report anything," Martin recalled. "This was the way he handled me: not restricting me to a single narrow category of stories, such as crime, but rather giving me leeway to report and write what I wanted to or what he was interested in. It was, really, an ideal editor-author relationship." Rose also proved to be a fine technical editor, someone who knew what he wanted from writers and how the articles should be organized. He sometimes returned Martin's manuscripts to him along with memos with instructions on how to reorganize them, paragraph by paragraph. Although not always understanding the reasons for Rose's decisions, Martin complied, and he found when reading the stories in proof "how right he had been."[54]

The *Post* often placed a five-thousand-word limit on its articles, which, said Martin, provided good discipline for a writer, forcing one to "write tightly, without an unneeded word." Some stories, however, could not be told within these limits, and Rose and Hibbs gave Martin the flexibility to expand his pieces when needed, often running them over several issues as a multipart series. Under Rose's guidance, Martin had begun writing on a wide range of subjects, and although the *Post* had a reputation as a conservative publication, with its articles and covers idealizing traditional American values of home and family, it gave Martin almost carte blanche on the stories he covered. Over the years he investigated sensitive and sometimes taboo issues such as divorce, abortion, mental illness, and school desegregation. "These were not midwestern stories," Martin said, "they were national stories." He found himself traveling all over the country, from Beverly Hills, California, to Brownstown, Indiana.[55]

The *Post* showed great courage in publishing many of his stories, said Martin, noting that at the time he wrote about abortion it was illegal in every state and was "never mentioned in polite society; the newspaper still called it 'illegal surgery,' not abortion." One of the few occasions when the magazine's nerve failed came when Martin proposed doing a series on the investigative methods of U.S. senator Joseph McCarthy, Republican from Wisconsin. McCarthy's probes into supposed communists within the American government in the early 1950s had produced cries of a witch hunt from his opponents, who accused him of recklessly taking advantage of Cold War tensions between the United States and the Soviet Union for his own political advantage. Although both Rose and Hibbs had approved of Martin's idea of exploring the phenomenon that became known as McCarthyism, someone in higher authority at the magazine, "no doubt at the corporate level," said Martin, nixed the idea. He noted it marked the only time the *Post* refused to let him "do a political piece on what I have to believe were political grounds."[56]

Martin repaid the *Post*'s faith in him with loyalty, writing "almost exclusively" for the magazine, sometimes spending as much as a year or more researching and writing a story. In doing so, he found his writing undergoing a change. In his earlier work, Martin had spent a lot of effort trying to include in his stories every single fact he had the space for, and, to a great extent, "letting the facts speak for themselves." As his writing matured, especially in the series he did on school desegregation and divorce, he began permitting himself to draw conclusions from the evidence he had gathered, and the stories were "more consciously *written,* were not simply agglutinations of facts." The change may have been a result of his growing confidence as a writer, as he had been working at the profession for many years, or it may have been because Martin was able to spend enough time on a story that when he sat down to write he felt he had "become an expert on the subject" and could reflect on the facts and shape the language to match what he had discovered.[57]

Martin became one of a handful of people (Ober estimated the number at fifty) pursuing a living as a full-time freelance writer of heavy-fact articles. Four times in a five-year period, from 1953 to 1957, he won the magazine industry's top honor, the Benjamin Franklin Award, for work published in the *Post;* he also received recognition for his writing in the Society of Professional Journalists' annual Sigma Delta Chi Awards. The *Post* reveled in its contributor's success, paying for Martin and his wife to travel to New York for the award ceremonies. Martin's career as one of the country's finest freelance reporters received mention in both *Time* and *Newsweek* magazines, with the reporter for *Time* noting that while Martin's style was "unpretentious," he had few peers as "a fact finder." Martin told *Time* that the common denominator in his work was his abiding interest "in the individual human being and what happens to him in a society that really doesn't work as well as it should. . . . Sounds kind of pretentious, but I think it's so." *Newsweek*'s headline for its story on Martin used just three words to describe him: "The Best Reporter."[58]

The freedom associated with the life of a freelancer meant much to Martin, as the *Post* soon discovered. Hibbs, recognizing Martin's worth to the magazine's continued success, paid him top scale for his stories and attempted to acknowledge his contributions in other ways, including adding him to its masthead as a contributing editor. Although deeply honored by the offer, Martin declined it after talking it over with his wife and agent and thinking about it for several days. When he had quit his job as a reporter on the *Indianapolis Times*, Martin wrote to Hibbs, he had embarked on something he said he had "wanted to do since childhood. And something which at the same time scared me to death, because of its insecurity." Martin had even turned down secure staff positions at *Collier's* and *Life* magazines to pursue his dream. If he agreed to be on the masthead, Martin believed he would be abandoning "something hardly won," important to him as well as important "symbolically to the country," a belief, he added, that might sound pretentious, as all exalted principles did. In spite of his personal feeling, Martin would have agreed to be listed if he thought it would "greatly benefit" the *Post*. To him, however, such an acceptance on his part might in fact diminish his value to the magazine, if readers questioned his objectivity after seeing his name on the masthead. Martin ended his letter to Hibbs by expressing the hope that declining the invitation would not affect his relationship with the magazine, as he had come to consider himself a *Post* writer. Whenever in his affairs any conflict arose between the *Post* and any other magazine, Martin wrote, he always resolved it, with no hesitation on his part, in the *Post*'s favor. "I've been more comfortable working for the Post than for any other magazine," he wrote.[59]

Hibbs responded to Martin's missive by writing back and telling him how impressed he had been, calling his correspondence "one of the finest personal documents I have read in a long time" and offering his respect for how well and forthrightly Martin had stated his case. The editor said Martin's decision to decline being listed on the magazine's masthead would in no way affect his standing with him and the rest of the staff. "There are a good many of us around this joint, John, who regard you with both esteem and affection," wrote Hibbs, "and a little difference of opinion on staff status isn't going to change that."[60]

Martin's strong belief in the value and independence of his position as a freelance writer, what he called "the loneliest trade," never wavered, but he did have plenty of opportunity over the years to experience what being part of a large organization and working with others might entail. Thanks to a chance set of circumstances, he left the life of the "dispassionate observer" and became an integral part of the national political career of the governor of his home state, Adlai Stevenson, a relationship that lasted until Stevenson's death in 1965 and even after. "All my life I had been a reporter, on the outside looking in," Martin noted. "Now suddenly I was on the inside looking out. . . . I was not reporting policy nuances; I was making them." Following Martin's involvement as a speechwriter with Stevenson's first campaign as the Democratic Party's presidential nominee in 1952 against GOP contender Dwight D. Eisenhower, nothing would be the same for him ever again.[61]

FIVE

All the Way with Adlai

ON SUNDAY, FEBRUARY 3, 1952, JOHN BARTLOW MARTIN AND his wife, Fran, took their daughter, Cindy, to dinner in downtown Chicago at the Pump Room at the Ambassador East Hotel to celebrate her tenth birthday, which fell on February 5. Later that evening the family adjourned to the apartment of a friend, well-to-do Chicago attorney Louis A. Kohn, whom Martin had met through his friendship with two other lawyers, John Voelker and Raymond Friend. Kohn had been an important part of the team that had elected Adlai Stevenson to the Illinois governorship in 1948 and had been encouraging Martin to edit a book of speeches Stevenson had made as governor that would also include a long biographical introduction about the Democratic Party's rising star. "I presumed he [Kohn] hoped to use the book in Stevenson's forthcoming campaign for reelection as governor," Martin recalled.[1]

During that winter, however, there were many political pundits who believed that Stevenson might run for the presidency, as President Harry Truman, beset by abysmal ratings in public opinion polls (only 32 percent of Americans approved of the job he was doing), seemed unlikely to run for re-election. Although Stevenson had used Martin's story about the Centralia mine disaster to attack his opponent, incumbent Dwight H. Green, in the 1948 gubernatorial campaign, Martin had never before met Stevenson, whose fifty-second birthday was also on February 5. Stevenson joined the gathering at Kohn's apartment and he and Cindy together cut a birthday cake made by Kohn's wife. "I remember feeling awed by him," said Cindy Martin Coleman years later. "He was, after all, the governor of the state of Illinois." She still remembered how happy he seemed and his "smiling eyes."[2]

The guests at Kohn's apartment tried to avoid the one subject that Democrats across the country were then pondering: Would Stevenson try to win the party's presidential nomination at the convention that summer in Chicago? A few weeks earlier, on January 22, Stevenson had met with Truman at Blair House in Washington, D.C., and the president had offered the governor his support as the Democratic Party's next presidential candidate. "I told him I would not run for President again," Truman said of the conversation, "and that it was my opinion he was best fitted for the place." Stevenson, however, turned down the president's offer, saying only that he wished to run for re-election as Illinois's governor. Privately he told friends that Democrats might have been in power far too long (the party had held the White House since 1932), and if the Republicans nominated General Dwight D. Eisenhower, he doubted he could beat such a nationally known figure. "Nobody needs to try to save the Republic from Ike Eisenhower, and couldn't if they tried," Stevenson told James Reston of the *New York Times*. Stevenson did relate to his staff that his decision could very well change if conservative U.S. senator Robert A. Taft ("Mr. Republican") of Ohio received the G OP nomination, as he strongly disagreed with Taft's noninterventionist foreign policy stands. According to Martin, friends and advisers of Stevenson did their best to avoid the subject of the presidency, almost like "anxious relatives hovering at the bedside of a patient they know is stricken with a fatal disease but who doesn't know it himself."[3]

At Kohn's apartment Martin and Stevenson ignored discussing the presidential boom then building for the governor and concentrated instead on talking about the book project. Instead of a collection of his speeches, however, Stevenson had a different idea. He said it was a shame that so few people were interested in state government and suggested that after his re-election Martin should come to the state capital in Springfield, spend several months with him to find out how his administration worked, and then write his book. Martin was intrigued by the suggestion, thinking he might even turn the idea into a series of articles for the *Saturday Evening Post*. He found the governor to be "a thoroughly engaging man," whose uneven features – a large, irregularly shaped nose, unruly eyebrows that gave him a quizzical expression, and large blue eyes – caught his attention from their first meeting. "I never had met a politician like him," Martin recalled. "He was quiet, intelligent, soft-spoken, and there was nothing insincere about him. I was greatly impressed."[4]

Adlai E. Stevenson II certainly had the proper pedigree for high political office. Born in 1900, he was the grandson of Adlai E. Stevenson I, who served as vice president during President Grover Cleveland's second term in 1892, was the vice presidential running mate of Democratic Party presidential nominee William Jennings Bryan in 1900, and ran (unsuccessfully) for governor of Illinois in 1908. Educated at Princeton University, Stevenson II had gone on to study at Harvard Law School, but withdrew to serve as an editor at his family's newspaper, the *Bloomington (Ill.) Pantagraph*. He returned to study law at the Northwestern University Law School, graduating in 1926. During the Great Depression and World War II, Stevenson served in governmental posts in Washington, D.C., working as a special assistant to secretary of the navy Frank Knox and as an adviser to the U.S. delegation to a conference in San Francisco from which the charter for the United Nations emerged. Encouraged by Kohn, who saw him as "the type of man that ought to run for high office," Stevenson, with backing from Cook County political boss Jacob M. Avery, agreed to run for governor in 1948 and won in a dominating fashion, defeating Green by more than half a million votes, at that time the largest majority ever recorded by a candidate in Illinois.[5]

After meeting with Stevenson, Martin consulted with his close friend and writing adviser, Francis Nipp, who expressed reservations about the project. Nipp feared that if Martin became too closely identified with Stevenson, he might endanger his position as an independent freelancer. "I wanted to go ahead anyway," said Martin, and Nipp agreed to help him research the governor's enormous speech file. Traveling to New York to find a publisher for the book (Harper and Brothers offered him a contract), Martin discovered that his friends in the publishing world were enthralled by Stevenson and believed him to be a liberal in the Democratic tradition of Franklin D. Roosevelt and Truman. "Actually, he [Stevenson] was not so liberal," Martin observed. "He was a man who favored balanced budgets, feared federal executive power, looked with favor on business, deplored what he considered labor's excesses." Time was of the essence as Martin learned from Harper and Brothers that another firm had talked to Noel Busch, a journalist, about doing a similar book on Stevenson. Interest in Stevenson as the Democratic Party's 1952 candidate for president had been heightened with Truman's announcement on March 29 that he would not seek re-election.[6]

In early April Martin went to Springfield and spent a week with the governor and his staff. He continued to be favorably impressed by Stevenson, especially his self-deprecating sense of humor and obvious intelligence. "He grumbled about the burdens of his office and his own weariness. Always he pretended to be not a politician but, rather, an amateur good-government man surrounded by politicians who probably wanted to do him in," said Martin. "He pretended astonishment and bewilderment at the presidential boom." Nipp and Martin came up with an outline for the book, expanding the biographical introduction and printing Stevenson's speeches as an appendix. Eventually Martin dropped the idea of using the speeches, and the book became a brief biography, not unlike a profile for *The New Yorker* magazine. Martin wrote a rough draft in just two weeks and delivered the manuscript to his publisher in mid-April. Harper and Brothers stalled on publishing the book after Stevenson issued a public letter on April 18 that seemed to take him out of the running for the nomination. In view of his prior commitment to run again for governor, Stevenson said he "could not accept the nomination for any other office this summer."[7]

With his Stevenson book on hold for the moment, Martin could turn to worrying about more personal matters, including buying a new house. On June 26 the Martin family moved to a white Victorian frame house at 185 Maple Avenue in Highland Park, Illinois, a residence that had been built on a wooded ravine lot about an acre in size a year after the 1871 Chicago fire. "It was what was then called 'an old clunk,' today 'a charming historic Victorian,'" said Martin, who added that the house had to undergo extensive (and expensive) renovations, including a new foundation. The family barely had a chance to move in before they were besieged with guests arriving for the Democratic National Convention, held from July 21 to 26 at the International Amphitheater in Chicago. A few weeks earlier the Republicans had met there and nominated Eisenhower as their party's presidential candidate, with U.S. senator Richard Nixon of California as his running mate. Attending the Democratic convention on a daily basis, Martin and his guests subsisted on turkeys cooked by Fran and eaten while sitting at a long, rough-hewn table Martin discovered in his new house's basement. On the convention's first day, Martin found himself on the main floor just below the podium during Stevenson's welcoming speech to the delegates. The governor's well-received remarks reignited the clamor for him as the party's presidential standard bearer.[8]

The fifteen-minute speech excited the delegates, and Martin called it one of the most thrilling political moments of his life. James Reston noted that the "reluctant candidate" had talked himself into being a leading contender for the nomination, as his address "impressed the convention from left to right." When balloting began on Friday, July 25, Stevenson trailed U.S. senator Estes Kefauver of Tennessee, but he won the nomination on the third ballot, boosted by the withdrawal of former secretary of commerce and ambassador W. Averell Harriman. U.S. senator John Sparkman of Alabama became the party's vice presidential candidate. The diverse coalition among the Democrats that had been held together by Roosevelt and Truman was, said Martin, rearranging itself, "and it could only rearrange around Stevenson." Also, for the first time, both the Republican and Democratic conventions were broadcast in their entirety on television, and millions of people across the country tuned in to watch the proceedings. Writer Bruce Bliven described 1952 as the year "television came to politics." Watching the convention on a television set propped on the dining room table at his new house in Highland Park, Martin saw Stevenson capture the nomination. One of Martin's guests, artist Ben Shahn, gave him the tally sheet on which he had been marking Stevenson's growing delegate count toward the nomination. On the back of the sheet Shahn had sketched a caricature of Stevenson; the Martins kept this and the other drawings Shahn had made during the convention for the rest of their lives.[9]

With the election only three months away, Stevenson set about organizing a national campaign and placing his personal stamp on the party. He replaced Democratic National Committee chair Frank McKinney, a Truman ally, with Stephen A. Mitchell, a Chicago lawyer who had been an early Stevenson supporter. In addition, Stevenson established his campaign headquarters not in Washington, D.C., where the DNC had its headquarters, but in Springfield. Many believed Stevenson did so to disassociate his candidacy from the Truman administration, which the Republicans had been hitting hard for the stalemate then occurring in the Korean War, corruption in some government agencies, and its supposed soft stance on communism. These issues became the GOP's formula for capturing the White House after years in the wilderness. C_2K_1: communism, corruption, and Korea. Carl McGowan, a member of Stevenson's staff as governor and a key part of his presidential effort, noted that sentiment played a role in the decision to pick Springfield as the headquarters, as the governor "felt that his identification really *was* with Springfield and he was a new face and that somehow it gave him more of a solidity to the people than if he had been working out of an office in New York or Washington."[10]

Martin had been vacationing at Three Lakes in the Upper Peninsula of Michigan when he received a telephone call from William J. Flanagan, Stevenson's press secretary. Flanagan beseeched Martin to join him in Springfield to help with magazine public relations, as he had been swamped with requests for information about the candidate; Martin agreed to help. He did not know it at the time, but Martin had set the stage for a long career on the national political scene. "A campaign," he noted, "is a watershed in your life and later you tend to date everything by whether it happened before or after a certain campaign." Arriving in Springfield on August 21, Martin felt an immediate sense of confusion, "confusion as to who was doing what, as to what I was supposed to be doing, and so on." Campaign staffers were spread all over town, with some working at the governor's mansion, some at a rented brick house on South Fifth Street, and others on two floors of the Leland Hotel. Martin, who had a desk in the dining room at the Fifth Street house, said that in the end "Springfield came to resemble a disaster area, a haven for refugees from a flood." He also noticed how young everyone on the staff seemed, with almost nobody looking older than forty and most in their twenties and thirties. "There just weren't any old men around during the campaign, almost never," Martin observed. The candidate shared the general bewilderment at what was going on. Seeing Martin at the headquarters, a surprised Stevenson asked him, "What are you doing here?" Martin said he was not yet sure, but was trying to help Flanagan with the crush of media then invading Springfield. "He [Stevenson] said rather plaintively, 'Nobody ever tells me anything anymore,'" Martin recalled. "He seemed glad to see me, as though I was an old friend, somebody he knew. I've noticed that in him on other occasions and with other people."[11]

Confusion also reigned at the Volunteers for Stevenson office at 7 South Dearborn Street in Chicago, where Fran spent one or two days a week sorting out the mess the files were in, according to Martin. "Desks were pushed into the big bare rooms helter-skelter," he noted, "piles of literature and buttons and ribbons littered the floor, and everybody was scurrying around talking on the telephones." Fran also tried to organize Stevenson volunteers and raise money for the campaign in Highland Park, but she ran into difficulties. Martin noted that while people in the community seemed willing enough to volunteer on Stevenson's behalf, they "did not want anything to do with the regular Democratic organization," or the rest of the Democrats running that fall, which, of course, antagonized party regulars. Still, both Martins remained excited about their work on Stevenson's behalf, and during his visits home to Highland Park Martin found it "impossible to talk about anything but the campaign." Their house brimmed with material on Stevenson, both Martin's research and Fran's volunteer paraphernalia. The desk in his office became piled high with unopened fan and business mail that Martin never got around to answering, even after the campaign ended. He had to resort to taking care of essential matters over the telephone.[12]

During his first few days in Springfield, Martin experienced what he called a "curious transitional state," as never before had he been part of such a large organization. "I always had been with the newspapermen, waiting outside the closed door of the conference room for the statement to be issued, the decision to be taken," he observed. "I always had been with the newsmen who were trying to sneak in the window or break down the door to find out what was going on behind the door. And I always felt comfortable with them." Martin also shared most reporters' "skepticism and even suspicions of all politicians." While in Springfield he naturally gravitated to fraternizing with the assembled reporters, spending his spare time with them, having drinks with them, and listening to them gripe about their problems with Flanagan, who never seemed to enjoy a close relationship with the candidate. "Fundamentally and deep down Stevenson just does not have much respect for or liking for the press," said Martin, "despite the fact that his press relations are by and large most excellent." Flanagan received much of the blame from the disgruntled reporters for matters that were beyond his control. "Nobody could have done much better," Martin later noted. At first, Martin tried to help with the complaints brought to him by reporters, but he later decided that many of them were "phonies, pretending to hate the assignment and complaining chronically of inept handling and unnecessary hardship, yet secretly delighted with the assignment and proud of it." As the campaign went on, Martin learned to avoid reporters and their questions whenever possible, as he "knew too much," and even viewed his onetime colleagues as "the enemy."[13]

In addition to having his illusions about his fellow reporters shattered, Martin discovered something about himself during this time: that he was a serious person and needed to be among like-minded people. Unhappy at the press office with Flanagan, where his position seemed "really more like a salesman's job than a writer's," he found himself gravitating toward Stevenson's speechwriters, called "speech researchers" by a campaign that wished to perpetuate the myth that Stevenson wrote his speeches without assistance from any ghostwriters. A *New York Times* article on the Stevenson campaign disingenuously reported that it was the job of the "research staff to dig out facts and figures and ideas for speeches." They did much more than that. John Fischer, editor at *Harper's* magazine and one of Stevenson's speechwriters, pointed out that it would have been physically impossible for one man to produce the material needed for a national presidential campaign. "During the 1952 campaign," said Fischer, "he [Stevenson] made up to seventeen speeches a day; sometimes two of them were major pronouncements running to about forty minutes, while the others were fifteen-minute whistle-stop talks." Moreover, Fischer noted, all of these speeches had to be different because Stevenson, who hated to give the same speech twice, as it "bored him," shunned the usual practice of having three or four basic speeches that could be used over and over again, with minor variations, at whistle-stops or other brief, less formal occasions on the campaign trail. "He wanted something fresh every time, even though the press services couldn't possibly report more than two speeches a day in any detail," Fischer added.[14]

The men responsible for crafting Stevenson's speeches gathered together at a building at 509 South Sixth Street in Springfield. Because their working area was on the third floor of the six-story Elks Club building, a few blocks from the Leland Hotel and the governor's mansion, the speechwriters became known as the Elks Club Group. The Elks included such prominent names as Arthur M. Schlesinger Jr., a Harvard University history professor and a Pulitzer Prize winner; W. Willard Wirtz, who taught law at Northwestern University and was an expert on labor issues; Robert Tufts, a former U.S. State Department official and economist from Oberlin College; and David C. Bell, who had been a member of Truman's staff since 1947 and served as a liaison between the administration and the Stevenson campaign. "Most of the speeches," said Bell, "were drafted for a given occasion, a given place and a given audience, and to include a policy stand on a given issue." Schlesinger and Bell shared responsibility for the speechwriting operation, and passed on completed drafts to McGowan, who forwarded them on to Stevenson for his changes. The candidate spent a lot of time "fussing and fiddling" with speech drafts, sometimes staying up in his hotel room until 3:30 A M "turning it [the speech draft] around, writing new paragraphs, until the final product, in a sense, was really a Stevenson-written speech," McGowan noted. Fischer agreed with McGowan's assessment, saying that none of the candidate's speechwriters tried to put "alien words" in his mouth. Fischer compared his task, and that of the other speechwriters, as serving as "literary tailors" for Stevenson, cutting and stitching material to fit his known measurements and according to a pattern and style on which all could agree.[15]

Schlesinger, in particular, impressed Martin, and the two men became lifelong friends. "He could, seemingly, simultaneously hold a telephone conversation, write a speech, read source materials, and talk to somebody across the desk," Martin said of Schlesinger. "He wrote rapidly and well. He wrote basic drafts on major speeches, did heavy rewrite on other people's drafts, and, from his friends around the country, obtained dozens of drafts." The tall, affable Bell, who had been in Truman's Bureau of the Budget and had written some speeches for the president, rarely wrote first drafts for Stevenson's speeches himself, but did rewrite almost everybody else's first drafts, "to the dismay of some writers," said

Martin. Bell had been told by McGowan that he had been selected for the assignment because of his "broad experience in the various elements of [Truman's] legislative program," and therefore was the natural person for liaison duties in the many different areas in which Stevenson would have to take a position during the campaign, including foreign and domestic policy, labor, agriculture, and education. According to Fischer, Bell clearly had more seasoned political judgment and administrative talent than anyone else, and the speechwriters were "glad to work under his direction – or, at least, accepted him less grudgingly than any alternative leader." Fischer added that Bell's peculiar talents combined the "tact of a hotel manager, the patience of a mother superior, and the relentlessness of a slave driver."[16]

The writers who were gathered at the Elks Club seemed to know exactly what they were doing, Martin said, and what they were doing was something he also knew something about – revising a manuscript. "I remember being somewhat surprised that you go about revising a speech manuscript just about the same way you go about revising an article: With a pencil and scissors, straightening out kinks in the line of thought, improving diction and syntax, getting rid of soft and dull spots and ambiguity, etc.," he said. During his first few days in Springfield some of the Elks had given him drafts of whistle-stop speeches for a campaign trip to Connecticut for his comments and suggestions, which he made and passed back. "Once I said something to Bell about thinking my work at Flanagan's was about ended and he said they were going to need a lot of help at the Elks," Martin recalled. By mid-September Martin had left the press operation for good and had joined the Elks Club Group, where he remained for the rest of the campaign. "I think that the real difference was that the men at the Elks were serious men and those at Flanagan's weren't," Martin said. One of the reasons the speechwriters welcomed him to their group was the breadth of Martin's knowledge about the country and its people he had gained while doing his freelance writing. "It got to be a kind of [an] office gag that everywhere the Governor went to make a speech," Martin said, "it turned out I'd once done a story about the place. It was truer than you'd think."[17]

A new world opened for Martin when he joined the Elks Club Group, a world he approached with some trepidations. After all, he had never written a speech and knew nothing about how a political speech should be structured, nor had he ever collaborated with another writer. Because of his previous work on the Stevenson book, however, Martin did know something about the governor's speaking style and could "tell when something sounded Stevensonian or didn't." Some of the writers at the Elks Club mainly worried about the quality of their prose, while others, including Schlesinger and Bell, possessed greater political instincts and worried instead about a speech's political effectiveness. "I began by worrying about the prose and soon learned to worry more about the politics," Martin said. He recalled being shocked at first when he heard Schlesinger and Bell talking about people – Jews, Catholics, African Americans, farmers – as voting blocs, as he considered such talk the language of political hacks in ward headquarters. "I came to see," Martin said, "that in a diverse pluralistic democracy like ours, a politician can approach the electorate in no other way." Under the tutelage of Bell and Schlesinger, Martin began to translate his emotions, instinct, and feeling for people, especially the disadvantaged in American society, into a rational system of liberalism that could be applied to writing speeches for a politician. "What I brought to liberalism and to the Elks Club was, in addition to writing, a life's experience and instincts," Martin said. Liberalism came almost automatically to him, and Martin cited such influences as his underdog feeling in childhood, the influence of his liberal-minded friends and the books he read in high school, and what Franklin D Roosevelt's New Deal policies had done for his family. He noted that when he worked for the *Indianapolis Times* and reported on a strike, he was "instinctively on the strikers' side."[18]

Early in the campaign Schlesinger believed that Stevenson overvalued the votes of independent Republicans, a group that had helped him win election as governor but would more than likely oppose him in his presidential race. Instead, Schlesinger wanted the governor to concentrate on obtaining every Democratic vote possible. He and many of the other speechwriters, including Martin, tried to make Stevenson "sound more liberal than he was." They were also uneasy at times about Stevenson's habit, in his speeches, of telling special interest groups what they did not want to hear. Stevenson had a "natural and honorable dislike," said Schlesinger, "of the kind of speech which seeks to buy votes by making promises." Stevenson lectured conservative American Legion members about the dangers of excess patriotism and flag waving ("Men who have offered their lives for their country know that patriotism is not the fear of something, it is the love of something"), and told liberal labor unions of his independence from their views ("no labor bosses are ever going to boss me"). "It was a brilliant device to establish Stevenson's identity," said Schlesinger. "As a permanent device, it was an error." Martin added that Stevenson was not unwilling to pursue policies as president that labor unions sought, but he was reluctant "to let it appear that he was anybody's captive, including the unions."[19]

Before the campaign began, Stevenson had informed a friend that he intended to keep his literary effort "on as high a level as I can." As he traveled around the country touting his candidacy, there were many, said Martin, who by mid-September began accusing Stevenson of "talking over the heads of the people." Martin himself received this complaint from people he knew in New York publishing circles, who were quick to add, "Of course *I* understand him." Years later, on another campaign, a tired and tense Stevenson admitted to Martin, "Oh, damn it, I never can say anything simply." Local Democratic candidates accustomed to being coddled and pampered by their presidential candidates grumbled that Stevenson spent too much time polishing his speeches when he should have been spending time with them, and others were put off by his sometimes biting humor. Perhaps influenced by Stevenson's baldness and both his and his staff's intellectual background, conservative columnist Stewart Alsop came up with a word to describe Stevenson, "egghead," that was quickly picked up by other journalists. "It became, as Senator McCarthy and Senator Nixon increased their attacks," said Martin, "a word of opprobrium, well suited to the anti-intellectual climate of 1952." Stevenson's speechwriters and other staff members worried about this issue, but, as McGowan once told Martin, "You can't change the Governor."[20]

As each week's campaign schedule became available, the speechwriters met to divide the schedule, taking an assignment if they were familiar with the location to be visited or had particular knowledge about a topic. When a writer received his assignment, said Martin, he usually made telephone calls to people in the community for their advice on local issues (being careful to weigh the validity of the information they provided), did further research, produced a speech draft, and turned it into Bell, who rewrote the draft and gave it to another speechwriter for his comments and revisions. "If it was a major speech, several Elks would gather around . . . and work on it collectively," Martin noted. "It was not unusual for a speech to go through half a dozen drafts, and some went through more. Rewriting sometimes merely honed language; sometimes it changed policy." Although Schlesinger had never met Martin before the 1952 campaign, he had known him through his writing, especially his work on the Centralia mine disaster, and the two men "hit it off at once," according to Schlesinger. "The brilliant reporter turned out to be a diffident, quizzical, humorous man whose gentleness of manner concealed a sardonic toughness of mind." Schlesinger and Martin developed a method of writing rough drafts of speeches together, with the Harvard academic writing the substantive center of the speech, while the magazine writer handled the "pleasantries and setup at the beginning and the rising rhetoric at the end; then we would trade drafts and mark them up, and put them together," Martin recalled. He discovered that he particularly enjoyed writing "rollicking rally speeches" for use before large, enthusiastic Democratic crowds. "They had a gay, rollicking quality," Schlesinger said of his friend's speeches for these occasions. Although Stevenson also seemed to enjoy delivering such talks, afterward he seemed apologetic about their partisan nature, no doubt, said Martin, because the governor's "friends in Republican Lake Forest chided him."[21]

One or two of the Elks Club speechwriters usually accompanied Stevenson on his campaign trips, and Martin soon became a familiar figure on these visits because, as McGowan noted, he was a professional writer and "could knock it [a speech] out fast at the last minute, particularly for short things, and a lot of these things came up, you know, at the last minute, unscheduled appearances here and there." The Elks rarely had the opportunity, however, to meet with the candidate as a group, not surprising considering how painful it was for Stevenson to rely on ghostwriters to help him with his speeches. "The Elks got instructions on policy by osmosis," according to Martin. "'Ghost candidate' seemed a better phrase than ghostwriters, from the Elks' viewpoint. They rarely knew, except by a cryptic sentence from McGowan, what subject Ste-

venson wanted to talk about or what he wanted to say on it." It was Mc-
Gowan who often came to the Elks Club to pick up the speeches before
heading out on the campaign trail, going over the major ones with the
speechwriters before returning to the governor's mansion. There, noted
Martin, McGowan edited the speeches, sometimes doing substantial
rewrites before giving them to Stevenson. "More than any other single
person, McGowan shaped the substance of the campaign," said Martin.
According to McGowan, there was little personal jealousy among Stevenson's campaign staff, particularly when it came to the writers at the
Elks Club, a fact he found "quite amazing since they have all this pride
of authorship that professionals have." The speechwriters were able to
submerge those feelings, he added, and were amenable to the changes
he suggested on their speech drafts. "They were wonderful – it was a
wonderful performance," McGowan said.[22]

Stevenson himself preferred to ignore his speechwriters' very existence. The best theory as to why Stevenson felt this way, said Martin, was
because he "really wished the writers weren't there. He was proud of his
own writing and once told a friend he wished more than anything else
he had been a writer." Martin believed that the candidate subconsciously
resented the speechwriters and "so seemed to take the attitude that if he
would just close his eyes we would just go away." On campaign trips the
writers literally slipped their drafts under Stevenson's hotel room door
in the middle of the night for him to find when he awoke. The governor
took the anonymous drafts, rewrote them, and made them his own. "It
was his way," said Martin. But he wondered why Stevenson behaved as
he did, because when he worked with Knox he had written speeches for
the secretary of the navy and must have been fully aware of "the absolute
necessity of a writer to a public man." Oddly, although the Stevenson
campaign attacked Eisenhower for merely "mouthing the second-hand
speeches of second-hand ghostwriters and thinking their second-hand
thoughts," nobody, according to Martin, ever accused Stevenson of uttering a word that was not his own. After the campaign had ended, Martin expressed his shock at how newspapermen ignored this "fantastic
fiction," either out of loyalty to Stevenson or, more likely, because the
reporters "were too lazy to figure out how many speeches were delivered,
how many written words were uttered, and how many hours there are in

a day." Anyone using simple arithmetic, he added, could figure out that Stevenson could not possibly have written every word for every speech he gave. "Yet we got away with this," Martin said.[23]

Members of the Elks Club Group had a big, bare room, about 650 square feet in size, in which to ply their trade. A long table ran down the middle of the room and on top of it were laid out the typed speech drafts and any incoming documents. Adjoining the workroom were four hotel-like bedrooms that some of them, including Martin, slept in for most of the campaign. During the day Schlesinger, Tufts, Bell, and Martin could be found scribbling in the workroom, while Wirtz, Fischer, and others preferred doing their writing in the back bedrooms. Scattered around the workroom were copies of such magazines as *Newsweek*, *Time*, *Foreign Affairs*, and the *Saturday Evening Post*, as well as issues of the *New York Times*, the *Saint Louis Post-Dispatch*, and several Chicago newspapers. For research purposes, the speechwriters could also turn to such basic documents as the Democratic Party's platform, Stevenson's messages to the Illinois legislature, the Illinois state budget, the voting records of Nixon and McCarthy, and even a Stevenson family genealogy prepared by Fran. Early in the campaign, Martin brought to Springfield briefcases full of research material from his own files, including hundreds of pages of his typewritten notes on the Midwest he had collected for a *Life* magazine assignment. "I found these mid-west notes particularly useful and put a great deal of material into various speeches from the notes," said Martin. The speechwriters also depended upon Martin's book on Stevenson, finally published in early September. According to Martin, his publisher had wanted to "play it safe" and waited to release the book until after Stevenson had won the nomination, which might have contributed to its poor sales (about nine thousand copies). It proved to be a valuable trove of information for the speechwriters, so much so that Martin wished the book had included an index.[24]

When he started working as a speechwriter, Martin attempted to follow the same schedule as he had during his freelance days, working from 9:00 AM to 5:00 PM with no actual writing being done in the evening, maybe only some light rewriting. Such a schedule lasted only a day or two before he started to work as the other speechwriters did. On a typical day Martin awoke at about 9:00 or 9:30 AM and walked down the street to a drugstore for a breakfast of coffee, orange juice, and a roll before returning to the Elks Club. The other speechwriters usually started work at 10:00 AM or a little later, and the group broke for lunch together at around 2:00 PM. Most of the time they ate at the Sazerac, at 229 South Sixth Street, a small, dingy bar equipped with a row of booths, a jukebox, and a big round table at which they sat. Sometimes a patron strolled over to drop a nickel into the jukebox to play a song, which blasted in the speechwriters' ears at the nearby table. On one occasion, Elks Club Group member John Kenneth Galbraith, hoping to enjoy a quiet lunch, told a patron about to drop his coin in the jukebox, "I'll give you a dime if you *don't* play it." A waitress named Mona, too young to vote, often took the speechwriters' orders and had to put up with continued complaints from Martin, Schlesinger, and Tufts that there was no chocolate sauce for their ice cream sundaes. They finally paid for their own private can and peace was restored.[25]

As they waited for their food ("always pretty bad," according to Martin) each day, the speechwriters discussed forthcoming speeches or talked about the campaign. "Sometimes at lunch we talked general opinions," Martin said. "We were growing to hate Eisenhower, mostly for his embracing of McCarthy and [William E.] Jenner [a conservative U.S. senator from Indiana], for his cynical rapprochement with Taft, for his obvious vote-seeking by any means, including promises of the most contradictory sort. . . . He seemed willing to scrap any principle, to do anything for a vote." To them, Eisenhower may have been "dollar honest," as Martin said, but the GOP presidential candidate was "intellectually and morally dishonest." The speechwriters were particularly infuriated by Eisenhower's willingness to iron out any differences he had with the conservative Taft and his bowing to pressure from Republican officials to drop from an October 3 speech in Wisconsin a planned tribute to his mentor General George Marshall, defending him from unjust claims by Jenner and McCarthy that Marshall served as "a front man for traitors." Eisenhower seemed like a man "willing to scrap every principle, to do anything for a win," said Martin. He later reflected that the speechwriters were far more opinionated than Stevenson, and before long he stopped wondering, even privately, how he, "an 'objective reporter,' could feel so partisan." After they finished eating, the speechwriters used to stop by the offices of the local newspaper, the *Illinois State Register*, to read the news bulletins written with crayon on sheets of newsprint hanging in its office window and review the newspaper's latest edition. "Sometimes we'd thus see where the Governor had just delivered a speech we'd sweated over; whoever wrote it got kidded about reading it now," Martin remembered.[26]

After lunch the speechwriters returned to their craft, working on their assigned speech drafts the rest of the afternoon. The noise in the workroom was constant, with ringing telephones, usually long-distance calls, and the clatter of typewriters. "I was the fastest typist and sometimes I guess I made so much noise at it that it disturbed phone conversations; once Dave [Bell] asked me to wait, he couldn't hear," Martin said. He also earned a distinction as the group's fastest writer and "a master of the whistle-stop speech," according to Galbraith, who added that nobody on the speechwriting staff could "say so much on two pages of triple-spaced typescript." When he reached an impasse in his work, Martin took to pacing around the large workroom. Fearing he might be disturbing the other writers, he switched to pacing around the corridor outside that ran in a square around the floor of the building. "This seemed to amuse the others," Martin noted. The speechwriters took a dinner break at about 7:30 or 8:00 PM, making their first stop at the Elks Club bar downstairs next to a bowling alley. "Every time we went in Dave Bell always stopped and looked longingly at the bowling alleys but I don't think he ever got time to bowl," Martin said. For dinner, the writers usually ate at the Leland or Lincoln hotels, a nearby restaurant, or sometimes shared taxis for trips to Stevie's, a steakhouse with the best food in town, according to Martin.[27]

After dinner, where they talked almost exclusively about the campaign, the speechwriters returned to the Elks Club, working at their assignments until midnight or two or three in the morning. Although Martin said that the Elks toiled "in remarkable harmony," the relentless pace took its toll. Most of the speechwriters became ill at one time or another; Schlesinger injured his leg during a campaign trip and Martin did not get over a cold he had caught until well after the election. One day Martin noticed Bell did not look well, and he later collapsed and had to be put to bed. A local doctor paid a visit and gave as his diagnosis overwork. Tufts suggested that the doctor give Bell an antibiotic; the physician agreed and gave Bell a shot of penicillin. Thereafter, Tufts became known around the Elks as Doctor Tufts, said Martin. He compared the experience of working in the campaign to being in the army again, as he could not leave and sometimes had to do things not by choice, including being away from his family for long stretches of time. "I remember once calling Fran and telling her to meet my train because that would give us another hour together, the hour driving home," said Martin, who added that he was away from home for so long his infant son, Dan, failed to recognize him.[28]

The pay Martin received failed to match the effort he expended or what he had been used to making as a freelance writer, about $500 a week. After the campaign had ended, Martin estimated he had incurred about $5,000 in bills largely because he had abandoned his profession for the summer and fall of 1952 to work for Stevenson, as had many people. When he first joined the campaign, Martin and Flanagan had agreed on a salary of $200 a week plus expenses, but up until early October Martin had not received a paycheck. "I had felt insecure in my general position, which was somewhat anomalous," Martin admitted. "There really hadn't been a job for me at the Elks; I had, in effect, just moved in and made one." Needing the money, however, Martin wrote a memo to Newton Minow, one of Stevenson's most trusted advisers who served as his surrogate on state matters while the governor campaigned, asking him to straighten out his payroll problem, including receiving the same per diem as the other speechwriters, about $10 a day. Upon his return from a campaign trip with Stevenson, Martin discovered a full payment for his time waiting for him, and he continued to be paid on schedule for the rest of his time with Stevenson. "If you wanted something done, Minow was the one," said Martin, who remained friends with Minow for years afterward.[29]

A good example of how the speechwriters cooperated, the extensive work that went into a speech, and how even the best intentions can go wrong in the heat of a campaign was a major talk given by Stevenson on October 9 before a large crowd at Kiel Auditorium in Saint Louis. Three weeks before its intended delivery, a tentative schedule had listed its subject as simply "Missouri Valley," later adapted to "Expanded Economy-Missouri Valley." On October 1 Tufts tackled writing the speech, scheduled for a nationwide broadcast on television and radio. "He [Tufts] spent a couple of days going through the mass of material that had been accumulated and began talking about the speech to other Elks," Martin recalled. Since he had done an article on the plains states several years before, Martin pondered several ideas for the speech: the Mississippi and Missouri Rivers, the Missouri Valley Authority, the liberalism of the *Saint Louis Post-Dispatch* newspaper, and the expanding economy. At about the same time he received in the mail from New Hampshire a leaflet arguing that the United States should approach foreign aid in a religious spirit. The leaflet included a quotation from French political philosopher and historian Alexis de Tocqueville saying that he only understood the secret and power of America when he went into its churches and "heard her pulpits aflame with righteousness. . . . America is great because she is good, and if America ever ceases to be good, America will cease to be great." Martin wrote a memo advocating using the quote as the starting point for a foreign policy speech and noted it might be useful as a starting point for the Saint Louis address. "A sort of Mississippi Valley and the World speech," said Tufts, who set to work producing a draft for the others to consider.[30]

Tufts finished his first draft on October 6, and another Elk rewrote it; Schlesinger took the result with him to work on when he left with Stevenson on October 7 for campaign stops in Michigan, Wisconsin, and Missouri. Believing his first draft better than the revised version, Tufts shared it with Martin, who thought "the substance . . . weak, some of the prose soaring." Martin believed that because the speech was set to be delivered at the campaign's halfway point, it should take advantage of that fact and sum up the positions Stevenson had taken in September, thereby opening an avenue for attacks on the Republicans in October. As Tufts and Martin worked separately on this idea, Martin, making notes for the speech and influenced by his reading of *The Frontier in American History,* came up with the phrase "new frontier." His notes read, "Theory of a frontier that never closes. 1890 they said frontier closed. They were men who dealt with figures. We say never. New frontier. New frontier for America." Going over their notes, Tufts and Martin decided the Saint Louis talk should be "the New Frontier speech – Adlai

Stevenson's New Frontier, his vision of an America to be." This was eight years before John F. Kennedy, in accepting the Democratic nomination for president at the convention in Los Angeles, delivered his own New Frontier speech. According to Martin, Ted Sorensen, Kennedy's speech-writer, had not been aware of Stevenson's use of the phrase. Martin drafted a three-point outline for the role of government in the expanding frontier, that of a "policeman" (later changed to "umpire") to restrain greed and monopoly, of support for new enterprises such as what the Roosevelt administration had done with the Tennessee Valley Authority, and of creating an economic climate in which enterprise flourished because of safeguards against another financial depression. Tufts, whom Martin called "one of the best writers and clearest thinkers" in the Elks Club Group, worked on a ten-point Stevenson program that summed up positions he had already espoused. On the evening of October 7 the two men pasted together their three drafts. Martin believed the Saint Louis speech would be important for future historians, as it contained, he noted, the "clearest exposition of Stevenson's view of the proper role of government and of the 1952 Democratic program."[31]

While Martin and Tufts worked on reconciling the different drafts, they received a telephone call from McGowan and Schlesinger, then in Detroit. Tufts told them he and Martin had written an improved version of the Saint Louis speech and they would mail him a copy so it would be at his hotel in Milwaukee upon his arrival the next day. Martin and Tufts, with aid from a secretary, Nona Cox, worked in the early hours of the morning to finish the speech. With the last plane scheduled to leave the Springfield airport at 2:45 AM with the day's mail, the Elks had persuaded the local post office to hold the mail there until 2:25 AM. Cox finished typing the new draft, handed to her page by page by Martin and Tufts, at 2:20 AM and ran the three blocks to the post office to meet the deadline. In a telephone conversation the next day, Schlesinger told them he had safely received the speech and liked what it had to say. "The opening paragraphs on the Louisiana Purchase and the American future were [Bernard] DeVoto's as reworked by Tufts; the peroration was derived from [David] Cohn; and the rest, the central substance of the speech, was from the Tufts-Martin draft," said Martin. "The central substance began, 'I would speak to you tonight about our opportunities. I would

speak to you of America's new frontier.'" The speech had this to say about
the three roles of government:

> First, government is an umpire, denying special privilege, ensuring equal rights,
> restraining monopoly and greed and bigotry, making sure that the game is
> played according to the rules. On this point the Republicans agree – so long as
> they write the rules.
>
> Second, government has the duty of creating an economic climate in which
> creative men can take risks and reap rewards, so that our economic life will have
> a continuous flow of fresh ideas and fresh leadership; and, of course, it means the
> building of solid defenses against the greatest threat to that flow – depression. . . .
>
> Third, government has the duty of helping people develop their country.
> Have any great frontiers in human history ever been opened without the
> help of government? Christopher Columbus discovered the New World, but
> it was the Queen of Spain who provided his ships. The American govern-
> ment not only bought the Louisiana Territory but subsidized the railroads
> that spanned it, opened government lands to homesteaders, built TVA so
> the middle South could lift itself out of the quagmire of want. Government
> achieved the miracle of atomic power which is the new dimension for both
> good and evil in the world of tomorrow.

The speech also included Stevenson's ten-point program on the issues,
including repealing and replacing the antilabor Taft-Hartley law, supporting agricultural prices for farmers, widening and expanding Social
Security, working to eradicate racial discrimination, expanding housing opportunities, improving education, reducing inflation, reviewing
federal tax policy, encouraging the growth of small businesses, and
developing and conserving the country's natural resources. Although
Schlesinger, McGowan, Martin, and Stevenson made minor changes
to the speech, the candidate delivered it "substantially as it left the Elks
Club," said Martin.[32]

Just a few hours before Stevenson took the stage in Saint Louis,
Martin joined the campaign there and, with the help of a DNC radio and
television technician, timed the speech. It was twenty-eight minutes,
too long for the scheduled broadcast as well as allowing no time for an
introduction or interruptions by applause from the crowd. McGowan
approved cuts in the speech made by Martin, but he said he thought he
might have difficulty persuading Stevenson to accept these changes,
as the candidate liked the speech as written. McGowan turned out to
be right. Stevenson did not make the cuts Martin had suggested and

seemed tired and distracted when delivering his remarks, probably because he had just finished a long and unsuccessful day of campaigning
followed by entertaining about twenty-five people at dinner. He failed to
finish the speech on time and the networks cut him off before he reached
his conclusion. The partisan crowd gathered in the auditorium had been
waiting, said Martin, for a chance "to cheer and instead of giving it to
them Stevenson was giving them a lecture on government." Upon his
return to the hotel, the governor believed he had spoiled an excellent
speech by his poor delivery. "Actually," Martin later observed, "it was
not really Stevenson's fault: It was the wrong speech for the audience."
Such a speech should have been delivered earlier in the campaign, said
Martin, before "crowds became enthusiastic – October crowds are always hotter than September crowds."[33]

Not everything went wrong for the Stevenson campaign on its trips
around the country. The new experience of traveling with a candidate
made a great impression on Martin, who likened it to being part of a
victorious army. "We were coming to a town to take it," he recalled, "and
we had a speech to do it with, and a candidate to deliver it. . . . You felt
determined to win and sure you could." For long trips the Stevenson
campaign flew on chartered American Airline aircraft, usually a four-
engine Douglas DC-6 with the words "Stevenson Special" emblazoned
on its nose and flown by Fred Jeberjahn, a senior pilot with the airline.
The press, numbering about a hundred by October, flew in separate air-
planes that took off after Stevenson's plane and landed before it did "so
that if he [Stevenson] crashed they would be on the ground to report
the accident," Martin noted. Stevenson sat in the rear of the cabin in an
office area with a desk, while the speechwriters with him on the trip rode
in front near the typewriters and mimeograph machines. Martin always
had a fear of flying, but he got over it during the campaign, that is, as long
as he was on a plane with Stevenson. "When the Governor was aboard,"
he said, "everything was all right."[34]

There was a curious family atmosphere among those on the plane,
said Martin, almost as if "we were all a bunch of relatives of the Governor, here to try to help him get elected." The casual atmosphere infected
even Jeberjahn, who on one flight left the cockpit and strolled through
the cabin, only to be followed by his copilot. "For Christ's sake," cried

an alarmed Flanagan, "who's steerin'?" The atmosphere changed when Stevenson had to approve a speech draft while still in the air, and it was up to the secretarial staff to type his remarks on the speech typewriter, equipped with oversize type. A stencil had to then be cut to run off about two hundred copies on the mimeograph machine for distribution to the press. Frequently, the secretaries were still assembling the speech when the plane landed, and visiting congressmen and even a U.S. senator were pressed into service to get the job done. Sometimes Flanagan had to hand out copies while Stevenson delivered his remarks, something that always irritated the reporters, as, noted Martin, "they had no time to digest the speech and find the heart of it, and they needed time; for unlike speeches which contained four-point programs, Stevenson's speeches were structured with complexity."[35]

After the plane landed, staff members were the first to disembark, followed by Stevenson, who "always looked surprised at the people being there somehow," said Martin. "Sometimes he had to say a few words over a PA [public address] system and usually came off pretty well, though in the confusion of the crowd and handshakers and people thrusting microphones at him he always looked confused and harried and terribly alone among hungry strangers." On brief visits, Martin usually stayed behind at the airport, finding desk space at airline offices surrounded by teletype machines and busy clerks. He had to do this because he wanted to smoke a few cigarettes while he worked on upcoming speeches and could not stay on the Stevenson plane because of the danger of a fire while the aircraft was being refueled. "Very often I saw nothing of the town but the airport and a desk there," he recalled. On an overnight stop, Martin's only introduction to a community would be what he could see from the window of a speeding car or from the window of his hotel room. He had always wanted to visit the states of Oregon and Washington, and got the chance while with the Stevenson campaign. Unfortunately, the only scenery he witnessed came from what he could see from various airports. "We really made, during the campaign, an astonishing journey across the nation – yet saw really almost nothing, learned almost nothing," said Martin. One incident stuck in his mind. He recalled looking down from his room as the Stevenson motorcade returned to a hotel late one night to be greeted by a cheering crowd while a band played.

"Strange feeling of power," Martin reflected, "looking over city under these circumstances; strange feeling of intimacy with the candidate, a satisfaction that though he belongs to the crowd of strangers on the street, they don't really know him at all; but I do. Must be somewhat like father feels toward famous son. Pride, possessiveness, power, etc."[36]

Stevenson's vaunted eloquence abandoned him when it came to the standard political campaign practice of whistle-stopping, at which both Roosevelt and Truman had been masters. These were brief speeches for short stops before crowds at train stations or on the steps of a county courthouse. The governor did not enjoy this kind of campaigning. "Most candidates develop a standard extemporaneous speech that they give repeatedly at whistle stops and even to large audiences," said Martin, "getting it firmly fixed in their minds and delivering it with good timing." Stevenson, however, refused to give the same speech twice, which meant more work for his speechwriters, who had to produce as many as ten to eleven speeches for a single day of campaigning. The press corps that followed Stevenson also disliked the candidate's habit of delivering different speeches, as they had to update their stories several times a day. Upon his return from a campaign trip that included stops in Evansville and Indianapolis, Indiana, as well as Paducah and Louisville, Kentucky, Martin reported to the other speechwriters that they were on the wrong track with how they were dealing with the courthouse-type speeches, which could not be the "lyrical, graceful" speeches Stevenson liked, or a substantive speech, or a rousing rally speech. "Rather, it should be partisan enough to arouse Democrats," said Martin, "but not so partisan as to offend Republicans; it must be an 'image' speech, creating an impression of the candidate, not an 'issue' speech, and if it must contain an issue that issue must be presented bluntly, in black and white; above all it must be simple." He advocated providing a memo for Stevenson with notes about the history and background of each community he visited and letting the governor offer extemporaneous remarks based on the notes. Stevenson, however, did not like the idea and instead asked for an all-purpose whistle-stop speech and a courthouse speech, as he felt uncomfortable without a prepared text in hand. "He said that if he attacked he must attack from the record specifically," Martin said. "He felt that in the main he must make 'positive' speeches."[37]

As he continued to travel with Stevenson, Martin became convinced that scheduling, deciding where a candidate visited, was the heart of a campaign. "Only scheduling brings together the candidate, the issues, and the audience," he said. "It involves, or should involve, the highest political strategy." They needed to ponder if it would be wiser to maximize the Democratic vote or try to win over independents and some Republicans, as well as identify what kind of audience best suits the candidate and what section of society does he need most (students, labor unions, businessmen, or suburbanites). The speechwriters needed to be more involved with scheduling, as too often the speeches they produced were inappropriate for the occasion. For example, if the speechwriters decided their candidate needed to deliver a foreign policy speech, his schedulers should take that into consideration and change his schedule to "give him a thoughtful indoor sit-down audience, not a state fair grandstand; and if the writers decide he should switch to the attack, the schedulers should provide hot partisan crowds," Martin noted. He vowed to himself that if he ever again became involved in a political campaign, he would try to bring speechwriting and scheduling together.[38]

The growth of television as a major part of political campaigning became another source of problems for Stevenson, who rarely watched television and knew little about it. The candidate came across poorly on television and his schedulers compounded the problem, said Martin, by broadcasting a partisan speech before a "rally of screaming machine Democrats" when half of the audience watching at home were Republicans. The Democratic Party was also slow to match the Republican's use of advertising to sell its candidate, much as a business would sell its product. During the campaign's last three weeks the GOP spent $1.5 million on radio and television commercials airing in forty-nine key counties in twelve states; 130 of these spots appeared on the air one day in New York. Most of these advertisements featured "Man in the Street" questions from average voters to Eisenhower, who offered brief, nonspecific answers to their questions, titled "Eisenhower Answers America." For example, for a question about the high cost of living, Eisenhower merely responded, "My wife, Mamie, worries about the same thing. I tell her it's our job to change that on November 4." The Elks had received a leaked document outlining the Republicans' plans for the radio and television advertisements. Martin described it as "the saturation stuff with which they did close their campaign – the 'ordinary citizen' asking 'Ike' the simple-minded questions, the one-sentence pronouncements from the oracle." Martin compared this "advertising slogan kind of campaign" to what the Democrats were trying to do with Stevenson, which was to talk sense to the American people, and he remembered being "frightened at the idea that they might possibly win, because their appeal to unreason would mean if successful that the country was really in very bad shape indeed and I did not have in mind just this election." Even Eisenhower had complained about being merchandised in this way to the American electorate, telling a GOP campaign associate when the plan had been outlined, "All they talked about was how to win on my popularity. Nobody said I had a brain in my head."[39]

Television's power to mold public opinion showed itself in what has become the signature moment of the campaign: Nixon's "Checkers Speech," broadcast live on television and radio to millions of viewers and listeners across the country on the evening of September 23. The speech came in response to a story in the liberal *New York Post* that as a U.S. senator Nixon had benefited from a secret slush fund of approximately $16,000 (the actual amount turned out to be $18,235) contributed by a "millionaire's club" of California businessmen. Nixon quickly tried to squelch any questions about the fund, noting that it had been established to help defray travel, postage, and other expenses that could not be charged to the federal government and that he in no way profited personally or had been swayed politically, but his opponents eagerly seized the chance to attack. Democratic Party chairman Mitchell called on Nixon to resign from the GOP ticket. Calls for Nixon's resignation also came from nominally Republican-supporting newspapers such as the *Washington Post* and *New York Herald-Tribune,* and reporters on Eisenhower's campaign train were almost unanimous (voting 40 to 2) in their belief that Nixon was an albatross around the general's neck and had to go. The scandal put Eisenhower in a bind politically. How could he defend Nixon's fund when he had been traveling around the country decrying the corruption in the Truman administration, promising to clean up the mess in Washington, and insisting his campaign would be spotless? Eisenhower appeared reluctant to commit one way or the other, telling

Nixon in a telephone conversation, "This is an awful hard thing for me to decide." An irate Nixon responded bluntly and profanely to Eisenhower's indecision, telling him, "Well, General, I know how it is. But there comes a time in matters like this when you either got to shit or get off the pot."[40]

In an attempt to save his political career, Nixon took to the airwaves to defend himself. The Republican National Committee raised $75,000 to pay for a half-hour broadcast following the popular *Milton Berle Show* on NBC television, as well as broadcasting the remarks on 194 CBS radio stations and 560 stations on the Mutual Broadcasting System's radio network. Flanked by his wife, Pat, on a simple set, a "GI bedroom den" at the El Capitan Theatre in Hollywood, he carefully outlined to the American people his family's modest finances (Pat did not have a mink coat, but "a respectable Republican cloth coat") and attacked his opponents, challenging Stevenson to explain the news that he had his own special fund, established to bolster the salaries of key executives working in the Illinois state government. "Not one cent of the $18,000 or any other money of that type ever went to me for my personal use," Nixon said. "Every penny of it was used to pay for political expenses that I did not think should be charged to the taxpayers of the United States. It was not a secret fund." What has gone down in history from Nixon's remarks, however, was his mention of a gift his family had received after the 1950 election from an admirer in Texas, a cocker spaniel dog named Checkers. "The kids, like all kids, love the dog; and I just want to say this right now, regardless of what they say about it, we are going to keep him," said Nixon, his voice choked with emotion.[41]

Martin and the other Stevenson speechwriters listened to Nixon's speech on a small radio in their workroom at the Elks Club. The consensus among them was that Nixon had presented "a weak defense," and they agreed with fellow Democrats that the broadcast had been nothing but a miniature soap opera. Since the story about the fund had broken, the Elks Club Group had been enthusiastic in their belief that it might ruin the Republican campaign. "The story got so big so fast that we became afraid Eisenhower would win the election right then," Martin noted, "by simply thus proving his own simple honesty [by firing Nixon]." In the days following Nixon's speech, however, the Elks discovered – mainly by talking with their wives, "always almost our only contact with the outside world," said Martin – that many people had apparently been "convinced by Nixon that he was really a nice guy." A bit of an understatement from Martin considering that the GOP National Committee had received 300,000 letters and telegrams from people all over the country urging Eisenhower to keep Nixon as his vice presidential candidate. Members of the Republican National Committee voted 107 to 31 to keep the GOP ticket as it was. Eisenhower also seemed convinced, telling an outdoor rally in Cleveland that he had seen "many brave men in tough situations" but had never seen anyone come through as Nixon had. The next day the two men finally met in Wheeling, West Virginia, and Eisenhower, perhaps trying to re-establish the campaign pecking order, told Nixon, "You're my boy."[42]

Another Republican speech, this one by Eisenhower, proved to be particularly damaging to any prospects for a Stevenson win in 1952. Throughout the campaign the GOP had hit the Democrats hard with critical comments about the stalemate in Korea, with American forces and their South Korean allies making limited headway in the fight against communist North Korea. Thinking of ways to answer his Republican critics, Stevenson had considered announcing in a speech that if he were to be elected he would go personally to Korea. He discussed the idea with McGowan and decided to abandon it. "We had just thought that it was thinking ahead to the time when Adlai would be elected, the same as talking about cabinet appointments would be premature," said McGowan. "This was no great strategy decision on our part. I think it was Stevenson's idea, thrown out casually. To us it seemed slightly ridiculous." Eisenhower, however, decided to take the dramatic step, telling a crowd of five thousand people at the Masonic Auditorium in Detroit that his administration's number one goal would be to end the war. "That job requires a personal trip to Korea, I shall make that trip," said Eisenhower. "Only in that way could I learn how to best serve the American people in the cause of peace. I shall go to Korea." Democrats criticized the pledge as a stunt, with Truman terming it "demagoguery," saying if Eisenhower knew how to end the war he could "save a lot of lives" by sharing his plan now and not after he was elected. Stevenson used his well-known wit, commenting, "If elected, I shall go to the White House." American voters, however, were thrilled that the general who had been one of the architects of America's victory in World War II would put his authority on the line in such a manner. McGowan said Eisenhower did not need to make such a pledge in order to win, but his statement did help to clinch the election for the Republicans. Although the Democrats seemed to have missed a golden opportunity, Martin believed that even if Stevenson had gone ahead and made such a pledge, it would not have had the same effect on the voters as Eisenhower's did, as Stevenson did not have his opponent's impressive military background. Years later Stevenson said he had abandoned the idea for such a sensational ploy because it sounded to him as merely a way to gain votes, and it might weaken his bargaining position if he had become president.[43]

Those who have been part of a national presidential campaign have sometimes compared it to being inside a giant bubble in which the staff is insulated from what is really happening in the outside world. Good news and bad news are magnified, and victory seems assured. It was that way on Stevenson's final whistle-stop train trip through Ohio and Indiana and on to Chicago the final weekend of the campaign. Stevenson's campaign staff was united in the belief that he would win the election, and they appeared to be "enthusiastic as well as very tired," remembered Martin. Martin got off the train when it stopped in Gary, Indiana, to hear Stevenson's remarks. "I have a clear recollection," he said, "of a working man from I would judge the Gary steel mills standing in the cinders by the railroad track holding up his small child to see the Gov and saying to him, 'There's the next president.'" An October 25 Gallup poll had given Eisenhower 52 percent and Stevenson 48 percent, and *Newsweek* magazine had reported, "The guessing is closer, and the 'experts' are more genuinely confused than in any other election of our times." Many from Stevenson's campaign staff made their predictions and chipped in $5 to a pool predicting the results in the Electoral College. Martin guessed that Stevenson would garner 400 electoral votes, while Tufts had about 450 and Schlesinger 330. Fran also contributed her money, guessing the lowest total possible to win the election for Stevenson. "In general I gave away the farm states, claimed Illinois, New York, California, Minnesota, the South, and Massachusetts," Martin recalled. "I gave the Republicans Iowa, Kansas, Maine, Michigan . . . Nebraska, New Hampshire, New Jersey, Ohio, Oregon, South Dakota, Vermont, Virginia, and Wisconsin."

While Stevenson slept on the train, the speechwriters continued to craft a speech he would give on Saturday, November 1, at Chicago Stadium, a talk they had been working on all week. Martin had written a draft with only the end usable, while Wirtz had submitted a draft of which only a portion of the middle could be used. Schlesinger, George Ball, and Wilson Wyatt put together a draft that included Wirtz's middle's section and an ending he had written, said Martin. To their "considerable astonishment," said Schlesinger, the result was "a bang-up speech. It was the last any of us had in us."[44]

Resting in his suite at the Conrad Hilton Hotel before his Chicago Stadium speech, to be broadcast nationwide on television and radio, Stevenson had been confident of victory. "Of course, I'm going to win," he told Schlesinger. "I knew it all the time. This is why I was reluctant to run. . . . I figure that I will get about 366 [electoral] votes. I don't see how I can lose." Stevenson's confidence received an extra boost from the turnout for his speech, as the vast stadium was packed, with only seats in the upmost balcony empty. Claiming there had been an "electric feeling of victory in the air" as his campaign came into the home stretch, Stevenson, with Martin standing alongside Fran with the working press just below the platform, read the ending Martin had written:

> I see an America where no man fears to think as he pleases or say what he thinks.
>
> I see an America where slums and tenements have vanished and children are raised in decency and self-respect.
>
> I see an America where men and women have leisure from toil – leisure to cultivate the resources of the spirit.
>
> I see an America where no man is another's master – where no man's mind is dark with fear.
>
> I see an America at peace with the world.
>
> I see an America as the horizon of human hopes.
>
> This is our design for the American cathedral, and we shall build it brick by brick and stone by stone, patiently, bravely and prayerfully. And, to those who say that the design defies our abilities to complete it, I answer: "To act with enthusiasm and faith is the condition of acting greatly."

By the time Stevenson had reached his "I see an America" ending, he had neared the end of his scheduled television time. The crowd, Martin noted, had begun to applaud at the end of each sentence, but Stevenson had held up his hand to silence them so he could finish on time. When he finished, the crowd "took the roof off the place," and some had tears in their eyes, according to one Stevenson staff member. The next morning the speech appeared on the *New York Times* front page. Martin said he believed that Stevenson's welcoming speech to the convention and his closing speech at Chicago Stadium "framed the lofty elegance and idealism of the campaign."[45]

On Election Day, Martin and Fran awoke early at their Highland Park home and voted at a nearby high school. The local precinct captain told Martin that turnout had been heavy at the polling place and believed it was a good sign for the Democrats' chances of victory. "It was a bright, beautiful election day," said Martin. They returned home; bid farewell to their daughter, Cindy; picked up their guests, including Tufts, Bell, and his wife, Mary; and drove to O'Hare Airport for a flight to Springfield to watch election returns at the governor's mansion. That afternoon they began hearing reports of heavy turnout all over the country, but nobody knew what to make of the report. McGowan knew it would not be the Democrats' night when, while still tying his tie before going over to the mansion from his home a few blocks away, he heard disappointing voting results from usually Democratic precincts in Connecticut. He commented to his wife, "We don't need to go over there, we can go to bed." Eisenhower won 55.7 percent of the vote in Connecticut. By 7:00 PM, with the early returns already coming in and the news all bad for Stevenson, a grim mood hit staff members gathered in the ballroom at the Leland Hotel. A surge of Democratic votes from Minnesota and other farm states raised hopes of a miracle come-from-behind victory for a time, but when Martin asked Bell, the political veteran, about this, he "just smiled in a kind of patronizing way. Looking back, I don't blame him." About 10:30 PM the Martins and others, about fifty in all, people who were Stevenson's personal friends or his close associates in the administration, gathered at the mansion. "I just went and sat in a corner with a small radio and listened to the returns," Martin remembered. "Other people would come and stop and listen a while and shake their heads and go away. It was more like a wake than anything else." At about 12:30 AM word drifted through the crowd that Stevenson had written his concession speech, which most of them watched on a television with poor reception. A composed Stevenson strayed from his prepared text and ended his concession with the same humor that had marked his campaign. He noted, "Someone asked me, as I came in, down on the street, how I felt, and I was reminded of a story that a fellow townsman of ours used to tell – Abraham Lincoln. They asked him how he felt once after an unsuccessful election. He said he felt like a little boy who had stubbed his toe in the dark. He said he was too old to cry but it hurt too much to laugh."[46]

Although Stevenson had received the second largest number of votes for a Democratic candidate in history, 27,314,992, he had been swamped by Eisenhower's total of 33,936,234; Eisenhower carried thirty-nine states with 442 electoral votes, while Stevenson had captured only nine states (Alabama, Arkansas, Georgia, Kentucky, Louisiana, Mississippi, North Carolina, South Carolina, and West Virginia) and 89 electoral votes. McGowan attributed Stevenson's defeat to a "very strong tide running for change" throughout the country. "Stevenson was not perfect," said Martin. "He made mistakes; lots of them. He wanted to be both the candidate and the campaign manager; as a result nobody managed the campaign." In Martin's opinion, however, no other Democratic candidate could have won more votes than Stevenson had against Eisenhower. The Democrats had been defeated because of voters' frustrations with the Korean War, corruption in government, and the fear, provoked by McCarthy and his allies, of communists in government, the three main themes of the GOP campaign. The campaign had also included a strong strain of anti-intellectualism that hurt Stevenson. "It is partly a revolt against 20 years of New Deal intellectualism and planning," Martin said. "It is not an accident the term egghead became popular and is used in a derisive way to denote anybody who had read a book. This caught on much faster than it should have." The Democratic Party also became a victim of its own success. Martin noted that as Americans prospered they had begun moving from the cities to the suburbs and abandoned voting for Democrats and turned instead to the GOP. "The shift to the suburbs has had an effect on this country that nobody in this country has fully explored or understood," Martin said at the time. He particularly recalled a conversation he had during the campaign with U.S. senator Joseph C. O'Mahoney of Wyoming. O'Mahoney had told Martin there was nothing Stevenson could say to the cattlemen of his state that would

sway them to his side, because twenty years ago "they had all been starving to death and now they were all driving two Cadillacs and voting
Republican." O'Mahoney also went down to defeat in the 1952 election,
losing to Frank A. Barrett, Wyoming's Republican governor.[47]

The landslide defeat crushed the spirits of those who had worked
so hard for Stevenson's election, but the candidate himself tried to raise
their spirits. The Martins and others, mainly from the Elks Club Group,
were preparing to leave the mansion, thinking Stevenson would want
to be alone with family and close friends. Seeing them leave, he stopped
them and said, "Come on upstairs and have a drink; let's celebrate my
defeat." He gave the first glass of champagne to Fran. A number of Stevenson's Lake Forest Republican friends, who had voted for Eisenhower,
were also there, and one said to him, "Governor, you educated the country with your campaign." Stevenson replied, "But a lot of people flunked
the course." Earlier in the evening, Martin had realized that Fran had
won the Electoral College pool, approximately $150, coming closest by
predicting a narrow Stevenson victory. "I told her we did not want the
money and we had to get rid of it," Martin recalled. "She agreed but did
not know what to do." Fran came up with an ingenious solution; upon
his return to the mansion she gave Stevenson her winnings, telling him
it was the first contribution for his 1956 presidential campaign. "I take
it shamelessly," said Stevenson, putting the cash in his pocket. "He was
by far the most composed man in the room – many of his supporters
[including Fran] were tearful," Martin noted. Most of the guests left the
mansion by 2:00 AM, but others returned to their hotel rooms and talked
until early the next morning.[48]

As the 1952 election came to an end, Martin observed a change in
Stevenson; his personality hardened and he appeared to be cold and
withdrawn. This disturbed Martin because he recognized it as a pattern
he had observed in other politicians he had met who seemed phony, cold,
glib, and unreachable. "The Gov had never seemed this way but now
that he was a candidate he did sometimes," Martin noted. He discussed
his concerns with Tufts, who told him that a candidate or a holder of a
public office is obliged to perform this "withdrawal," becoming remote
and suspicious, in order to save himself from being torn to pieces by the
countless people, some with selfish motives of their own, who surround

him. If a politician allowed his emotions to become entangled with the issues, he could not survive this "ordeal of power," Tufts observed. Martin also came to believe this, saying it explained why Stevenson had been "obscenely self-contained and unaffected by his defeat, while the rest of us were running around weeping." It was one of the reasons Stevenson was in public life, said Martin, and he and Tufts were not.[49]

On the morning of November 5, the Martins said their goodbyes to other Stevenson staff members, and Martin went to the Elks Club to arrange to have his things sent to him. "Everybody was in terrible shape," he said. Still, the Elks Club Group, along with Minow and Mc-Gowan, met for lunch at a restaurant at the edge of town. "It was a rather melancholy affair and I don't think anyone enjoyed it and we were all a little glad when it was over – at least I was," Martin said. After the lunch had ended, they gathered outside on the sidewalk in the cold sunshine and exchanged addresses. On the flight to Chicago, Martin and Tufts discussed what Stevenson might do next, and they pondered the possibility of collaborating on a daily or semiweekly newspaper column of political comment. "The idea was that Bob knew foreign policy and I knew the interior of America and between us we might get out a pretty good column," said Martin. Both of them felt at loose ends and neither man wanted to return to the work they had done before the campaign. After landing at O'Hare, the Martins had a final drink with Tufts at the airport, then took a taxi to Highland Park, arriving home in time to greet Cindy before she went to bed. Martin and Fran had talked about calling her earlier from Springfield when they knew they had lost the election, but they did not have the heart to do so. "She had felt as bad as we had," noted Martin. "In fact in some ways it was worse for her because she had gone to bed on election night before the returns were coming in very fast and had thought that we had won. It was a shock to her to learn on Wednesday morning that we had not." Both Martins expressed relief in being done with the campaign and having their lives center on Stevenson. "Politics, I think," said Martin after the election, "is not for me or for Fran. We seem unable to take politics in a non-serious way and nobody who is like that should be involved." Martin may have wished for a life away from the grind of politics, but in just a few short years he and his family were back at it again, and with a familiar candidate.[50]

SIX

The New America

ADLAI STEVENSON'S LANDSLIDE DEFEAT IN THE 1952 PRESIDENTIAL contest to Dwight D. Eisenhower had a demoralizing effect on John Bartlow Martin for months after the election. Martin tried to get back to his freelance writing career, traveling to Cleveland, Ohio, to do his usual heavy-fact legwork for a *McCall's* magazine assignment, but he had "no heart" for the story and abandoned the effort, returning home to Highland Park. "It was the only time I ever did that," said Martin. "I felt ill. I had not realized fully how emotionally involved I'd been in the Stevenson campaign." Eisenhower's elevation to the presidency, said Martin, had been a "repudiation of everything I believe in. All my life I have believed and tried to write certain ideas; Stevenson articulated them as a candidate; the people rejected them." He felt nothing but contempt for the advertising business that had helped to elect Eisenhower and the "implication you can sell a president precisely the same way you sell soap." Although he had always loved the United States and its people, his feelings after the election were so negative that he felt like "a stranger in my own country."[1]

In spite of the hurt he had felt after Stevenson's loss, Martin maintained his interest in the former Illinois governor's future. Stevenson had remained popular with Democrats and took on a new role as one of the party's leaders in opposition to the Eisenhower administration's policies. "A lot of non-vocal intelligent people," said Carl McGowan, a key Stevenson aide, "looked to Stevenson to articulate their hopes and thinking. This had a tremendous impact on young people. . . . When issues are floating around, it helps to have someone take a position."

Stevenson spoke out on such unpopular topics as the destructive influence of U.S. senator Joseph McCarthy; skillfully handled political problems within the party among its influential members, including U.S. senators Lyndon B. Johnson, Richard Russell, Hubert Humphrey, and John Kennedy; and helped raise money to pay off the party's substantial campaign debts. Organizations around the country clamored to have Stevenson speak at their meetings or, if he could not attend, send them a message. The requests were so numerous that Stevenson paid Martin to write the messages for him as well as assist him with drafts for speeches he delivered. Martin worked closely with William M. Blair Jr., one of Stevenson's law partners, along with W. Willard Wirtz and Newton Minow. Martin's wife, Fran, also helped. After attending meetings every Thursday as a board member of the Illinois branch of the American Civil Liberties Union, she volunteered in Stevenson's law office on the eighth floor of the Continental Illinois Bank Building in Chicago, drafting responses to some of his correspondence. "In drafting messages and letters, Fran and I learned to imitate Stevenson's eloquent and rather arch style," Martin recalled, "and he once told Fran, 'You sound more like me than I do.'"[2]

The Martins were part of a group that gathered with Stevenson in his living room to watch on television as returns were reported for the 1954 midterm elections. "He was less tense, or seemed so, than his guests," Martin said of Stevenson, who had campaigned for Democratic candidates around the country, delivering eighty-eight speeches in thirty-three states. "Toward the end he was covering thousands of miles by air, touring the countryside in an open car, speaking several times a day, sidestepping local factional feuds, receiving delegations in hotel rooms till late at night, then working on a speech, then arising early to begin the next day's labors," Martin noted. The results were a triumph for the Democrats, as the party regained control of both the House and Senate from the GOP and turned a 30–18 Republican lead in state governorships to a 27–21 advantage. At around 11:00 PM, Martin told Stevenson that his twelve-year-old daughter, Cindy, would not go to bed until she had learned if U.S. senator Paul Douglas, Democrat from Illinois, had been re-elected. Stevenson picked up the telephone, dialed the Martins' number, reached Cindy, and told her to go to bed as "everything's going to be all right." His prediction was on the mark, as Douglas defeated his Republican opponent, Joseph T. Meek, by more than 240,000 votes.[3]

Martin had some concerns about resuming his freelance trade. Although academic professionals who worked for Stevenson, such as Arthur M. Schlesinger Jr. and John Kenneth Galbraith, could return to their university teaching posts with few worries about being welcomed back, many serious newspapers and magazines were reluctant to take back writers who had been involved in political campaigns for fear they might have abandoned their objectivity. Editors at the *Saturday Evening Post,* who backed the Republican Party for the most part, continued to seek and buy Martin's contributions, as did editors at other magazines. "And I found that I could understand some stories the better for having been in the Stevenson campaign," Martin noted. The *Post* gave Martin a tremendous amount of leeway when it came to his support for Stevenson, perhaps wanting the exclusive details only an insider like him could deliver. In 1955, when it became clear that Stevenson would again run for his party's presidential nomination, the *Post* bought a story from Martin on what Stevenson had been doing since 1952 and his chances with the voters in 1956. "It was a nice affectionate piece yet a highly political one," said Martin, "and I was greatly pleased when the *Post* published it as I wrote it." The backing he received from the *Post,* plus continued encouragement from his agent, Harold Ober, helped him to finally put Stevenson's 1952 loss in the past and "restored my confidence in myself as a writer," said Martin. It also established a pattern for the rest of Martin's career, as he continually juggled freelance writing with his speechwriting work on behalf of a variety of Democratic Party candidates.[4]

In addition to keeping in close contact with Stevenson, Martin advanced his political education by examining the machinations of an organization – the Cook County Democratic Party – he had come to know while prowling Chicago's streets, slums, and criminal courts looking for stories. He was lucky enough to be there for the rise to the mayor's office and control of the city's Democratic organization by one of its best and most controversial chief executives: Richard J. Daley. Chicago's Democratic organization had its start during the Great Depression under the control of Mayor Anton Cermak, who was killed on February 15, 1933, during an assassination attempt against president-elect Franklin

D. Roosevelt in Miami, Florida. The organization continued to prosper under Mayor Ed Kelly and became, as Martin noted, "the most powerful of the old-fashioned big-city machines in America." He described it as embracing all sorts, "black men and white, Irish and Jews, Poles and Lithuanians, good citizens and crooks." The organization exerted its control over the city's 50 wards and 4,157 precincts through ward committeemen, who appointed a captain for each precinct. These were highly sought-after positions, as they offered one of the few ways out of the slums for many. Martin described a typical precinct captain as uneducated but intelligent, hard-working, and a longtime resident of a ward. "The captain is the man a citizen telephones if the garbage isn't collected or a dead tree needs cutting down," he related in the first of a two-part series he did on the 1955 Chicago mayoral election for the *Post*. "The City Hall government is remote; the precinct captain lives down the street. He is the government." They were particularly useful in slum wards, where residents were often in trouble with police and needed legal help and favors. At each election, captains were responsible for bringing in about 350 voters. Those who had yet to vote before a polling place closed received reminders of past favors from the captain of their precinct, and the grateful recipients of the machine's largesse dutifully followed the instructions. "That's the effectiveness of an organization," a ward politician told Martin. "And a man who hasn't got an organization is just in a hell of a fix."[5]

By 1955 members of the Cook County Democratic Central Committee had grown tired of incumbent mayor Martin H. Kennelly's lackadaisical leadership (he was "more disposed to reign than rule," said Martin) and believed he could not win another election. As party chairman for the county, Daley had handpicked the committee responsible for selecting the machine's candidates. It came as little surprise, then, when the committee unanimously picked Daley as the Democratic candidate for mayor. "Professional politicians want above everything else a winner," Martin observed. The move prompted a rare primary fight for the Democrats, pitting Kennelly, the businessman, against Daley, the prototypical machine politician. In Daley, the machine had picked a man it knew and could trust to look after its interests and the interests of the city he loved. "My opponent says, 'I took politics out of the schools; I took politics out of this and I took politics out of that.' There's nothing wrong with politics," Daley proclaimed in a speech to his fellow Democrats. "There's nothing wrong with good politics. Good politics is good government." Daley also regarded the Cook County machine "with the fierce protectiveness of a mother bear," said Martin, who found the professional politician to be liberal-minded, friendly, and fast-thinking. Later, he realized that Daley possessed two flaws: he had "an ineradicable blind spot" when it came to race relations, especially when it came to African Americans, and before he died he had failed to groom a successor.[6]

Martin covered the last two weeks of the Democratic mayoral primary. "This entailed hanging around the candidates' headquarters, attending ward rallies where they spoke and where they didn't speak, attending big rallies, riding with the candidates whenever possible, talking to their aides and to other politicians – ward leaders, precinct captains, etc.," he said. During his time on the campaign trail in February the temperature in Chicago dropped well below zero and he often did not get back home until 1:00 AM or later. On one typical day he attended a lunch featuring the candidates sponsored by the League of Women Voters, spent the afternoon with Republican mayoral primary candidate Robert E. Merriam (a former Democrat), attended the opening of Volunteers for Daley headquarters, had dinner at Henrici's (a popular restaurant frequented by politicians) with Kennelly's press agent and other reporters, and accompanied Kennelly to four or five rally appearances. "During a campaign," Martin observed, "the candidates live on the run, and you have to do legwork the same way. Mayoralty campaigning is a good deal like presidential whistle-stopping. There are few advance mimeographed texts; arrangements change from minute to minute; you have to get your notes when and where you can."[7]

Daley seemed to be everywhere during the Democratic primary, visiting each of the city's fifty wards, changing his itinerary several times an evening, and paying particular attention to establishing close relationships with ward committeemen and precinct captains. Kennelly's strategists preferred to use the airwaves to state their case, referring to television as "their precinct captain," Martin noted. An unimpressed Daley had scoffed, "Can you ask your television set for a favor?" The incumbent could also count on the support of every newspaper in Chicago.

"On television and in the papers, Kennelly was doing fine," said Martin. "But not in the wards." Democrats, including Douglas and Stevenson, were rallying behind Daley's campaign. A week before the voters went to the polls on February 22, Martin went with Daley to a ward meeting and in a bar across the street met a yellow-shirted precinct captain who told him, in a manner he likened to a doctor offhandedly discussing preparing for a minor operation, "I run a precinct here, and Kennelly's going to get killed." Daley received 369,362 votes to 266,946 for Kennelly, winning the right to face off against Merriam, the Republican nominee, whom Martin depicted as "the very epitome of the decent young man in politics."[8]

From March 25 to Election Day, April 5, Martin followed the Merriam-Daley race, spending most of his time with Merriam, whom he had neglected during the Democratic primary battle. Merriam had served eight years as an alderman for the Fifth Ward, which included in its area the University of Chicago and Hyde Park. "His manner, curiously formal for one so young [thirty-six]," Martin said, "was that of a boyish young man eager to please his elders." Martin collected enough research material and notes to fill four drawers in one of his filing cabinets, and he produced for the *Post* a stirring account of Daley's ascendancy to the mayor's office. Throughout the campaign, Merriam, the darling of good government reformers and businessmen, attacked Daley as the "machine candidate" and hinted at dark deeds to be uncovered involving ties between the machine and Chicago's notorious crime syndicate. "The whole idea was to have a fusion ticket of independent Democrats, independents, and what there was of the Republican Party, which wasn't very much," Merriam recalled. To highlight the possibility of vote fraud in the election, the Merriam campaign mailed dummy letters to registered voters in sixty-five strong machine precincts. Of the 31,986 letters sent, 2,982 were returned marked "Moved, left no address" or "Unclaimed." For his part, Daley accused Merriam of using "the big-lie technique and tossing around wild charges," and he promised voters that as mayor he would "conduct himself according to my conscience and my God." Martin believed Merriam had fallen into the hands of bad advisers, especially an advertising agency that had prepared television commercials that showed Chicago traffic jams, uncollected garbage, and, worse, bodies of hoodlums in the trunks of cars, which, he noted, "seemed to have little to do with Daley." Paddy Bauler, a north side alderman, said Daley's candidacy had fired up his precinct captains "like they ain't been in thirty years," as they appreciated "a guy who takes care of them."[9]

Martin spent the last Sunday of the campaign with Arthur X. Elrod, committeeman for the twenty-fourth ward, the "pre-eminent Democratic ward in Chicago, the cradle of the machine," said Martin. On that Sunday Elrod toured his ward in his red convertible with the top down, checking in on his precinct captains, with one predicting that Merriam would be lucky to get twenty-five votes in the ward. Elrod, however, kept the pressure on, wanting every vote possible. When one of his captains said his helper was in his car, a perplexed Elrod noted, "He's in his car? Who's he going to find in his car?" Martin spent Election Day following Merriam on his tour of precinct polling places, which "was made at breakneck speeds in autos, as most campaigning is indeed done." After the polls closed, Martin checked in with the Democrats gathered at the Morrison Hotel and ended the evening with the leaders of the Democratic machine at Fritzel's restaurant. When the votes were counted, the precinct captains had delivered for Daley, as he received 708,222 votes to 581,555 cast for Merriam. Analyzing the results for the readers of the *Post,* Martin proved prophetic when he wondered, barring some national Democratic disaster comparable to the Republican debacle of 1932, if the GOP could ever again elect one of their own as mayor in Chicago (William Hale Thompson, who left office in 1931, is still the last Republican to serve as mayor). "The campaign proved the power of the machine," said Martin. Looking back on the election years later, Martin also took from it the lesson that sometimes reformers "turn out no better than what they seek to reform and that politics is best left to the professional politicians." As a liberal partisan Democrat, he also discovered that all virtue did not reside with his party, nor wickedness with the Republican Party, and that many legislators and public officials "were better than their constituents thought, that they were at least as good as their constituents deserved, that the best got too little credit, and that not enough of the worst ones got caught."[10]

Several months after the Chicago mayoral battle, Martin learned he might be involved in presidential politics again when, on November 15,

1955, Stevenson officially announced his intention to obtain his party's nomination for president for a second time. Stevenson faced serious opposition in his quest from U.S. senator Estes Kefauver of Tennessee, who had decided to enter a series of state primaries hoping to win enough of them to convince Democrats to turn to him as their nominee. Although there were not yet, as today, enough delegates available in state primaries for a candidate to capture the nomination before the convention, poor showings in these races could help derail a campaign, as had happened to Republican Wendell Willkie in 1944 when he lost the Wisconsin primary to New York governor Thomas E. Dewey. Martin noted that Kefauver, in spite of his law degree from Yale University, possessed the "common touch" that former president Harry Truman had been known for, helped, no doubt, by his habit of sporting a coonskin cap on the campaign trail and his self-portrayal as "an underdog frozen out by the party organization." Stevenson realized the threat Kefauver posed and believed that although the Tennessee senator could not win the nomination, he could "very well eliminate [me]." The Democratic nomination had achieved additional significance earlier that fall when Eisenhower suffered a heart attack. Nobody knew for sure if Eisenhower would seek a second term in office, and if he decided to retire from politics, Democrats believed they had a good chance to win back the presidency if the GOP turned to Vice President Richard Nixon as its presidential nominee. Eisenhower's antipathy toward Stevenson and some of the other Democratic presidential contenders, whom he charged did not have the "competency to run the office of President," might have convinced him to stand for another four-year term. He announced his intention to do so at a special news conference on February 29, 1956.[11]

During the early skirmishes among the Democratic presidential contenders, Martin had embarked on a different campaign: ending a cigarette smoking habit he had started in high school. The connection between cigarette smoking and lung cancer had begun to emerge, and Martin decided to quit. After Martin had been tobacco-free for seven months, his doctor, Sylvan Robertson, told him, "There are some things worse than lung cancer, and one of them is your disposition when you're not smoking." The stress of his attempt to stop smoking, combined with the pressure of making a living as a freelance writer, led to a gastric ulcer bad enough to put Martin in the Highland Park Hospital in early 1956. "It was the beginning of an ulcerated existence I led, off and on, for some fifteen years – restricted diet, in and out of bed, in and out of hospitals," Martin recalled. "It did not, however, seriously interfere with my work." While he was still hospitalized, Martin had been visited by Wirtz, who asked him to come to work for Stevenson again as a speechwriter after he was discharged, joining Harry Ashmore, *Arkansas Gazette* editor, as the "principal writers on-hand during the primaries." Paid a salary of $1,500 a month, Martin began his duties on March 20, 1956, and stayed on the job until Election Day in November, with only, as he remembered, "a single two-day holiday. For me, as for Stevenson, it was the longest campaign."[12]

The same day Martin joined Stevenson's staff, the candidate received the shock of his life when Kefauver fooled everybody and handily won the Minnesota primary with 56 percent of the vote (he also captured twenty-six of the state's thirty delegates to the Democratic National Convention that August in Chicago). "He outpromised me," Stevenson said of his opponent, who had grabbed the underdog mantle and took to campaigning with an engaging enthusiasm that charmed Democratic primary voters. As Martin observed in a letter to a friend, Kefauver "is peculiarly well situated in any Democratic primary to reap the benefit of whatever discontent the little guy feels – and there's not much but little guys registered in any Democratic primary." Former Stevenson supporters complained that in his speeches Stevenson had begun to sound more like a political science professor than a candidate fighting for public office. Jim Finnegan, Stevenson's campaign manager and a thoroughgoing political professional whom Martin found to be a "congenial funny man," and other top staff members gathered the night of the Minnesota disaster to discuss whether Stevenson should withdraw from the upcoming primaries in Florida and California. Although rattled by this setback, Stevenson had no intention of quitting, and his staff made plans for him to go to California to "put out the Kefauver fire," said Martin, as well as repair the candidate's damaged reputation there.[13]

On March 28 Martin accompanied Stevenson as he flew to California to deliver two televised speeches, one in Los Angeles and one in San Francisco, that for the moment halted his campaign's descent into irrelevancy. Stevenson hit back at Kefauver for attempting to "weaken and divide" the party and, therefore, help the Republicans. "For four years I've done my level best to unite the Democratic Party, not to tear it apart," said Stevenson. "And I propose to keep on thinking that the party's welfare is just as important as my own candidacy." Finally, said Martin, Stevenson had begun to transform himself from "the visionary philosopher-statesman" into a "hard-hitting candidate" fighting for his political life. Stevenson's Republican friends may have not liked this partisan version of the man they knew, said Martin, believing he somehow was demeaning himself, but after his defeat in Minnesota Stevenson had no choice, as "Kefauver had pulled him off the pedestal and he had to fight on the ground." Martin, however, realized that the campaign continued to suffer from disorganization, as the writers were spending far too much time and effort into "polishing the big prestigious speeches in the East, where Stevenson was entered in no contested primaries, and not enough into the day-to-day political stuff for Florida and Oregon and California, where he was." They had also failed to divide the states up, but they eventually did, with Martin taking California, remaining there for the most part until the day of the June 5 primary. The state was the key, Stevenson staff members agreed, to the nomination.[14]

Martin began his time in California on April 26, meeting with such key Stevenson supporters as Edmund G. Brown, the state's attorney general; Fred Dutton, Brown's assistant and later a key aide for Robert F. Kennedy; Don Bradley, a Democratic Party organizer; and Alan Cranston, chairman of the California Democratic Council and later a U.S. senator from the state. After discussing with them preparations for Stevenson's upcoming trip there, Martin did what he did best: legwork. He interviewed all kinds of Californians to see what was on their minds. Martin worked closely with Bradley and his assistant, Jack Abbott, and they established Stevenson's schedule in the state and agreed on the issues he should address at each campaign stop. "Thus, for the first time in a campaign," said Martin, "I was able to bring schedule and issues together."[15]

Four years earlier, again in 1956, and "seemingly forever," said Martin, Stevenson had beseeched his speechwriters to fashion for him an "all-purpose" whistle-stop speech that could, when needed, be divided into an attack on the Eisenhower administration and an outline of the positive programs the Stevenson campaign offered to voters. Stevenson admitted to Martin that without a manuscript in his hands, ideas ran wild inside his head and he could not sort them out. He would start talking about three subjects, get too interested in the first, talk for fifteen or twenty minutes about it, then realize he had no time to talk about the other two subjects, which might be of equal or even greater importance. The result, said Stevenson, was a bored audience and a disgusted candidate. Providing such a speech, however, proved to be an impossible task – "it can't be written," Martin said. Even if such a speech could be crafted, there was no certainty that Stevenson would deliver it as written. He hated to give the same speech over and over again, even if crowds reacted positively, because he rebelled against repeating himself. At the same time, Martin pointed out, when Stevenson insisted on new material from his writers, he would turn around and complain about having little time to learn it well enough to present to campaign audiences.[16]

As a solution to Stevenson's search for an "all-purpose" speech, Martin hit upon a system he used in subsequent Democratic presidential campaigns, what came to be known as editorial advance. With Stevenson scheduled to make as many as sixteen whistle-stops a day in California, and with the burden of writing those speeches his alone, Martin realized he could not provide the candidate with a different speech for each appearance. He began preparing briefing sheets for Stevenson to use at each whistle-stop, a page or two outlining such information as the nature of the setting (for example, a picnic in a wooded grove or speaking from the back of a truck with a public address system), the size of the expected crowd, the crowd's composition (whether farmers, laborers, blacks, general public, etc.), whether the meeting was indoors or outdoors, which issues to raise and ones to avoid, and a few lines about the community that Stevenson could use to make connections with his audience. Martin also included the names of local heroes and politicians to be mentioned, sometimes including a one-sentence identification if the individual presented a problem, say, for example, "not to mention his lovely wife, he's divorcing her." If an issue was a new or dangerous one, Martin wrote language to smooth over any difficulties. If it was an old issue, he simply copied material from previous Stevenson speeches. To gather information needed for these briefing sheets, Martin talked to Dutton, Bradley, and Abbott, and, instead of state party chairmen, "local people of all sorts." By then, however, he had learned to be wary of the advice offered by local experts, preferring to keep in mind not their interests, but the interests of his candidate.[17]

On May 1 Martin met Stevenson in California and told him about his idea for the briefing sheets. Although dubious at first, as all political candidates are about anything new, Stevenson agreed to give them a try. The next day the briefing sheets were put to the test in San Francisco, where Stevenson had a "murderous" campaign schedule that included press conferences, a fund-raising lunch, and appearances from 9:45 AM to 9:30 PM. Just before Stevenson arrived at each stop, Bradley handed him the correct briefing sheet and, noted Martin, Stevenson "read them, then turned them over and scribbled notes in longhand, making the pages his own, and he used them, speaking, in effect, extemporaneously from notes, and the crowd liked it." Martin said that the briefing sheets kept Stevenson on track, as he never arrived at an event "without knowing what to expect and what was expected of him." It turned out to be one of "the best days of whistle-stopping" in Stevenson's life, said Martin, with cheering crowds delighted with his offhand comment that the United Nations should have never moved its headquarters away from San Francisco for New York. Newspaper reporters following the candidate began to write about a "new Stevenson" who had suddenly learned to enjoy campaigning. "Always uneasy when speaking without a highly polished, typewritten text in front of him, he learned to talk with rough-hewn notes – and in so doing, he freshened his delivery," noted *Time* magazine. Martin, however, made sure to stick close by his candidate so when he questioned, as he often did, why he had to say something about a particular subject, Martin could be there to present arguments for doing so based on what he had learned from local sources. "But it was necessary to be at his side," Martin said.[18]

The "new" Stevenson proved to be a hit with voters. On June 5 he won an overwhelming victory in the California primary, exceeding even the most optimistic staff estimates by defeating Kefauver by more than 400,000 votes. Martin compared it to Stevenson's landslide victory for the Illinois governorship in 1948 and believed that Kefauver had erred in attacking his opponent, as it threw away his greatest strength, his image

The Martin family, circa 1917, Laura, J. W., and John. As a youngster, Martin had as his highest ambition obtaining a job as a garbage collector. "I thought that it might be fun to drive a wagon around the city all day," he said. *Courtesy of Cindy Martin Coleman.*

At the age of eight, Martin, seen here with his mother, nearly suffered a fatal accident. He was playing marbles in the alley behind his house on Brookside Avenue in Indianapolis when an automobile came around the corner. The car's bumper struck Martin in the head, but fortunately the only serious result was a scar he kept for the rest of his life.

Courtesy of John Bartlow Martin Papers, Manuscript Division, Library of Congress.

Martin during his days as a student at Indianapolis's Arsenal Technical High School.

Courtesy of John Bartlow Martin Papers, Manuscript Division, Library of Congress.

Martin and his new bride, Frances Rose Smethurst, pose with their wedding party on the steps of the Congregational Church in Elmhurst, Illinois, August 17, 1940.

Courtesy of Cindy Martin Coleman.

Crouching at the far right of the second row, Martin poses with fellow
U.S. Army recruits at Fort Sheridan in Illinois in the fall of 1944.

Courtesy of John Bartlow Martin Papers, Manuscript Division, Library of Congress.

Martin smiles down on his young daughter, Cindy, while
stationed in San Antonio, Texas, during World War II.

Courtesy of Cindy Martin Coleman.

Martin and Fran on vacation in Colorado, circa 1946–47.

Courtesy of Cindy Martin Coleman.

His former employer, the *Indianapolis Times,* used this photograph of Martin to illustrate a July 31, 1946, story the newspaper did on his research for what became his book *Indiana: An Interpretation.* The article noted he started his freelance career because "he hates offices. Even now he hesitates to interview people in their offices, prefers instead to talk with them in their homes or, say, a nice cool bar."

Courtesy of Gary Yohler/Frederick Vollrath, Tiffany Studio, Indianapolis Times *Collection.*

While her parents look on, Cindy Martin (seated at right) smiles for a photographer at a dinner at Chicago's famous Pump Room in the Ambassador East Hotel to celebrate her tenth birthday. Joining the Martins for the occasion was Jean Goldberg, a friend of Cindy's. It was after this dinner that Martin met Adlai Stevenson for the first time.

Courtesy of John Bartlow Martin Papers, Manuscript Division, Library of Congress.

Flanked by Indiana governor Henry F. Schricker, Democratic presidential candidate
Adlai E. Stevenson waves to the crowd greeting his arrival at Indianapolis's Weir
Cook Airport during a campaign appearance in 1952. Stevenson later spoke on
economy in government at the Indiana State Fairgrounds, a talk that Martin, who
accompanied Stevenson on the trip, described as "the budget with a heart speech."

Courtesy of Indiana Historical Society, Bass Photo Company Collection, p. 130.

Seated at the far left, Martin attends a February 19, 1953, meeting of the
Chicago Headline Club. Seated from left to right: Martin; Al Orton,
Chicago bureau chief of the Associated Press; and Ken Clayton of the
Chicago Tribune. Standing, left to right: William J. Conway, Chicago
AP feature writer; and Carroll Arimond, Chicago AP city editor.

Courtesy of John Bartlow Martin Papers, Manuscript Division, Library of Congress.

David Dodds Henry, University of Illinois president, presents Martin with the 1955 Benjamin Franklin Award, then the magazine industry's highest honor, for the article best depicting a person, living or dead, for his series in the *Saturday Evening Post* on Nathan Leopold.

Courtesy of John Bartlow Martin Papers, Manuscript Division, Library of Congress.

Martin meets with Stuart Rose, *Saturday Evening Post* associate editor, in Philadelphia's Independence Square (*above*) and in the editor's office at the *Post* to discuss the writer's series on Leopold (*overleaf*). Martin said Leopold possessed "insight and perspective on himself to a degree unusual in people generally, and extraordinary in somebody who has been in prison for so long."

Courtesy of John Bartlow Martin Papers, Manuscript Division, Library of Congress.

Martin at the height of his powers as a freelance magazine writer in the 1950s, equipped with the tools of his trade: research material, typewriter, pencils, pencil sharpener, and edited manuscript.

Courtesy of the University of Illinois Archives,
Benjamin Franklin Magazine Awards File, RS 13/1/15.

President John F. Kennedy meets with Martin on March 2, 1962, in the Oval Office at the White House before the new ambassador takes up his post in the Dominican Republic.

Courtesy of Abbie Rowe, White House Photographs,
John F. Kennedy Presidential Library and Museum.

Fran Martin in the yard of the family's home on Maple Avenue in Highland Park, Illinois.

Courtesy of Cindy Martin Coleman.

Martin and Fran talk with Rafael Bonnelly, president of the Dominican Republic, at a reception following the marriage of Martin's daughter, Cindy, to Anthony V. M. Campbell, a Shell Oil Company executive.

Courtesy of John Bartlow Martin Papers, Manuscript Division, Library of Congress.

Ambassador Martin tries his hand at farming during a visit to the interior in the Dominican Republic. Those watching include Martin's sons, Dan, with his hand to his face, and Fred, standing and looking down at the far right of the photo.

Courtesy of John Bartlow Martin Papers, Manuscript Division, Library of Congress.

Martin poses with a Dominican farmer.

*Courtesy of John Bartlow Martin Papers,
Manuscript Division, Library of Congress.*

Martin shakes hands with Lyndon B. Johnson during the vice president's visit to the Dominican Republic for Juan Bosch's presidential inauguration in 1963. The day before Johnson arrived, the Central Intelligence Agency told Martin that U.S. immigration officials had stopped two communist "terrorists" from leaving New York for Santo Domingo.

Courtesy of John Bartlow Martin Papers, Manuscript Division, Library of Congress.

Martin and friends, including novelist John Voelker (seated with coffee cup in hand), pose for the camera during a hunting trip in Michigan's Upper Peninsula in the mid-1960s.

Courtesy of John D. Voelker Papers, Central Upper Michigan Peninsula and Northern Michigan University Archives.

Martin at work in his Highland Park home, circa 1970s. Longtime
friend Newton Minow called Martin the "most gifted and the
greatest perfectionist in writing" he had ever known.

Courtesy of Northwestern University Archives.

Overleaf: Views of the Martin family's camp on Smith Lake
in Michigan's Upper Peninsula taken in 2013. In Martin's day
the view from the porch had been obscured by trees.

Courtesy of the author.

as "the friendly handshaker. Worn out, he went too far in his attacks. He also went too far in his promises – his purpose became transparent and hurt *him*." Stevenson's decisive win in California, combined with his victories in primaries in Washington, D.C., New Jersey, Illinois, Oregon, and Florida, convinced Kefauver to drop out of the race in July, making Stevenson the front runner for the presidential nomination at the Democratic National Convention.[19]

To Martin, however, the California triumph backfired and was the worst thing that could have happened to Stevenson, as it made him over-confident. In the months to come he reverted to his 1952 style of "lofty rhetoric on grand issues," said Martin, who along with other staff members believed that Stevenson could only defeat Eisenhower by campaigning throughout the country as he had done in California. The governor had to leave his lofty perch and mingle with the voters to see their problems firsthand. Martin wanted him to conduct a major whistle-stop campaign in "areas of disaffection, a 'pothole' campaign, rubbing the raw nerves of discontent in a generally complacent country, maximizing his support among workingmen, Negroes, coal miners, and others." Instead, Stevenson wanted to make foreign policy his main issue, even though Martin and others told him there were no votes for him there and that he should hit hard from the campaign's outset on Eisenhower's health. "The conflict was never really resolved," said Martin. He was surprised to find himself and Schlesinger urging "hard-nosed political views" in meetings, while professional politicians such as Finnegan took the "lofty idealistic position."[20]

On August 16 at the International Amphitheater in Chicago, Stevenson received his party's nomination for president on the first ballot. What happened next shocked delegates, party officials, and reporters covering the convention. Stevenson decided to throw open the choice of his vice president to the convention. Party leaders such as Speaker of the House Sam Rayburn of Texas were disgusted with the idea, arguing it only added fuel to the fire of those who saw Stevenson as indecisive, but others saw it as a bold move, providing a contrast to the GOP convention's lockstep renomination of Vice President Richard Nixon. "Throwing the convention open also focused public attention on the vice presidency," said Martin, which in subtle ways made voters think about Eisenhower's fragile health. Kefauver became the leading candidate, but he was in a tight battle with U.S. senator John F. Kennedy of Massachusetts, a Catholic who had given the principal speech nominating Stevenson for president. Kennedy came close to winning, falling only 18½ votes short. Kefauver became Stevenson's running mate. Kennedy's graceful remarks asking the convention to make Kefauver's nomination unanimous only cemented his status as the Democratic Party's rising star and placed him on the fast track to be a contender for the presidential nomination in 1960.[21]

For Martin, the 1956 Stevenson presidential campaign did not have the fun and excitement of four years before, but was "just hard work," as he and other staff members spent most of their time at the Stevenson for President headquarters in Washington, D.C. "The research and writing operation of 1956 was less happy-go-lucky, less brilliant, but far more solid than the Elks Club of 1952," said Martin. Schlesinger and Wirtz joined Martin as full-time speechwriters, while Robert Tufts and William Lee Miller served on a part-time basis. From time to time such well-known figures as John Kenneth Galbraith, John Hersey, Seymour Harris, and Chester Bowles also offered their writing expertise. Martin had a premonition of the long road ahead when he and Fran watched Stevenson's acceptance speech from the rear of the gigantic International Amphitheater. From that distance, Stevenson appeared to be "a remote figure, disembodied, almost a puppet, uttering the tired phrases of the Democratic faith," said Martin. The speech, in comparison to those Democrats had been used to from Stevenson, "lifted few hearts," he added. The assembled delegates wanted to cheer, but Stevenson gave them nothing in his remarks to cheer about. "He had not won in 1952 but he had lifted hearts," Martin said. "Now he did not."[22]

Many of his staff considered it a losing cause from the start, but Stevenson made a herculean effort to unseat Eisenhower, giving three hundred speeches and traveling 55,000 miles across the country. Stevenson persevered in spite of complaining throughout the fall of a "residual weariness" from the battles he had fought to win the Democratic nomination, noted Galbraith. A research staff that had been spearheaded by John Brademas, later a longtime Indiana congressman, had come up with a list of 180 issues to be addressed. The writers prepared policy position papers on each issue, along with material for Stevenson to consult before press conferences. "A great deal of work went into each one – sometimes a day was spent on a single sentence," Martin remembered. Stevenson was then able to buttress the "New America" theme he had introduced at the convention with what Martin called a "programmatic affirmative campaign" with programs that foreshadowed Kennedy's New Frontier and Lyndon Johnson's Great Society, including a call for a national insurance program for the elderly long before the establishment of Medicare. Stevenson also flouted the conventional wisdom of the day regarding national defense issues by calling for an end to the military draft and the establishment of a volunteer army, as well as supporting a limitation on the testing of nuclear weapons in the atmosphere to help prevent deadly radioactive fallout. Martin believed that Stevenson ran a better race in 1956 than he had four years earlier, with the staff more experienced, more purposeful, and "less out on a lark than bent on winning an election. Its amalgam of professionals, semi-pros and amateurs worked together better than any outsider supposed." Martin and other staff members, however, were continually frustrated by Eisenhower's "apparently indestructible popularity." One anecdote typified Stevenson's uphill fight against the president. Stevenson remembered a time when he met a farmer unhappy about Eisenhower's farm policy. When asked why people did not seem to be mad at Eisenhower, the farmer replied, "Oh, no one connects *him* with the Administration."[23]

Stevenson attempted to sway voters a final time during a November 5 national broadcast from Boston, when, now desperate, he made Eisenhower's health a major issue. He noted that "every lesson of history and experience, indicates that a Republican victory tomorrow would mean that Richard M. Nixon would probably be president of this country within the next four years." It did not work; two tense international incidents had already sealed Stevenson's fate. In the final stages of the campaign the Soviet Union sent 200,000 troops and 4,000 tanks into Budapest, Hungary, to crush a citizen rebellion against Russian control of that Eastern bloc country. In addition, troops from France and Great Britain, ostensibly responding to an invasion of Egypt by Israel but in fact seeking to win back control of the Suez Canal that had been nationalized by Egypt in July, had triggered an ominous threat of retaliation in the Middle East by the Soviet Union. As these overseas calamities dominated newscasts, American voters turned to Eisenhower to steer the country away from war. Stevenson said that the Suez crisis alone cost him four million votes in the election. Even with these votes in hand, the Democratic candidate would have gone down to defeat, as he eventually lost by more than 9.5 million votes, with Eisenhower receiving the largest popular vote total in history (35,590,472). Suez turned "certain victory" for Eisenhower into a rout, said Martin. The incumbent president also dominated in the Electoral College, winning 457 electoral votes to 73 for Stevenson, who won only seven states (Missouri, North Carolina, South Carolina, Georgia, Mississippi, Alabama, and Arkansas). "All in all," said Martin, "it is impossible to conclude that Stevenson could have won, no matter how he campaigned. Eisenhower in 1956 was simply invincible."[24]

Although he had played a greater role in the 1956 campaign than he had four years earlier, Martin believed that Stevenson's second presidential loss had put an end to his participation in politics, and he returned to writing for national magazines. A series he did for the *Post* on a government investigation of one of the country's largest and most powerful unions – the International Brotherhood of Teamsters, Chauffeurs, Warehousemen and Helpers of America, more commonly known as the Teamsters – set him on the path, however, to becoming part of another Democratic presidential campaign.

Journalists had been investigating rumors that Teamsters officials had been enriching themselves at the expense of their members, and gangsters, salivating over the union's large pension fund ($250 million), had made inroads into its operations. During the 1956 California presidential primary, when Martin had found himself "swamped with too many speeches to write" for Stevenson, Pierre Salinger, a former newspaper reporter for the *San Francisco Chronicle* and then the West Coast correspondent for *Collier's* magazine, offered his help. According to Martin, Salinger produced a few speech drafts, from which he used little, but one day Salinger brought to Martin's hotel room in San Francisco a *Collier's* editor, who asked Martin to research and write an article on the Teamsters (the union was not then under investigation). "I told him I couldn't undertake it till after the election; he said he couldn't wait; I suggested he get Pierre Salinger to do it, and he did," Martin recalled.[25]

Salinger jumped at the chance to write about such a powerful organization. As one Teamsters official told him, discussing the union's firm grip on the country, "When a woman takes a cab to the hospital to have a baby, the cab is driven by a Teamster. When the baby grows old and dies, the hearse is driven by a Teamster. And in between we supply him with a lot of groceries." Unfortunately for Salinger, just when he finished his article, *Collier's* went out of business. He had two job opportunities waiting for him, one as public relations director for the Teamsters, and the other as an investigator with a U.S. Senate subcommittee created on January 31, 1957, the Select Committee on Improper Activities in the Labor or Management Field, which came to be widely known as the Rackets Committee. In addition to the Teamsters, the committee investigated other unions as well as the growing influence of the Mafia and the Chicago syndicate. Salinger went to work in February 1957 for the committee, chaired by conservative Democratic senator John L. McClellan of Arkansas, and shared what he had learned about the Teamsters with its chief counsel, Robert F. Kennedy, the younger brother of John Kennedy. Another journalist, Clark R. Mollenhoff, a Pulitzer Prize–winning reporter for the *Des Moines Register,* had for months been badgering Kennedy to probe the Teamsters possible illegal activities.[26]

Martin had first become acquainted with Robert Kennedy during Stevenson's 1956 presidential campaign, which Kennedy had joined to learn how to run such an organization in anticipation of his brother seeking the Democratic nomination for president in 1960. "He told me later he had learned how *not* to run one," Martin noted. Robert Kennedy described the Stevenson effort as a disaster and told Martin he had never seen such a poorly run operation. "He should have seen 1952," said Martin. The two men's paths crossed again when Martin received word from Stuart Rose at the *Post* that the magazine was interested in a series of articles on the Rackets Committee's more than two-year-long investigation of the Teamsters and its top officials, including Dave Beck (convicted of federal tax evasion charges in 1959) and James R. Hoffa (convicted of bribing a grand juror in 1964; he disappeared from view in 1975 and was never seen alive again). When the committee held public hearings, newspapers had published "scrappy reports," said Martin, but as Rose pointed out, nobody had yet been able to "put the whole story together," and he suggested Martin take on the task.[27]

The resulting seven-part series, published in the *Post* from June 27 to August 8, 1959, was Martin's longest yet, taking him nearly a year to put together and setting a mileage record for his legwork, as he traveled seventeen thousand miles around the country. In conducting his research, he filled twenty 150-page notebooks and wrote a first draft that ran 1,500 pages and 336,000 words; his final manuscript totaled 40,000 words. Martin had unearthed a remarkable study in power: the vast economic power wielded by the Teamsters, the largest labor union in the world with more than 1.5 million members, versus the great political power wielded by the U.S. Senate. The resulting investigation stood as one of the largest by a government entity since the days of the Teapot Dome scandal of the Harding administration of the 1920s and the banking and securities fraud inquiries of the 1930s. "They exposed wrongdoings in big business; the McClellan committee alone has gone after big labor," said Martin. The Rackets Committee's work (1,366 witnesses questioned produced a printed record of testimony that ran to 20,000 pages) sent shock waves through both political parties, as well as the labor movement in America, and raised essential questions still being argued about today: the use of and abuse of the Fifth Amendment, the authority of Congress to investigate, the rights of individual working men in a labor union, and the rights of an individual testifying before Congress. It also pitted the titanic personalities of two men, Robert Kennedy and Hoffa, who became "bitter antagonists," noted Martin. Hoffa viewed Kennedy as a rich, "spoiled jerk," while Kennedy's determination to uncover the labor leader's criminal activity became "a holy crusade" to him, one of his friends confided to Martin. Kennedy himself said the manner in which Hoffa operated the Teamsters meant it no longer served as a bona fide union: "As Mr. Hoffa operates it, this is a conspiracy of evil."[28]

To report on the investigation, Martin traveled to Washington, D.C., staying there off and on for more than half a year and becoming a familiar presence at the Rackets Committee's offices in Room 101 at the Old Senate Office Building. For his story he spent more time with Kennedy than with anyone else, sometimes visiting with him all day in his private office and going with him at day's end to Hickory Hill, his home in

McLean, Virginia, for dinner; it was often a hair-raising ride, as Kennedy, recalled Martin, "loved to drive his big convertible fast from office to home, his hair flying." On weekends at Hickory Hill Martin played, "not very well" he admitted, the traditional Kennedy family sport of touch football, swam with Kennedy in his pool, and accompanied him as he made trips around the country pursuing leads from whistleblowers in the union. "I liked Bobby Kennedy from the start," said Martin. "Though born to wealth and power, he had about him not a trace of superiority or affectation." Although dedicated to his work – Martin said he "seemed almost obsessed" – Kennedy infused his office with a youthful, light-hearted atmosphere. Martin remembered coming into Kennedy's office and seeing him and Kenneth O'Donnell, his administrative assistant, passing a football back and forth as they discussed the investigation (the two men were on the football team together at Harvard University). "He moved fast, handling his body well, like an athlete," Martin said of Kennedy. "He ran upstairs and downstairs. He scheduled himself remorselessly, and he drove his staff just as hard." Driving Kennedy's determination was the worry in the back of his mind that if the investigation proved to be a flop, it might have a negative effect on his brother's political future, both his re-election to the U.S. Senate in 1958 and his try for the Democratic presidential nomination in 1960. "A lot of people think he's the Kennedy running the investigation," Robert said of John, one of the four Democratic senators who served on the Rackets Committee. "As far as the public is concerned, one Kennedy is the same as another Kennedy."[29]

When Robert Kennedy's work took him to the Chicago area, he and some of his investigators sometimes stayed with Martin at his home in Highland Park, including one trip when Kennedy and his men were in the area to dig up a body in a cornfield near Joliet, Illinois. Walter Sheridan, whom Martin considered to be one of Kennedy's best investigators, later indicated that Kennedy and his staff had been looking for the body of a woman reporter from Joliet allegedly killed for daring to expose labor racketeering in the city. They had been tipped off by a convict in the prison there who said he knew where the body had been buried. It turned out to be a bogus tip, but Kennedy and those with him turned over a lot of earth in a farmer's field before realizing "the prisoner was just stringing them along," Sheridan said. "They did a lot of digging." While staying in the Martins' home, Kennedy played cops and robbers with their two small sons, Dan and Fred, while they were clad in their long flannel Doctor Denton pajamas, "chasing them noisily upstairs to bed," Martin remembered. Fran, who enjoyed betting on horse races, had to be on guard when the man investigating the mob's influence on unions stayed at her house. Once when the laundryman came to collect her two-dollar bet to pass along to her bookie in Highwood, a town north of Highland Park filled with taverns controlled by the Chicago syndicate, she had to ask Martin for the money in front of Kennedy. Thinking fast, she said to her husband, "I owe the laundryman two dollars." Understanding her real meaning, Martin handed over the cash. "Bobby never knew," he said. Martin proudly noted that Fran had a knack for picking successful long shots, and word soon spread throughout Highwood that she must have connections with "the mysterious 'they' who fixed the races, and the laundryman and others respectfully solicited her picks."[30]

As Martin got deeper and deeper into his story, he discovered that there seemed to be two different Robert Kennedys (a theme picked up on by many other journalists during Kennedy's subsequent career). There was the person few in the public saw – the family man who went home to Hickory Hill and loved having his children swarm over him when he opened the front door. Those who watched the Rackets Committee's hearing on national television, however, only witnessed the relentless prosecutor, hectoring hostile witnesses who dodged his questions on Fifth Amendment grounds, which earned Kennedy a reputation for ruthlessness that dogged him until the end of his life. Instead of seeing a cold-blooded individual, however, Martin thought of Kennedy as "hard driving, tenacious, aggressive, [and] competitive," a person who said his long and eventually unsuccessful campaign with the Rackets Committee to put Hoffa behind bars was "a little like 1864, when [General Ulysses S.] Grant took over the Union Army to go back into the wilderness – to go back slugging it out." Unlike some of his friends who were concerned about possible infringements of civil liberties, Martin did not believe Kennedy persecuted Hoffa or denied him his constitutional rights. "As a crime reporter, I had seen far worse prosecutions," said Martin. "Indeed, I thought he treated Hoffa fairly, on the whole." What Martin could not understand was Kennedy's conviction that the labor leader represented America's biggest problem, a notion that sounded odd to someone who had only recently been involved in a presidential campaign concerned with helping rein in the worldwide threat of nuclear destruction. Kennedy believed that if someone did not do something about Hoffa's damaging influence on the Teamsters, gangsters would soon have a stranglehold on the country's economy. During the investigation Kennedy had also grown to admire the rank-and-file members of the Teamsters, and he believed that Hoffa had engaged in sweetheart contracts with employers, receiving kickbacks in return and denying workers their fair due. Kennedy also possessed, like some politicians Martin had known, an almost mystical faith in the democratic system, a faith readers of the *Post* likely shared. "Like them [other politicians]," noted Martin, "he links it with the righteousness of his own cause. He feels that, although Hoffa may win a battle, he can never win the war, because justice and right will prevail, owing to the excellence of this democratic system and the good sense and decency of the American people."[31]

Martin held a much harsher opinion of the investigators who worked for Kennedy. Most of them were in their late twenties and early thirties and had previously worked as newspapermen, FBI agents, or policemen. Kennedy had, at the inquiry's peak, forty-two investigators on his staff, aided by forty men from the government's General Accounting Office. "These men," Martin noted in his articles for the *Post*, "condemn wrongdoing unequivocally. For many of them the crusade against Hoffa is their first cause, important as first love. There is something a little chilling about their moral certitude and zeal." They lacked, Martin later reflected, the tolerance for human weakness he had seen in the work of big-city detectives he had known. The investigators' ardor for justice did translate into meticulous evidence gathering. Kennedy told Martin that for every witness called to testify before the committee, twenty-five people had been interviewed, and they examined tens of thousands of documents for every one placed into the record. During one inquiry, Salinger and two other investigators went through more than 600,000 checks from one company alone. Sheridan noted that as long as those on staff did their work to the best of their abilities, they could always count on the leader's support, something he had not had in his previous job. "The big difference – it was just a phenomenal difference to me – of going from the FBI to work for Robert Kennedy was that with the FBI you knew that J. Edgar Hoover would never back you up," said Sheridan, "and with Robert Kennedy you knew that he would. It was all the difference in the world."[32]

Kennedy's cooperation with Martin was part of the chief counsel's ongoing effort to cultivate good relations with the press, especially with columnists and magazine writers. Edwin O. Guthman, a reporter with the *Seattle Times* who later became Kennedy's press secretary at the Justice Department, said that in his journalism career he had never encountered someone in public life who had answered his questions "as candidly and completely as he [Kennedy] did," and Kennedy often briefed reporters in considerable detail about the evidence to be presented at a committee hearing. Kennedy developed "special relationships" with certain reporters, noted Guthman during the investigation of Beck, and these writers always had access to him and received tips on stories and verification of information when needed. As a reporter, Martin said it made him "a little nervous" to see journalists who had completed independent investigations on the Teamsters, such as Mollenhoff, exchanging information with Kennedy about what they had uncovered. In a draft for his *Post* series Martin had included a passage, cut from the published piece, pointing out that some newspapermen had become so close to the investigation that they attended committee staff parties almost like members of the staff themselves, and some shared their "zeal for getting Jimmy Hoffa." As a representative of the *Post,* one of the country's leading magazines, Martin said he could count on Kennedy's full cooperation, as he "was anxious that the *Post* story come out well; it was the first full-dress account that tried to pull the whole investigation together."[33]

To gain a broader perspective on the Teamsters investigation, Martin also talked to some of the senators serving on the Rackets Committee, including McClellan and the leading Republican member of the panel, Barry M. Goldwater of Arizona, whom he found to be "an amusing, engaging man." Martin found himself spending a lot of his time with John Kennedy, seeing him alone in his Senate office, having breakfast with him at a New York hotel, and eating dinner with him and his wife,

Jacqueline, in Washington, D.C. When they were alone together, Martin remembered that he and the Massachusetts senator "talked politics almost entirely." Kennedy had been gearing up to run for president in 1960, and the primaries would begin in little more than a year. Although winning primary races did not translate into a clear path to the nomination, they were important to Kennedy as a way of showing to party leaders skeptical of his youth and religion, as well as grassroots Democrats, that he could win support from a broad spectrum of voters. Knowing of Martin's experience in Stevenson's two presidential efforts, Kennedy picked his brain on what kind of campaign staff he might need, his opinion on various issues, and how to connect with the academic world when it came to developing policy ideas and position papers. "Jack Kennedy struck me as an extremely attractive and extremely intelligent young man," Martin said. "He presented a lighthearted funny exterior, sometimes almost frivolous, but inwardly he was deadly serious and he had an astonishing fund of information about all manner of subjects, such as France's problems in Algeria and the number of Nigerian exchange students in the United States." He also seemed, unlike Stevenson, to "welcome challenges, not be burdened by them," Martin noted. Many people Martin ran into that spring and summer in Washington, D.C., including some former Stevenson supporters, had begun to proselytize on Kennedy's behalf. Martin still had his doubts about Kennedy, as he was unsure if he was presidential material, noting, "He was so young."[34]

For the other part of his story for the *Post*, Martin had to somehow convince a suspicious and hostile Hoffa to talk with him. It would not be the first time in his journalism career that Martin had come up against a recalcitrant Teamsters official. During his time as a young reporter with the *Indianapolis Times,* Martin had covered a truck strike and attempted to interview Daniel J. Tobin, then the Teamsters president, at the union's headquarters at 222 East Michigan Street in Indianapolis (the union moved its headquarters to Washington, D.C., in 1953). Martin remembered that Tobin's office had a door that "was locked and steel-barred, like a prison cell." He had to stand in the corridor and shout his questions at the union leader, who yelled his answers back to Martin, usually responding with such curt statements as, "No," "No comment," or simply "Go to hell." No reporter, Martin ruefully noted, had ever "got much out of the Teamsters." With this experience behind him, Martin decided to use his status as a reporter with the *Post,* and the possibility of finally telling his side of the story in an unbiased manner to the American people, to convince Hoffa to open up to him about his life and work. He adopted the stratagem of calling Hoffa not from his home, but from the *Post*'s Chicago advertising office, having the switchboard operator place the call, and leaving the *Post*'s telephone number for Hoffa to call back. "Moreover," said Martin, "this kept my home telephone number, and hence my address, out of Teamsters headquarters, which seemed only prudent in view of the reputation of Hoffa's associates." The strategy worked; after a week of telephone calls, Hoffa finally called Martin back and agreed to an interview at Teamsters headquarters in Washington, D.C.

Ushered into Hoffa's plush office, Martin spent two hours interviewing the Teamsters president, mindful that their talk was probably being recorded. He was able to convince Hoffa that he wanted to hear his point of view on the union controversy. Hoffa agreed to tell other union officials to talk to Martin, and he allowed the reporter to follow him as he did his job, including negotiating contracts with Midwest truckers in Chicago and accompanying him on a flight from Chicago to Miami for the Teamsters' annual meeting. Martin, who refused to accept an airline ticket Hoffa had bought for him (Martin had anticipated such a move and had bought his own), sat by him for the entire flight, and the two men talked all night with few interruptions, except for one by a stewardess who recognized Hoffa, "which secretly pleased him," noted Martin. Instead of asking questions about the investigation, which he knew Hoffa would either be unresponsive about or refuse to answer, Martin concentrated on details about the union leader's life and his views about the U.S. labor movement. "I liked him," he said of Hoffa, perhaps because the two men viewed themselves as fighting for the underdog. At one point in his life Hoffa had been arrested eighteen times in one day for his union activities, but he persevered to become president of Teamsters Local 299 in Detroit. The local served as his power base as he clawed his way to the union presidency using often brutal tactics and counting on allies who had no qualms about using force to get their way. "I'm no damn angel," Hoffa said. As Martin insightfully pointed out in his *Post* series, the image of Hoffa as "the cocky little underdog battling the United States Government is not false; it is his natural role." In fact, he went on to write, if Robert Kennedy of the Rackets Committee had not existed, Hoffa "would have had to invent him." Hoffa, a devoted family man who had no hobbies and who neither smoked nor drank, concentrated all his efforts on behalf of the Teamsters, working to gain its members better working conditions and more money. "Running a union is just like running a business," Hoffa told Martin. "We're in the business of selling labor. We're going to get the best price we can."[35]

In evaluating the Rackets Committee's investigation of the Teamsters, Martin reported that it produced a demand for reform legislation to stem in part the influence of racketeers in the labor movement, and he also had an overall good opinion of the work done by Robert Kennedy and his staff. "There was remarkably little politics in the committee's work," Martin wrote. "McClellan stood firm against pressure and made no mistakes. Indeed, had all congressional committees conducted themselves so well, congressional committees would have received less criticism in recent years." But the federal investigators had failed in one task. Hoffa remained Teamsters president and had been acquitted in the two criminal trials resulting from the committee's work. In his time with both Kennedy and Hoffa, Martin also discovered that the two fearsome antagonists shared similar qualities, as they were both "aggressive, competitive, hard-driving, authoritarian, suspicious, temperate, at times congenial and at others curt." They were also physical men who sought to keep in shape, often by doing push-ups, and in spite of their wealth and power "eschewed frivolity or indulgence and both seemed oblivious of their surroundings. Both were serious men and, in their own ways, dedicated," Martin later observed. As for their opinions on the long investigation, Martin wrote that Hoffa shrugged off the committee's relentless focus on his union, saying, "You just put in your time. And when they get tired of kicking us around they'll adjourn and forget about it." Kennedy admitted to the writer, "It's been a real struggle."[36]

When he had finished his story, Martin offered to show his manuscript to both Hoffa and Kennedy so they could correct any factual errors, but not his interpretations of events. Hoffa turned down Martin's offer, but Kennedy spent the better part of a day and well into the night

going over the manuscript point by point with Martin at the writer's
hotel room in New York. It proved to be "not an easy negotiation," said
Martin. Kennedy was as tenacious with the reporter as he had been with
reluctant witnesses appearing before the Rackets Committee. "What
bothered him the most about the MS [manuscript], I think, were the
similarities I noted in the piece between him and Hoffa," said Martin.
"He was amazed and simply could not understand; it had never occurred
to him; he had thought of himself as good and Hoffa as evil; I was looking at them from a different angle." Once during the discussion Kennedy asked Martin why he had not included statements that could be
damaging to Hoffa. "I asked if he could prove them by sworn testimony,"
Martin noted. "He said he could not but he knew they were true, he
couldn't understand why I wouldn't put them in." The reason Martin
was cautious was of course because of a possible libel action against the
Post by Hoffa and the Teamsters. As a lawyer himself, Kennedy should
have known this, but Martin put this misunderstanding down to the
chief counsel's youth.[37]

The sometimes contentious back and forth between Kennedy and
Martin on the Hoffa story did not diminish Martin's respect for the
investigator, or Kennedy's esteem for the reporter. Years later, Martin
reflected that no matter how much Kennedy viewed Hoffa "as evil and
himself as good, he never once objected to my attempts at impartiality.
Nor did he ever let those attempts impair our own personal relationship."
After the series appeared in the *Post,* Kennedy, who became the day-to-
day manager for his brother's presidential campaign in 1960, approached
Martin and told him he had not wanted to mention it while the story was
still pending, but he wanted him to be a speechwriter for his brother.
By the spring of 1960, John Kennedy and fellow U.S. senator Hubert H.
Humphrey were battling one another in a series of Democratic presidential primaries. On April 5 Kennedy had squeaked by Humphrey to
win the Wisconsin primary, setting up a rematch in West Virginia to
see if the Roman Catholic Kennedy could win a race in that Protestant-
dominated state.[38]

Although he had made no formal announcement of his intentions,
Stevenson had not declared himself out of the running for the nomination. "Deep down he wants it," a close friend of Stevenson's told journal-

ist and author Theodore White during the winter months of 1959–60. "But he wants the Convention to come to him, he doesn't want to go to the Convention." If Stevenson faltered, other candidates appeared ready to step in to stop Kennedy from obtaining the nomination, including Senate majority leader Lyndon B. Johnson of Texas and U.S. senator Stuart Symington of Missouri. Martin and other Stevenson advisers, including Newton Minow and William M. Blair Jr., had urged him not to run again and instead to endorse Kennedy. By doing so, Martin and the others argued, Stevenson would ensure Kennedy's nomination and he would then have a solid claim on being secretary of state in a Kennedy administration. "I told Stevenson I did not think he could be nominated," Martin recalled, "and even if he were, he might lose to Richard Nixon, who seemed certain of the Republican nomination, and losing to Nixon would break his heart." Martin remembered Stevenson raising several objections, including his belief that Kennedy was too young and, as a Catholic, could not hope to become president. He also cited his obligations to former first lady Eleanor Roosevelt and his other supporters who wanted him to be available if the Democratic convention, held from July 11 to 15 at the Los Angeles Memorial Sports Arena, could not agree on a nominee. "Or at least this is what he said," noted Martin. He and others believed that "in his heart Stevenson wanted the nomination." By this time, Martin had become a supporter of John Kennedy's candidacy, but he told Robert Kennedy that as long as Stevenson "refused to take himself out, I felt bound by ties of loyalty to help no one else." Martin said that Robert Kennedy understood his situation, as "all the Kennedys understood loyalty," and Martin informed him the day after the convention nominated his brother, which Martin predicted it would do, he would go to work for John Kennedy. Robert Kennedy arranged for Martin to have Sunday breakfast alone in New York with his brother to share his intentions for the fall campaign.[39]

In June Martin met again with Robert Kennedy and afterward produced a ten-page memorandum with suggestions, based on his experience with Stevenson in 1952 and 1956, on how a speechwriting group for a presidential campaign should be organized. From the outset, he warned Kennedy that no matter how carefully advance preparations were made, a campaign was "a fast-developing constantly changing affair, and so

most speeches that get delivered are, with a few exceptions . . . written almost immediately before delivery. Therefore, a certain amount of helter-
skelter confusion is inevitable." In addition to establishing a competent
research staff at campaign headquarters, which Martin assumed would
be in Washington, D.C., he said that when it came to speechwriters,
too many "writers-in-residence are an embarrassment, and they tend to
talk, not write." He advised having no more than six full-time writers
on the campaign staff, with two based at headquarters producing major
speeches a week in advance of their delivery by the candidate. Another
two writers should travel with the candidate, revising speech drafts "in
the light of current developments." These writers, noted Martin, often
might have to set aside a prepared speech and produce a new one at
a moment's notice. "It will probably turn out that a great deal of what
actually gets delivered will be written by these writers who travel with
the candidate, particularly as the pace increases toward the end of the
campaign," he said.[40]

The final two speechwriters, whom he described as "legmen and
writers," would be responsible for the position Martin pioneered while
with Stevenson in the 1956 California primary: editorial advance. They
would be responsible for talking to local political leaders and other
sources to find out what should be discussed in a speech, what local
luminaries to mention, what kind of crowd to expect, what the physical surroundings would be, and "what the local pitfalls and beartraps
are," Martin explained. Although it might not seem so at first, the work
of these writers "is extraordinarily important," he said, as a candidate
could not deliver a thoughtful speech on a difficult subject if he had been
scheduled to appear at, for example, a boiler factory. If the editorial advance men did not do their jobs well, "the headquarters writer may dump
the candidate into this trap." Martin also counseled Kennedy to be open
to accepting speech drafts from writers who were not part of the staff,
particularly during the end of the campaign. "At that time everybody
is exhausted, running out of ideas, running dry on language; and it is
extremely helpful during the last two weeks of October to be able to call
on somebody wholly new," Martin said. Just a few days after receiving
Martin's memo, Kennedy responded, saying what he had provided was
"very helpful and much appreciated. It brought back some vivid memo-

ries of the [Stevenson] campaign." Kennedy also added that his brother was "very enthusiastic" when he told him Martin might work on a draft of an acceptance speech to be given in Los Angeles.[41]

As Martin conferred about campaign strategy with the Kennedy brothers that June, he put politics aside for the moment to host a visit by his parents, J. W. and Laura Martin, and Aunt Verl Garrison, who came to Highland Park to be on hand for Cindy Martin's graduation from high school. Over the years Martin had repaired his relationship with his father and had come to "like and understand him," and J. W. took great pride in his son's accomplishments as a writer, as well as his association with such nationally known figures as Stevenson and John Kennedy. With his contracting firm on solid financial ground, J. W. had sold the family's former home on Brookside Avenue and had moved to a Lannon stone house at 208 East Kessler Boulevard on the north side of Indianapolis. During his visit to his son's home, J. W. reluctantly shared with him that he had not been feeling well, and Martin, with difficulty, persuaded him to see his physician, Doctor Sunoll Blumenthal, who had taken over the practice of Martin's previous doctor, Sylvan Robertson. After examining the senior Martin, Blumenthal discovered he had experienced a "heart episode" and urged him to go to the hospital for further tests. "He refused," said Martin. "I tried to persuade him. He was adamant." Martin could tell that his father feared a prolonged hospital stay or, worse, being confined in a nursing home. "Can you imagine that big strong man in a nursing home?" Martin asked. On the morning he left for home, J. W. shrugged off his illness, ate a big breakfast, called out in a booming voice, "Anybody going to Indianapolis?" and drove off in his car with his wife and sister-in-law.[42]

During the Fourth of July weekend Martin had taken his family to their camp at Three Lakes in Michigan's Upper Peninsula. Four days later, at dawn, Martin heard a knock on their screen door. He could see their best friend, Earl Numinen, his face "as gray as the presunrise dawn," standing at the door. Over the years Numinen had become good friends with J. W., and he had reciprocated, telling his son, "I like that Earl Numinen," which was about the highest compliment his father had ever given anyone, noted Martin. Numinen broke the news to Martin that J. W. had died the previous night. Martin later learned from his mother that in the middle of the night J. W. had half raised himself from the bed, looked over at her, and said, "poor dearie," a term of endearment he often used for her, and fell back in the bed, dead from a heart attack. That day Martin drove his family the approximately six hundred miles to Indianapolis, mindful of what his father had once told him: "'More demmed fools get killed goin' to funerals' – grief stricken, they become heedless." After the funeral, Martin and Fran stayed on in Indianapolis, helping his mother and convincing her to stay in the Kessler Boulevard house, offering financial assistance if she needed any help; she remained there until her death ten years later.[43]

On July 11, the day Martin buried his father at Indianapolis's Crown Hill Cemetery, the Democratic National Convention began in Los Angeles. Although Kennedy and his supporters were urging the 4,509 delegates and alternates gathered at the Sports Arena that it was "time for a new generation of leadership," the old guard seemed unwilling to depart the stage. Former president Harry Truman said Kennedy lacked "maturity and experience," and Johnson had announced six days before the convention opened that he, too, would seek the nomination. Those wishing to stop Kennedy from winning the nomination – Johnson, Symington, and Stevenson – believed that if they could prevent a first-ballot nomination, many delegates would abandon the Kennedy cause and look to one of them as the Democratic Party's nominee. There were signs, however, that Kennedy was quite close to obtaining the 761 delegates needed to win the nomination, as both the vital Pennsylvania and Illinois delegations had broken in his favor, with Stevenson's home state pledging him only two delegates to fifty-nine for Kennedy. Those working on Kennedy's behalf were optimistic that even if he failed on the first ballot, their candidate had enough strength to eventually win the nomination. Although there were wild, clamorous demonstrations on the convention floor and in the galleries on Stevenson's behalf, the outpourings of emotion for the party's two-time presidential candidate failed to change the outcome, and Stevenson himself did little to push the issue, a grave disappointment to his devoted supporters. Late on Wednesday evening, July 13, near the end of the roll call vote, Wyoming pledged its fifteen delegates to Kennedy, clinching for him the nomination.[44]

From the beginning of Robert Kennedy's approach to him about being part of his brother's speechwriting team, Martin had expressed some uneasiness. It seemed to him that Theodore Sorenson, who had joined John Kennedy's staff as his chief legislative aide when he started his work in the U.S. Senate in 1953, had already become Kennedy's main writer through his close contact with the senator as the two of them had traveled around the country for the past several years wooing local party leaders. "Bob said that situation would have to change – Sorensen simply could not, in a presidential campaign, remain the only one [speechwriter], and he intended to persuade Jack of this," said Martin. At the campaign's outset there did seem to be a division of labor that followed the model Martin had outlined in his memo to Robert Kennedy.[45]

Shortly after the convention ended, Archibald Cox, a Harvard University law professor who had headed an academic advisory group for John Kennedy before his nomination, met with the candidate at his home in Georgetown. Kennedy asked him if he "would spend full time heading up a unit which would be sort of an intellectual apparatus, preparing speeches," Cox recalled. "And he was very candid in talking about Ted Sorensen and Ted Sorensen's fear that somebody was going to elbow his way in between him and Kennedy, and did I think I could get on with Ted Sorensen. And I didn't see why not, that I could think of only one person in my life that I hadn't been able to get on with at all. So why shouldn't I be able to get on with Sorensen?" Cox established a speechwriting and research team based at 1737 L Street in Washington, D.C., and he hired a staff that included William Atwood, a former Stevenson speechwriter and editor at *Look* magazine; Joseph Kraft, a former reporter with the *New York Times* and *Washington Post*; James Sundquist, a former Truman speechwriter; and Robert Yoakum, a newspaper columnist. The plan, said Kraft, was to try to set up in advance "certain fixed speeches, and he [Cox] assigned those out as soon as we got there. The idea was that these would be done in August before the Senator went on the road." Longtime Kennedy assistant Myer "Mike" Feldman headed the research team, housed in the same building as Cox's group, and collected reams of material on their Republican opponent, Vice President Nixon. Sorensen and his chief assistant, Richard N. Goodwin, who had joined the Kennedy staff in the fall of 1959 after working as special counsel for a congressional investigation of improprieties in tele-vision quiz shows, handled speechwriting chores for Kennedy while he traveled on his private plane, a Convair 240 series twin-engine propel-ler aircraft named *Caroline* in honor of his daughter. The plush, for the times, sixteen-seat aircraft did yeoman work during the 1960 presidential campaign, transporting the candidate, his staff, and selected members of the press on flights totaling 225,000 miles.[46]

The Kennedy team did not forget Martin's editorial advance idea. They sent Goodwin to Highland Park to talk to Martin about issues and positions for the fall campaign, as well as informing him that John Kennedy wanted to try out his system during a whistle-stop trip down California's Central Valley in mid-September. Before joining the cam-paign, Martin traveled to Philadelphia to share his plans with his editors at the *Post*, Stuart Rose and Ben Hibbs, who offered no objections. Mar-tin then went to California, spending a week there doing legwork and writing briefing sheets in advance of Kennedy's visit. Once done on the West Coast, he journeyed to Detroit to do the same thing for Kennedy in Michigan. "On Labor Day, I stood in the crowd in Cadillac Square, watching Kennedy speak, as I had watched Stevenson speak," Martin said, "and I was struck by how much more forceful, even aggressive, Ken-nedy was. He seemed to assume this labor crowd was with him, and if it wasn't he would convert it, and he did, to cheers." Martin accompanied Kennedy aboard the Southern Pacific's New Frontier Special (named for the theme Kennedy had outlined in his acceptance speech at the con-vention) as it hauled the fifteen-car campaign train for its two-day trip through the Central Valley, with stops in Redding, Sacramento, Rich-mond, Roseville, Oakland, Bakersfield, and ending with a Democratic rally jammed with seven thousand supporters and another two thousand waiting outside the Shrine Auditorium in Los Angeles. At each of the whistle-stops, Kennedy gave a five-minute speech from a platform at the train's rear, and before each one Martin supplied him with the briefing sheet he had prepared for the occasion. Kennedy liked what Martin had done with the briefing sheets he provided and asked him to continue doing so throughout the rest of the campaign.[47]

In the end, Martin spent about half of his time out ahead of Ken-nedy doing his editorial advance work and the rest of the time with the candidate on the *Caroline*. There was plenty of work for the speechwriters, noted Sorensen, as Kennedy spoke eight to ten times a day, sometimes in four or five states. In one week of eighteen- to twenty-hour days, the candidate visited twenty-seven states. On the first full campaign weekend alone Kennedy visited Massachusetts, New Hampshire, Maine, California, Alaska, and Michigan. Looking at the packed schedule for the next few months up to Election Day, Martin realized he could never do all the briefing sheets by himself, so he trained Kraft, whom he described as "very bright, a good writer, a good reporter," to do the work. Kraft, who got on well with both Sorensen and Goodwin, turned out to be an excellent pupil, and he joined Martin in the editorial advance assignment the second week of the campaign during a tour of Texas.[48]

Kraft had been a Kennedy supporter since seeing him at a meeting of Maryland Democrats in January 1960, so when he received the call from Cox to join his "speech factory," he was glad to offer his assistance. After doing the editorial advance work in Texas, Kraft returned to Los Angeles with the idea that he would be shuttling back and forth from the Cox group to the speechwriting team (Sorensen, Goodwin, and Martin) with Kennedy on the campaign trail. "I never went back to the Cox factory," Kraft recalled. "I stayed doing the advances and largely being on the plane all the way through the campaign." He and Martin played leapfrog, with one of them doing advance work in a state, then accompanying the candidate as he made his campaign appearances there, while the other writer did the same in a different state. Kraft said both Martin and Sorensen advised him on people to see, and reporters in the area also offered suggestions. There were some difficulties in the beginning for Kraft, particularly during his first trip into Texas, where he remembered Kennedy saying to him after one visit, "You can't leave me naked here like that." An appearance in Lubbock, Texas, had turned into a near-disaster because Kraft failed to tell Kennedy how to pronounce the name of the town. "He knew about the German town on the Baltic [Sea] and started out . . . saying, 'It's great to be here in Lubeck.'" Kraft, however, soon developed a better feel for his position, and it became easier and more routine for him. "A large part of my job was getting to know Sorensen and Goodwin, getting to relax with them, getting to relax with the Senator," Kraft noted. "He [Kennedy] really liked a relaxed relationship, and you had to know him a little bit in order to achieve it. I only achieved it with time." The editorial advance system meshed well with the candidate, said Kraft, as Kennedy proved to be adept "at taking a fast briefing, just very, very good at switching gears and picking up something."[49]

In addition to finding an editorial advance partner in Kraft, Martin had discovered by the end of the California trip that he had a candidate for president he truly believed in. He had begun his work with some misgivings about Kennedy, a man younger than he was and who appeared to be "a totally different man from Stevenson, and I had admired Stevenson so long. Transferring political loyalty is not easy." Sometimes when he watched Kennedy delivering a speech, Martin felt nostalgic for Stevenson's "graceful prose." He soon realized, however, that Kennedy was far more effective than Stevenson had been in rallying the country behind his candidacy and, unlike the man from Illinois, spent less time agonizing about the content of his speeches and more time meeting with local politicians. Kennedy also did not mind repeating the same stump speech over and over again. In working for Stevenson, his speechwriters had placed their emphasis on good writing, Martin observed, while for Kennedy, the emphasis was placed on the speech's political effect. "His speeches did not soar and capture the imagination as had Stevenson's 1952 speeches," Martin said of Kennedy, "but they got his message across – that he was young, vigorous, and could get this country moving again." Kennedy, who rarely followed the prepared text word for word, did not seem to mind whether or not people admired him for his oratorical skills, but he did care "a great deal about whether his speeches made people want to follow him, to vote for him," Martin noted. The candidate also had a keen ear on what language worked in a speech and what failed to move audiences. "When a line proved successful at one stop," recalled Sorensen, "whether planned or improvised, he [Kennedy] used it at the next and many times thereafter." Ironically, Stevenson perfectly captured the difference between Kennedy and himself when, introducing the candidate at a rally, he had pointed out that in classical times when Cicero finished speaking people remembered how well he spoke, but when Demosthenes finished speaking people were moved to take action. "It was so apt it stung," Martin recalled. In the end, Martin found Kennedy much easier to work with than Stevenson, as he maintained an even keel during the campaign's rigors and proved to be far more accessible. "He took advice more readily, made decisions faster," Martin said. "He wasted no time. He used his staff well."[50]

Connecting with the candidate was not the only hurdle Martin had to face during the campaign. He also had to forge a relationship with Sorensen, who zealously guarded his closeness with Kennedy and wrote, rewrote, or reviewed every speech. When he had first gone aboard the candidate's plane, Martin recalled that Sorensen had taken him aside to remind him, "A Kennedy speech has to have class." In a memorandum to speechwriters he distributed in late July 1960, Sorensen had established the basic theme for campaign speeches that included "the action, summoning every segment of our society; the result, to restore America's relative strength as a free nation; and the purpose, in order to regain our security and leadership in a fast-changing world menaced by communism." He continued that a speech should leave the audience the general impression that a Kennedy administration, unlike a Nixon one, could "be trusted to 'get things done' on all the new problems that are coming up on 'the new frontier' of the '60's . . . through specific steps that require effort by all the people as well as vigorous Presidential leadership, characterized by both courage and compassion." Sorensen and Kennedy had developed such a symbiotic relationship that they communicated "almost by shorthand," said Martin. He remembered how when the *Caroline* stopped for brief appearances at local airports, Kennedy, who viewed Sorensen as "indispensable," paused before his speech for a word or two from Sorensen, who would "look up at him [Kennedy] and utter a sentence or two, suggesting a speech theme, and Kennedy would think, nod, remember, and go out and deliver it." Some of the most eloquent campaign prose in his time came from Kennedy, said Martin, who particularly admired the ending of his speeches, which he compared to parables. And when the candidate spoke about such weighty issues as foreign affairs, he did not seem to be tentative and burdened as Stevenson had been. Instead, Kennedy appeared to know "exactly where we should go and how we should get there," said Martin.[51]

Sentiment played no role during the campaign. "The Kennedys played with a hard ball," said Martin. He remembered how Sorensen sat outside the door to the senator's private cabin on the *Caroline,* "the keeper of the portal," personally approving anyone who entered. "It was a no-nonsense campaign, work to be done, no time wasted on people's feelings," said Martin. He had received a call from his old friend Schlesinger, offering his speechwriting assistance on Kennedy's travels. Martin passed the request along to Sorensen, but he nixed the idea, believing the candidate might be criticized by the Republicans (in his speeches Nixon had denounced the Democrats as "the party of Galbraith and Schlesinger and [Chester] Bowles) and the press as being a captive of the liberal Americans for Democratic Action, a group with which Schlesinger had long been associated. "It was a hardboiled political decision," said Martin. Schlesinger said he had offered to do anything the candidate wanted, including joining him on tour, and Sorensen had reacted by telling him he wanted him to do some major speech drafts, but "it was evident that he wished them done at a distance." Sorensen and Goodwin had "managed to maintain a stranglehold on the speech situation," Schlesinger said, including blocking for the most part speeches from the Cox group. Cox tried to funnel ideas through Kraft, but it never worked. "A lot of it was spitballing, it had to be spitballed. It would have been impossible really to integrate the Cox operation with the plane operation," said Kraft. "In a sense it would have been like trying to funnel Niagara into a hose." It was not, Cox recalled, a "happy time" in his life. Goodwin did note that the material provided by the Cox group made a valuable contribution during the campaign, as it became a sort of traveling library he carried along on the *Caroline* in a Sears and Roebuck footlocker and a suitcase. "I don't know what the hell we would have talked about without it," Goodwin said.[52]

The pragmatic Martin must have passed muster with Sorensen, as he became, as Kraft noted, the only person closely associated with writing for Stevenson to be a regular part of the Kennedy speechwriting team on the plane. Sorensen had complained that at times the candidate believed the material arriving from the Cox group in Washington, D.C., had not been "responsive to what he wanted." Still, Kennedy, Sorensen said in his memoirs, had insisted that he find some way to accommodate the speeches Cox and his group produced. "I very much wanted to do so," said Sorensen. "But Archie was many miles away, out of touch with the ever-changing tempo of the campaign." The same could not be said of the information provided by the able editorial advance team of Martin and Kraft, who were, Sorensen noted, collecting local color, opinion, and commentary, as well as providing "draft introductions, notes, conclusions, and themes for the final speeches to be delivered by the candidate. We almost always made good use of their material." Pierre Salinger, who handled press relations for the Kennedy campaign, noted that Martin's local speech inserts were often given more attention by the community's reporters than were the central theme of the candidate's remarks.[53]

Amidst the endless toil of the campaign trail, there were some light-hearted moments, particularly at the expense of Kennedy's opponent. On September 26, Kennedy and Nixon faced off in the first-ever tele-vised debate, which was witnessed by an estimated seventy million people; by this time 88 percent of American families owned television sets. "We knew the first televised debate was important," said Sorensen, "but we had no idea how important it was going to turn out." Kennedy, tanned from campaigning outdoors, refused makeup, as did Nixon ini-tially. Nixon's advisers, however, realized something needed to be done and used some shave stick to cover up his five o'clock shadow. It did not work; viewers could see on their television sets a tanned, calm, and confident Kennedy, while Nixon, who had injured his knee during the campaign slamming it on a car door, appeared ill and sweaty under the harsh glare of the television lights. Theodore H. White, whose book on the campaign, *The Making of the President, 1960*, became an instant clas-sic, was astounded about the contrast between the two candidates' faces, with Nixon appearing "tense, almost frightened, at turns glowering and, occasionally haggard-looking to the point of sickness."[54]

On election night, November 8, Martin and his wife were at the Kennedy compound in Hyannis Port, Massachusetts, where they spent a long and tense evening watching and waiting to see if their candidate won. Campaign staffers converted Robert Kennedy's house, next to his father's mansion and across the back lawn from John Kennedy's cot-tage, into a "communications and vote analysis center that included an array of telephones staffed by fourteen operators to keep in touch with party leaders and poll watchers from across the country." The operators, all women, were kept quite busy that night. Although the ballot counting went on into December, Kennedy won a narrow 112,803-vote victory over Nixon out of the nearly sixty-nine million votes cast; the Democrat's margin was greater in the Electoral College, where he had 303 votes to 219 for Nixon. The vice president had captured more states (twenty-six to twenty-three) than Kennedy, but the Democrat's strategy of focusing on the more populous states had paid off, as he won Illinois, Texas, Michigan, Pennsylvania, and New York. Kennedy's controversial choice of Johnson for vice president proved to be a fortunate one, as the Democrats won back some of the southern states they had lost to Eisenhower in previous elections, with the big prize being Johnson's home state of Texas. The Kennedy-Johnson ticket also won in North Carolina, South Carolina, Georgia, Louisiana, Arkansas, and Missouri.[55]

On his third try, Martin had finally been on the winning side of a presidential contest. He spent less time in celebrating Kennedy's victory, however, than in pondering what his time with the campaign had done to him. In a sense, he said, he had "grown up politically" during his work for Kennedy. Looking back on Stevenson's 1952 presidential campaign, and even during his time as governor of Illinois, Stevenson had maintained, according to Martin, a particular "amateur attitude toward politics," an attitude most certainly not shared by the Democratic candidate in 1960. "From him [Kennedy] and his staff and his campaign strategy, I learned hard politics. And this was backed up by what I had learned writing about politics," Martin noted. For the first time, he began thinking of himself as, while not a professional politician, "at least no longer an amateur." The only regret Martin had after Kennedy had been confirmed as the nation's thirty-fifth president and he and Fran had been on hand in Washington, D.C., for the inauguration, was that his father had not lived just a few months longer to see another Democrat in the White House. And, as Franklin D. Roosevelt had been the president of his father's life, Kennedy became the president with whom Martin most identified.[56]

SEVEN

The Honorable Ambassador

NAMED FOR THE COUNT OF PEÑALVA, EL CONDE STREET IN Santo Domingo in the Dominican Republic is a cobblestone pedestrian road that stretches from the Parque Colón to the Parque Independencia. On the morning of March 8, 1962, young demonstrators, angry that two alleged enemies of the people had been allowed refuge on American soil, ranged up and down this popular shopping district, smashing windows, wrecking storefronts, and looting merchandise. Spying a car belonging to the new U.S. ambassador, whose driver had gone to a Spanish tailor's shop to pick up a white linen suit for the diplomat to wear when he officially presented his credentials the following day at the National Palace, the mob pulled the driver from his seat, then smashed and burned the automobile. They went on to torch two other vehicles belonging to the U.S. government and attacked the school the ambassador's two sons attended. The boys watched from their upstairs classroom window as the demonstrators, brandishing chains and manhole covers, tore down the American flag and wrecked the school's first floor before finally being driven away by two truckloads of Dominican soldiers armed with machine guns. Realizing the danger, adults at the school quickly hustled the boys away from the scene, and they escaped unscathed.[1]

The next day, March 9, John Bartlow Martin, relieved that his sons, Dan and Fred, had escaped harm, presented his credentials as the first American ambassador to the Dominican Republic since the assassination nearly ten months earlier of the country's brutal dictator, Rafael Trujillo. For years as a freelance journalist and speechwriter for political candidates, Martin had preferred to remain out of the limelight, re-fusing to make many speeches, explaining to those who asked, "I do not like to present myself." Now he had to. Surviving a brief slip on the polished marble floors as he started up the palace's broad interior stairs, and conscious of his uncomfortable white linen suit that "felt like ply-wood armor," Martin shook hands with Rafael Bonnelly, president of the Consejo de Estado, the Council of State that now ruled the Dominican Republic, and proclaimed, "Mr. President, I have the honor to present my credentials as the Ambassador of the United States to the Dominican Republic." Bonnelly introduced him to the other six "presidents" of the council. Next came an elaborate diplomatic ballet of Martin introduc-ing his staff to the council, and before it was over "some of us," noted Martin, "Dominicans and Americans, were half-smiling; yet though it was awkward, even foolish, it was touching too." Although Bonnelly did not formally apologize for the mob's burning of the ambassador's car, he did express his regret about the incident, and after a formal protest from the United States, the Dominican government paid to replace the vehicle. Returning after the ceremony to the residence at the U.S. Em-bassy, Martin, with his wife, Fran, read his copy of the credentials he had presented. More like a form letter and using diplomatic language seemingly dating from another century, it expressed President John F. Kennedy's confidence in Martin's ability to advance the interests of both his country and that of the Dominican Republic. Martin remarked to his wife, "I hope he's right."[2]

Martin's long journey from his comfortable home in a Chicago sub-urb to the turmoil of a newly democratic and unstable Caribbean nation had begun more than a year earlier, after Kennedy's presidential inaugu-ration on January 20, 1961. At that time Washington, D.C., appeared to be "suffused with an atmosphere of youth, of vigor, of hope," said Martin, a transformation he credited to the young president. The new administra-tion included many people Martin had known during his days with Adlai Stevenson's two unsuccessful presidential campaigns and his time as a Kennedy speechwriter. Although bitterly disappointed at being passed over for the secretary of state position that had gone instead to Dean Rusk, Stevenson had accepted a job as the U.S. ambassador to the United Nations. Stevenson's law partners also joined the administration, with

Newton Minow serving as chairman of the Federal Communications Commission, Bill Wirtz as undersecretary of labor, and Bill Blair as ambassador to Denmark. Theodore Sorensen, Pierre Salinger, Richard Goodwin, Arthur Schlesinger Jr., and Kenny O'Donnell were on the White House staff, while Robert F. Kennedy joined his brother's cabinet as attorney general. "Never before had I known so many important people in an administration," said Martin. "It was an aspect of political campaigning to which I had given no thought."[3]

After the turmoil of the campaign season, Martin had relaxed with Fran by vacationing in Puerto Rico, a trip paid for by a public relations company promoting the commonwealth. The firm hoped Martin might write about his experiences there for the *Saturday Evening Post.* "I checked with the *Post* then went," he said. Martin found no story there, which did not bother his hosts, as they were patient; Martin did later write some articles about Puerto Rico. When he and Fran were about to leave, he suggested that on their way home they should visit the Dominican Republic – a place Martin had not been to since the winter of 1937–38, on a trip with his first wife, Barbara. "I had always wanted to go [back]," Martin noted, "for I had liked the Dominican Republic and its people better than any other in the Caribbean, but, since I had published my anti-Trujillo piece [in *Ken* magazine] I had not thought it entirely safe." Although Trujillo continued to maintain an iron grip on the country and its people, Martin thought he might be safe because of his connection to the Kennedy administration. He took no chances, however, writing letters to Schlesinger and Sorensen in the White House giving them his detailed itinerary and letting them know when he and Fran expected to return. Because he entered the country as a journalist and expected Trujillo's secret police to search his hotel room, he kept carbon copies of his letters to the White House in his briefcase, hoping to forestall any reprisals for his previous supposed transgressions against the dictator.[4]

The Martins spent a week in the Dominican Republic, visiting tourist sites and, more quietly, talking to people and getting their insights and opinions about Trujillo's reign. The entire country, especially its capital, Ciudad Trujillo (Trujillo City), named by the dictator after himself, appeared to be "unusually tense," according to Martin. Upon his safe return to the United States, Martin produced a memorandum about Trujillo, the country, the effect of economic and diplomatic sanctions imposed on Trujillo by the Organization of American States after the dictator had dispatched agents to assassinate Venezuelan president Rómulo Betancourt, and the possibility of subversion inspired or instigated by Fidel Castro's communist government in Cuba. Once he finished the memo, Martin sent it off to Schlesinger.[5]

Refreshed by his trip, Martin returned to producing well-researched stories for such national magazines as the *Post* and *Look,* including a four-part series on how the Midwest had changed in the years since the end of World War II and an in-depth examination of an obviously disturbed young New Jersey man who had murdered someone after receiving little or no help from his school and a state hospital. They were good stories, Martin noted, but he realized that he had begun to repeat himself; the Midwest series seemed to mirror what he had done on Muncie, Indiana, so long ago for *Harper's* magazine. "It was getting too easy, too expectable," he said. "I have always worked best when I worked against a resistance, writing something new, something hard." Martin began wondering if it was perhaps time for him to take a risk with his career. This restlessness might have been fueled in part by an offer broached by Schlesinger, who asked him if he might be interested in serving as ambassador to Switzerland. A startled Martin said he knew little about that country but believed it was "a rather dull place." He also demurred about serving as America's top diplomat in Morocco, whose ruler, he noted, still cut off the hands of thieves – "not a pleasant prospect." Undisturbed at his friend's rebuffs, Schlesinger advised him to take time and think more about the job offers, as it was hard to find capable people to staff the new administration.[6]

Although he had turned down two diplomatic posts in Kennedy's New Frontier, Martin did make contributions to the administration, including writing speeches for Robert Kennedy and Blair. His most lasting involvement, however, came in work he did for his good friend Minow in his role as the new FCC chairman. Martin helped craft a phrase that has entered the American lexicon and that Minow expects to be in the first sentence of his obituary when he dies. Minow had at first turned down an offer for a job in the Kennedy administration, but he had agreed to help the president's brother-in-law, Sargent Shriver, recruit people to fill the many open positions in the new government. Minow did make it known that the only job he might be interested in was FCC chairman because of his interest in the television industry, and to his "great surprise" he became Kennedy's first appointment to a federal regulatory body. Established by Congress in 1934, the FCC had the power to issue broadcast licenses in the "public interest, convenience, or necessity," but for many years had been lax in its oversight and sometimes corrupt in its practices. Minow believed that broadcasters had not been meeting their public interest obligations as outlined in their licenses to use the airwaves. In March 1961 he was preparing to make his inaugural speech as the head of the FCC to industry executives at the thirty-ninth annual convention of the National Association of Broadcasters, the industry's trade association, set for May 9 in Washington, D.C. Broadcasters were expecting the worst, as Minow had said at his confirmation hearings before the U.S. Senate that the FCC should have a role in "encouraging better programs" and had expressed a determination "to do something about it." If a television network decided to put a "lousy Western" on the air it was none of the government's business, Minow told the senators, but if a network "put on nothing else for three years, then it is." He also had two attributes that made him eminently qualified for the job: he had no interest in being reappointed and sought no job in the television industry after leaving government employment.[7]

According to Minow, Martin approached him and volunteered to produce a speech draft. "I wouldn't have imposed on him," Minow said years later. Before Minow took over the FCC, Martin recalled, the two men "discussed the office, and I promised to help him with his speeches if I could." Martin realized the importance of the NAB speech for Minow and the FCC, as the commission alone had the power to reform television. He wrote Minow in March that he expected to have some ideas to pass along to him in a few weeks and suggested he refrain from leaking any information about what he intended to say to reporters, including Jack Gould, a noted television critic for the *New York Times* whom Minow admired. "I suggest you store everything up until May then drop the bomb," wrote Martin. Minow responded by thanking Martin for his assistance and said the staff at the FCC had all become great fans of Martin. The great debate among them, Minow added, was whether Martin resembled Ernie Pyle or Abraham Lincoln.[8]

Before volunteering to aid Minow in his effort to give the television industry a much-needed jolt, Martin had for several months been researching and writing a series for the *Post* on the state of American commercial television, a business that had grown by leaps and bounds since the end of World War II. In 1946 in the United States, eight thousand homes had television sets, but by the time Kennedy took office as president that number had skyrocketed to forty-seven million homes; nearly nine out of ten households had one or more television sets and the average American spent six hours a day watching programs. Advertisers had taken notice of television's penetration into family life and had spent more than $1.5 billion on commercials in 1959. Minow noted that the public seemed to spend more time with television "than it does on anything else except working and sleeping."[9]

To gain a sense of television's quality and its effect on American society, Martin decided to spend almost an entire day, twenty hours, watching television. He woke up at 5:30 AM, ate a hasty breakfast, tuned his family's television set to Chicago's WNBQ Channel 5, sat down, and kept his eyes glued to the set until the NBC station ended its broadcast day at 1:52 AM. "The channel and the day were chosen at random," Martin noted. After watching Dave Garroway on the *Today* show, Martin was besieged by a seemingly endless slate of "game shows," programs that had disappeared for a time after the quiz show scandals of 1959. "Now they are back," he said. By the end of the morning Martin had also seen approximately seventy commercials advertising such products as soap, detergents, lipstick, orange juice, salad dressing, baby food, hair cream, hair spray, vitamins, soup, headache remedies, bleach, frozen food, appliances, and patent medicines. "The commercials, loud and frequent and long, seemed stupefying," he said. In the afternoon, after watching television for nine straight hours, Martin observed that except for news broadcasts and two brief interviews on the *Today* program, "nobody on Channel 5 had discussed a single idea." He persevered, enduring such banal hit programs as *Sing Along with Mitch* and *The Jack Paar Show*, as well as the violence of a show called *Official Detective*, which featured several fistfights, three shootings, four killings, and a suicide. "After Paar,"

Martin laconically noted, "it was a pleasure." All in all, he wrote in a draft for his *Post* article, what he had seen had been "a vast wasteland of junk." Obviously, Martin added, no one would normally watch television as he had done, just as few people would sit down and in one day read an entire issue, cover to cover, of a magazine such as the *Post*. "Nonetheless," he said, "this is what was sent over the airwaves by one television station, owned by a leading network in a big city. The station is licensed by the Government to use the people's air; this is how it used it that day."[10]

On April 8 Martin sent Minow a first rough draft of his proposed NAB speech, which he admitted might be "too tough" on the industry. He also shared the draft with Schlesinger, asking him, if he had the time, to "mark it up and return it to me or to Newt direct." In his letter to Minow, Martin said the broadcasters expected the new FCC chairman to "tell them to clean house or you'll do it for them. I would do it – but at the same time not do it." Instead, Martin advised Minow to take a conciliatory tone, because if he "hit them on the nose" it might have a negative effect on the new NAB president LeRoy Collins, the former governor of Florida, who had been a supporter of reform in the industry. Martin advised elevating the controversy between the industry and its critics by calling the broadcasters attention not only to their "mundane failings – too much violence – but to the larger context of intercontinental TV. At present the broadcasters' main concern is that there is too much mayhem and sadism on TV. They also bear a great guilt burden because of the quiz-payola scandals. . . . All this seems beneath you. I would like to see you enlarge enormously the whole context of the TV controversy." Minow appreciated Martin's work, writing him on April 17: "I cannot, cannot, cannot thank you enough. I'm deeply moved by your giving me so much of your thought and time, and the country will benefit from it – and so will I!"[11]

In addition to Martin's contribution for his NAB speech, Minow also had assistance from Tedson Meyers, an FCC aide; Stanley Frankel, his brother-in-law and a former newspaper reporter and magazine publisher; and others. Of all the drafts he received, however, "the best one by far" came from Martin, said Minow, who noted he was a much better editor than he was a writer. Minow's editing skill came in handy and ensured him everlasting fame when he cut two words from one of Martin's drafts.

The original draft, which owed much to Martin's experiences watching channel 5, included the following: "I invite you to sit down in front of your television set when your station goes on the air and stay there . . . and keep your eyes glued to that set until the station goes off. I can assure you that you will observe a vast wasteland of junk." According to Martin, Minow "had the wit" to cut "of junk" and retain "vast wasteland," a phrase inspired in part by T. S. Eliot's long poem, "The Waste Land." A good portion of what Martin wrote remained in the forty-minute speech Minow gave before the approximately two thousand broadcasters assembled for lunch at the Sheraton Park Hotel. The part that received the bulk of the media's attention was the following:

> When television is good, nothing – not the theater, not the magazines or newspapers – nothing is better.
>
> But when television is bad, nothing is worse. I invite each of you to sit down in front of your television set when your station goes on the air and stay there, for a day, without a book, without a magazine, without a newspaper, without a profit and loss sheet or a rating book to distract you. Keep your eyes glued to that set until the station signs off. I can assure you that what you will observe is a vast wasteland.
>
> You will see a procession of game shows, formula comedies about totally unbelievable families, blood and thunder, mayhem, violence, sadism, murder, western bad men, western good men, private eyes, gangsters, more violence, and cartoons. And endlessly commercials – many screaming, cajoling, and offending. And most of all, boredom. True, you will see a few things you will enjoy. But they will be very, very few. And if you think I exaggerate, I only ask you to try it.[12]

Minow's speech, which left many broadcasting executives looking like "refugees from an atomic blast," reported one magazine, received attention for all the wrong reasons and was "badly misinterpreted," noted Minow. "Today that speech is remembered for two words – but not the two I intended to be remembered," he later said. "The words we tried to advance were 'public interest.' To me, the public interest meant, and still means, that we should constantly ask: What can television do for our country? For the common good? For the American people?" Minow said he wanted the broadcasters to know that there was a new team in town who really cared about the public interest, and that if television failed in that area they would find themselves in difficulty with the government. At the same time, he added, the FCC stood ready to back television executives if they decided to tackle controversial issues in their programming.[13]

The speech made Minow, noted Martin, a symbol of the "newness and boldness of the Kennedy administration." The overwhelming media attention, however, caused Martin some trouble with his *Post* series on television, as he had to alter his original passage describing television as a "vast wasteland" as not his own summary of what he had seen, but instead quoting Minow as the source of the phrase. For his concluding article for his *Post* series, Martin profiled Minow, his NAB speech, and its aftermath, including one television executive issuing a "call to arms" against the FCC chairman. Nowhere in the article, however, does Martin reveal the key role he played in the "vast wasteland" address. In his memoirs Martin acknowledged that in this instance he had approached a conflict of interest, but he concluded, "It didn't bother me." The *Post*'s flexibility when it came to Martin's connections with the FCC chairman might have been prompted by the threat television posed to its very existence, especially the loss of advertising revenue and circulation as more and more Americans turned to television for their entertainment. Broadcasters and their allies lamented the way print journalists lionized Minow, and they accused print journalists of being overly critical of television out of spite because of the threat the industry posed to their business. Martin took great pains in later years to note that his origination of the "vast wasteland" phrase took nothing away from Minow. "This thing happens all the time," he said, noting that Louis Howe came up with "the only thing we have to fear is fear itself" for President Franklin D. Roosevelt's first inaugural address. "It is the business of holders of high public office to broker ideas to the public; Newt Minow had the wit to recognize a good phrase and the courage to throw it in the teeth of the broadcasters and thus show the public the need for reform," said Martin.[14]

A few weeks after Minow's speech, Martin learned of a dramatic event that changed the course of his career. On May 30 on a road outside of Ciudad Trujillo, then the capital of the Dominican Republic, seven assassins ambushed and killed the dictator. Those directly involved in the dictator's killing, and the other conspirators, had all previously been associated with Trujillo's rule and were inspired in their action by everything from patriotism to revenge. The murder sparked retaliation from Trujillo's relatives and remaining supporters, who tracked down and killed all but two of the assassins. The country slowly plunged into chaos as rival groups, including Trujillo's son, Ramfis, and the dictator's puppet president, Joaquín Balaguer, jockeyed for control. Democratic elements in the Dominican Republic took to the streets to seek the removal of the dictator's family from the country once and for all.[15]

The news of Trujillo's fall from power prompted Martin to ask Fran, while they sat on their home's back porch having a drink, "How would you like to be the wife of the ambassador to the Dominican Republic?" Although he had not spent a lot of time thinking about what Schlesinger had earlier said about being an ambassador, the chance to establish true democracy in the Dominican Republic after thirty-one years of Trujillo's despotism had inspired Martin to start thinking about seeking a diplomatic post. It also marked a chance to be a part of the Kennedy administration's Alianza para el Progreso (Alliance for Progress), a program for economic aid and political reform instituted shortly after Kennedy had taken office to do for countries in Latin America what the Marshall Plan had done for Europe following World War II. Kennedy said the alliance represented a "vast cooperative effort, unparalleled in magnitude and nobility of purpose," to satisfy such basic needs in Latin America as homes, work, land, health, and schools. Also at the back of the president's mind was the fear that the region, ripe for revolution, might embrace communism as Cuba had done when Fidel Castro overthrew pro-American dictator Fulgencio Batista. Kennedy told his aide Richard Goodwin, who worked to fashion many of the alliance's details, that the "whole place could blow up on us," and he considered the region to be, for his administration, the "most dangerous place in the world." In the aftermath of Trujillo's killing, Kennedy saw three possibilities for the Dominican Republic: the development of a democratic regime, a continuation of the government established by Trujillo, or the growth of a Castro-style leadership. "We ought to aim for the first," the president told his aides, "but we can't really renounce the second until we are sure that we can avoid the third."[16]

Martin called Schlesinger to express his interest in becoming the American ambassador to the Dominican Republic, and Schlesinger appeared enthusiastic about the suggestion, but cautioned patience. The Kennedy administration had yet to decide whether or not to send a new ambassador; the United States had cut diplomatic ties with Trujillo on August 26, 1960, and OAS sanctions against the Dominican Republic were still in force following the dictator's assassination. As he later wrote Schlesinger, Martin believed he was particularly equipped for the job because he had a long-standing interest in the country, had written about it, studied it, and visited. "I love it and its people and would like to help it realize its potentialities," wrote Martin. "What is more, it seems to me that if somebody with my experience can serve this country abroad, it is primarily because he can do legwork, can find out what is going on; and the Dominican Republic seems to me to be a place where it could be a good idea to have someone who can do legwork." In June 1961 Martin met with Robert Kennedy, who had become increasingly involved in foreign affairs on his brother's behalf since the Bay of Pigs disaster, at a fund-raising dinner. Before the dinner and after, Martin met with Kennedy in his room to talk about the Dominican post. "In brief," Martin wrote Fran about the meeting, "he was for my appointment and was sure the President would favor it and he would get busy on 'working something out' and we would keep in touch." Kennedy did tell Martin that there existed strong opposition within the government, especially within the State Department, on recognizing the new regime and that nothing would happen anytime soon. Even if the administration decided to send an ambassador, the State Department was certain to have its own candidate in mind for the job. "This is all a long way from happening," Martin wrote. "But I would think that tonight's conversations moved the affair out of the realm of day dreaming and into the possible. I couldn't be more pleased."[17]

Other members of the administration offered their support for Martin, including Chester Bowles, undersecretary of state, who wrote Schlesinger that Martin, whom he knew from Stevenson's 1952 and 1956 presidential campaigns, would make "an excellent ambassador to the Dominican Republic when and if we restore normal relations." Robert Kennedy spoke directly to Rusk about Martin's wishes for a diplomatic assignment, and Kennedy told Martin that the secretary of state appeared to be "enthusiastic about it." Schlesinger informed Martin that

support had been coming in "from even the remote precincts," and jok-
ingly said that "we confidently expect your nomination on the fourth
ballot." When Schlesinger asked Stevenson whether Martin was a good
choice, Stevenson initially said he would have to think about it for a time,
but he eventually wrote a letter of support on Martin's behalf to Rusk.
Sounding particularly Stevensonian, he wrote, "I hear that John Bartlow Martin is under consideration for Ambassador to the Dominican
Republic. I am not sure why anybody would want to be Ambassador to
the Dominican Republic, and John has not approached me personally.
But if he wants to be, I can underline, endorse, recommend, sponsor,
and get madly enthusiastic about his appointment. I don't know whether
you know him, but he's a gifted writer and thoughtful student and perceptive reporter – and a damn good liberal Democrat!" Rusk responded
to Stevenson's correspondence by noting that his enthusiastic support
for Martin placed him in company with Robert Kennedy, George Ball,
Roger Tubby, and others who shared his high opinion of Martin. "I can
assure you that his desires will be given every possible consideration,"
Rusk wrote.[18]

With no decision forthcoming from Washington, in early August
Martin, accompanied by Fran and their sons, traveled to Three Lakes
in Michigan's Upper Peninsula for a vacation. On Friday, September 1,
after a day spent exploring the dense woods in the family's Jeep, Martin's
friends in Michigamme, Earl Numinen and Maurice Ball, greeted him
with the news that President Kennedy had been calling all over town
trying to reach him and wanted him to return the call as soon as possible.
By the time Martin reached the White House, Kennedy had left for the
Labor Day weekend and instead he talked to the president's brother-
in-law, Stephen E. Smith, who said Kennedy wanted Martin to travel
to Washington as soon as he could for discussions on the Dominican
Republic. Upon his arrival, Martin met with Smith and Robert Kennedy,
who told him that the president wanted additional facts to deal with the
OAS sanctions against the Dominican Republic. "The main question
was: Should we urge the OAS to lift its sanctions against the Republic?"
noted Martin. "This, in effect, would mean that we regarded the sanctions as directed against the Generalissimo personally and that, with
him gone, we now accepted his heirs as rulers of the Republic." Kennedy

wanted Martin to travel to the Dominican Republic, learn what he could, and report back to him. Smith gave Martin a sheaf of classified information to study, and when Martin pointed out he had no security clearance, Smith, knowing the urgency of the situation, told him, "You've got Smith clearance – take them."[19]

Martin spent a week going over the material and gaining his bearings in the State Department before traveling to the Dominican Republic, arriving there for his presidential fact-finding mission on September 10 and staying in the country for three weeks. Accompanied by an interpreter, Joseph G. Fandino, a State Department career officer who later married Martin's daughter, Cindy, Martin did most of his work in the Dominican Republic's two major cities, the capital and Santiago. He spoke "adequate" Spanish, but always depended upon an interpreter when conducting official business. Martin did what he had always done in his magazine legwork, talking to all sorts of people – businessmen, working men, doctors, lawyers, militant university students, widows whose husbands had been murdered by the secret police, army officers, government officials, leaders of the underground political parties, and Trujillo's son, Ramfis. Everywhere he went, Martin was besieged by Dominicans pleading with him for visas so they could leave their country for the United States. The wife of a young member of the oligarch, then in prison, spoke for many of her fellow countrymen when she told Martin that Ramfis had been making a great show of democratizing the country but that nothing had really changed. "There's been thirty-one years of murder," she said. "People now don't want any more Trujillo. There's a feeling that if you don't help us, we'll let anyone else do it. But we don't want to." She urged that the OAS sanctions remain in place. Ramfis insisted that only he could control the military, and he expressed surprise at the opposition's impatience with his attempts at democratization. He promised Martin that if a clash came, the opposition, and not his supporters, "would get the worst of it. I see the future as very, very dark."[20]

Trujillo's decades of rule had left the Dominican Republic in shambles, both economically and politically. In Martin's estimation the worst thing the dictator had done was to damage almost beyond repair the Dominican character, destroying the people's confidence in themselves and in each other. "Nobody trusts anybody down there," Martin noted. "They're afraid to talk out loud . . . in restaurants. They whisper. To relatives, a man to his wife." In his years in power Trujillo had unraveled the mutual trust that "creates civilization," Martin said, "the glue that holds society together." The dictator left behind a harmful legacy that affected the Dominican people as they moved toward self-government, and it made things extremely difficult for the Kennedy administration as it attempted to aid the country through the Alliance for Progress. "They have no confidence in themselves because for thirty-one years they looked to the palace for everything, to Daddy [Trujillo]," lamented Martin. "They don't think they can do a thing." The Dominican Republic's history provided little hope for future stability; between 1844 and 1930 the country had had fifty presidents and suffered through thirty revolutions.[21]

Upon his return to the United States Martin produced a 115-page report for the president and State Department outlining what he had discovered and setting out the choices for the administration moving forward: "all bad," he noted. Martin described the Dominican Republic as "a sick, destroyed nation, to be viewed as one ravaged by a thirty-years war, even one to be occupied and reconstituted." Ramfis had begun to enjoy the feeling of power, Martin continued, and he described him as "pretty cold and tough," while Balaguer's moves toward democratization were merely window dressing; the rightist military, not the communist left, posed the greatest danger to establishing democracy in the country. The alternatives Martin proposed to Kennedy were, in a rising order of involvement for the United States: do nothing, an impossible choice given America's interest in establishing a pro-Western, reasonably stable, and free government in an important region; support the regime as it then existed, which would cost the United States "the support of the Dominican people for years to come," Martin noted; or help establish a broad-based provisional government until, with OAS assistance, free elections could be held, and negotiate Ramfis out of his economic power and out of the country. If the last option, the one Martin supported, was selected, the Kennedy administration would also have to be prepared to loan the Dominican Republic funds to get its economy on track and send in numerous civil and military missions to establish order. "It amounted," Martin said of this final choice, "to negotiating the Trujillos out if possible and, if not, throwing them out. I recommended sending a high-level negotiator immediately and sending the fleet to the horizon to back him up." The political risks in this option were extreme for Kennedy because, if the administration tried but failed to establish democracy in the Dominican Republic, it faced the danger of "another Castro in the Caribbean," noted Martin.[22]

On October 5 Martin and a host of administration officials, including Rusk, Goodwin, and Schlesinger, as well as representatives from the Central Intelligence Agency and Alliance for Progress, met with President Kennedy in the Cabinet Room at the White House. As Kennedy came into the room and gestured for those waiting for him to be seated at the long, gleaming, six-sided cabinet table, he saw Martin and said to him, "I've been reading your novel, John." A speed reader, Kennedy had perused Martin's report, according to Schlesinger, "with relish" while he also listened to a World Series game between the New York Yankees and Cincinnati Reds. Kennedy told those gathered that none of the alternatives looked attractive, and he asked questions as they discussed the issue. State Department officials George Ball and George McGhee had worked out a plan whereby the Trujillos would deed their vast land holdings to the Dominican Republic, and in return the United States would help the Dominican government raise the needed funds to pay off the dictator's family. In the end, Kennedy adopted the proposal Martin had recommended and sent McGhee directly from the White House to the airport to put the policy into action. As Martin left the meeting to return home to Highland Park, Kennedy thanked him for his work. "Seeing President Kennedy made you feel good all the rest of the day and for several days thereafter," noted Martin. "There *was* hope. If ever a man was a leader, John F. Kennedy was." Of course, the policy chosen by the president meant that the United States would not be sending an ambassador, Martin or anyone else, to the Dominican Republic for quite some time, a fact he explained to Fran in talking about his trip.[23]

Although negotiations in the Dominican Republic started well and the Trujillos apparently agreed to leave the country, the Dominican armed forces balked and threatened a coup against the Balaguer government. Sporadic rioting broke out and troops began shooting students in the streets, the secret police continued a campaign of terror against those viewed as enemies of the state, and two of Ramfis's uncles returned from "vacations" abroad to take matters into their own hands. Moving swiftly, Kennedy dispatched a fleet of American warships to the country; the fleet sailed just offshore of the capital, ready to support Balaguer if he needed help in stopping a military coup. "The day we sent the fleet," said Martin, "is the only time in our recent history, so far as I can recall, when we threw our weight, including the threat of force, solidly against a rightist dictatorship." After further unrest and military uprisings, including strikes and looting in the capital, Ramfis flew to Paris, followed by the body of his father; Bonnelly succeeded Balaguer as president; the United States and a number of Latin American nations recognized the new Council of State, which took power on January 1, 1962, and was charged with leading the country until democratic elections could be held; and the OAS lifted its sanctions.[24]

As matters reached a climax in the Dominican Republic, Martin pored over reports about the negotiations he had received from his friends in the State Department and White House. The establishment of the Council of State finally gave the American government a chance to do something positive in the Caribbean after the crushing failure of the CIA-sponsored Bay of Pigs operation. Because of Trujillo's damaging influence, the country had no experience with democracy or politics, noted Martin. "They realize this," he said of the Dominicans. "They seek guidance. If we do not provide it, the communists will. Now we have what may be a last chance to teach the moderate Dominicans how to lead." He remembered in particular a conversation he had during his fact-finding mission with a young Dominican lawyer, ignorant of politics, who wanted to form a new political party and had asked him for copies of the U.S. Constitution and political party platforms. When Martin suggested that the lawyer obtain the documents at the library, the Dominican had looked at him "as though I'd lost my mind – didn't I know Trujillo hadn't allowed such subversive material into the Republic?" Appointing an ambassador to the Dominican Republic, Martin added, would show America's moral support for the council and "symbolize our intention to offer it political as well as economic aid. It would give us a fresh start to match the regime's fresh start.... Only an ambassador can make America's purpose clear." Martin wanted to be that ambassador.[25]

With the way now seemingly clear for the Kennedy administration to send a new diplomat, however, Martin received some disappointing news from Ball. The State Department had a candidate of its own, a career Foreign Service officer. Instead of the position in the Caribbean, Ball offered Martin a post as ambassador to the newly independent African nation of Tanganyika (today the United Republic of Tanzania). A frustrated Martin traveled to Washington to personally lobby for the Dominican post with administration officials, talking with Ball and Minow, who advised him to seek help directly from Robert Kennedy. According to Martin, Minow had earlier told Kennedy that Martin badly wanted the Dominican position, and Kennedy had responded, "But John knows he can have any job in this administration he wants." Martin went to Kennedy's office in the Justice Department and arranged to meet with the attorney general. "I've never asked you for anything in my life, Bobby," Martin said in the meeting, "but I want the ambassadorship to the Dominican Republic, and they're about to give it to the [State] Department's candidate." Kennedy looked at him "for a long time," then told Martin he would speak to the president on his behalf. Martin waited in the apartment of his friend, Congressman Sidney Yates of Chicago, to learn about his fate. After six days, he received a call from a deputy undersecretary of state for administration telling him he was being appointed as the U.S. ambassador to the Dominican Republic and he should come to his office to start filling out the necessary paperwork. It marked quite a change for the forty-six-year-old self-employed freelance writer. "I'm going to have a job and a boss – something I haven't had for 25 years," Martin noted.[26]

After being confirmed by the U.S. Senate and sworn into office by McGhee, Martin paid a courtesy call at the White House on President Kennedy, who from the start acknowledged that the new ambassador's job would not be an easy one. The two men discussed the problems facing the Dominican Republic, and Kennedy noted his intent to send Vice President Lyndon B. Johnson to the country for a visit in mid-April (later postponed), warning Martin that he did not want any riots during Johnson's stay. On more than one occasion the president said Martin should let him know directly if he needed anything. As Kennedy showed Martin out the door, he displayed his well-known mordant wit, saying to Martin, "If you blow this, you'd better not come home."[27]

Accompanied by Fran and their sons, Fred, nine years old, and Dan, eleven years old, Martin took a plane to New York, where the family spent the night at Stevenson's embassy residence. The next day, March 4, they flew from New York to the Dominican capital, restored to its historic name, Santo Domingo, where Martin assumed his diplomatic duties on behalf of the United States. "Now I was really on the other side – was no longer a journalist, was in government; was not on the outside looking in, was on the inside looking out; was not writing about politics but making it," Martin reflected. As an ambassador in what the State Department determined to be a Class IV post, the lowest ranking on its scale, Martin received a yearly salary of $20,000, later raised to $22,500 when the department upgraded the posting to Class III status as the embassy and its collateral missions grew to include more than three hundred people. This number included 160 Peace Corps volunteers who were drawn to service in a foreign country hoping to overcome the legacy of American imperialism in the Caribbean. "The Dominican Republic was small, but it was a testing ground," said Martin. "The success of U.S. policy in the Caribbean swung on the Dominican hinge."[28]

In Santo Domingo the Martin family lived at the American embassy residence, a large, white, oblong concrete building of two stories with more than twenty rooms and surrounded by a low stone wall. Knowing of the Dominican Republic's instability, in a closet in his bedroom Martin kept a canister of tear gas and a walkie-talkie for emergencies, as well as a shotgun he owned. "The Dominican Republic (or DR as we called it) was exotic and exciting for the whole family," recalled Fred, who added that both he and his brother were well aware of the country's volatility. "Massively different to anything we boys had ever seen – poor, hot, noisy, colorful, and all life conducted in a foreign language." The boys' parents did their best to include their sons in many of their official duties, which, noted Fred, was "kind of them to do and great fun for us." The boys constructed a shack in the embassy garden that they turned into a miniature fortress complete with a concrete floor, wooden walls, and a palm-thatched roof. There they and their friends, according to Martin, "played guerrilla warfare." The boys, who were quite adept at picking up the Spanish language, also produced a mimeographed newspaper, imaginatively titled the *American Embassy News*, and, according to their mother, kept on hand a "collection of goats, burros, parrots and puppies in the yard and all in all seem to be growing up as normal red-blooded Ambassador's sons should." Although the residence appeared to be well-suited for official functions, Martin considered it "unadorned and bland," and his wife considered it "big and cold and dull." The Martins attempted to add some warmth and color by hanging on its walls pictures they had purchased over the years, as well as adding a revolving display of paintings by Dominican artists. "We are loaded with sun-porches downstairs, and screened porches upstairs, and bathrooms, and guest-suites, and servants' wings, and all that stuff," Fran wrote friends in the United States. "The grounds are absolutely magnificent – much more impressive than the house – with flowering hedges and old stone walls and tremendous trees and a huge swimming-pool which occasionally harbors a small lizard or two." In the mornings, Martin and Fran drank their coffee on the upstairs porch off of their bedroom and before going to bed at night had a drink in the same spot, discussing "what this country could be if we could only get it to work," remembered Martin.[29]

At the residence, the Martins hosted frequent receptions and cocktail parties for 250 to 300 guests at a time, including members of the Dominican government and military, the foreign diplomatic corps, and American businessmen in the country. "I always had my senior staff attend," said Martin, "and before the guests arrived we would meet in my study and divide up the guests – who would talk to whom, what we were trying to find out, whom we were trying to influence." The gatherings were also a way for Martin to placate the restless Dominican military, which recoiled at taking orders from the council and wished for a return to the days of Trujillo when it had enjoyed absolute power. "Scarcely a week passed that rumors did not sweep the capital that the military was plotting a coup," Martin recalled. Coup warnings usually started popping up on Wednesday evenings, he noted, and by Thursday they gained enough traction so that by Friday a credible plot against the government might be afoot. In response, Martin raced around the capital trying to halt the uprising, wondering by Saturday if this would be the one to succeed. By Sunday "you'd get it [the coup] stopped, and then Monday you'd mop up," said Martin, "and then try to rest on Tuesday and Wednesday and then on Thursday you'd start all over." Hoping to stem the tide, and directly authorized to do so by President Kennedy, Martin passed along a warning to military officials that the United States would find it "extremely difficult to recognize and almost impossible to assist any regime which took power by force or threats of force." The presidential caution did work for a time, but tension still existed. At an embassy reception, a Dominican colonel who had downed several drinks let down his guard and scornfully threatened the ambassador, saying to Martin, "You and your little bow tie – we'll show you and your democracy." Quite a "nice group" to deal with, Martin wryly noted.[30]

Martin maintained his office in the little chancery, the embassy office building at the rear of the residence's grounds. There he attempted to keep track of his diplomatic staff and the various American missions scattered all over the capital city, including the Agency for International Development, Peace Corps, U.S. Information Service, and Military Assistance and Advisory Group. He considered some of the career Foreign Service officers "terrible" at their jobs, but others were "first-rate," including Harry W. Shlaudeman, head of the political section, whom Martin described as "imaginative, analytical, precise, yet he had kept a young man's passion." Shlaudeman had a distinguished diplomatic career, serving as American ambassador to Venezuela, Peru, Argentina, Brazil, and Nicaragua before receiving the Presidential Medal of Freedom in 1992. In his office Martin talked privately with key Dominicans and wrote long cables to Washington, D.C. About every six weeks he produced a summary of the situation in the Dominican Republic for the State Department and the White House. He also tried, whenever possible, to improve his staff's writing, banning from any communications two words then fashionable in the State Department: "viable" and "counterproductive." As head of the U.S. mission, Martin signed all outgoing cables and refused to put his signature to what he referred to as "gibberish."[31]

In his early days in the Dominican Republic, Martin coordinated his activities to meet the three main policy objectives of the United States: to keep the Council of State in office, to help the Dominicans hold free and honest elections, and to help the "winner into the Palace alive and on schedule." In his public speeches and privately, Martin attempted to make American policy in the Dominican Republic clear to "the nervous military inherited from Trujillo and to leaders of the

[Catholic] church, oligarchy, business middle class, press, and political parties." Martin realized both he and those Dominicans trying to keep the country from blowing apart were inexperienced. He quickly developed a frank relationship with Bonnelly, whom Martin thought of as "a decent, sensible, patriotic, upright, intelligent man." Bonnelly seemed determined to hold the line against any attempts at overthrowing the government. "He often told me he would never leave the Palace before his term expired, February 27, 1963, unless he was killed," said Martin. "He also told me he would not seek to extend his term. I believed him, though many did not." Meeting with Bonnelly at his modest home just down the street from the embassy, Martin told him, "I've never been an ambassador before." Bonnelly responded, "That's all right – I've never been a President before."[32]

Since Trujillo's assassination, twenty-six Dominican political parties had sprouted into being, ranging from the extremist left to the extremist right. Two of these parties appeared to be the favorites in the upcoming election: the Unión Cívica Nacional (National Civil Union, or UCN), led by Doctor Viriato Fiallo, representing the middle and upper classes, and the Partido Revolucionario Dominicano (Dominican Revolutionary Party, or PRD), considered by many to be to the left of the UCN and representing the lower classes, the *campesinos,* the rural poor. Juan Bosch, a respected writer and anti-Trujillo dissident who had spent many years in exile in pre-Castro Cuba, Venezuela, and Costa Rica, had helped form and now headed the PRD. "Our purpose," Bosch said of his party, "was to organize the great masses of the people and lead them into the political arena, where they could claim and obtain, by democratic procedures, what they had never had – liberty and social justice." The American intelligence community had been wary of Bosch, believing he might be secretly procommunist or even a party member, but a later evaluation of him by the CIA more accurately described him as belonging "to the reformist, nationalistic, democratic left." To each leader of the parties, Martin insisted upon holding elections on schedule, encouraged participation by all, and tried to dissuade them from any extreme measures. "We could live with any of them, at least any that had a chance of winning," he said. As the election campaign progressed, Martin came to regard Bosch as a far superior campaigner to his opponent. "Fiallo probably would make a better president than Bosch," Martin mused. "But the way he is going he will never have an opportunity."[33]

The two main Dominican political parties, as well as the council, seemed helpless when it came to stopping rioting by disenchanted youths and thugs who could receive anywhere from fifty cents to a dollar a day for participating in the disruptions, often paid for by extreme leftist parties, especially those supporting Castro's Cuban brand of communism. "An ordinary *turba* [the local word for a street riot] cost $150," said Martin, "but if one wanted cars burned and store windows smashed, the cost went up to $500." Particularly confusing to the ambassador and his wife were Dominican teenagers who had grown up under Trujillo's tyrannical regime and now "confused liberty with license," said Martin. One of these teens told Fran he liked the Americanos well enough, but he hated the Yanqúis. Cindy had joined her family in the country on summer vacation from Sarah Lawrence College to teach conversational English for three hours a day to Dominican students at the Bi-National Cultural Center. One of her brightest students, a seventeen-year-old who was a member of a far-left political party, told her he had worked hard to make the money for the English lessons. He needed to learn enough English so he could better his life by leaving the Dominican Republic for the United States. Fran remembered that when Cindy asked her promising student how he had earned his wages, he replied, "by being in '*turbas*'. . . most of them directed at the Americans, and some, in particular, at the American Embassy! But it's that kind of illogical country."[34]

When the council refused to crack down on the rioters, Martin urged other methods be used, ones he had seen up close while reporting on crime in Chicago and which would spark protests from any host country if tried by a U.S. diplomat today. "There [in Chicago], if a policeman saw an ex-convict or a known hoodlum on the street, he picked him up 'on suspicion,' took him to the station, held him the legal limit, then released him – only to raid his flat that night, roust him out of bed, and start all over; time after time harassing him, hoping finally to drive him out of town," he recalled. Martin knew these methods amounted to illegal detention and were among the worst abuses of a citizen's constitutional rights, abuses he had railed against as a writer. But now, trying to support a faltering Caribbean government possibly on the brink of being supplanted by Castro-supporting communists, he favored using such unsavory tactics. "The alternatives simply seemed unacceptable – a leftist takeover, a military takeover in reaction, or a slaughter in the streets," Martin said. A slaughter seemed likely because Trujillo had trained his police, when facing rioters, to shoot to kill – something the council forbade. With the police unsure what to do, chaos reigned on the streets. With the approval of President Kennedy and assistance from his brother, the attorney general, Martin imported a couple of Spanish-speaking detectives from the Los Angeles Police Department. "They trained the Dominican police in riot control, gave them nightsticks, tear gas, and gas masks, and white helmets – they became known as the *Cascos Blancos,* white helmets – and in a few weeks the Council re-won the streets, thanks almost entirely to those two detectives," said Martin. He later noted it seemed "incredible" to him that he had to go all the way up to the President of the United States to stop teenage rioters, but that is what he had to do.[35]

Often Martin felt like a prisoner in the air-conditioned embassy residence, unable to break down the walls between himself and the average Dominican, as he dealt almost exclusively with politicians, members of the government, and the oligarchy. "I am in touch with all the people who have their hands on the levers of real power," he noted at the time. "But I am not in touch with anybody else. This is one of the gravest limits imposed on power. In the past it has often been the fatal flaw that has betrayed the person that holds the power." From time to time Martin did mingle with the Dominican people, taking his wife and sons to Parque Colón for a Sunday evening band concert, eating an occasional dinner at a Santo Domingo restaurant, and shopping at the local market. "Invariably we were well received by ordinary Dominicans; some, who seemed to feel that we were taking part in their national life, as at a band concert, appeared proud and grateful," he noted. The Martin family also made numerous trips into the country's interior, trying to visit every provincial capital and a number of other towns.[36]

They traveled in the family's Jeep, imported from their camp in Michigan's Upper Peninsula. They filled the Jeep with a large batch of

Alliance for Progress comic books to give to children in the villages they visited, as well as such "delicacies," Fran noted, as "canned, smoked oysters and French mineral water, band-aids, dysentery pills, bug bombs and the like; a cooler-hamper filled with hams and turkeys and hard-boiled eggs, all of which usually spoils by the second day out." Martin viewed these journeys as "whistlestopping, campaigning to promote Dominican-American relations and our policies." In most places the American visitors were cordially received by the Dominicans. During the day the Martins went into a community, met the governor or city officials, and told them they "wanted to see whatever they wanted us to see, because we wanted to know what their problems were, and so on," said Martin. At night the Americans would hold a town hall meeting, with everyone in the area invited to come. Usually anywhere from a hundred to two hundred people attended these gatherings. After being introduced by the governor, Martin would "just say very briefly who I was and what I was here for: to learn about their problems and do anything I could to help, and then invite them to ask me questions about our policy or about their problems, and see what they wanted and what they'd like to have done in this country now that Trujillo was gone." The responses Martin received were often about inadequate housing, lack of jobs, poor roads, the need for agrarian reform, the lack of electricity, and unsafe drinking water. The ambassador took these complaints to Bonnelly or the U.S. Agency for International Development director and, now and then, could get something done about them.[37]

For his trips into the interior, Martin had been urged by Dominican government officials to have bodyguards on hand to ensure his safety. "I never would do it," he recalled. "I had the feeling that if the American Ambassador had to take a bodyguard, he'd better stay home." On a visit to La Vega, approximately seventy-five miles north of Santo Domingo, Martin might have wished he had a bodyguard along. While Martin met with local officials in one room, Fran, Dan, and Fred were in another room and could hear a crowd gathering outside and chanting anti-American slogans, including "Yankees go home." In response, Dan and Fred yelled out of a window to the crowd below, many of them primary and high school students, "*Viva los Dominicanos,*" meaning "Hurray for the Dominicans." At first the crowd seemed good-natured, bantering back and forth with the ambassador's children. When the Martins, accompanied by Fandino, decided after consulting with nervous local authorities to leave the building and get into their car, however, the situation got ugly in a hurry. "The instant we appeared, the crowd changed: Not friendly, hateful," said Martin. "And it moved: Surged forward through the police line to the car. We walked fast toward the car but did not run and told Dan and Fred not to. I waved to the crowd, but it was too late – now at best we could only escape." The Americans did escape from their predicament unharmed, but not before a few tense moments, including having the crowd shake and pound on the car with their fists and throwing what seemed to be stones at the boys (Martin later realized they were actually mango pits). In addition, someone in the crowd heaved a heavy bundle into the car that Fran and her sons feared might be a bomb, but it was only a bundle of leaflets. Never again, try as he might, did Martin feel quite the same way "about the Dominican people after they had threatened our children."[38]

On the evening of the day Martin underwent the frightening episode at La Vega, he met by prearrangement with the local leaders of political parties, including the leftist organization, the Movimiento Revolucionario 14 de Junio (Revolutionary Movement June 14), which, according to Martin, was the nationalistic young people's party infiltrated by communists that had been responsible for the anti-American demonstration. Martin had a difficult time connecting with the group's young leaders, as they could come up with no specifics when it came to how the United States could help with social reform in the Dominican Republic. "Then I asked them what the hell they thought they were doing throwing rocks at my kids," Martin recalled. He added that anyone teaching teenagers to go into the streets to throw stones at other children "was doing his country no service." The young men seemed untroubled after Martin's lecture. He came away believing they were "brainless, posing as intellectuals but only mouthing slogans and speeches," he said, one of which was "Culture or death." There seemed to be, Martin concluded, no way to reach them on a personal level. Some Dominicans, however, did appreciate Martin's efforts. Dan Kurzman, a foreign correspondent for the *Washington Post* who reported on the nation's fledgling democracy, remembered that the ambassador's "informality and earthiness had deeply impressed the people, even those at the village level."[39]

In spite of the gulf that existed between the Americans and Dominicans, there were a few bright spots. On her visits to Dominican villages Fran had been shocked at the poor health of infants, often because their mothers had not been taught the basics of hygiene or nutrition. Although she had no training, except for some time working in a baby clinic in the capital's Upper Town, Fran decided to establish a similar clinic in Higüey, the small and remote capital of the La Altagracia Province on the country's east coast. Backed by a Chicago friend's $500 donation to purchase medicine, Fran traveled to Higüey and met with church leaders, government officials, police and military commanders, and what local health professionals there were. "What she wanted, she told them all," recalled Martin, "was to help them set up a clinic that they themselves could run. Not an American charity but a Dominican clinic." The facility, which came to be known as La Pequena Clinica de Higüey (The Little Clinic of Higüey), not only treated sick children, but also educated their mothers in matters of diet, nutrition, and infant care. Selecting a site where the poor would not hesitate to come – a muddy square behind the public market – Fran had plenty of help to get her dream off the ground. Two male Peace Corps volunteers poured a fifteen-by-twenty-foot concrete slab, the Dominican military donated a tent, and local citizens gave lumber to make tables and chairs. Five local doctors agreed to donate one afternoon of their time each, and about twelve housewives in the area volunteered to do the same.[40]

On the clinic's first day of operation, thirty to forty mothers visited, and gradually, noted Fran, it handled twenty-five to thirty babies every afternoon. "They are brought in from the *campo* [countryside] by their mothers or fathers on horseback, on foot, or on burro," noted Fran, who made the 109-mile journey to the clinic weekly and eventually twice a week. Martin admired his wife's resiliency as she managed to carry on in spite of witnessing "babies with swollen bellies and copper-colored hair and skin shredding off of tiny legs, all signs of malnutrition; babies with acute and often fatal diarrhea; babies so tiny that when she unwrapped the scrap of torn bath towel in which they were swaddled she found little sticks of hands and feet that resembled more a bag of chicken bones than human life." Undaunted, Fran set up a tax-exempt foundation on the clinic's behalf in the United States, lobbied friends back home for contributions, and successfully cajoled enough donations of medicine from American pharmaceutical companies that they soon filled the embassy residence to overflowing. Contributions included a film projector from Bell and Howell in Chicago, multivitamins from Smith Kline and French in Philadelphia, and a case of Dial soap from an anonymous donor. "Please tell everybody, all those wonderful blessed generous Americans," Fran wrote friends back in the United States "that their money is being spent for such items as wood for benches, water pipes, paint, nails or 'hot plat[e]s or sterilizing needles' or 'one gallon of worm medicine' or 'one gallon of Kaopectate, $14.90' or 'bought in market, two bin funnels, 50¢.'"[41]

The Higüey clinic persevered through a variety of difficulties. Rain often flooded the clinic, volunteers did not always show up for their work, medical supplies ran short, and on one windy day the tent blew down. A card-index system developed to keep track of a baby's weight to help ensure they were at the proper weight for their age languished because the housewife volunteers charged with tracking the information were often as illiterate as their patients' mothers. Once a riot almost broke out over a planned mass inoculation against whooping cough, diphtheria, and tetanus. Fran had wrangled a donation of 350 shots from an American church agency in Santo Domingo and had announced the program in advance, using a sound truck in the *campo*. Unfortunately, on the day of the inoculations, two thousand mothers and their babies showed up. The crowd almost brought down the tent once again. Fran's hardest task, said Martin, came in making clear the idea of self-help, as Dominicans were used to charitable help and governmental largesse from their time under Trujillo's thumb but had no experience with citizen participation. Each day brought small victories for the clinic, described by Martin as "a sort of Alliance for Progress in miniature, with all its promise and difficulties." A young boy came in for a bandage for a cut finger and in return for the aid donated three cents. A local radio station spent fifteen minutes of air time explaining the clinic's purpose and pleaded with the community to support it with both volunteer service and monetary contributions. A young bartender in a Higüey hotel – someone "popularly supposed to be heading for Communism, the young liberal university-type," said Fran – offered to type copies of a list of medicines available at the clinic with five carbon copies so that each doctor could know what he had to dispense. Once he had finished that job, he asked Fran if she would help him establish facilities for teenagers so he could help combat delinquency in Higüey.[42]

On December 20, 1962, more than a million Dominicans, approximately 70 percent of the electorate, went to the polls in a national election supervised by the OAS. In what was the first free and honest election in the country since 1924, Bosch received 628,044 (59.5 percent) votes for president to 317,764 (30.1 percent) for Fiallo, who failed to help his cause when he condescendingly referred to a crowd he addressed in a poor neighborhood as *"mis negritos"* ("my little negroes"). Bosch's PRD also had success in winning seats in the national assembly, capturing twenty-two of the twenty-seven seats in the Senate and forty-nine of the seventy-four seats in the Chamber of Deputies. Although there were predictions of riots and even gunfights in the streets, the election went off without a hitch, cleaner, said Martin, than most elections in Chicago. He called the election truly "revolutionary," as it had brought to the surface of Dominican life an entire class of people, the *campesinos* – "the small shopkeeper in the roadside store, the workingman, the poor" – who had never before been involved in helping to run the country. Martin knew a provincial governor swept into power with Bosch who could not sign his name, as well as a mayor who had never before worn shoes. "To the upper middle class and the middle class of the Republic, therefore," said Martin, "the Bosch victory felt a good deal like an invasion by a foreign force, not only because he [Bosch] was in exile and so were his party leaders, but because suddenly the other leaders, the congressmen, the senators, the mayors, the aldermen in towns and villages, were all people who had never had any part in government before."[43]

From the beginning of his administration, Bosch was seen as "unacceptable to many people in the business and professional classes," noted Martin, as well as anathema to the political leaders he had defeated. UCN members refused to become part of the new government. "I wanted to form a national coalition cabinet, but they all refused," Bosch recalled. The Catholic Church and military leaders also viewed the new president with suspicion. In spite of these rumblings of discontent, Martin said that the United States's policy objectives had been served "rather well," as the provisional council had survived its term in office, the election had been successful, and it appeared that Bosch would be sworn in as president with little trouble "owing to the magnitude of his sweep. Thus on the surface we have achieved our broad goals. We were pleased by the election because it produced a large vote, because the winner had a big majority, and because the election was peaceable."[44]

As a liberal Democrat Martin was sympathetic to Bosch's progressive outlook and program. With his overwhelming victory, Bosch had the opportunity, said Martin, to assume leadership of the democratic left in Latin American and to make an example of Dominican democracy in comparison to Castro's totalitarian regime in Cuba. Two incidents during the campaign, however, made Martin wary about the new president's character. On two occasions, one involving the use of colored ballots for different parties because of the high illiteracy rate in the Dominican Republic, and the other claims by Catholic Church leaders that Bosch was a Marxist-Leninist, Bosch had responded by threatening to quit the race. His reaction was not surprising given that a church-supported radio station had made the ridiculous announcement that if Bosch won "all the nation's priests would die on their altars, that Dominican children would be snatched up and packed off to Russia, from whence they would return converted into enemies of God." Working behind the scenes, Martin defused the situation, kept Bosch in the race, and avoided becoming entangled in his quarrel with the Catholic Church. During the crisis Martin lost a bit of respect for Bosch as a man because he detested his tactic of threatening to quit unless he got his way. "However my respect for his nerve and his skill as a political manipulator did increase," said Martin, "and I am bound to say that he handled the issue magnificently, forcing everybody to do precisely what he wanted and to play into his hands." In Martin's view the church issue turned what would have been a Bosch victory into a landslide. "Bosch emerged from the campaign as a masterful politician although by no means an admirable one," said Martin. In private notes he kept while ambassador, Martin worried about Bosch's character, viewing him as "temperamental, moody difficult. At times of crisis he is likely to hide out and consult no one and be by himself. He is a plunger, a risk-taker, a desperate gambler." Although he called Bosch "brilliant," Martin also viewed him as possessing intellectual arrogance and contempt for "stupidity and ineptitude," qualities that would not "serve him well as President, for he is going to be confronted with and surrounded by inexperience and ineptitude at their best." Martin also theorized that Bosch's years in exile hurt him. A "dark and conspiratorial mind" might be essential when dealing with the sometimes murderous plots of Caribbean exile politics, Martin noted, but it was unhelpful for the Dominican Republic's leader.[45]

Even before his inauguration on February 27, 1963, Bosch had antagonized the entrenched opposition to his government. A leaked copy of a draft for a new constitution that included such liberal measures as guarantees for basic civil liberties, prohibitions against deporting political dissidents, and legalized divorce outraged the oligarchy and the Catholic Church. "It prevented," said Bosch of the document, "any reintroduction of the gigantic landholdings that were familiar in the old days of the dictatorship, and the enslavement of the worker, who risked being killed as an accused Communist if he presumed to ask for a raise in wages. . . . It was the Constitution of a democracy, and democracy does not recognize privileges of the cradle or the bankbook – all of which is considered criminal in a country that earned social privilege by birth and economic privileges by a dictator's favor." Bosch defended the draft constitution in a speech before his inauguration in which he also attacked the council; the sometimes rambling remarks further frightened those who opposed him. The tensions that existed in the country had an effect on Martin. Four days before Bosch's inauguration, he made the following notes:

> You can only be a virgin once. I'll never again feel the eagerness, enthusiasm, eagerness to help, hopefulness for a better day, willingness to take risks, vigor, almost naïve belief in opportunity here, confidence of cooperation of the Consejo, goodwill, boundless goodwill – that I felt a year ago arriving here. . . .
>
> Bosch is a divider, a splitter, a schemer, a destroyer. Can he build? I doubt it. Not unless he gets good advice. And he won't take advice.
>
> He is more a [Charles] DeGaulle than a Castro.
>
> A year ago, while recognizing problems, I felt optimistic, for I never doubted my own or the Consejo's goodwill. Nor the people's. Nor the capacity of any of these three, except maybe the people.
>
> Now I doubt them all.

Years later, Martin believed he may have judged Bosch too harshly, as it was unfair of him to compare him to the only other presidents he had known: Kennedy, "born to wealth and influence in Massachusetts," and Bonnelly, who had been "nourished in the Santiago oligarchy."[46]

The Bosch government faced long odds against its success as it took office. The country lacked any democratic tradition, its economy faced collapse, and the *campesinos* had unrealistically high expectations for change. Nobody worked harder than Bosch to make the new government a success. Regularly rising before dawn, he made his way to his palace office by 5:00 AM, working there until early afternoon before returning home for lunch and a brief nap, noted Martin, then returning to his office and working until midnight. Unfortunately, Bosch accomplished little, according to the ambassador, because his aides failed to keep away the hundreds of callers who besieged the new president and wasted his time. "No wonder he was exhausted," said Martin. "The Consejo had been confused, but the Bosch government, especially in the beginning, was chaotic."[47]

When Martin visited Bosch during his first few weeks in office, he often found him bent over a stack of papers with figures, making cuts to the budget with a pencil, "running the government like an old lady saving string in a country store." Although fiscal responsibility seemed a laudable goal, there were more pressing matters to which Martin could not attract Bosch's attention, especially a rising unemployment rate that hit 30 percent. "I thought the times demanded, the voters demanded, a government that would spend money, redistribute income, put people to work, and give them an opportunity to create a better life – in short, a New Deal," Martin said. Bosch refused, becoming, Martin noted, the only revolutionary he knew who enshrined free-market economist Adam Smith. The new president also wasted a month, in Martin's estimation, threatening to go to war with the Dominican Republic's neighbor, Haiti, and opened himself up to criticism by allowing Dominicans the freedom to travel to Cuba and refusing to shut a school run by a suspected communist. "Although these activities were of little real importance," Martin observed, "they did give Bosch's enemies on the right a pretext to attack him." Bosch's administration, however, Martin be-

lieved, stood as "one of the most dollar-honest governments" in the nation's history, better in that area than many governments in Latin America and the United States. In addition, during Bosch's administration
"the state killed no one" and almost none of the country's citizens were
arbitrarily imprisoned, said Martin. But the lack of social progress hurt
Bosch with his political supporters. "Wherever I went, I myself heard
poor people saying, 'Juan Bosch is good for nothing,'" said Martin.⁴⁸

Bosch's slow start also hurt him with American officials in Washington, fueled in no small part by unsympathetic portrayals of the new
president in the American press as soft on communism, including a
series of articles by Hal Hendrix, Latin America editor for the *Miami
News*. Hendrix's views on Bosch were not surprising, given that he had
also been critical of President Kennedy's decision to appoint Martin as
ambassador to the Dominican Republic, believing the former newspaper reporter and freelance writer to be unqualified for the position. In
his private journal, Martin expressed a different point of view about the
country's new president: "It boils down to this: While everyone else is
nervous because they think he [Bosch] is moving too far left, I am worried because he is doing nothing revolutionary at all. And we are not
helping him. And it is in truth damn hard to help someone who doesn't
want to be helped." He feared that the Dominican Republic had the fate
of being a "hard-luck country" and that Bosch, in some ways, had the
misfortune of being a "hard-luck President."⁴⁹

Although never comfortable with Bosch's fitness to be president,
Martin went to often extraordinary lengths to support the new Dominican government, always keeping in mind that while propping up a provisional government such as the council might have been essential in
the chaos after Trujillo's assassination, "presuming to give advice to an
elected President starting a four-year term" was quite another proposition. The ambassador offered both professional and personal advice and
help, suggesting what legislation might be appropriate, giving tips to
Bosch about how to staff his administration, mediating between the
president and a leading opposition newspaper, and tendering to Bosch
his valuable skills as a speechwriter. Martin even arranged a dinner party
to help bridge the divide between Bosch and Dominican professionals
and businessmen, the *civicos*. Although the dinner produced nothing

but "small talk," noted Martin, at least it had not been a disaster. On a personal level, Martin helped Bosch sign with his own New York literary agent, Harold Ober Associates, and when the president's teenage son, then a student in New York, suffered an injury that needed an operation, Martin successfully sought permission to have him treated at a U.S. government hospital. Looking back on Martin's work in the Dominican Republic, a fellow American diplomat observed that he functioned in office "much as would the authoritative coach of a rather backward football team." According to Sam Halper, Caribbean bureau chief for *Time* magazine, in action Martin was "an unforgettable sight." Although the ambassador, said Halper, did not possess a flare for politics or economics, on the "people to people level he was simply great – a diplomatic doctor with a marvelous bedside manner: always concerned (even to the detriment of his own health), always available for consultation, always trying."[50]

Bosch appreciated all that Martin tried to do for his country and his government, as he did the efforts of Newell Williams, head of the U.S. AID mission. Both men, said Bosch, did not appear to be agents of the U.S. government, but rather "two Dominicans as anxious as the best of Dominicans to accomplish the impossible for us. They were anything but coldblooded officials looking out only for the interests of their own country and government." A number of serious problems that needed difficult solutions were quickly resolved by Martin and Williams, sometimes within twenty-four hours, said Bosch. Bosch welcomed the services offered by the Americans because he realized he was not an easy person to deal with. "I was sensitive to anything that might affect Dominican sovereignty," he said. Bosch once told Shlaudeman that one of his dearest wishes would be to cut the Dominican Republic across its border from Haiti and have the island float away "several thousand miles from you," away from America's dominating presence. During his childhood, Bosch had witnessed the Dominican flag being lowered from public buildings to give way to the U.S. banner. "No one will ever know what my seven-year-old soul suffered at the sight," he said. Perhaps Martin and other American officials would have realized the problems to come with Bosch if they knew who had been his boyhood hero: Pancho Villa, a general of the Mexican Revolution who bedeviled American forces sent to capture him in 1916 and 1917. At night as a youth Bosch had prayed "for the appearance of a Dominican Pancho Villa, someone who would do in our country what Pancho Villa had done in Mexico."[51]

In early June 1963 Martin traveled to Washington to seek additional assistance from the Kennedy administration for Bosch's tottering government, including a $15 million loan for agricultural development, and to present his case to members of Congress and the media. "In short," said Martin, "I would make one more try to save Bosch. For I thought if we did not, he would run into serious trouble, probably in September. September is a month of high seasonal unemployment, a traditional time of troubles, and Bosch had indicated he would propose radical legislation in September." If Bosch could survive his first year in office, there was a strong possibility of him keeping a hold on power for his full four-year term, said Martin. The ambassador warned officials in the nation's capital that if they did nothing, Bosch would have to move politically to the left to stem the drift of his young voters from the PRD to the 14th of June Movement, a move that might include an agrarian reform program confiscating private land holdings without compensation, something that would outrage Bosch's opponents in the Dominican Republic as well as conservative and liberal lawmakers in Washington. Martin also asked for assistance in training "an effective antisubversive force for Bosch – and, as a double check, I wanted a greatly stepped up CIA covert operation of our own, one capable, if necessary, of keeping several people inside and outside the Bosch government under close surveillance."[52]

At a meeting with President Kennedy and his advisers in the Oval Office, Martin warned that the administration gambled in supporting Bosch, but the alternatives – a rightist coup or a leftist takeover – were far worse alternatives. Kennedy offered a sympathetic ear to Martin's problems, approving additional AID programs for the Dominican Republic, but he worried that expropriating private land holdings could cause trouble for Bosch no matter how he did it. For a brief time the two men discussed whether Martin would return to help with the 1964 presidential campaign, but Kennedy, after thinking about the possibility, told Martin, "Maybe you can do more for us holding that place together. Well, we'll see." Getting ready to leave, Martin asked the president if he had any message for Bosch. Kennedy responded that there might come a time when Bosch would need to deport suspected communists and, if that day came, the United States stood ready to assist, even offering to accept those he kicked out. After Martin shook hands with Kennedy and started walking out past the desk of Kenny O'Donnell, the president's appointment secretary, Kennedy pointed his finger at Martin and quipped, "There he goes – the Earl E. T. Smith of this Administration." Smith had been the American ambassador to Cuba in the Eisenhower administration when Castro came to power. "I was so startled," Martin remembered, "I could only say to him, 'What a thing to say,' and he grinned and waved, and I left." In spite of Kennedy's wisecrack, Martin felt his confidence renewed after his trip, with the president responsible for this feeling due to "his intelligence, his confidence that made anything seem possible, even Bosch's success."[53]

Martin's efforts on Bosch's behalf failed to gain any ground, and he described the situation as "a desperate holding operation." He continued to fight as hard for Bosch's survival as he had done for the council, realizing that he now battled not for the president himself, but to uphold the principle of representative government and the right of the Dominican people to elect their leaders. By August 23, however, Martin had completed a lengthy contingency paper outlining direct action the United States could undertake instead of continuing to support Bosch's democratically elected government. The alternatives included conniving with the military to force Bosch out and replacing him with a civilian junta that would hold elections in a year or two; tacitly consenting to Bosch's ouster by the military; attempting a "behind-the-scenes" takeover, offering Bosch money plus a guarantee of U.S. armed intervention to keep him in power if he agreed to have the United States "pick his Cabinet, dictate his policies, and run his government"; instigating a clandestine operation to achieve the same ends; or persuading or pressuring Bosch and his vice president to leave the country quietly and convene a national assembly to elect a new president. "I concluded that all alternative policies were so unacceptable that they should be adopted only in dire necessity," he noted. "'Dire necessity' meant an imminent danger of a Castro/Communist takeover or 'clear demonstration that Bosch would fail and imminently fall or flee.'" In case of such a "dire necessity," Martin recommended that the Kennedy administration begin plans for either a "covert power takeover or an overthrow with our tacit consent." He emphasized that the American government's interest still lay in supporting Bosch's presidency, and it dared not "give an inch, in public or in private, in all-out support for him, either in the Dominican Republic or in Washington." Martin shared his findings with two embassy officials, including Shlaudeman, but he never transmitted the complete proposal to the State Department or White House, keeping it instead locked away in his private safe. "I did not send it because it might become known, I doubted the [State] Department would adopt it, and therefore it could only further undermine Washington's confidence in Bosch," said Martin.[54]

On September 25, 1963, after only seven months in office, Bosch was overthrown in a bloodless military *golpe* (coup) backed by rightist groups in the Dominican Republic; a three-man civilian junta, the Triumvirate, presided over the government, but the army retained real power. Bosch left the country for exile in Puerto Rico. Until the end, Martin had done everything possible to forestall the coup, including producing a fake instruction from the State Department he could share with the Dominican military if the need arose. "In a tight situation, it might help me bluff," he noted. The bogus "incoming cable" had a statement saying that the U.S. government was "unequivocally opposed to any attempt by anyone to overthrow the legally constituted and democratically elected government of President Juan Bosch," and went on to warn it would be "virtually impossible to assist any regime which might come to power in the Dominican Republic as a result of the overthrow of President Bosch." Words, however, failed to halt the military's takeover. Although Bosch had been a poor president, Martin said that fact did not justify the coup, as it overthrew not only Bosch but constitutional government in the Dominican Republic. "This was the real Dominican tragedy," he said. "All that work, all that money, all that caring for the people – now it was all swept away in a few minutes by a bunch of machine gunners in the night in the preposterous peach-colored Palace." The Kennedy administration refused to recognize the new regime and recalled Martin, who returned to the United States on September 28. "At times in the Republic," he said, "I had felt that everything in my past life had prepared me for this job – my reporting, my writing, my work in politics. Now all that, along with Bosch, had failed."[55]

The chaos surrounding the coup reached beyond Santo Domingo to the Little Clinic of Higüey. After Martin had left the country, Fran, who had remained behind with the boys, went several times to the clinic. She took with her more than a hundred cartons of used clothing donated by the U.S. Navy. Local people decided to hold a rummage sale, with the proceeds going to the community center. The sale proved to be a disaster. When the clothes were gone, several hundred enraged women, joined by groups of hostile young men, ransacked the building and stole educational materials and supplies for the baby clinic. A Peace Corps nurse had slipped out a back door with the proceeds from the rummage sale, but everything else, said Martin, "baby scales, medicines, books, tools, vitamins, crochet hooks, yard goods, soap, cabinets – everything they had built and used in all the community projects – was gone." A disheartened Martin could not bear to share the terrible news with Fran, but he later learned that she had known about the calamity at the clinic and "hadn't the heart to tell me." Martin compared what had happened to the clinic with what had occurred following Trujillo's assassination, when Dominicans, in "inchoate rage," had sacked the dictator's houses after his fall and moved into them.[56]

Martin spent seventy-seven days in Washington in consultations at the State Department and White House on what course to take with the Dominican situation (Fran and the boys finally rejoined Martin in Washington on October 18). At a meeting at the White House that included officials from the State Department, the Pentagon, the CIA, and AID, President Kennedy told Martin, "I take it we don't want Bosch back." Martin agreed, and when Kennedy asked why, the ambassador had a simple explanation: "Because he isn't a President." The group agreed on a "tough statement," said Martin, condemning the military coups in the Dominican Republic and one in Honduras that had occurred on October 4, and saying that there then existed "no opportunity for effective collaboration by the United States under the Alliance for Progress or for normalization of diplomatic relations" for either country. As the meeting broke up, Martin asked Ralph Dungan, a White House aide, if he could have time to explain to the president how Bosch had fallen. Dungan assured Martin that Kennedy had not lost confidence in him. "I was grateful, but it wasn't that," Martin recalled. "It was a guilty need to give him an accounting. I never got the chance."[57]

That fall in Washington, a time Martin remembered as being always cold and wet, Martin worked on Dominican matters in a temporary office on the third floor of the State Department. Initially, the Kennedy administration refused to recognize the Triumvirate, attempted to persuade other countries to follow the same course, and tried to put pressure on the Dominican regime to return to a constitutional government. These efforts failed, and officials "began to fear that a collapse of the triumvirate might bring back a harsh military dictatorship; we feared a communist uprising; and we feared we might encourage young noncommunist leftists to fight and die uselessly," remembered Martin. Finally, President Kennedy had decided on a policy of granting U.S. government recognition to the Triumvirate if it would establish a reasonable timetable for new elections. "The Dominican regime only had to sit tight, maintain control, and wait," said Martin. "We on the other hand were being pushed hard to settle."[58]

On November 22, 1963, Martin, now alone in Washington after his family had returned to Highland Park, went to work in his office at the "antiseptic Department – with its clean desks and locked files it always looked deserted." On that day he met with a young Harvard student writing a paper on the Dominican Republic and handled several telephone calls about a secret trip he was planning to meet with former Dominican president Rafael Bonnelly to discuss a new constitutional scheme for the country, including a referendum on a new constitution. At about 1:50 PM he heard from Bob Sayre, a young Foreign Service official, that Kennedy had been shot while visiting Dallas, Texas. Later that afternoon Martin learned that the president had died. As he sat staring out the window of his office, watching as the flags around the city were lowered to half-mast, Martin remembered thinking: "One shit-head with a squirrel rifle can change the fate of mankind." He later joined a State Department staff meeting in which there was a discussion about preparing lists of what problems were most urgent and what ones could be delayed to pass along to President Johnson – "how strange it sounded!" said Martin.

Someone remarked that Latin American officials were already talking about making the Alliance for Progress a monument to the fallen president. "I got up and almost ran from the room," said Martin. "It was the first time I had wept."[59]

The tears came again a month later when Martin returned to Washington to tie up some loose ends after spending Thanksgiving with his family in Highland Park. At home he explained that they would not be going back to the Dominican Republic as ambassador, but might someday travel there again as private citizens, a goal Fran and Martin later accomplished. "The world was a different place now," said Martin, whose resignation as ambassador was accepted by the Johnson administration on January 14, 1964, to be effective on February 15. On December 14 the Johnson administration had announced its recognition of the new governments in the Dominican Republic and Honduras. Such recognition had been agreed upon before President Kennedy's death, but the assassination had delayed such a step because Johnson did not want to make one of his first acts to be seen as a policy shift to the right. Making his final goodbyes in Washington, Martin could not leave town without seeing Robert Kennedy, staying only a minute or two to thank him, to offer his help in the future, and noting he planned on writing a book about his experiences in the Dominican Republic. "With that odd tentative half-smile, so well known to his friends, so little to others, he murmured, 'Everybody's writing a book,' and 'All right, thanks, John,'" Martin recalled. "And then, 'Well, three years is better than nothing.'" Canceling a plane reservation he had made, Martin decided instead to travel home by train. That night he had trouble sleeping and awoke when the train pulled into a city somewhere near Pittsburgh. "I wept, and kept thinking, 'Why, oh why, did they kill him. Why him,'" said Martin. At that time he had grown disenchanted with both the Dominican Republic and his own country, one too weak and evil, the other too powerful and evil. Martin no longer felt the youth and confidence he had possessed at the start of the Kennedy administration. "I felt old and without hope, with heart for nothing," he said. "It was all gone. And destroyed by blind malevolent chance. That was what hurt the most of all."[60]

What made the hurt so intense for Martin was his sense that the tragedy in Dallas had robbed the country of hope and faith, something it "did not know it had until it lost it." He also suffered a loss in the Dominican Republic, where the U.S. government's good intentions and dedication proved not to be enough to save the fragile Dominican democracy. For Martin, writing had always been a search for meaning, and it deeply troubled him to find no such meaning in the events of 1963. "What happened in the Dominican Republic shook me badly," he said, "because I failed, but shook me worse because I could not understand why. The pure politics of it, of course, is clear. But there is more – the awful incalculable." Was it merely blind chance or a malevolent fate? He did not know the answer. To find some solace, Martin turned to a place that had been a salve for his soul and a sanctuary for his troubles for many years, the wild country of Michigan's Upper Peninsula. After Christmas, he and his family, including Cindy and her husband, Anthony V. M. Campbell, a Shell Oil Company executive she had met and married while in the Dominican Republic, traveled to their camp in Three Lakes, Michigan. During their stay the Martins went rabbit hunting, rode a toboggan in the bitter cold (25 degrees below zero) down a hill onto the frozen lake, and observed a herd of deer while taking a Jeep ride in the deep woods. Martin had also decided that the Three Lakes area had become too crowded for his tastes, and while he was there he found a tract of rough, rocky, and uninhabited land on Smith Lake that he decided to purchase. At the beginning of January his family went home, but Martin stayed behind to snowshoe, visit friends, dream about building a camp far out into the woods on his new property, and think about his life, "at night alone in the camp in front of the fire, healing. I kept warm." Martin noted that for his entire life, when he had been hurt or needed healing, he wanted to be alone.[61]

EIGHT

LBJ and Adlai

DURING HIS SERVICE AS U.S. AMBASSADOR TO THE DOMINICAN Republic, John Bartlow Martin had shunned the usual trappings of power that came with his high diplomatic post and had concentrated instead on his work. Martin had some trouble, however, transitioning from public office to private life and admitted that he missed "some of the perquisites of power." Instead of being driven to his office in a chauffeured limousine, he had to endure Chicago-area winters with other commuters, and there were no U.S. Marine Corps guards on duty to snap to attention when he arrived every day at his office. Martin now faced the ultimate question: What would he do with the rest of his life? Martin could write – it was, as he said, "all I knew how to do" – but he could not return to his old freelance trade, producing heavy-fact stories for magazines, as the industry had fallen on hard times as television began to draw away its advertisers. His interests had also shifted away from writing about crime and its effect on society to such issues as national politics and foreign policy. "One doesn't go back," he noted.[1]

Martin decided to write, as a memorial to both President John F. Kennedy and the Alliance for Progress, an account of his work in the Dominican Republic, deciding on the title *Overtaken by Events,* one of the "few good phrases to come out of the State Department bureaucracy," he noted. In March 1964 he accepted an appointment as a Fellow at the Center for Advanced Studies at Wesleyan University in Middletown, Connecticut. The university gave him the rank and salary of a full professor without any teaching responsibilities except for an occasional seminar or lecture (he gave a regular seminar on "The Limits of American Power"), and it expected him to be engaged on a serious piece of work of his own, his book on the Dominican Republic. "I was writing the rough draft at a furious pace," he noted, "eighty-five pages a day." Martin also did a good deal of reading and thinking, trying "to make sense out of what happened in Santo Domingo, Washington, and in Dallas." The Martin family, including his wife, Fran, and their two sons, Dan and Fred, lived in a small two-story shingle house provided by the university across the Connecticut River from Middletown and the campus. "The atmosphere at the center was what one had always hoped a university atmosphere would be – a civilized community of serious scholars who could be fun," said Martin. He particularly enjoyed interacting with the other Fellows – Edmund Wilson, Jean Stafford, and Sir Herbert Read – and believed his interactions with them helped make *Overtaken by Events,* eventually published by Doubleday and Company in 1966, a better book than if he had written it at his Highland Park home.[2]

Every Monday evening the Fellows gathered for a dinner on campus that also included interested faculty members and Paul Horgan, the center's director and a noted novelist and historian, who presided over the Fellows "with grace and elegance." After dinner, the Fellows listened to and discussed a paper read by one of their company or a member of the Wesleyan faculty. Wilson in particular had taken a liking to the Martin family. Horgan said the Martins, with their "two appealing young sons," more than anyone else at the university "tapped Edmund's feelings." The sometimes caustic critic and man of letters felt more at home with Martin than he did with the academics at Wesleyan, describing him as in the "Lincolnian Illinois tradition," and he said Martin's work as a journalist was of a "high order." Wilson also enjoyed the time he spent with Fran, and he treated her sons with respect. "She has a reckless, crackling, sparkling wit which amuses me extremely," he said. Martin noted that Wilson, who usually drank martinis before dinner and wine with dinner, often slept through the reading of papers. He was awake, however, to hear a "dreadful" paper by a young university psychologist on the psychology of mice. Wilson playfully wrote a letter of complaint against the professor from the offspring of one of the rodents the psychologist had experimented on, which he sent to Martin. For several weeks they sent dispatches back and forth parodying the psychologist's paper.[3]

Later during his residency at Wesleyan, when Martin was called away to undertake a dangerous assignment in the Dominican Republic for President Lyndon B. Johnson, those he left behind in Connecticut, both his family and his colleagues at Wesleyan, worried about his safety. "The concern of everyone at the Center was acute," said Horgan. Fran, Dan, and Fred, however, found comfort from Wilson, who lavished on the boys, recalled Horgan, "an almost paternal tenderness." Horgan remembered a dinner he had with Wilson in which the curmudgeonly critic saw the Martins enter looking forlorn, worried, no doubt, about Martin's well-being. Wilson invited them to join him and for the next two hours had Dan and Fred "laughing at his jokes and stories," Horgan recalled. Wilson quizzed the boys about their hobbies and tastes in books and music, and he promised that later he would show them his magic tricks (Wilson was a practiced amateur magician). Horgan could see gratitude in Fran's eyes for the way Wilson distracted her sons from the "dread of the danger that had their father in its idiot grip," and he always fondly remembered the "lovely tact" Wilson displayed that evening, becoming for the Martins "a new family hero."[4]

In the summer of 1964 Martin, accompanied by his family, took a break from writing his book to explore the remote tract he had purchased at Smith Lake in the Upper Peninsula of Michigan. For Martin and Fran, the hourglass-shaped lake became an important part of their lives, as both of them, noted Dan, loved "the wildlife, the remoteness, the sense that they were in touch with nature." Starting from L'Anse on Lake Superior, the Martins drove their Willys Jeep for an hour and a half along an old logging road to within a mile of Smith Lake. It took them the rest of the day to carry their tents, boat, and other supplies the last mile through the woods to the site of their planned new camp (as cabins are called in the area) on top of a high, granite cliff sixty feet above the lake. Enormous white pines towered over the hemlocks on the cliff, and not far from the water's edge the Martins discovered the ruins of an old trapper's shack. "This, we decided, we would rebuild into a temporary camp," recalled Martin. The rustic shack, rebuilt by Dan and Fred, still stands at the camp. From there, as the sun set, they heard the cry of loons on the lake, and when their fire died away the howling of coyotes filled the air; a few nights later they "heard the commanding howl of a timber wolf," said Martin.[5]

The Martins stayed at the site for several days, mapping their lake and their land. Martin conferred with his friend, Earl Numinen, a highway engineer, and together they laid out a route for a mile of road to the clifftop camp. "We did not want a good road passable by passenger cars – that would encourage curious visitors, and one reason we had come to Smith Lake was to be alone," said Martin. "What we wanted was a Jeep road." He and Numinen walked the mile from the logger's road to Smith Lake through alder swamps and around hills, selecting a route at the base of hills and at the edge of swamps. On Numinen's advice, Martin went to the nearby town of Herman, about twelve and a half miles from the lake, and talked with Charley Dantes, a local leader and owner of a small sawmill that he ran with his son. When Dantes, himself a Democrat, learned that Martin was friends with Adlai Stevenson, he "could not do enough to help us," including using his bulldozer to clear a path for the Jeep road to the Martins' new camp. On the day Dantes's yellow bulldozer set out to do its job, the Martin family walked behind the powerful machine as it plowed the earth, only falling behind at noon when they stopped to eat sandwiches for lunch. When they caught back up to the bulldozer, Martin said, "a doe and two fawns had joined our procession. I suppose the soft, fresh-turned earth felt good beneath their feet."[6]

Starting in 1966 and ending two years later, Martin oversaw the construction by Finnish carpenters of a thirty-by-thirty-foot log cabin with a large living room, kitchen, bedroom, indoor bathroom, and an enormous fireplace built out of fifty tons of native rock. Initially, Martin and his sons, while living in tents, rebuilt the one-room trapper's shack. When it was ready, the Finnish carpenters used it as a temporary camp, "living in it while they constructed the big camp up on the cliff, built it slowly, painfully, log by chipped and fitted log, a beauty." Every board and every nail that went into its construction, as well as the equipment for building it, had to be hauled to the site either by Jeep or by hand. "We learned a good deal about carpentry and plumbing, building Smith Lake," said Martin. "Not until 1968 were Fran and I able to use the big camp, and work on its interior and its outbuildings [including a sauna] continued for several years. But we succeeded." Nestled amid hemlocks on the edge of a high cliff overlooking the lake, the camp became a sanctuary for the Martin family, the place they "retreated to in times of trouble," noted Dan, but also because they all enjoyed the woods and lake. "Dad was an avid fisherman, loved shoreline casting for bass, and we caught 24 bass in other lakes and introduced them into Smith Lake, where they took, and the bass fishing became excellent," said Dan. "Dad usually fished every day and we fished with him." For years every June the family dropped what they were doing to vacation at Smith Lake, staying there until Labor Day. "Nothing was better than to spend all day exploring back logging roads in our Willys Jeep, getting it stuck and winching out several times, and making it back to camp long after dark, splattered in mud and exhausted," recalled Fred.[7]

Martin began to realize that a subtle transformation had taken place, from a time when he took care of his sons to a time when "they took care of me." The first year at Smith Lake, Dan and Fred had been responsible for such simple chores as washing dishes, hauling water, finding kindling for the fire, and taking his direction at rebuilding the trapper's shack. "In a few years they were taking initiatives – had learned what needed doing and did it, without being told," Martin remembered. "It became they who staked out the tent, who rowed the boat, who made the campfire." By the time they had finished building at Smith Lake, Dan and Fred were not only doing the heavy work but were participating in such important decisions as where to fish. One day, when the three men had driven by Jeep to another remote lake in the woods to fish, Dan, without a word, started hauling the boat Martin had carried for so many years, and Fred picked up the oars, tackle box, and packs, asking his father to bring along the fishing rods. "I was grateful," Martin said, "but never felt older."[8]

As it had since 1952, politics intruded from time to time on Martin's work, both at Smith Lake and at Wesleyan. Vice President Johnson's ascension to the presidency after John Kennedy's death had disheartened many members of the administration. Their poor opinion of the former Senate majority leader might have been exacerbated by his being from the state in which their leader had been gunned down and his often antagonistic relationship with Robert Kennedy. Three of Martin's friends from the 1960 presidential campaign – Arthur M. Schlesinger Jr., Theodore Sorensen, and Pierre Salinger – had resigned from their White House jobs by the time the 1964 presidential election season began, and Robert Kennedy left his post as attorney general to run for the U.S. Senate seat in New York. Martin also mourned John Kennedy's tragic death, but he had in his heart a soft spot for Johnson because of an incident at the 1963 inauguration of Juan Bosch as president of the Dominican Republic. During the festivities, Dan had broken his arm after being thrown from his burro. A Dominican doctor had set the arm and put a cast on it, but Martin wanted the arm X-rayed by an American doctor onboard the USS *Boxer,* an American aircraft carrier on hand to provide helicopter air cover for the vice president. Martin told Johnson that his wife, Fran, could not accompany the vice president's wife, Lady Bird, on a scheduled visit to the Dominican School for the Blind because she had to be with Dan when he went to the carrier. "Why don't you let me take the boy, and his mother, too, up to Washington with me Thursday?" Johnson spontaneously asked Martin. "They can take better care of him at Bethesda [Naval Hospital] than here."[9]

Ever since that time, whenever anyone asked Martin about his view of Johnson, his mind turned back to that occasion and the vice president's compassionate gesture. Johnson, he noted, helped save his son's arm, as the break had occurred near the growth center at the elbow, "and if it had not been reset properly it would not have grown." When Johnson asked for his help in his presidential effort against his Republican opponent, conservative U.S. senator Barry Goldwater from Arizona, Martin agreed. The veteran speechwriter had high hopes for the campaign and believed the 1964 election could be a means to discuss fundamental issues of American policy, including war and peace in the nuclear age and the proper role of government in a free society. Unfortunately, he later observed, the election turned out to be "one of the silliest, most empty, and most boring campaigns in the nation's history."[10]

In the late summer of 1964, Bill Moyers, special assistant to Johnson, took Martin to see the president and the two men discussed the upcoming campaign for a few minutes. Johnson believed that Goldwater had a chance to capture the election by winning the South; adding Indiana, Illinois, and Iowa, the conservative Midwest; and winning New

Mexico, Colorado, and the mountain states. Martin told the president about his background in the Midwest, and he agreed with Johnson that the region's conservatism might swing voters to the Goldwater camp as a backlash against gains made by African Americans, highlighted by the Civil Rights Act Congress passed on July 2 after much wheeling and dealing from Johnson. White working men in the Midwest, said Martin, particularly those of Eastern European extraction, felt threatened by black men and feared they might lose their jobs to them. There were also vestiges of the McCarthyism of the 1950s and the isolationism of the 1930s in reaction to America's growing power and foreign commitments, including troop increases in Vietnam, he added. "At the fringe were lunatics who hated communists, Jews, Catholics, Negroes, waste, or big government (or any government, it sometimes seemed) indiscriminately," Martin noted. With all these difficulties, the Midwest might well prove to be "the battleground" in the election, according to Johnson strategists. Martin remembered the president telling him, "We need you. You write it and tell me what to say and I'll say it." Martin later observed that Johnson was the easiest candidate he ever worked for as far as speechwriting was concerned, far easier than either John Kennedy or Adlai Stevenson had been, because Johnson "would say what you wrote." As he left his meeting with Johnson, the Texan called out to Martin, "Get some new ideas, John," words he had heard from past Democratic presidential candidates.[11]

That fall Martin had an office in the Executive Office Building, next to the White House, where he worked under the direction of Moyers, who was in charge of the campaign's speechwriting staff. Unlike his previous experience with John Kennedy's presidential campaign, Martin did not always travel with Johnson, but spoke to him occasionally in the White House and passed along strategy recommendations to Moyers. Martin also worked with the other speechwriters, including Dick Goodwin, his companion on the Kennedy campaign plane, and William Wirtz (secretary of labor in the Johnson administration), with whom he had worked on Stevenson's two unsuccessful tries for the presidency. As the incumbent, Johnson had an enormous advantage over his opponent, and he and his advisers decided he should "stay presidential," initially running his campaign from the White House, ignoring his opponent, touting the surging economy and his legislative successes with Congress, and possibly reassessing his strategy in October. "I guess the best thing for me to do," said Johnson, "is to stay around here and let people know I'm real busy tending the store, that I'm taking good care of their business." It seemed to be a sound strategy, as a Gallup poll had 77 percent of eligible voters supporting Johnson to only 20 percent for Goldwater. Johnson advisers planned, noted Jack Valenti, to treat their GOP rival "not as an equal, who has the credentials to be President, but as a radical, a preposterous candidate." This was not hard to do given Goldwater's acceptance speech at the Republican convention, where he had said, "I remind you that extremism in the defense of liberty is no vice. And let me remind you that moderation in the pursuit of justice is no virtue." Goldwater's statements about selling the Tennessee Valley Authority, making Social Security voluntary, withdrawing the United States from the United Nations, and using low-yield nuclear weapons against Chinese supply lines in North Vietnam only reinforced his reputation as an extremist. "Our overriding issue in 1964 was very simple," noted Larry O'Brien, a Kennedy aide who had remained to work with Johnson. "In one word, Goldwater."[12]

While Johnson remained above the fray, using the presidency as his "greatest asset," his staff set out to convince voters that Goldwater could not be trusted to hold high office, and they used his extreme statements against him. With the assistance of a New York advertising agency – Doyle Dane Bernbach – the Johnson campaign spent $3 million on television advertising hitting Goldwater on his intemperate remarks on Social Security, opposition to the Nuclear Test Ban Treaty, and his view that the country would be better off if the Eastern Seaboard could somehow be cut off from America. One commercial in particular, which has gone done in history as one of the most famous, or infamous given one's political leanings, in presidential campaign history, treated Goldwater "as a bloodthirsty mad bomber." The "Daisy" advertisement, as it is now called, featured a young girl in a field picking petals off of a daisy and counting – sometimes inaccurately – from one to nine. When she reached nine, a menacing male voice took over, reciting a countdown. The camera zoomed in on the child's right eye, followed by a bright flash and roar of a nuclear explosion. As the immense fireball grows and boils in fury, Johnson's voice can be heard, saying, "These are the stakes, to make a world in which all of God's children can live, or go into the dark. We must love each other, or we must die." The spot ends with a voice-over urging, "Vote for President Johnson on November 3. The stakes are too high to stay home."[13]

According to Martin, Johnson had decreed that no speech of his during the campaign could be longer than seven hundred words. "With commercials like that to explain complicated issues," asked Martin, "who needs long speeches?" Years later, he learned that while Johnson campaigned as "the candidate of military restraint," behind the scenes the president had made plans to increase the American combat presence in the Vietnam War. Although he met frequently with such senior presidential advisers as Clark Clifford and Abe Fortas, saw the president occasionally and saw Moyers, Goodwin, and Wirtz on a daily basis, Martin said he had no inkling of any such move to widen the war, and he doubted if any of his colleagues did either.[14]

Although many Democrats were extremely confident of victory in November, Martin, still nervous about Johnson's chances in the Midwest and elsewhere, did some legwork in several states (by car across Wisconsin, Indiana, Ohio, Pennsylvania, and West Virginia in early September, and Oklahoma, Texas, New York, and Connecticut in late September), and discovered that almost nobody seemed to be paying much attention to the campaign. He found that Democratic voters admired Johnson and believed him to be the safer candidate than Goldwater, but many did not have the same enthusiasm they had previously displayed for Kennedy. Consequently, Johnson could count on "very broad but rather shallow support," and Martin worried that the president's lead in the polls could very well breed "overconfidence and indifference among Democrats." He wrote a memorandum for the president telling him that people in the Midwest were saying that the election had come down to a choice between "a kook and a crook," with Goldwater being the kook and Johnson the crook. Martin advised Johnson that he should let the voters see him in action and "convince them he was not a crook; and the best way to do that, I thought, was personal, whistle-stop campaigning." Johnson took action to broaden his support, wishing to win over every possible voter and achieve the largest popular vote victory in presidential history, surpassing the 60.3 percent attained by Warren Harding in 1920 and the 60.8 percent garnered by Franklin Roosevelt in 1936. "He not only wished to win bigger than John Kennedy had won in 1960, but bigger than anybody had won ever," said Martin. "Moreover, he wanted people to vote for him, not against Goldwater; he wanted all the American people to vote for him because they loved him."[15]

To achieve such a historic victory, Johnson set out on a whirlwind tour of the country at the end of September, traveling sixty thousand miles over a forty-two-day period and making two hundred speeches in the Northeast, Midwest, and Upper South. With bullhorn in hand, the president attracted enormous crowds (seventy thousand in Peoria, Illinois, and forty thousand in Indianapolis), stopping his presidential motorcade to shake hands and encourage voters, "Come on folks, come on down to the speakin'. You don't have to dress. Just bring your children and dogs, anything you have with you. It won't take long. You'll be back in time to put the kids in bed." For Johnson's appearances in the Midwest, Martin did what he had done during John Kennedy's presidential campaign, producing for the candidate editorial advance memorandums giving information on where the speech would be held, what political notables might be in attendance, and the background on each community.[16]

The Johnson juggernaut rolled on to what seemed to be a certain victory. The only bump along the way occurred in the middle of October, when the story broke that a key Johnson adviser, Walter Jenkins, had been arrested and charged with disorderly conduct with another man in the basement restroom at a Washington, D.C., Young Men's Christian Association facility. The incident seemed tailor-made for the Goldwater campaign, as its candidate had focused on the morality issue and had attacked the morals of the president himself. "What had looked like a landslide suddenly promised to be a debacle," said Martin. Jenkins resigned, and international events, including the fall from power of Soviet premier Nikita Khrushchev and the explosion by Communist China of its first nuclear weapon, conspired to knock news about the White House aide's homosexual tryst from newspaper's front pages. By the end of October Martin said the Johnson campaign had entered a "holding" pattern, but it probably did not matter as he had received "fantastic" reports from reporters and political insiders about Johnson's chances in the Midwest, including the key states of Illinois and Ohio, as well as states in the East and the West. Martin's reports were accurate; Johnson defeated Goldwater in a landslide, carrying forty-four states and the District of Columbia. Martin's warning about paying more attention to the Midwest paid off in particular, as the president swept the region, capturing even the normally Republican-leaning Indiana (no Democratic presidential candidate had won the state since Roosevelt in 1936, and none would do so again until Barack Obama in 2008). Johnson received more than 43 million votes, or 61.1 percent of the total vote cast, then the largest in American history. Accompanied by Fran, Martin watched the election returns in Moyers' White House office, while the president learned of his great triumph at his Texas ranch. Martin reflected that the great conservative crusade that year had begun with Goldwater's slogan "In Your Heart You Know He's Right." Democrats had responded, "In Your Guts You Know He's Nuts." These two slogans "composed a fitting epitaph on the 1964 campaign," he said.[17]

After the election, Martin returned to working on his book about his time in the Dominican Republic, but a crisis in that Caribbean nation saw him called back to Washington to help the Johnson administration in an undertaking that if not for the thousands of Dominican dead and wounded, might be likened to "a comedy of errors and inconsistencies, a mixture of Hamlet and the Marx Brothers," said a reporter who covered the unfolding tragedy. On April 24, 1965, just three months after Johnson's inauguration, supporters of exiled Dominican president Juan Bosch and reformist members of the military, who became known as the Constitutionalists, rebelled against the civilian junta installed after the 1963 coup now dominated by Donald Reid Cabral, a former vice president of the Council of State. Since Kennedy's death, the moderate social reforms supported by the Alliance for Progress for Latin America had given way to a more pragmatic, probusiness approach that called for supporting dictators if they remained friendly to American businesses, a policy promulgated by Thomas Mann, Johnson's choice as assistant secretary of state for inter-American affairs. Martin viewed Mann as "a right-wing fellow. He had a Texas attitude toward Latin America, the Tex-Mex attitude, the paternalistic, 'Oh, they're all just a bunch of little kids. They have their little revolutions, but they don't mean much.'"

Mann's associates also believed that he operated under a single judgment when it came to Latin Americans, asking the question, "Is he a Communist or isn't he?"[18]

Both Mann and the new American ambassador to the Dominican Republic, W. Tapley Bennett, a career Foreign Service officer, were comfortable with Reid and had funneled $100 million in direct and guaranteed loans to his regime. Reid's influence in the Dominican Republic had suffered, however, due to economic troubles, worsened by the worldwide fall in the price of sugar, a crop that constituted 70 percent of the country's economy. Many Dominicans were also uneasy with Reid's close ties to the United States (many living in Santo Domingo derisively referred to him as "el Americano") and had grown tired of the widespread corruption in their government. To cut costs for sugar production, Reid laid off thousands of workers, increasing unemployment and worsening the lives of ordinary Dominicans. "We seemed to have few ties to the young people and to the left," noted Martin. "And where did we go politically if Reid failed?" He also worried that Bennett had no dealings with Dominicans opposed to the ruling government, including those who supported Bosch's return, particularly members of his Partido Revolucionario Dominicano (Dominican Revolutionary Party, or PRD). "The ambassador should always be in touch, not only with the regime in power, but with the opposition to the regime," said Martin. "He's not doing his job if he's not." After the crisis, Bennett came under fire from some administration officials in Washington, with one source telling a reporter that the ambassador did not seem to know anyone in the country "who was to the left of the Rotary Club," and an embassy associate saying Bennett seemed ill at ease with people "who were not well dressed and to whom he had not been properly introduced."[19]

The countercoup struck while Bennett was away; he left the country for consultations at the State Department the day before the uprising, stopping along the way to visit his mother in Georgia. In addition, eleven of the thirteen officers in the U.S. Military Advisory and Assistance Mission were out of the country, attending a conference in Panama. With the rebels distributing captured weapons to the general populace, anarchy seemed to reign in the capital, with public order collapsing and fighting intensifying into a full-scale civil war with thousands of casualties. Consisting of much of the regular Dominican military and business class, the Loyalists forces, fearing the possibility of defeat, called upon the United States to intervene. Worried about the potential threat to American citizens and the danger that the rebellion might be infiltrated with Fidel Castro–style communists, Bennett pressed the Johnson administration to dispatch American troops to restore order. "If the present loyalist efforts fail," Bennett cabled Washington, "the power will go to groups whose aims are identified with the Communist Party. We might have to intervene to prevent another Cuba." The United States had had a chance to exert its authority earlier and put an end to the fighting when military and political figures from the Constitutionalist cause had met with the ambassador and asked him to mediate an end to the fighting. Through a representative, Bosch had even broached the possibility of resigning as "constitutional president" in favor of José Rafael Molina Ureña, Speaker of the Dominican House and next in line for the presidency. Believing that the Loyalists would have no trouble crushing the rebellion, Bennett declined to intercede and instead tried to convince the Constitutionalists that their cause was hopeless and that they should lay down their arms.[20]

The rebel representatives later told journalists that Bennett had been unnecessarily insulting when speaking to them, responding to their request for him to intercede with the comment, "this is not the time to negotiate, this is the time to surrender." Bennett maintained, however, he told the rebels that he did not have the authority to serve as a mediator in the conflict but would pass along their request to the Loyalists so the two sides could start talking with each other. After being rebuffed by Bennett, an angry Colonel Francisco Alberto Caamaño Deño, who became the popular leader of the insurgent forces, vowed to fight to the death. Bennett remembered that as the rebel leaders were about to leave the room, Caamaño, whom he had never met before that day, stopped and said, "Let me tell you, we shall go on fighting no matter what happens."[21]

On April 28 a force of approximately five hundred Marines landed, followed a few days later by army troops from the 82nd Airborne Division under the overall command of General Bruce Palmer, in a mission code-named Operation Power Pack. They were the first American forces in the Dominican Republic since U.S. Marines occupied the country in

1916 under the orders of President Woodrow Wilson; that occupation lasted until 1924 and left a long legacy of bitterness. Johnson knew his action would be criticized as gunboat diplomacy, but he also realized that doing nothing would open him up to rebukes, noting, "When I do what I am about to do, there'll be a lot of people in this hemisphere I can't live with, but if I don't do it there'll be a lot of people in this country I can't live with." Undersecretary of state George Ball said Johnson's decision might have been influenced by what Ball called "highly dubious" reports from J. Edgar Hoover, Federal Bureau of Investigation director, of a large number of communists in the Dominican Republic. Hoover himself was convinced that Bosch and his allies were "either communists or fellow travelers."[22]

Reading about the intervention, which grew to approximately twenty thousand American troops, Martin felt disheartened by the turn of events in the Dominican Republic. "I feared that once more we had ranged ourselves on the wrong side – *for* an unpopular regime, *against* the people," he noted. Martin could not "make heads or tails" of American policy, telling a newspaper reporter he did not know why U.S. troops were in the country. "I said that if we wanted to really just protect the lives of American citizens," Martin remembered, "it seemed to me that the thing to do would be to take them out of the country and get our troops out." With the benefit of hindsight, Martin criticized Bennett for failing to broker an agreement between the warring factions when he had the chance. "Bennett should have, in my view, kept them talking," said Martin. "As long as they're talking, they're not shooting. And all he would have had to have done would have been to bring them together with somebody from the government and have them sit down in somebody's neutral office, and try to work out a settlement, which we've done before, there and elsewhere." Once the ambassador refused to use his influence to broker a settlement, many of the civilian politicians from Bosch's PRD, including Ureña, abandoned the cause and sought the safety of asylum in foreign embassies. "Civilians, they respect the right of asylum; the military, they don't," Martin said. "So the military men had no choice, but to go back to the street and fight, you see? They had no political leadership or guidance from the Bosch people; they were all in asylum. And this is the vacuum that the communists filled."[23]

Although Johnson had attended Bosch's presidential inauguration in 1963, he had little confidence in Bosch's ability to bring any stability to the Dominican Republic if he were to regain office. Perhaps influenced by its desire to keep Bosch from returning to power, the Johnson administration, which by far preferred former president Joaquín Balaguer, passed along to the press misleading claims from the American Embassy about communist infiltrations into the Constitutionalist's cause. American journalists were quick to ridicule and undermine a list circulated by the embassy (prepared by the Central Intelligence Agency) with names of "Communist and Castroist leaders" among the rebels, a list that included a number of errors. "It was terrible," said Martin, "just sloppy work by the CIA." Bennett had also disseminated to reporters sensational accounts of atrocities committed by the rebels given to him by Loyalist generals, including a wild tale of a police officer having his head cut off, stuck on a pole, and paraded through Santo Domingo's streets. Martin believed that Bennett did not "lie deliberately to them [the media], but they thought he did. From then on, they didn't trust him, and they didn't believe the United States' line. They didn't believe anything we said." Johnson later further inflamed the issue with his extreme rhetoric. The president's own national security advisor, McGeorge Bundy, later admitted that although there was "a mess in Santo Domingo," the graphic accounts the president shared with the media did not "correspond precisely with the evidence that was available to substantiate his proposition." These miscues undermined the Johnson's administration's credibility with the media and helped to spark opposition to the intervention from liberal members of the Democratic Party.[24]

On Thursday, April 29, Martin received telephone calls from Moyers and Ball telling him that Johnson and secretary of state Dean Rusk wanted him to travel to Washington to consult on the Dominican crisis. "I went gladly," said Martin, "grateful for an opportunity to advise and participate." Early the next morning he traveled from Connecticut to Washington via a U.S. Air Force Lockheed Jet Star aircraft, arriving about 6:30 AM and immediately going to the White House Situation Room, where he reviewed the cables and papers about the situation in the Dominican Republic. He also met with Johnson and key officials – Ball, Rusk, secretary of defense Robert McNamara, the

Joints Chiefs of Staff, members of the CIA, and other administration officials – in the Cabinet Room to discuss what American forces should do if the Loyalist forces collapsed. Should U.S. troops then fire upon the rebels? Martin remembered that Rusk pointed out to the president that it was a serious matter to start shooting up a foreign capital with American troops. "I said quickly, 'Yes Mr. President, that's the last thing we want to happen,'" Martin noted. Johnson looked across the table at Martin and responded, "No it isn't. The last thing we want is another Castro in the Caribbean."[25]

The president asked Martin to go to the Dominican Republic and make contact with the rebels; work with Monsignor Emanuele Clarizio, the Papal nuncio (Vatican envoy), to negotiate a cease-fire to stop the bloodshed, something the OAS had requested; and find out what the facts were and report back to him. In addition, Martin believed that one of the main reasons Johnson sent him to the Dominican Republic was to try to re-establish the administration's credibility with American journalists reporting on the crisis, including Tad Szulc of the *New York Times* and Dan Kurzman of the *Washington Post*. "It was a political move," said Martin, "domestic politics." A Johnson adviser told columnist Marguerite Higgins that if Martin, a "liberal's liberal," found out on his mission that communists had overtaken the rebellions, and said so officially, the administration knew it would not "be given a hard time by the Arthur Schlesingers and other liberals of that ilk." Martin had a more humanitarian reason, however, for his decision to serve as a presidential envoy: "to prevent a hell of a lot of Dominicans getting killed by United States troops. Because this seemed to me, clearly, to be the way the government was headed, the way our government was headed."[26]

Taking Harry Shlaudeman, his political officer during his time as ambassador and then the State Department's Dominican Republic desk officer, with him as his aide, Martin hurried from his meeting with Johnson to Andrews Air Force Base to fly to the Dominican Republic. As he left the Cabinet Room, Martin asked Bundy how much time he had before American troops might have to start a shooting war. Bundy said he might have, at most, forty-eight hours to discover what was going on. Martin saw four dangers facing the Dominican Republic: "a Communist takeover, a full-scale U.S. military occupation, an entrenched

Dominican dictator supported by us, or a U.S. Hungary – a frontal assault on the rebel stronghold in Ciudad Nueva, with U.S. troops slaughtering thousands of Dominicans, including innocents" (in 1956 Soviet troops had brutally crushed a rebellion by Hungarians seeking greater political autonomy from Russia). Martin was still unconvinced that communists had actually taken control of the rebel movement, and believed he had the Johnson administration's blessing to say so if he found that to be the case. On their flight, Martin and Shlaudeman compiled a list of the people they would need to see, including American embassy officials, Bosch supporters, Loyalist generals, and numerous others. "At that time," said Martin, "we had no idea how difficult it would be to locate people and get to them in the war-wrecked Republic." He began to realize the difficulty he faced as he witnessed the mess in Santo Domingo, with parts of it burning and the palace a wreck from the fighting. "Seeing thus the city I loved was painful," Martin noted.[27]

Arranging a cease-fire amid the chaos of a civil war proved to be a sometimes dangerous task for Martin. He also had to swallow his distaste for working with Dominican military leaders, including General Elías Wessin y Wessin, who had conspired to overthrow Bosch's democratically elected government. These "gutless Generals," Martin later cabled Washington, seemed to be more than happy to "wait for the U.S. to do the job for them" in taking on the armed rebels. The bitterness engendered by the fierce fighting torpedoed Martin's initial efforts at achieving a cease-fire during his April 30 meeting with Loyalist generals and Lieutenant Emilio Conde, the Constitutionalist representative, at the San Isidro Air Force Base. "This was hate, real and naked," Martin recalled. The sides could not even agree to stop the shooting for a few hours to collect the dead bodies now rotting on the capital city's streets. News of an attack from rebel troops threatened to derail the talks before they had a chance to get started. Taking direct action, Martin approached Wessin, whom he believed had the most power of any of the generals because he controlled the military's tanks, and said they should forget their past differences and instead work together. "President Johnson is deeply concerned about the senseless killing of the Dominican people," Martin told Wessin. "He has sent me here to try to help stop it." He asked the general, who carried a submachine gun into the meeting with him, to be the first to sign the cease-fire. Wessin hesitated for a bit, then went with Martin to Monsignor Clarizio and signed the agreement, followed by other Loyalist generals and Conde. The next day, Saturday, May 1, Martin planned to discuss details of the cease-fire with Caamaño.[28]

While Clarizio broadcast a news announcement about the cease-fire agreement over the radio, Martin, Shlaudeman, and Bennett flew in a helicopter to the U.S. Embassy, where they talked for a bit before the presidential envoys dined on C-rations, found some desks to work at, and set out separately to meet with people they knew. Because gunfire made it impossible to venture into the rebel zone at night, Martin went to see several Dominicans in the International Zone, the perimeter of which was now patrolled by American forces. "The night was black. There were no streetlights," said Martin. "No houses were lit. My driver stopped at checkpoints manned by shadowy men with guns. . . . Sometimes far away, sometimes close, we heard gunfire – sniper fire, machine gun fire, and heavy fire, mortars and 106 mm recoilless rifles." While Martin rode in the front seat with his driver, two U.S. Marines sat in the back holding automatic rifles, serving as his bodyguards on his perilous assignment. One of the Dominicans Martin visited was Antonio Imbert Barrera, a national hero for his part in assassinating Rafael Trujillo, an honorary brigadier general (giving him a military escort for protection), and a conservative man who had kept himself apart from the military officers at San Isidro. Imbert had transformed the Dominican National Police Force of about twelve thousand men into almost his own private army, and he also informed Martin that he controlled three hundred counter-insurgency troops, bragging they were the only worthwhile soldiers in the country. "Imbert is a brave man," Martin noted at the time, "shrewd, blunt, with sources everywhere." While the two men talked at Imbert's house on Sarasota Venue about what had prompted the uprising, Martin received an urgent message from American officials that Bosch had been trying to get in touch with him from his exile in Puerto Rico. Martin hurried back to the embassy to call Bosch, who appeared upset over reports that U.S. Marines had attacked Constitutionalist forces to make it easier for Wessin's troops to advance. "I told him that, so far as I knew, this wasn't true (it wasn't)," said Martin. "I would inquire, and hoped to see his rebel commander . . . [Caamaño] tomorrow." Bosch passed along to Martin possible telephone numbers to reach Caamaño and told him that his arrival in the Dominican Republic had been "the best news he had received."[29]

The danger inherent in Martin's mission became apparent upon his return to Imbert's home at about 1:00 AM. When his driver pulled up to the gate, Martin noticed it was closed and could not see any guards in sight, but knew they were hiding behind the hedge and wall. He told his driver to turn on the inside dome light and "made a 'pssst' sound." In a couple of minutes a guard appeared out of the darkness and approached the car with caution. Not recognizing Martin, the guard returned to the sentry post to call the house for instructions. "At that moment a string of shots went off behind my ear," Martin remembered. "I dived for the floor, began calling out to the guards not to shoot, that it was an accident." Fortunately, Imbert's guards were well-trained and did not return fire. One of Martin's Marine guards had been attempting to put the safety on his weapon, and his hand had slipped and the weapon had gone off by mistake. "Had they been any other Dominican troops they'd have killed me," said a relieved Martin. That was not the last of the gunfire he experienced early that morning. As he and Imbert talked in the dining room, lit with a kerosene lamp, they heard heavy automatic weapons fire that sounded as if it was coming from across the street. Imbert told Martin to get on the floor and the two men "went crouching low to the living room." Imbert believed that the PRD had lost control of the rebellion to the communists, and he seemed confident the war could be ended without a frontal assault on the rebel stronghold at Ciudad Nueva. Martin asked him to see if he could learn more about the rebel leadership. "The thing I want to do," Martin recalled saying to Imbert, "is to stop the killing, stop the bloodshed. That's the first thing."[30]

The morning after his meeting at Imbert's home, Martin began what he called "an elaborate charade" to arrange a meeting with Caamaño, who refused to talk anywhere but at his headquarters behind the rebel lines. "We called him, he called us, we called the Papal Nuncio, he called us, and so on," Martin noted. Finally, Martin and Shlaudeman set out for the rebel stronghold in the southern part of the city in the nuncio's black sedan, its hood covered by a large yellow and white Vatican flag and driven by Clarizio, dressed in his long white robe and red cap. Clarizio, described by a reporter as "a veritable dynamo and a dauntless truce negotiator," drove slowly so any potential snipers could plainly see him, and he also kept the car's windows rolled up so they "would know we did not intend to shoot," said Martin. Reflecting on the trip years later, Martin believed that the instruments of U.S. policy in the Republic – the nuncio and the U.S. Marines – were similar to those employed by the Spanish who had ruled the country for three centuries, "subduing and pacifying the natives by using both the cross and the sword."[31]

At their meeting, Caamaño indicated that he intended to honor the cease-fire, but Martin had difficulty connecting with the colonel because of interruptions by Héctor Aristy Pereyra, a former official with the Council of State and someone Martin had considered to be "a playboy, a smooth operator in both business and politics, intelligent, ambitious, joining party after party and movement after movement." Based in part on this meeting and on information he gleaned from "thoroughly trustworthy sources," Martin came to the conclusion that the political leadership of the Constitutionalist cause had been overtaken by communists and other extremists, and he also worried that the colonel's growing power might go to his head. "In all my time in the Dominican Republic, I had met no man who I thought might become a Dominican [Fidel] Castro – until I met Caamaño," said Martin. "He was winning a revolution from below. He had few political advisers in Santo Domingo at that time but Communists." The people then at the center of the rebellion may not have been, in the well-known phrase of the 1950s, "card-carrying members of the Communist Party," said Martin, but they were extremists who were "committed to violent revolution and would have ended up with a Castro-style government if they succeeded."[32]

As the American envoys and the nuncio left the meeting, they were greeted with wild cheers by a crowd of about two hundred who had gathered on the spot and who previously had heard a speech from Aristy praising Martin's friendship for the Dominican people. "I had hoped to avoid being used by either side," said Martin. "Now I was caught." As they pushed through the crowd and were able to get into the nuncio's car, ordinary people in the crowd thrust their hands inside to shake their hands, crying out, "We trust you, Mr. Martin," "We have faith in you," and "We want democracy." While moved by the demonstration, Martin knew it had been well-organized, and Shlaudeman had noted that a black-shirted young man, a member of a far left political party, had been yelling "Yankee go home" before being jerked out of sight. "He had used the wrong script," noted Martin. Still, the plight of the Dominicans weighed heavily on Martin's mind, and he told Shlaudeman that night that he had never done a "dishonorable thing until that day." He said he had accepted the friendship of the rebels and the ordinary people gathered at their headquarters, but they might all be slaughtered in the coming days, possibly even by gunfire from U.S. forces, a horrible thought for Martin. Shlaudeman, however, held out hope that the cease-fire they had negotiated would hold, saving thousands of lives, and that now they had to work to avoid another Hungary. "I doubted that we could," said Martin, who remembered overhearing young marines bragging about achieving their first kills. "They had been so trained. What a world."[33]

In spite of Martin's fears and sporadic gunfire throughout the night, the cease-fire held. Because of the animosity between the two sides, however, he saw no chance for a political settlement at that time, and he sensed a "rising determination" from U.S. officials and Loyalist generals to use American troops in direct action against the rebels. "I began to think our gravest danger lay in being provoked into a massacre," Martin said. "Indeed, now that the U.S. troops had landed and the Communists knew they could not win, perhaps the Communists' new objective was to provoke us into just that." The only hope he saw was to gain time by maintaining the hard-won cease-fire and hope that Dominicans "might come to their senses" in time and reconciliation could come through the rise of new political leaders. Martin shared his conclusions by telephone with Johnson, who had been keeping a close watch on events in the country, running the operation "like a desk officer in the State Department." The president, who had been pushing the line that the rebel cause had been infiltrated and controlled by communists, expressed his satisfaction with Martin's work, telling him, "I'm very, very proud of you and what you have done." Johnson also instructed his envoy to pass the word along that there had been "no gunboat stuff about this. ... I think you ought to tell about your sympathies and your feelings and how you are opposed to dictatorship.... Maybe you, as a man that's not

responsible for this operation, could talk better than somebody else."
Martin had also reported his conclusions about the rebel movement falling under control by "Castro Communism" and its democratic elements
"destroyed" at a joint press conference with Bennett on Sunday, May 2,
the first time, noted Kurzman, that an American official had "gone on
the record with so unequivocal a statement." Caamaño was quick to tell
reporters that the rebel movement did not "have a Communist problem." He accused American embassy officers of having "Communists on
the brain." The rebel colonel did say that there were some communists
who attempted to "latch on to the movement," but they had no power
and were not in a position to gain any. Those supporting the Johnson
administration were quick to piggyback on Martin's assessment, with
one official saying, "It is one minute to midnight and if we do not act at
once in the political field the movement will really become Communist
and we shall have to maintain a permanent military occupation in this
country."[34]

Perhaps remembering their earlier experience with the list of communists supplied by the U.S. Embassy, reporters greeted Martin's announcement with some skepticism, although many believed him to be,
as Kurzman called him, "a scrupulously honest man." Interviewing Martin while he ate a hasty lunch at the embassy residence, Kurzman said
that when he asked him if he could offer any concrete evidence about his
charges, Martin would only say that such "evidence existed but could
not be divulged." The reporter noted that Martin looked much older
than he remembered him looking when he last saw him a year before.
"His thin face was more wrinkled and his frail body more bent, and his
hands trembled slightly," Kurzman noted. In spite of his frail looks, however, the reporter said that Martin had driven himself relentlessly while
on his mission. The physical strain on the envoy, Kurzman added, paled
in comparison to the emotional strain of being in a country wracked
by bitterness and hatred as a result of the civil war. Tad Szulc, another
reporter who interviewed the former ambassador, believed that Martin's
bitter disappointment at Bosch's overthrow two years before and now
seeing the chaos and bloodshed in a country in which he had placed
his hopes had made him "slide too easily into despair." According to
Kurzman, Martin's suspicions of alleged communist influence in the

rebel cause were not necessarily wrong, but they did seem to be based on "impressions and assumptions rather than facts, unless the facts were among those he was unable to divulge." Later, in his book *Overtaken by Events*, Martin did list the names of those he believed were Castro communists who had jointed the rebellion, including leading officials of the Partido Socialista Popular and Movimento Popular Dominicano, as well as the extremist wing of the June 14th Movement. "During the Civil War," said Martin, "our intelligence agents saw many of these men at rebel headquarters or strongpoints. Independently, Shlaudeman and I were told by thoroughly trustworthy sources that they were there."[35]

On the evening of May 2 Martin journeyed to Puerto Rico, where he met with Bosch at the home of Jaime Benítz, chancellor of the University of Puerto Rico. Before the gathering, Johnson had told him that all options were still open, and he did not rule out reinstalling Bosch as president. "Just go explore everything and see what you can get," Martin quoted Johnson as instructing him. In his talks with Martin, Bosch insisted that a meeting of the Dominican legislature should be held to vote on a general amnesty and install Ureña as the new president. Martin tried to explain to Bosch that such a meeting would be impossible given the chaos still gripping Santo Domingo. In a subsequent talk with Martin, Bosch also expressed a reluctance to return to his country, feeling he had been "burned" by previous events, including accusations from some American officials that he was a communist. When Martin asked him if he might be willing to go to the Dominican Republic to advise and assist on rebuilding the nation, Bosch responded, "No. I cannot. If I return, I am the president. The Constitution provides for only one president." The meeting was interrupted by a telephone call to Martin from Abe Fortas, a Johnson friend and aide, asking him to obtain a statement from Bosch indicating the United States had saved the Dominican Republic from a communist takeover. "I told Fortas I didn't think there was a chance in the world he'd do this," Martin recalled, but Fortas asked him to try anyway. As Martin had thought, Bosch refused to have any part of such a statement. "Bosch isn't stupid," Martin later said. "He's a lot of things, but he isn't stupid."[36]

On Monday, May 3, Martin returned to the Dominican Republic, where he worked to find a third force to help make peace, as he believed that Caamaño and the rebels would never reach an understanding with Wessin and the San Isidro generals. The United States, however, could not completely sever its ties to the previous Dominican government controlled by the generals, as that would leave American troops facing off against the rebels, something Martin wanted to avoid at all costs. The answer came in a telephone call from Imbert, who asked Martin to his house to discuss forming a new government. The two men discussed the matter, and Imbert agreed to lend his support. On May 7 a Government of National Reconstruction came into being with Imbert as president; other members of the new junta included Colonel Pedro Bartolomé Benoit; Alejandro Zeller Cocco, whom Martin did not know but who had impressed Bennett; Carolos Grisolía Poloney, a lawyer described by Martin as "honest, intelligent, level-headed, an impressive senator in my time"; and Julio D. Postigo, a close friend of Bosch's and a bookstore owner and publisher. Martin now viewed Imbert as a "necessary bulwark against anarchy" and said a government under him now seemed to be the best solution for the Dominican Republic, a determination backed by the White House, which he said had encouraged him to make the arrangements with Imbert. "I didn't want [the United States] to fight the rebels," he recalled. "I wanted some Dominican to fight the rebels. And Imbert was the guy; he was the only one with any guts, the only one with any troops."[37]

Even with the Imbert government now in control, Martin continued to try to craft a political solution, meeting once again with Caamaño in an attempt to get talks started between the rebels and Imbert. To help break the impasse, Johnson sent a new negotiating team to the country in mid-May that included Bundy, Mann, deputy secretary of defense Cyrus R. Vance, and Peace Corps director Jack Hood Vaughan. These negotiators, said Martin, "cut the ground out from under Imbert and tried to install a president of more liberal coloration," selecting Antonio Guzmán, the former minister of agriculture during Bosch's administration. "He had been my first choice to enter the Imbert government; I had tried unsuccessfully for hours to persuade him to do it," Martin noted. Caamaño agreed to step aside in favor of Guzmán, but Imbert, enraged at what he saw as American perfidy, refused. Martin speculated that Johnson decided to dump Imbert because he had received criticism from the U.S. press about Imbert being "another Trujillo, a kind of gangster, an assassin, and a rightist." Supporting such an individual might damage the president politically, Martin added, and might explain why the administration decided to try to build a new government around Guzmán.[38]

The Guzmán gambit, as Martin called it, eventually failed, and on May 18 Martin left Santo Domingo with Mann for Washington, staying there for an additional ten days. Ironically, Mann, usually considered a conservative, Martin noted, had been working with Bundy on installing the liberal Guzmán government, while Martin, a liberal sent by Johnson to the Dominican Republic to talk to the rebels, had ended up helping set up the conservative Imbert regime. On May 19 Martin participated in a tense meeting with Johnson, Humphrey, Rusk, McNamara, and other administration officials on whether to favor Imbert or Guzmán. "After the meeting had been going on for more than three hours," Martin recalled, "it began to relax simply because of the passage of time, and some of us caught ourselves forgetting we were addressing the president of the United States, he seemed more like a county board chairman running a courthouse meeting on a sewer bond issue."[39]

In early June the OAS sent a new negotiating team to the Dominican Republic that included representatives Ilmar Penna Marinho from Brazil, Ramón de Clairmont Duenes from El Salvador, and Ellsworth Bunker (American ambassador to the OAS) from the United States; the negotiators were supported in their efforts by a contingent of troops from Latin America, as the United States slowly reduced the number of its forces in the country. By the summer of 1965 all sides had agreed to an Act of Dominican Reconciliation with a provisional government headed by Héctor García-Godoy, formerly foreign minister under Bosch. On June 1, 1966, Dominicans elected Balaguer as president with approximately 57 percent of the vote. He defeated Bosch – who had returned to the Dominican Republic on September 25, 1965, the second anniversary of his overthrow – amid charges of intimidation and fraud among PRD supporters and their allies. Over the years Martin had tended to think of his days in the Dominican Republic as a failure, but in the years from Trujillo's assassination to 1986, discounting the 1965 civil war, the Dominican people, he noted, lived "in peace and freedom, the longest period of peace and freedom in all Dominican history. Our military intervention turned out far better than we had any right to expect."[40]

As Johnson's envoy to the Dominican Republic, Martin had, in spite of the mess with the Imbert government, accomplished two of his main goals: obtaining an initial cease-fire and preventing any "massacre of the Dominicans by the Americans." Such service sometimes translates into a job with a president's administration, and Johnson seemed amenable to the idea. Several times since he had left the Kennedy administration Martin had thought about going back into government, but he had turned down a request from Sargent Shriver, Peace Corps director, to head the program's effort in Brazil and had rejected an offer from the State Department to be the U.S. ambassador to Jamaica. Now, after performing several missions for Johnson, Martin saw him alone in the Oval Office, and the president proposed that he move to Washington permanently as a consultant to him and the State Department. "I didn't want to do it and made some noncommittal response," Martin remembered, "and we talked on, then he asked if there was anything else I wanted to say to him. I told him I'd be interested in another embassy but not a sinecure like Jamaica, an important one and one where we had a chance of success." The president indicated Martin was "entitled" to such a position, adding, "I'd like to see you have it." Asking him where he might want to be posted, Martin suggested to Johnson somewhere like Venezuela, and as he left the president said he would try to keep in touch. Subsequently, Moyers pushed Martin to accept the consultant position, saying he would have only nominal contact with the State Department and instead would actually be "the president's principal speechwriter and one of his principal advisers, and he indicated it might well lead to a very good embassy." Later, talking with Fran, Martin began to realize just how carefully Johnson had phrased his response. "He'd said I deserved an embassy but he hadn't said he'd see that I got one, he'd said he'd like to see me have it," Martin recalled. Such an offer never came, and Martin presumed he never received an ambassadorial appointment because he had declined to show the personal loyalty Johnson demanded when he declined the offer to join the president's staff.[41]

In the aftermath of the American intervention in the Dominican Republic, Martin spent a lot of his time talking with reporters and his liberal friends and trying to explain the reasons behind the intervention (writing an article on his experiences in the Dominican civil war for *Life* magazine). Many of them opposed the Johnson administration's decision to send troops to the Caribbean, including Schlesinger, who refrained from publicly criticizing Martin. Other friends in the media trusted Martin's assessment about the situation in the Dominican Republic, with Jack Fischer, editor of *Harper's*, speaking for many when he said he put his "complete faith in his [Martin's] skill as an investigator, reporter, his basic decency and his judgment." One of these encounters helped to set the course for a project that consumed much of Martin's time for several years to come. During a July 1965 luncheon at the home of Katharine Graham, publisher of the *Washington Post*, Martin met with Adlai Stevenson. Although Stevenson had been attempting to explain America's actions in the Dominican Republic as the American ambassador to the United Nations, he remained "bewildered" about the reasons behind the move. "Nothing has caused me so much trouble," Stevenson had written Schlesinger, "since the Bay of Pigs and it goes on and on." For an hour or more after lunch, Martin attempted to explain what the United States was trying to do through its military intervention, and Stevenson "seemed to accept the explanation." The former presidential candidate also asked Martin to come to New York because he wished to talk to him about a major writing project he had in mind. "I got the impression," said Martin, "that he wanted me to help him write his autobiography."[42]

Martin, who considered Stevenson to be "one of the most important figures" in his life, never had the opportunity to discover what Stevenson might have had in mind for their collaboration. On July 14, 1965, Stevenson was in London following a speech in Geneva, Switzerland. During his stay, Stevenson had met with British prime minister Harold Wilson and had visited friends. That day after lunch he and Marietta Peabody Tree, his confidante and lover, went for a walk in Grosvenor Square near the U.S. Embassy; he wanted to show her the house he had lived in while working on the UN Preparatory Commission following World War II. The house, however, had been torn down and replaced with a modern building, which caused Stevenson to sigh and comment, "That makes me feel old." The duo walked on toward Hyde Park, but Stevenson asked

Tree to slow down before uttering his final words, "I am going to faint." He fell over backward, hitting his head on the pavement, unconscious. Although passersby, including a heart doctor, tried to help, and an ambulance arrived to take him to the hospital, Stevenson died of a massive heart attack.[43]

News of Stevenson's death reached Martin while he and his family were staying at Smith Lake. That night he and Fran took a train to Chicago, where they spent time in Adlai III's office working with Newton Minow and others on funeral arrangements before taking a flight to Washington to attend a service for Stevenson at the National Cathedral. There, offering his condolences to Martin on the loss of his friend, Johnson said of Stevenson, "He showed us the way." Flying back on the presidential plane taking Stevenson's body home to Illinois, Martin fell into a conversation with Schlesinger, who told Martin he should write a biography on the two-time Democratic presidential candidate. Initially, however, Martin put that idea aside and told Stevenson's sons during a wake that he hoped they would not "merely name an expressway after him but would do something like establish an institute, perhaps at a university, that could train promising young leaders from the Third World, the Third World whose importance Stevenson had been early to realize." An expressway in Chicago was named in Stevenson's honor, but Martin's wishes came true in part when in 1968 the Adlai Stevenson Institute for International Affairs was founded at the University of Chicago. "It is a terrible thing in so many ways," Martin wrote his daughter, Cindy, about Stevenson's death. "He meant so much to so many people he never heard of, and did so much for them. And there are so few as half as good." Martin noted he felt a bleak feeling of loss and emptiness, but he realized his sorrow would be softened in time "by the memories we have – the privilege of the friendship of a great human being – the laughter and the victories as well as the tears and defeats, all shared – and the knowledge that a nation that can produce him and President Kennedy too may yet become the place they worked to make it."[44]

At first, the Stevenson family turned to another person close to their father, Walter Johnson, a longtime University of Chicago history professor, as its choice to write the definitive Stevenson biography. Johnson certainly had the necessary knowledge, as he had been national cochairman for the movement to draft Stevenson as the Democratic presidential candidate in 1952 and became a close friend of the former governor. Instead of tackling the biography, however, Johnson decided to serve as editor of a collection of Stevenson's letters, writings, and speeches. "I felt it was time to get the solid material out," Johnson later said. "When I began I was thinking of two or three volumes. But there was so much good material, and it soon became evident that it would require several more volumes." *The Papers of Adlai Stevenson*, published from 1972 to 1979 by Little, Brown and Company, grew to eight volumes under Johnson's editorship, assisted by Carol Evans, Stevenson's secretary for many years.[45]

According to Martin, Adlai III, a few months after his father's death, had sought his advice about the biography, asking him if any writer the family selected might be willing to share royalties to help support the establishment of a Stevenson Institute. "I told him that I myself had never split royalties but that in these circumstances, to help the institute and because of my feelings for his father, I probably would," Martin recalled. He suggested names of several writers as possibilities, but none of them panned out, and after a time Adlai III asked Martin to take on the project. "I've always been a fact writer and I've always written about people. These two elements come together better in biography than in any other form," Martin noted. In October 1965 he wrote Ivan von Auw Jr., one of his agents, along with Dorothy Olding at Harold Ober Associates, that he had been in talks about the biography with Adlai III and Minow. "They're for me, and so are most others, but I think two important people [Martin did not name them] are not; and while Adlai and Minow seem to be all but certain that I will be anointed, I'm somewhat less so."[46]

Fran had counseled her husband to reject the assignment, as she considered doing the Stevenson biography as "going back," and she wanted him not to "relive the past but to move forward." She added that to do a proper biography of Stevenson would take a long time and the family might prove to be difficult. Fran's reservations had some validity in the end, but Martin decided to forge ahead with the biography on someone he considered to be "an extraordinarily appealing civilized human being." Doubleday and Company, publisher of Martin's *Overtaken by Events*, agreed to back the project, offering financial support of approximately $200,000, with a due date for the book of January 2,

1969. Martin approved splitting his royalties with Stevenson's sons and gave Adlai III, acting for the family, the right to review the manuscript before publication. They also established a procedure to follow if they could not reach agreement on suggested changes, with the issue going for binding arbitration to Carl McGowan, a federal judge and Stevenson's former chief of staff, or if McGowan was unavailable to Minow, Stevenson's former law partner. These legal precautions were spelled out ahead of time to avoid the problems William Manchester had experienced with Jacqueline Kennedy and Robert Kennedy in writing about John Kennedy's assassination in *The Death of a President,* eventually published in 1967 after long, tense negotiations and a lawsuit prompted by Jacqueline Kennedy. Martin later said he did not like the idea of the book being Stevenson's "official" biography, as the word conveyed the "idea that the [Stevenson] family controlled the manuscript, and therefore the book cannot be trusted entirely. That's not the situation."[47]

Martin started his work on the Stevenson biography in December 1965. For a few months, he and his family rented and lived in Stevenson's farm in Libertyville, Illinois, where Martin had visited him often during his lifetime, finding the place to be "light and airy, filled with sunshine, cheering." Martin kept expecting to see Stevenson's "dumpy figure waddling up the sloping field from the Des Plaines River, picking up dead tree branches as he came; to enter through the sun porch, blue eyes wide, cross the living room and, looking slightly perplexed, hesitate by the fireplace; then, grumbling about 'this appalling task,' go into his study to work on a speech." With the assistance of his old friend Francis Nipp, who worked for a time as his research assistant, Martin catalogued Stevenson's library and discovered reference books, bound copies of Stevenson's speeches, family histories, and numerous items on Abraham Lincoln and Illinois. "He was a man of Illinois, always; even after he belonged to the world," Martin said of Stevenson, "Illinois history, the Illinois prairies, and above all these seventy acres held him." Scattered about Stevenson's office were a bust of President Kennedy, "gorgeous" pictures of a cruise Stevenson had taken on a private yacht during his UN years, an autographed picture of President Johnson, a collection of plaster donkeys (the Democratic Party's symbol), and mementos of Stevenson's travels around the world. "Under his desk blotter was a scrap of paper containing in his handwriting a notation that Artie, his Dalmatian, was buried by a tree outside his study window," Martin recalled. The biographer found that his subject had been "a string saver; he almost never threw anything away." On the wall of the basement stairs Martin saw a lithograph from the 1892 presidential campaign, when Stevenson's namesake had been elected vice president as the running mate of Grover Cleveland, plus one from 1900 when the elder Stevenson lost with Democratic presidential candidate William Jennings Bryan. The basement also included an old filing cabinet with one drawer stuck tight. "I finally pried it open – and found Stevenson's daily appointment books covering his entire four years as Governor," remembered Martin.[48]

In addition to the items he uncovered at Stevenson's home, Martin explored materials at the Illinois State Historical Library in Springfield; the State Department in Washington; the U.S. Mission to the UN in New York; and Princeton University, where Stevenson had graduated in 1922. Martin also received a grant from the Rockefeller Foundation to work on the book while staying with Fran and Fred at the foundation's Villa Serbelloni on Lake Como in Italy. Fran brought with her seventeen footlockers crammed full of items on Stevenson. During his search of what Martin called Stevenson's "enormous" archive, he found not only the longhand first drafts of the presidential candidate's famous speeches, old love letters, campaign contribution lists, and income tax returns, but such minutiae as ticket stubs to Princeton football games and old dance programs. Martin and Nipp copied several hundred thousand pages of Stevenson's papers, placing the copies into loose-leaf binders, each containing upwards of two hundred pages. They numbered the binders and gave each one a special symbol designating whether it contained correspondence, speeches, or other material. "We indexed the copies, making an average of perhaps a thousand 5-by-8-inch cards on each of the sixty-five years of his life, and arranged them chronologically," said Martin, who used the cards to write the rough draft, as they guided him to material in the binders. "I write from the actual documents," he noted. Martin acknowledged that there was "a certain amount of accountancy to this type of research," but it was the way he worked. "It's clumsy, it's awkward, it's slow – it takes a lot of time – but you don't make many mistakes this way," he noted. "And that's the whole purpose." To fill in any gaps in the information, Martin interviewed nearly two hundred people involved in Stevenson's life, dictating his interview notes and indexing them in binders as well. The interviews included some he did in the summer of 1966 in Bloomington, Illinois, with Stevenson's family and friends. These were especially important because Martin believed that nobody could understand Stevenson unless they understood the town where he grew up. "It was there that I discovered that Stevenson's childhood, far from the happy time usually pictured, had been a horror," said Martin, including a tragedy in which Stevenson accidentally killed a young friend with a rifle.[49]

In the fall of 1966 Martin and his family moved to Princeton, New Jersey, and it was there that he realized the "generous" royalty advance, which he had invested "for my future," and the research grant he had received from Doubleday would not be enough to finish the book Martin had originally estimated it would take him three years to write; it ended up taking a decade. Looking for supplementary income (he estimated it would cost him $30,000 more in research funds to complete the Stevenson biography), Martin thought of writing once again for the magazine market, writing Olding that he did not mind borrowing "more money from the bank to carry expenses if there seems a good chance of writing pieces that will sell for enough to repay the loans and keep me going." Martin, however, had the good fortune to receive a one-year appointment as a visiting professor in public affairs at the Woodrow Wilson School of Public and International Affairs at Princeton. "After that, Arthur Schlesinger had me appointed visiting professor at the Graduate Center of the City University of New York, where he himself now taught," said Martin. He commuted to CUNY from Princeton to teach his seminar, which dealt with the limits of American power in foreign policy, something he had been obliged to think about while writing *Overtaken by Events* and researching Stevenson's UN work. He particularly remembered something President Kennedy had said to him while they had talked about Bosch's overthrow in the Dominican Republic. "There are some things," Martin remembered Kennedy as saying, "we simply cannot do." Students in Martin's seminar were required to write a paper on a foreign policy emergency, for example, the Cuban Missile Crisis or the Korean War, "laying out the policy alternatives among which our policy makers had been obliged to choose and identifying the factors that had limited American power and thus helped force the policy choice."[50]

The limitations on American power were often on Martin's mind, and not just because of the seminar he taught. In addition to working on the Stevenson book, he had been delivering speeches to several groups, including universities and political organizations, on foreign policy topics, especially the Dominican intervention. Americans had begun to link the intervention in the Caribbean to the country's growing involvement in Vietnam, where the 189,000 U.S. troops stationed there by the end of 1965 had doubled by the end of the following year. "I was careful to explain our Dominican policy but stay clear of the Vietnam War," said Martin, who had instead been preoccupied by Johnson's 1964 presidential campaign and the Dominican civil war. By late 1966 or 1967, however, he had joined his friends, among them Schlesinger, in opposition to the Vietnam War. That war would, in many ways, interfere with his work on the Stevenson book, as student protests against the Johnson administration's Vietnam policies helped ignite a fight in the Democratic Party for its 1968 presidential nomination, to be decided in late August 1968 at the party's convention in Chicago. That battle drew Martin into his old role as a speechwriter, saw him once again be part of a Kennedy's campaign for the presidency, and returned him to the state where he had grown up and which he had left behind so many years before.[51]

NINE

The Return of the Native

IN THE 1960S THE MAROTT HOTEL, LOCATED ON THE NEAR north side of Indianapolis at 2625 North Meridian Street, had faded from its original glory days of the 1920s and 1930s, when it had hosted key political and social events for the community and welcomed such famous guests as Winston Churchill, Clark Gable, and Herbert Hoover. On the evening of April 4, 1968, however, the hotel hummed once again with activity as staffers for U.S. senator Robert F. Kennedy strolled up and down its hallways. They were staying there after the end of a long first day in Kennedy's quest to win Indiana's Democratic presidential primary. Kennedy's senate speechwriters Adam Walinsky and Jeff Greenfield, along with a new member of the team, John Bartlow Martin, were busy discussing the details of a foreign policy speech their candidate was slated to deliver later at Louisiana State University when they were interrupted by a secretary, who told them that civil rights leader Martin Luther King Jr. had been shot in Memphis, Tennessee. Later, while at dinner, they heard that King had died.[1]

Kennedy's staff scrambled to decide if the candidate should cancel his schedule, which included the opening of his downtown campaign headquarters and a speech at an outdoor event at Seventeenth and Broadway Streets in a predominantly African American neighborhood. In a squad car at the curb near the Marott, Martin came across an Indianapolis police inspector and asked his advice about whether or not Kennedy should appear at the rally. "I sure hope he does," Martin remembered the policeman fervently saying. "If he doesn't, there'll be hell to pay. He's the only one can do it." The policeman feared that a race riot might break out in Indianapolis when African Americans learned of King's death, and Kennedy was one of the few white politicians blacks would listen to. Martin suggested to the officer that he call headquarters, and the officer learned that Kennedy was on his way to the rally. "The inspector said he'd go there," Martin remembered. "Walinsky went with him to be sure Bobby knew [about King's death]. Greenfield and I went to our rooms to draft a statement on King's death for Bobby."[2]

Arriving at the rally, Kennedy, wearing a black overcoat once belonging to his brother, John, climbed onto a flatbed truck in a paved parking lot near the Broadway Christian Center's basketball court. After asking for those waving signs and banners to put them down, he informed them that King had been killed. The audience packed in tight near the makeshift stage had been anticipating a raucous political event and for the most part were unaware of the shooting, and they responded to the announcement with gasps, shrieks, and cries of "No, No." Facing the now stunned and disbelieving audience, some of whom were weeping at their loss, Kennedy gave an impassioned, extemporaneous six-minute speech that has gone down in history as one of the great addresses in the modern era. He said in part: "What we need in the United States is not division; what we need in the United States is not hatred; what we need in the United States is not violence or lawlessness; but love and wisdom, and compassion toward one another, and a feeling of justice toward those who still suffer within our country, whether they be white or they be black." Hearing about the candidate's moving words from campaign aide Fred Dutton, Martin and Greenfield threw away the statements they had so carefully written for Kennedy. "What he had said was so much better than anything we had written," Martin remembered.[3]

Kennedy's dramatic speech was just the opening salvo in a whirlwind two-month campaign. "It was tough. Indiana is not Kennedy country," Martin recalled. "It was fun, too, because it was so helter skelter. And because, since I knew the state, I exerted influence." When he decided to enter the primary there, Indiana marked the first test of Kennedy's long-shot effort at wresting the Democratic presidential nomination from incumbent Lyndon B. Johnson, as well as fellow U.S. senator Eugene McCarthy of Minnesota, who had been the first to challenge the president. In addition to Indiana, Kennedy looked to primaries in other states, including Nebraska, Oregon, South Dakota, California, and New York. Martin sensed that the time might be right for a candidate like Kennedy because of the country's mood. "The people didn't want programs. They wanted leadership," he said. "They had programs running out of their ears and look at the mess they were in? They wanted a man. This is what ignited the Kennedy crowds." The primary campaign in his old home state was, in many ways, Martin noted, the "climactic event" in his life, bringing together "writing, politics, and Indiana." And yet the entire matter had "rather sneaked up" on him.[4]

Before the political uproar began in 1968, Martin had started the year in his rented house in Princeton, New Jersey, where he worked steadily on his biography of Adlai Stevenson, also commuting once a week to teach his seminar at the City University of New York. There were interruptions to his routine, such as when a search committee at a small college in Illinois approached him to gauge his interest in becoming president of the institution and when representatives from the Gulf and Western conglomerate asked him to serve as a consultant on its plans to buy a sugar plantation in the Dominican Republic; nothing came of either offer.[5]

Even before Kennedy's risky decision to enter the 1968 presidential contest, Martin had maintained close ties to the former attorney general. In the spring of 1964 Martin had participated in an oral history program with the new John F. Kennedy Presidential Library in Boston, Massachusetts, whereby members of the Kennedy administration were interviewed for their insights on their time in office. "A Kennedy-style campaign," said Arthur M. Schlesinger Jr., "was organized to conduct interviews while memories were still vivid." At Robert Kennedy's request, Martin helped out, interviewing the attorney general during some long sessions in February, March, and April 1964, a time when Kennedy was still struggling to come to grips with his brother's death and also harbored bitter feelings for the man who had replaced him as president, Johnson. Kennedy's feelings were still raw about the assassination. When Martin asked him if he wanted to discuss the events of November 22, 1963, Kennedy responded, "No, I don't think I need to go into that." Martin remembered the interviews as being "excruciatingly hard work for both of us. He both wanted and feared to have me ask hard questions about his brother, and I felt much the same way, not boring in as I would have in a different sort of interview, but at the same time conscious that I could not escape an obligation to history."[6]

The interviews became particularly valuable for those attempting to unearth the hostility that developed between Kennedy and Johnson. Johnson had always believed that Kennedy had tried to deny him the vice presidential nomination in 1960, while Kennedy viewed the Texas politician as someone incapable of telling the truth. "He lies even when he doesn't have to," Kennedy told Martin. In an interview with Martin on May 14, 1964, in New York, Kennedy said there were a number of matters that arose between November 22 and November 27, 1963, that had made him bitter, or at least unhappy, with Johnson, including the new president's treatment of Jacqueline Kennedy on the flight from Dallas, Texas, to Washington, D.C., and the rush removal by Johnson of his brother's items from the Oval Office. Later, Kennedy believed that Johnson received too much credit for passing legislation that his brother had initiated. Martin and Kennedy also engaged in a substantive discussion on the merits of Kennedy's obtaining the vice presidential nomination under Johnson in the 1964 election. While Kennedy appeared skeptical about the possibility, Martin argued forcefully for him to seek the post, saying he had a "unique position – and not just in the party but in the minds of the American people." That argument failed to sway Kennedy, who believed it would be "an unpleasant relationship" if it happened and that he would not have any influence on Johnson and would lose his ability to make independent decisions. Johnson eventually sidestepped the difficult choice of accepting Kennedy as his running mate by excluding from consideration all members of his cabinet, or those who met regularly with it, which eliminated Stevenson. "I am sorry that I had to take so many nice fellows down with me," said Kennedy, who instead ran for and won the U.S. Senate seat from New York.[7]

By the fall of 1967 liberal activists in the Democratic Party opposed to the war in Vietnam had begun seeking an alternative candidate for the next year's presidential contest. Urged on by some members of his senate staff, Kennedy had also been flirting with the possibility of opposing Johnson. "How can we possibly survive five more years of Lyndon Johnson?" Kennedy asked Schlesinger. "Five more years of a crazy man?"

Other advisers, however, warned him that if he ran for the presidency against Johnson he would be committing political suicide. During his time at Lake Como in Italy working on his Stevenson biography, Martin had joined the chorus of those urging Kennedy to tackle Johnson, who Martin believed might not be electable. He urged Kennedy to think about lining up second-choice convention delegates for himself in 1968. "Yet the thought of his running made me uneasy," said Martin. "I had vague stirrings of the fear he might be assassinated." Those fears might have prompted Martin to later advise Kennedy that he should work to establish a senatorial subcommittee to investigate the handling of the war in Vietnam, modeled on the committee headed by Harry Truman during World War II. "Whatever one thinks of the morality or wisdom of the war in Viet Nam," Martin wrote Kennedy, "widespread misgivings exist among the American people that the war has been mishandled in a number of ways." The subcommittee's purpose, said Martin, should be to produce "reliable facts; to confirm or allay once and for all the public misgivings; to reduce and if possible eliminate waste, extravagance, and corruption; and to inquire in general into how well the war is being conducted." Kennedy did explore the establishment of a special presidential commission composed of influential figures in politics and the military to study and provide recommendations on the war to the Johnson administration, but Johnson and his new secretary of defense, Clark Clifford, rejected the plan as unworkable.[8]

Kennedy turned down an offer by a group of student activists, the Conference of Concerned Democrats, to take on the president on behalf of its "Dump Johnson" movement. Rebuffed by Kennedy, the activists, Allard K. Lowenstein (later a U.S. congressman) and Curtis Gans, both involved in the liberal organization Americans for Democratic Action, considered a number of possibilities, including U.S. senators Frank Church and George McGovern, before finally getting their man: McCarthy, the poetry writing, gray-haired, fifty-one-year-old senator from Minnesota who had been growing more and more doubtful about his country's role in Vietnam. As early as 1967 McCarthy, joined by fourteen other Democratic senators, had signed a public letter urging the president to continue a bombing halt over the Christmas holiday. He had also been infuriated by testimony from Nicholas Katzenbach, undersecretary of state, at a Senate Foreign Relations Committee hearing that Johnson had the constitutional power to do whatever he wished in Vietnam. "There comes a time when an honorable man must raise the flag," McCarthy said of his decision to face off against Johnson in Democratic primaries.[9]

After a rough start – 60 percent of the American public had never heard of McCarthy when he started his campaign on November 30, 1967 – the senator quickly picked up support from college students across the country, energized in their opposition to the war after the shocking Tet Offensive by North Vietnamese soldiers and their Viet Cong allies at the end of January 1968. Although the offensive was a military defeat for North Vietnam, the breadth and ferocity of the assault stunned the American public, especially images of the U.S. Embassy under attack in Saigon and graphic footage of a suspected Viet Cong guerrilla being executed by the chief of South Vietnam's national police. With the Johnson administration suffering from a growing "credibility gap" between reality on the ground in Vietnam and its carefully groomed, optimistic pronouncements about the war's progress, McCarthy's insurgent campaign blossomed. On March 12 McCarthy came within an eyelash of defeating Johnson, an incumbent president, in the New Hampshire primary, finishing only 230 votes behind Johnson with the aid of 5,511 Republican write-in ballots. (Richard Nixon easily won the Republican primary.) "I think I can get the nomination," an ecstatic McCarthy told reporters as he prepared to move his campaign to Wisconsin for the primary there on April 2.[10]

The day voters made their choices in New Hampshire, Martin received a telephone call from Kennedy, who told him he intended to announce his own candidacy for the presidency on Saturday, March 16, from the Senate Caucus Room – the same room from which John Kennedy had begun his race for the Democratic nomination for president eight years before. Robert Kennedy asked for Martin's help in drafting an announcement statement and also sought his assistance for the race to come. It was a natural fit, as the two men shared a compassion for those Martin once described as "*los de abajo,* those from below." Especially since his brother's death, Kennedy had developed a need to speak on behalf of the disadvantaged in American society, said Martin, a group that included African Americans, poor Appalachian whites, starving Native Americans, and Hispanic migrant workers. "He had no contact with, no rapport with, no feel for, the petit bourgeois, the suburbanites," said Martin, something that came back to haunt the candidate in the Oregon primary. Martin worked on a statement and telephoned what he had written to Kennedy's secretary, Angie Novello. When Kennedy made his announcement about his candidacy for the presidency, he said his decision to challenge Johnson reflected "no personal animosity" toward the president, but did point out the "profound differences over where we are heading and what we want to accomplish." Martin's help became particularly important when the Kennedy campaign decided to test its strength with voters by entering the Indiana primary, with voting set for May 7.[11]

In the Indiana primary Kennedy faced off not only against McCarthy but also against the state's popular governor, Roger D. Branigin, who was running as a stand-in for the president. Kennedy knew the difficulties that faced him in Indiana and in primaries to come. There were not enough delegates at stake in primary states to secure the Democratic nomination (only 966 delegates were available, and 1,312 were needed to win), but Kennedy believed strong showings in the primaries would demonstrate his electability to powerful Democrats, such as Chicago mayor Richard J. Daley, and grassroots workers. Warned by his advisers that entering the Indiana primary would be a gamble because of the state's well-earned conservative reputation, Kennedy replied, "The whole campaign is a gamble." He likened his first primary test to the one his brother faced in 1960 when he attempted to prove to disbelieving political pundits by running in the West Virginia primary that a Roman Catholic could win the support of Protestant voters. "Indiana is the ball game," said Robert Kennedy. "This is my West Virginia." Martin advised Kennedy to tone down such remarks as "they risked too much on a doubtful state." Kennedy argued that Hoosiers should be reminded that as president his brother had never forgotten the boost West Virginia had given him, hinting at favors to come for Indiana if he won the primary. "I said he could say this privately to politicians but not publicly," Martin recalled. Finally, the candidate, upon the advice of Ted Sorensen, one of his campaign directors, decided to include a line in his speeches informing Hoosiers that they had a chance to pick a president. "I liked this – Indiana's presidential primary had never before been important," Martin recalled. "He [Kennedy] began saying in almost every speech, 'Indiana can help choose a president.'"[12]

If he had been consulted, Martin said he would have advised against entering the Indiana primary, as the state was "redneck conservative country." In a March 29 memorandum to Kennedy, Martin warned that Indiana was a state "suspicious of foreign entanglements, conservative in fiscal policy, and with a strong overlay of Southern segregationist senti- ment." There was some hope for Kennedy, he added, as Indiana might respond "to a new and strong hopeful leader in time of trouble." To this mix had been added in recent years "a new, liberal, partly Jewish, mana- gerial, upper middle class in the northeastern Indianapolis suburbs," but the candidate, Martin said, should not forget the "hillbilly backlash of production line workers in southwestern suburbs and such manufac- turing towns as Muncie, nor the Polish backlash in Gary suburbs." White backlash voters believed African Americans were pushing too hard and too fast for equality and feared the gains made by blacks meant losses for them. He later described Hoosiers to Kennedy staff members as "phleg- matic, skeptical, hard to move, with a 'show me' attitude." These were the voters Kennedy counted on to give him enough of a mandate to knock McCarthy out of the race for good. A defeat in Indiana would be disas- trous for Kennedy's budding presidential effort. Campaign aide William Haddad remembered realizing, "if we lose Indiana we lose everything."[13]

Just two days after Martin's memo, the political world was turned upside down when Johnson, in a nationally televised address, made the shocking announcement: "With American sons in the fields far away, with America's future under challenge right here at home, with our hopes and the world's hopes for peace in the balance every day, I do not believe I should devote an hour or a day of my time to any personal partisan causes or to any duties other than the awesome duties of this office – the Presidency of your country. Accordingly, I shall not seek, and I will not accept, the nomination of my party for another term as your President." The pressure of the war and the campaign had been weighing heavily on the president, and his family, especially his wife, Lady Bird, worried about his health if he ran again (Johnson had suffered a serious heart attack in 1955). The final straw came when the one thing the president had feared from the first days of his presidency had come true: Robert Kennedy had announced his intention to seek the job once occupied by his brother. "And the American people," said Johnson, "swayed by the magic of the name, were dancing in the streets. The whole situation was unbearable to me."[14]

Anticipating Vice President Hubert Humphrey's entrance into the presidential contest (he officially announced his candidacy on April 27, too late to enter any of the primaries), Kennedy acted quickly, calling a number of Democratic Party leaders poised to play important roles at the August convention. He failed, however, to receive any firm pledges of support. "I have to win through the people," Kennedy said. "Otherwise I am not going to win." Martin did not see Johnson's withdrawal from the race as benefiting Kennedy's cause, as it cost him two of his best issues, "the unpopular president and the unpopular war." Johnson's decision not to seek re-election had also failed to dislodge Branigin from the race in Indiana, as the deadline had passed for his name to be removed from the primary ballot. The governor decided to campaign as a favorite-son. Even without support, financial or otherwise, from the Johnson administration, Branigin and his advisers believed he could win over Hoosier voters. With a victory in his home state, the governor could control the Indiana delegation and bargain from a position of strength at what looked to be a wide-open Democratic convention in Chicago, perhaps even trading the state's sixty-three delegates in return for a spot on the ticket as vice president. From the beginning of the contest in Indiana, Martin had considered Branigin, not McCarthy, to be the toughest foe to beat. "I figured Governor Branigin would come in first; what we had to do was beat McCarthy in the three-way contest," said Martin.[15]

On Wednesday, April 3, while Martin was at CUNY, Sorensen called and asked him if was free to travel with Kennedy the next day to campaign in Indiana. Martin agreed, and the next morning he met Kennedy and his wife, Ethel, at Washington, D.C.'s National Airport for a flight to Indiana on a prop jet jammed with about forty-three reporters and twenty Kennedy staff members. "Bobby looked fine and relaxed. He always looked slight, slender, even thin, with a wry grin. But he no longer looked boyish," said Martin. "He had aged a great deal since his brother's murder five years ago. He aged even more as this spring campaign wore on." Kennedy's regular speechwriters, Greenfield and Walinsky, both seemed unhappy at Martin's presence, an attitude he viewed as natural. Permanent staff people were always possessive when it came to their candidate.[16]

As the airplane made its way to South Bend for a Kennedy speech at the University of Notre Dame's Stepan Center, the candidate, dressed in a gray, plaid suit, his standard garb on the campaign trail, sat beside Martin and asked, "Do you think it can be done?" Martin said he thought so, and the two men discussed what speeches might be needed. Kennedy requested that Martin stay with him on the entire eight-day trip, which included stops in Indiana, Ohio, Louisiana, West Virginia, Kentucky, Michigan, Alaska, and South Dakota. He also reminded the veteran speechwriter that what he produced could not be "Stevensonian, [it] had to be simpler, suggested I travel the whistlestops with him for a few days and listen, 'to get the rhythm.'" Martin shared a draft of an earlier speech he had sent Kennedy along with a statement saying the question before the country was whether there would be one nation or two or none. "He especially liked three or four sentences in it, one quoting Adlai Stevenson as saying that self-criticism is the secret weapon of democracy," Martin noted. Kennedy liked the line so much he told Martin to give it to Greenfield to include in his Notre Dame talk. Unfamiliar as yet with the campaign staff, Martin gave the quote by mistake to Walinsky, who could not believe Kennedy wanted to use a Stevenson quote in his speech and left it out. Martin later noted that after the speech Kennedy grew angry with Walinsky and Greenfield for cutting part of his speech without first informing him. "This campaign promised to be like others I'd been through," said Martin. One great difference, however, was that Martin had vowed to avoid getting into any arguments with other writers about speeches, as he had been producing them since 1952 and the thrill of hearing a candidate utter his "golden words" had long passed. In this campaign, as he had for Johnson's 1964 race, he simply turned in his speeches and paid little attention to whether or not they were used.[17]

Following his appearance in South Bend, Kennedy transferred to a small plane to fly to Muncie for a talk at Ball State University. Martin and most of the other Kennedy staff members stayed aboard the Electra for a flight to Indianapolis. That evening, after Kennedy had calmed the crowds at the outdoor rally in Indianapolis with his poignant remarks following King's death, he returned to the Marott. Various members of the campaign staff gathered in his room while Kennedy called the newly widowed Coretta Scott King to offer his airplane to fly to Memphis to retrieve her husband's body. "When the call came in, he asked, 'What should I say to her?'" Martin remembered. "Since no one else answered, I said, 'Just tell her how you feel. It has to come from you.'" Young members of Kennedy's staff were distraught about King's death, and many were openly crying. Martin, however, remained dry-eyed. "I'd done all my weeping in 1963, when President Kennedy was killed," he said. Kennedy staffers discussed what the candidate should do, with some arguing he should cancel his appearances, while others believed he should stick to his schedule. Martin remembered Kennedy saying, "There's a lot of people who just don't care." Finally, they decided to cancel the rest of the trip except for a Kennedy speech the next day at Cleveland's City Club, a sober address crafted by Sorensen, Walinsky, and Greenfield on the "mindless menace of violence in America," which, Kennedy said, "again stains our land and every one of our lives."[18]

The news of King's violent death at the hands of a white gunman, James Earl Ray, had sparked outrage and violence across the country. Riots exploded in a number of cities, including the nation's capital, Washington, D.C. Regular army troops were called into action by President Johnson to bring the situation under control. Flying into Washington from Cleveland on the Kennedy plane, Martin could see smoke rising from the fires burning in the city. "Before our eyes," said Martin, "the American civil rights movement was turning into the Negro revolution." Kennedy wanted to go into the riot-torn streets, believing he could help stem the violence, a plan that both Martin and Dutton argued against. Dutton pointed out that Kennedy could do nothing without first consulting with Mayor Walter Washington, and Martin warned he could do little while people were still rioting, and he also argued that going into the streets at this time would look like a cheap political stunt on Kennedy's part. A reluctant Kennedy agreed to return to his home at Hickory Hill in McLean, Virginia.[19]

On Sunday, April 7, Martin attended a strategy meeting at Hickory Hill with Kennedy's campaign team, including Dutton, Sorensen, Richard Goodwin (who had switched to Kennedy after being with McCarthy for a time), and those responsible for television advertising. The meeting lasted from 4:00 PM to 10:00 PM with the advertising people doing much of the talking, and little of what they said made sense to Martin. A frustrated Kennedy finally agreed with Martin's assessment that "everybody ought to go to Indiana," and he overruled a request by the advertising representatives to stay in New York. "He *was* decisive. He ran a meeting hard. When he decided something, that ended it," recalled Martin. Before he left, Martin gave Kennedy two speech drafts he had been working on, including one on foreign policy (part of which was later used in a talk at Indiana University) and another on leadership. Martin recalled that the candidate said he had to start spending more time giving substantive speeches and less time in wild motorcades with huge crowds. "I've got to stop looking like Frank Sinatra running for president," said Kennedy.[20]

While Kennedy returned to Indiana and other states for campaign visits, Martin spent the next week at home in Princeton. On Sunday, April 14, he received a call from Sorensen, telling him that Kennedy had requested he talk to Martin and urged him to give his full-time effort to the campaign. "Kennedy had told Sorensen he wanted me to do for him in Indiana what I had done for his brother in 1960 in various states – editorial advance," said Martin. He left the next day, stopping in Chicago to have a tooth fixed before going on to Indianapolis, where he stayed until the primary election on May 7. During his time back in his home state, Martin stayed at his mother's house on Kessler Boulevard with Fran, who joined him on the campaign. Fran worked with Arthur M. Schlesinger Jr.'s wife, Marian, speaking to the wives of college professors "who favored McCarthy and managed to move some of them over to our side, especially in Bloomington," Martin noted. John W. Douglas, a former State Department official and a troubleshooter for the Kennedy campaign in Indiana, said the two women "did a wonderful job" in the state, concentrating their efforts on universities and the suburbs. "They were impressive personalities," said Douglas, "spoke very well and, as a result, were able to eliminate or soften hostility to Bob among these groups." On April 17 Martin went to the Kennedy campaign's headquarters, in a

loft upstairs over the old Indiana Theater downtown, "surely one of the
dreariest places in dreary Indianapolis," Martin noted. He met with Joe
Dolan, a Kennedy aide in charge of scheduling the candidate, and two
young staff writers and researchers, P. J. Mode and Milton Gwirtzman,
to help map out strategy for the rest of the Indiana campaign.[21]

Martin counseled that the frantic nature of Kennedy's early days on
the campaign trail should be avoided at all costs in Indiana. He sensed
that the ordinary Hoosier watching television at home each night was
"tired of excitement and, after watching pictures of killing in Viet Nam
and rioting in the cities, doesn't want to watch pictures of kids pulling
your [Kennedy's] clothes off. Instead of competing with McCarthy for
young college students who opposed the Vietnam War, Martin wanted
Kennedy to appeal to a broader constituency, including blue-collar workers. "The people, I thought," said Martin, "did not want to be excited." He
reasoned that the 1968 election resembled 1952, the year of Stevenson's
first presidential campaign. Then, the electorate, weary after years of the
New Deal and two wars, sought calm and had turned to Eisenhower.
After eight years of what Martin called Eisenhower "do-nothingism,"
the voters were ready to follow a fresh, exciting, young leader, and had
turned to John Kennedy. "Not in 1968 – once more they [voters] wanted
change," said Martin, "change from Vietnam and from riots, but change
and calm, not a summons to great adventures."[22]

To eliminate the frenzied pace that had marked Kennedy's campaign to that point, Martin urged the senator to change his style to appear "sober and responsible" to Hoosiers. "For the middle-aged voters,
and to be contemplative, Bob should try to identify with Indiana's past
greatness," Martin wrote Sorenson. Martin wanted Kennedy, accompanied by some of his children, to visit the George Rogers Clark and
William Henry Harrison memorials in Vincennes, followed by a visit to
the grave of Abraham Lincoln's mother, Nancy Hanks Lincoln, where
he could "walk around and kick leaves and muse about saving the Union,
the house divided, kids, etc." Later, Martin advised and Kennedy agreed
to visit the Indianapolis home of one of the state's greatest icons, the
Hoosier Poet, James Whitcomb Riley. To avoid being identified too
closely with the concerns of Hoosier African Americans, Martin also
wanted Kennedy to schedule stops at industrial communities he labeled

as "redneck backlash factory cities," including Kokomo, Muncie, and Marion. To play to Hoosier nostalgia, the Kennedy staff came up with the idea of an old-fashioned railroad whistle-stop trip to several cities using the route of the Wabash Cannonball, including Logansport, Peru, Wabash, Huntington, and Fort Wayne.[23]

Others on the Kennedy staff recognized the worth of what Martin did for the candidate. "John Martin made a real contribution in Indiana," said Douglas. "He made suggestions about topics and places that would appeal to the Indianans as Indianans and just as members of the larger national community. John was trying to take the candidate's approach, his personality and his views on issues and placing them in some kind of historical setting or geographical context that would be attractive to Indiana voters." Martin spent most of his first week in Indiana working on scheduling with Dolan and seeking support for his ideas with Goodwin, Ted Kennedy, and Larry O'Brien, who had resigned his job as postmaster general in Johnson's administration to help run Kennedy's campaign. "Most of the stuff in the briefing sheets came from interviewing I did from my book on Indiana [*Indiana: An Interpretation*], and from Indiana fact books and the world almanac," said Martin. Kennedy later praised the Hoosier journalist for the documents, claiming they were a lifesaver that gave him a sense of confidence anywhere he appeared in Indiana. "When he came to a strange town," Martin noted, "he knew what to expect – what kind of town it was, who was in his audience, what kind of people they were, what was on their minds, and so on."[24]

On Saturday, April 21, Martin and Dolan had finished the schedule and briefing sheets for campaign stops at the Hoosier historic sites to begin at the start of the week. On Sunday, Martin traveled to Washington, D.C., and then on to Kennedy's Hickory Hill home, where a number of his key staffers had gathered. That evening at dinner, Martin told Kennedy about the schedule for the next week, and the senator expressed little enthusiasm for visiting the historic sites and balked at taking any of his children along. With the help of Dutton, Martin convinced the candidate to include his children on the ground that "every Hoosier takes his wife and kids to visit the Lincoln sites." Kennedy also expressed his dislike for Tuesday's schedule. Martin explained that the white backlash vote in the central Indiana factory communities differed in composition from the Poles and other ethnic groups that had settled around Gary. In cities like Kokomo the white backlash vote consisted of workers who had come to Indiana from Kentucky and Tennessee ("red-necks and Klansmen," Martin called them) during World War II to find jobs in the war industry. "Why am I going there then?" Kennedy asked. Martin replied, "Because there are a lot of Democratic votes there and you've got to convince them." Kennedy, after reviewing Martin's briefing sheets, agreed to the schedule and even decided to take three of his children, David, Courtney, and Michael, and his pet dog, Freckles, to visit the Hoosier historic sites. "When we first started talking, he was quite sharp and irritable with me," Martin recalled, "and didn't like the ideas or the schedule. As we went on, however, he accepted them." Staff members could get Kennedy to do something he did not like if they could convince him it was important. "He would take advice if he trusted the advisor's judgment and knowledge," Martin added. "He still made the decisions – too much so, probably – but he could be persuaded."[25]

To attract the support of Hoosier voters, Martin also argued that Kennedy had to alter his message and speak out against rioting and violence and emphasizing his law enforcement experience as attorney general. At the same time, Martin and others on the staff stressed, Kennedy should not neglect to include statements that injustice could also not be tolerated. Gwirtzman noted that the candidate was trying out a few phrases along these lines and he suggested that instead of saying "attorney general" – a government position many people do not understand – Kennedy should just say he was the former chief law enforcement officer of the United States. Kennedy liked the recommendations, nodding and saying, "I can go pretty far in that direction. That doesn't bother me." According to Gwirtzman, Kennedy "just wanted to point out the fact that he had faced these kinds of problems in 1962, in 1963, even in 1964, that he had had some experience with it and that it was perfectly possible to preserve civil liberties . . . while enforcing the law." Martin also urged Kennedy to talk more about government working with private enterprise, along the lines of his effort as senator to revitalize New York City's largest ghetto, Bedford-Stuyvesant, by working with white business leaders. On the issue of Vietnam, Martin wrote for Kennedy a line that the senator wanted to end the fighting and stop spending money in Vietnam and use it instead for programs in the United States, including some in the Hoosier State. "This played to Indiana's natural isolationism and chauvinism and penny-pinching," Martin said. "It always got applause.[26]

Kennedy's decision to emphasize a more conservative tone in his stump remarks for the Indiana campaign caused some dissension among his staff, particularly Walinsky and Greenfield. Martin remembered finding the young men one night working together to compose limericks about Kennedy coming to Indiana and becoming a member of the KKK. Douglas noted that some on the staff believed Kennedy spoke too strongly on law and order and not enough on social justice. An article by *New York Times* reporter Warren Weaver Jr., titled "Kennedy: Meet the Conservative," observed that Martin and Goodwin (who was not involved) had seemingly turned the liberal Kennedy into a Democratic version of George Romney, the Republican governor of Michigan who had dropped out of the presidential race. Although some in the media and on Kennedy's own staff viewed these changes as a struggle for the candidate's soul, Martin "conceived of it as an effort to win the Indiana election." He said that Kennedy could not hope to achieve a victory in the Indiana primary by making speeches pleasing to the ears of liberals on the East Coast, something Martin said his friend, Arthur Schlesinger, understood. (Schlesinger did call Martin during the campaign to tell him that the speeches made "curious reading in the East.") Only Kennedy had the moral authority to take a firm stand against violence and rioting before white backlash voters because he stood as one of the few white men in America whom African Americans trusted implicitly, noted Martin. "They knew that in his heart he was for them," he said. Kennedy also always followed his statements about intolerance for violence and rioting with pleas to end injustice. "This may be viewed as a cynical effort to have it both ways; it may also be viewed as an effort to heal the country's wounds, to bring us together again," said Martin. There was nothing the candidate said in Indiana that he would have to later take back if elected, insisted Martin, and nothing he would have to disavow in other primary states. Martin added that Kennedy "said and did what was essential to win Indiana." Douglas noted that in the light of the political rhetoric that followed the 1968 primary campaign, Kennedy's statements "were models of moderation and good sense."[27]

Martin made sure to gauge what effect the ideas he presented to Kennedy had on Hoosiers. During the candidate's stops at county courthouses around the state, Martin often wandered around the edge of the crowds. There always seemed to be a group of young girls screaming in the front rows, but most of the townspeople hung back with their hands in their pockets, as though they were daring Kennedy to make them respond. "He emphasized that violence could not be tolerated; and got big applause; then when he went on and said injustice could not be tolerated either and everybody was entitled to jobs and schools, they didn't applaud but they didn't mind – they had heard what they wanted to hear, that he was against violence in the streets, and that was enough," said Martin. During these campaign stops, Kennedy usually climbed onto the trunk of the convertible he rode in before speaking. "Previously he had been using a bullhorn; I objected that the bullhorn had become a symbol of southern sheriffs during the civil rights troubles and of Lyndon Johnson," said Martin, "and a small microphone was substituted." When he finished, Kennedy tossed the microphone back to Martin, and then came the difficult task of maneuvering through the massive, "savage crowds," as Martin described them, who tore off Kennedy's cufflinks and ripped his clothes. One of the hardest tasks for the campaign staff during these mob scenes involved getting Kennedy's car moving again after the speech, which became, Martin said, a "bruising business." He noted that Dutton usually placed himself in front of the convertible, faced it, and then inched his way backward into the crowd. The car's driver slowly moved forward as Dutton beckoned, and Martin made it a habit to tell children in the crowd to be careful to not get their toes run over.[28]

One thing was always on the minds of Martin and other Kennedy staffers that spring: the grim specter of another assassination. Even before Kennedy had decided to enter the primaries, his family and friends worried about his safety. Martin remembered that Jacqueline Kennedy had told Schlesinger of her brother-in-law, "If he gets in, they'll kill him, just as they did Jack." In the days before the Secret Service provided protection for major presidential and vice presidential candidates, Kennedy depended upon a former FBI agent, Bill Barry, as sort of a one-man security detail. "He only accepted as much protection as he got because he liked me," remembered Barry. "He wouldn't have had anybody if really left to his own choice." All that spring, as his candidate rode, exposed, in the back of an open convertible while campaigning, Martin found himself scanning the windows of surrounding buildings and watching people in the crowds, trying to anticipate any signs of trouble. If he did spot a potential threat, Martin was prepared to knock Kennedy down, away from any danger. "I wanted to talk to Kennedy about it, and did talk to Barry and Dutton, but it was no use – he [Kennedy] had a fatalistic view that if he was going to get killed he was going to get killed and there was nothing to be done about it," Martin recalled. Kennedy tried to put a brave face on the hazards he faced, paraphrasing a quote from French author Albert Camus: "Knowing you are going to die is nothing." Martin argued that there were measures to cut down on the odds of anything happening, including putting the candidate in a closed car during motorcades, having more police on hand to precede the campaign caravan and searching buildings on the route, and avoiding publicizing the route ahead of time. "It was no use," he said. "They were all for it but they knew he [Kennedy] wasn't, so nothing was done." Martin remembered that Fran, prophetically as it turned out, had compared Kennedy to Manolete, the Spanish bullfighter, and the mob scenes from the campaign were "a little like a bullfight," said Martin. The crowds who came to see Manolete perform, he remembered, demanded more and more of him, and he kept giving more and more of himself until there "was nothing left to give but his life, and he gave them that."[29]

Martin believed Kennedy turned the corner in the campaign with his visits to the Hoosier historic sites in southern Indiana on Monday, April 22, and backlash factory cities in the central part of the state on Tuesday, April 23. "Before then it had lacked direction, had been all razzle dazzle and high pressure, had not been in tune with the Hoosier voters," Martin recalled. "On those days, and thereafter, he got on the same wavelength with the Indiana voters, he felt at home with them, and they with him. He started an upward surge on those days that continued until the end." For all the resources at his disposal – his fortune; a large, dedicated staff devoted to ensuring his success; and the mystique of his family's name – Kennedy worked harder than anyone else to capture the

hearts and minds of Hoosier voters. Douglas observed that probably no
national candidate in modern times worked as hard as Kennedy did.
"He came across as authentic, direct, and straightforward – a person in
whom people could have confidence," Douglas remembered. Martin
could see firsthand the effort Kennedy had made in the state, turning
voters attitudes around to his cause through the passion of his words and
the depth of his commitment to bettering the lives of those who needed
help. Martin noted:

> He went yammering around Indiana about the poor whites of Appalachia and
> the starving Indians who committed suicide on the reservations and the jobless
> Negroes in the distant great cities, and half the Hoosiers didn't have any idea
> what he was talking about; but he plodded ahead stubbornly, making them
> listen, maybe even making some of them care, by the sheer power of his own
> caring. Indiana people are not generous or sympathetic; they are hardhearted,
> not warm and generous; but he must have touched something in them, pushed a
> button somewhere. He alone did it.[30]

On Tuesday, May 7, all of Kennedy's hard work paid off, and he
won the Indiana primary. The final returns had Kennedy winning with
42.3 percent of the 776,000 votes cast. Branigin finished second with
30.7 percent, and McCarthy trailed the field at 27 percent. In winning
nine of Indiana's eleven congressional districts (losing only the fifth
and sixth districts to Branigin), Kennedy captured fifty-six of the state's
sixty-three delegates to the Democratic National Convention, with Branigin winning the remaining seven. Kennedy swept fifty-seven of the
state's ninety-two counties and also captured the majority of Indiana's
largest urban centers, including Indianapolis, Gary, Hammond, South
Bend, Kokomo, Muncie, Fort Wayne, Terre Haute, and East Chicago.
"I've proved I can really be a leader of a broad spectrum," Kennedy observed to a staff member. "I can be a bridge between blacks and whites
without stepping back from my positions."[31]

Kennedy's victory in Indiana failed to knock McCarthy out of the
race for the Democratic presidential nomination, but Martin remembered being satisfied that his candidate had not only beaten his fellow
U.S. senator but also a popular incumbent governor in his home state.
"Going home to my mother's house, Fran and I said it was nice to win
one. It seemed so long since we had," Martin said. For the first time since

1963, he and Fran felt good about the future, as they were both involved in something they thought important, were doing it together, and it had worked, they had won. Kennedy offered people hope, he noted. "Somehow with him, you really felt it didn't all have to be race riots at home and war in Southeast Asia and crap from the White House and the rest of the government," said Martin. "The United States could become again what it ought to be, a great nation able to live with itself and with the rest of the world." But Kennedy was not attempting to return to the solutions of the 1950s and 1960s, as they would not work in the late 1960s and 1970s, and he was not his brother, according to Martin, but unique. Liberals might have believed Kennedy had repudiated Democratic programs from the New Deal era when he discussed in his speeches returning government to the people and restoring local control over federal programs, but they had forgotten that the best of the New Deal – rural electrification and soil conservation – had been locally controlled, Martin said. "The button he [Kennedy] was trying to push," he said, "was individual worth and importance; the enemy he fought was the feeling of helplessness so many Americans have come to have about problems big beyond their grasp."[32]

The day after the Indiana primary Martin and other campaign staffers flew back to New York with Kennedy. On the flight, Martin looked ahead to primary campaigns in Nebraska, Oregon, and California (a large prize with 174 delegates at stake in the winner-take-all contest) and asked Dutton what he planned on having him do next. Dutton said he wanted him to do in California what he had been doing in Indiana, as "the briefing sheets were the best stuff Kennedy had been getting – Kennedy told me this too – and wanted me to do the same in California," Martin remembered. He agreed to do so, but he realized it would be a major time commitment, as he would have to fly back to the East Coast every Wednesday to teach his seminar on the limits of American power. At a dinner with Ivan von Auw, one of Martin's agents, the two men discussed how his work with Kennedy might affect his writing of the Stevenson biography. Von Auw assured Martin that since the manuscript was not due until next June or July, he could safely interrupt work on it to campaign through the California primary, set for June 4. During this time, Kennedy also captured the Nebraska primary with 51.5 percent of the vote; 31 percent went to McCarthy. "The idea of Robert Kennedy, a city man if there was one, campaigning among farmers seemed ridiculous but it wasn't," said Martin. "He did well with them, as I had also noticed in Indiana."[33]

In analyzing the primary season, Martin had theorized that McCarthy, after losing in Indiana, had decided to ignore the Nebraska primary and place everything he had on defeating Kennedy in the Oregon primary on May 28, which in turn might hold down the Kennedy vote in California enough for the Minnesota senator to win there as well. "California was a truer test," Martin noted, "big and diverse, a nation and an empire in itself." Oregon proved to be inhospitable territory for Kennedy. As he candidly admitted to a reporter for the *National Observer,* "Let's face it. I appeal best to people who have problems." Kennedy's campaign floundered under the direction of Oregon congresswoman Edith Green. Just a month before the May 28 primary, Kennedy's headquarters had just three people and only two desks. The mostly middle-class, suburban, well-educated, prosperous citizens of the state responded favorably to McCarthy as a candidate. In Oregon, campaigning for Kennedy once again alongside Marian Schlesinger, Fran informed her husband that it was not going well, as "she and Marian couldn't move votes, the campaign seemed disorganized, there was little enthusiasm compared to Indiana, she was uneasy." said Martin, who received similar pessimistic reports from advance men in Oregon.[34]

Martin had been in and out of California since May 9, writing briefing sheets for Kennedy's appearances in the state while living at the Ambassador Hotel in Los Angeles and working in an office at Kennedy headquarters on Wilshire Boulevard in an abandoned bank building. Ominous reports from Oregon prompted him to fly to Portland on Thursday, May 23. While looking for Fran at the Benson Hotel, he looked out a window and saw Kennedy walking back from a street rally a few blocks away. "Somebody said it had been a good rally but it didn't look good to me," said Martin. "He shouldn't be able to walk down a street in the center of town without anybody paying attention." Meeting with Kennedy in his room, Martin could see from his face that things were not going well in the state. "He was really pulling these campaigns out of his guts, and he looked it, drawn, nervous," said Martin. He asked the candidate if he wanted him to stay with him in Oregon or go back to

California. Kennedy thought about the question for a long time before finally offering a noncommittal response, adding that it might be too late to pull out a victory. "I think he knew he was going to lose Oregon," said Martin. McCarthy captured 44.7 percent of the vote, with Kennedy coming in at 38.8 percent, marking the first time a Kennedy, in twenty-seven previous tries, had gone down to defeat in an election. "He took it very hard," Martin said of Kennedy's reaction to the Oregon primary. "It really flattened him to lose." Since the Indiana primary, McCarthy had been calling on Kennedy to agree to debate him, a challenge he finally accepted, with the debate set for June 1 in San Francisco.[35]

When Martin returned to his duties in California, there had been a shakeup among the campaign staff. Dutton had left Kennedy's side to iron out scheduling difficulties in the Golden State and had lambasted the writers for producing speeches that lacked news value and "sounded either like position papers or Senatorial speeches," Martin recalled. To help whip the writing back into shape, Martin called upon Schlesinger's assistance. Schlesinger, along with Fran, joined Martin at the Ambassador Hotel in Los Angeles on Wednesday, May 29. That evening the two men met with Kennedy and urged him not to say, as he had intimated, that he would drop out of the race entirely if he lost the California primary. "Arthur argued cogently that there was a good chance the Paris peace talks would break down, that this would result in a resurgence of pressure for escalation of the Viet Nam war," Martin remembered, "and that if Kennedy dropped out there would be none but McCarthy to oppose and McCarthy would be the sole beneficiary politically."[36]

On Thursday, May 30, Martin, joined by the Schlesingers, accompanied Kennedy as he flew to Fresno to begin a railroad whistle-stop tour through the San Joaquin Valley that included visits to Madera, Merced, Turlock, Modesto, Stockton, Lodi, and Sacramento. "On the way I got him to do his homework – read his day's briefing sheets," Martin said of Kennedy. Along with Schlesinger, they also discussed how they could make some news on the trip, discarding several possibilities before Kennedy came up with the idea of sending Humphrey a telegram challenging him to join the June 1 debate. The stop in Fresno, however, did not go well, with a small, unresponsive crowd, and Kennedy appearing nervous; Martin noticed that the candidate's legs were shaking. Kennedy started out by reading aloud his telegram to Humphrey, then began kidding the crowd. "After Fresno, I told him to turn the speech around – kid the crowd first, then go into the issues including the telegram," said Martin. After the rough start in Fresno, Kennedy improved his performance, and Schlesinger remembered being enchanted by the "mixture of banter and intensity with which he [Kennedy] beguiled and exhorted his hearers." The candidate used the Humphrey telegram throughout the day, but he kept losing it and asking Martin for a copy, one time asking, "Where's that damn telegram?" This was heard by the crowd, which produced plenty of laughter. Finally, at one of the stops, Martin gave Kennedy a copy of the telegram before he spoke and informed him it was the last one he had and "if he lost it this time he was on his own." Kennedy also kept forgetting or losing the briefing sheets Martin had meticulously prepared and did not "know what crop was grown at each stop, and Dutton or I had to write them out in big block letters on scraps of paper at the last minute." As the trip progressed, the crowds grew larger and much more responsive to Kennedy's message, and the candidate also improved on his performance, working the crowd to perfection with what Schlesinger termed "wonderful travesties of stump speeches," as well as clever use of information on the communities the campaign visited, provided by Martin in his briefing sheets.[37]

Although people in the McCarthy campaign that spring had been talking about the "politics of participation" and "the new politics," prompted by the many college students who flocked to help the antiwar candidate, Martin had little use for such academic chatter and preferred a more pragmatic stance. He noted that the Kennedy staff campaigned in the "old politics" method of scheduling their candidate in his areas of strength – African Americans, blue-collar workers, ethnic groups, and Catholics, for example – and pitched his speeches straight at his audiences. The core of any political campaign, Martin said, included what he termed "old-fashioned gut politics – appealing to diverse groups of voters in one way or another, sometimes by telling them what they want to hear, sometimes by doing the reverse, sometimes by kidding them, but always making the pitch."[38]

To prepare for his June 1 debate in San Francisco with McCarthy, Kennedy gathered with his advisers and briefing books at the Fairmont

Hotel, but the sunny weather seemed to distract him from his task. "There was no sense stuffing the candidate's head full of facts from speeches he had already given," said Martin. "There is always danger in over-briefing." After the debate, most observers believed the two Democratic candidates had battled to a draw. "It was a conversation rather than a debate," according to the *New York Times,* "and it demonstrated that the two rivals are in substantial agreement on every major issue." But with expectations high that McCarthy, known for his caustic wit and intellectual vigor, would easily defeat his opponent in such a setting, Kennedy gained most from the encounter. "My own impression was that Kennedy had at least held his own," said Martin, "and looking back I think the debate probably put out the McCarthy fire which had been ignited by his Oregon victory and Kennedy's bad reaction to that victory."[39]

On Monday, June 3, the day before the primary election, Martin worked on two statements Kennedy could issue if he lost in California. One declared that he would stay in the race and the other announced a halt to his campaign except for the New York primary and stated that Kennedy would decide his future course at the Democratic convention. Martin also prepared a long memorandum outlining suggestions on what Kennedy should do in the months leading up to the convention. For the next primary in New York, Martin urged the candidate to attack McCarthy, as the Minnesota senator was not an ally, but an enemy. "There is no hope he will throw to you at the convention," Martin said. "Counterattack him earlier than you did in California." Once the New York primary had been decided, Martin wanted Kennedy to buy time on national television in order to speak out when events warranted, for example, if the peace talks between the United States and North Vietnam broke down. Using tactics that had worked in Indiana and California, he also suggested a transcontinental whistle-stop railroad tour from the East Coast to the Midwest, then by airplane to the West Coast. "Make it a 'whistle-and-listen' trip – announce you are traveling to listen to the people's views as well as to present your own," Martin noted. Mayor Richard Daley of Chicago could be the key to Kennedy's success or failure at the convention, and Martin urged the New York senator to visit with him after the California primary, give a few speeches while in the city, and plan a motorcade through African American or Polish neighborhoods. "Daley probably would not approve heavy motorcading," said Martin. "But a show of strength in Negro and backlash wards would impress him and people he sees." Above all, stressed Martin, Daley wanted to be able to support a Democratic candidate who could win in the November general election.[40]

On Tuesday, June 4, California voters went to the polls. A nervous Martin feared that during the last week McCarthy had caught up to Kennedy. "I thought the debate had dampened him down a little but was afraid he might catch us on Sunday, Monday, and election day," Martin remembered. His fears almost came true, but Kennedy held on to win the primary, garnering 46.4 percent of the vote to 41.8 percent for McCarthy. Trying to relax at his suite at the Ambassador in Los Angeles, Kennedy received good news from the South Dakota primary, which was also being held that day. He had won a smashing victory in that state, winning 59 percent of the vote to just 20 percent for McCarthy, with the rest going to a slate pledged to President Johnson and Humphrey.[41]

At about midnight Kennedy began preparing to go down to the hotel's Embassy Ballroom to address his happy group of supporters that had been singing "This Land is Your Land" and chanting "We Want Kennedy." Earlier in Kennedy's hotel suite, Martin gave him a memo he had prepared on what to do after the California primary, and the candidate had begun to read it, but Martin told him to stick it in his pocket and peruse it later. As Kennedy passed Martin and Fran in the hotel hallway, she gave the candidate a memo analyzing the Oregon defeat, and he also placed it in his pocket. "Later," Martin regretfully noted, "we said if he'd been shot in the chest, the memos would have saved him." A reporter following Kennedy down to the ballroom asked Martin if he would be joining Kennedy "into the burning pit, or some such phrase," Martin recalled. "I said no, I'd been there before, I'd wait here."[42]

Standing behind a lectern decorated with one of his bumper stickers, Kennedy first expressed his regard for the work of Los Angeles Dodgers' pitcher Don Drysdale, who had pitched his sixth straight shutout that day, adding that he hoped his campaign might have such good fortune in the future. Emphasizing once again his campaign's main themes, Kennedy told the crowd, "I think we can end the divisions in the United

States. What I think is quite clear is that we can work together in the last analysis. And that is what has been going on within the United States over a period of the last three years – the division, the violence, the disenchantment with our society, the division, whether it's between blacks and whites, between the poor and the more affluent, between the age groups or in the war on Vietnam – that we can start to work together." Ending his speech, the candidate thanked his supporters, flashed a "V" for victory sign with his fingers, and said it was "on to Chicago and let's win there," before skirting the crowd and walking through the kitchen on his way to attend a press conference in the hotel's Colonial Room. He never made it; Sirhan Sirhan, using a .22 caliber Iver Johnson revolver, shot and hit Kennedy in the neck and head, mortally wounding him.[43]

Martin had watched part of Kennedy's talk on a television in a small room adjoining the candidate's suite before wandering out into hallway to get some fresh air. He saw Greenfield running by and heard him say something that ended with "shot." Running after him, Martin asked what he had said, and Greenfield angrily replied, "You heard me." When Martin said he had not, Greenfield told him that there was a rumor that Kennedy had been shot. Returning to the small room, Martin watched "the horror" on television, and when the announcer said that Kennedy had been shot in the head, everyone in the room responded with an agonized "Oh no." As he heard sirens wailing outside, Martin saw many of the staff, young and old, begin hurrying to the elevator to go down and see what had happened, and he started to run as well. As he turned the corner, however, he stopped and thought to himself, "What the hell am I going there for, he needs a doctor, not a writer; if I can do anything it's for Fran." He remembered that after John Kennedy had been assassinated, he had stayed alone in Washington and had not had Fran join him there, which had hurt both of them. Martin returned to the room where Fran had stayed and the two of them watched television coverage of the shooting and grieved together for their fallen candidate until finally going to bed at about 4:00 AM. "I kept wondering," said Martin, "if I could have helped if I'd gone down with him."[44]

Kennedy ended up at Good Samaritan Hospital, where he underwent three hours of surgery and never regained consciousness. The morning after the shooting, Martin and Fran had missed their flight to

New York as they tried to learn more about Kennedy's condition. Fran told her husband she could not leave without seeing Ethel, so the two of them went to the hospital. "I felt helpless," Martin said. While at the hospital they saw Ted Kennedy and were able to talk to him for a few minutes. Martin wrote a short note to Ethel that read, "Dear Ethel, we are praying. God bless you and yours. Fran and John," and Ted agreed to deliver it to her. They also talked to Kennedy press aide Frank Mankie-wicz, who said Kennedy's condition did not look good. The Martins re-turned to their hotel, spending the day watching for news on television and trying to make arrangements with their sons, Dan and Fred, both attending East Coast prep schools (Fred at Phillips Exeter Academy, Dan at the Putney School), to pick them up as planned on Friday, June 7. Early in the morning on Thursday, June 6, Martin received a telephone call from his friend, Newton Minow, who woke him to tell him that Kennedy had died earlier at 1:44 AM. "Fran and I hoped that if he could just get through that one night he might make it," said Martin. "He hadn't."[45]

More than two thousand people gathered at Saint Patrick's Ca-thedral for a high requiem mass held in Kennedy's honor on Saturday, June 8. Late in the evening before the service, Martin had stood vigil alongside Kennedy's casket with Goodwin, Jacqueline Kennedy, Burke Marshall, and others. "Late as it was," Martin recalled, "there must have been a million people on the streets just standing and staring toward the cathedral." After the hour-and-forty-minute ceremony, Kennedy's coffin was taken by hearse to the train at Pennsylvania Station for what was supposed to be a four-hour journey to its final destination, a gravesite at Washington's Arlington National Cemetery. Robert Kennedy's fi-nal resting place was just a few feet from the grave of his elder brother, John.[46]

From New York, the Penn Central train carrying Robert Kennedy's coffin traveled slowly to its destination through Newark, Trenton, Phila-delphia, and Baltimore. All along the route people stood silently along the railroad tracks, paying tribute to Kennedy, whose coffin rested on top of chairs in the last car. Along the railroad right-of-way people held signs, many saying merely "Good-bye Bobby," while in New Brunswick, New Jersey, a bugler on a station platform played "Taps" as the train sped by.

Accompanied by Fran and his sons, Martin called his time on the train both "terrible and great," and he "broke up a couple of times" upon seeing such Kennedy stalwarts as Larry O'Brien and Kenny O'Donnell. He added that it was fitting that his friend's last trip came on a train, as he had loved whistle-stop campaigning. The railroads ran through poorer neighborhoods, the homes of African Americans and factory workers. "They were his people," said Martin. "The disadvantaged. Old men stood with their hats over their hearts. Young women held babies. Factory workers stopped work and leaned out of windows and climbed up on roofs." Because of the throngs of people lining the tracks to pay their respects, the journey from New York to Washington took more than eight hours. Upon the train's arrival at Union Station, more masses had lined city streets along the five-mile route from the station to Arlington Cemetery. At the end of the brief service, astronaut John Glenn presented a folded flag to Kennedy's wife, Ethel, and his son, Joe.[47]

Attempting to regroup after the tragedy with his family in Michigan's Upper Peninsula, Martin took up work again on his Stevenson manuscript, but he could not concentrate. Martin felt nothing but "bleak despair," and both he and Fran said they were through with politics (only Fran followed through on the threat). After all, the only three candidates Martin had ever cared about – Stevenson and the two Kennedys – were dead. "There *is* a point in working for the principles of Robert Kennedy," said Martin, "but no Robert Kennedy." The five years since the death of John Kennedy had been bad, he noted, but always, in the back of his and others' minds, had been the thought, "'Well, there's always Bob.' Now there isn't. There's nothing. . . . This time the bastards have finally beaten me." To exorcise his pain, he returned to the one thing that had always been his salvation: writing. Martin began writing a journal of the Indiana and California primary campaigns, putting down on paper "the Bobby Kennedy I had loved." Although winning the Democratic nomination would have been an uphill battle, Martin said the Kennedy forces would have gone into the convention with wins in California and New York, and they might have gained a victory in Illinois, Michigan, Ohio, or Pennsylvania, and if they had accomplished that, Kennedy would have been nominated. "I have no doubt at all that if nominated he would have been elected," Martin said. "And if elected a great President, maybe even greater than his brother." He ended his speculative history, however, with a dark thought: "But they would have killed him."[48]

As Martin tried to deal with his grief in the wilds of the the Upper Peninsula, Democrats prepared to gather for their convention at the International Amphitheater in Chicago from August 26 to 29. Although their nominee was still in question, they knew the person they would face in the fall. Earlier that month at the Miami Beach Convention Center, the Republicans had nominated as their presidential candidate former vice president Nixon, who had beaten back challenges from Governor Nelson Rockefeller of New York and Governor Ronald Reagan of California. The convention had gone off with few problems, and the television networks, with their equipment already in Miami, had called upon the Democratic Party to also hold its convention there. Under pressure from Mayor Daley, however, the Democrats remained in Chicago. The choice proved to be a poor one, as thousands of peace activists descended upon the convention to protest the Vietnam War. Daley, however, had refused to grant the protestors any permits to hold demonstrations or permission to camp in city parks. "No thousands will come to our city and take over our streets, our city, and our Convention," Daley declared, and he established an 11:00 PM curfew. Fences and barbed wire ringed the amphitheater, and vehicles were stopped and checked blocks from the convention. A confrontation seemed inevitable, and police and protestors clashed in the city's streets and parks and even in the hotels housing delegates and leading Democrats, including Humphrey and McCarthy. Protestors responded to the beatings by police and stinging tear-gas canisters with cries of "The whole world is watching." British reporters were aghast at what they witnessed, noting that the police "went, quite literally, berserk," beating not only protestors but newsmen and innocent bystanders as well.[49]

In the days leading up to the convention, Martin received a request from an old friend from his days with Stevenson, George Ball, that he work directly for the Humphrey campaign. Martin demurred for the time being, but said in a July 10 letter to Ball that down the road he could do for the vice president what he had done for both Robert and John Kennedy – not writing set speeches, but "going out ahead of the candidate, talking to local people, then advising him on what issues to discuss and what approach to take to them in each place." Martin also noted his role in thinking up "happenings" for Robert Kennedy and his close work with the campaign's schedulers to try and "make the schedule fit editorial and political needs rather than be devised arbitrarily by advance men, geographers, and local politicians." Martin told Ball he thought these activities might be useful to Humphrey, if at all, more in September and October rather than in July. "In the meanwhile," said Martin, "I gather that he [Humphrey] does have serious problems, not so much in winning the nomination as in getting nominated in such a way as not to lose the election." He offered to produce memos from time to time leading up to the convention addressing possible problems facing the candidate and what he could do to solve them. Martin was more direct when dealing with attempts by Adlai Stevenson III and Minow to have him join the Citizens for Humphrey Committee in Illinois, saying he was not yet ready to do so, as he did not know the vice president's position on Vietnam and wanted to see what Ted Kennedy might do at the convention. "I can't imagine that my abstention will be a crippling blow to the committee," Martin told Stevenson.[50]

On August 4 Ted Van Dyk, a close assistant to Humphrey and the vice president's chief executive officer during the presidential campaign, wrote Martin to say that his offer to write memos was "certainly a welcome one" and to send them directly to him. Van Dyk also hinted at working something out with Martin's offer for doing editorial advance work for the vice president in the fall campaign. Five days later, Martin crafted a four-page memo to Humphrey, through Van Dyk, offering some of the same advice he had given Robert Kennedy on what he should do after the California primary. Martin wrote that the vice president seemed too much a creature of Johnson and the Democratic Party machinery and needed to establish his independence without a direct break with the president. To do so, Martin suggested, as he had for Kennedy, a whistle-stop trip across the country before the convention, what he called a "whistle-and-listen" journey, staying out of large cities for the most part and hitting instead small towns and suburbs. "You would not so much speak to the people as listen to them, find out what's on their minds, what their concerns are, what they think should be done about them," said Martin. "You should not meet with local political leaders but with private citizens – businessmen, working men, farmers, housewives, etc."[51]

Although Martin had established some ties to the Humphrey campaign, he still had no real enthusiasm for any Democratic politician after Kennedy's death. Martin attended the party's convention and drifted, as many former Kennedy people did, into the last-minute campaign of U.S. senator George McGovern of South Dakota, who had entered the race for the nomination on August 10 after peace advocates in the party had grown frustrated with McCarthy's inaction after losing the California primary. Schlesinger, who helped with McGovern's cause, believed that he would be "a better President than Humphrey or McCarthy." The Kennedy people converged on McGovern's candidacy not so much because of McGovern, although Martin noted he was "a very decent man," but because they had grown to despise McCarthy and because Humphrey represented to them the Johnson administration's position on the Vietnam War. Martin never forgave McCarthy for saying the weekend before the Oregon primary that undoubtedly rumors would spread that an attempt would be made to assassinate Kennedy. "It was a terrible thing to say," Martin said. In spite of his connection with McGovern, Martin did have some contact with Humphrey. Walking down Michigan Avenue one day during the convention, Martin saw a limousine pull to the curb near him and the vice president stuck his head out of the window and called out his name. "We shook hands," Martin recalled, "and he said, grinning but his jaw thrust out at the same time (something no other man can do), 'I'm going to get it [the nomination] and I want you to help me in the fall.' . . . He was always direct, he never hesitated to ask for help." Martin said he equivocated on Humphrey's offer, saying something like, "We'll see how this one comes out," meaning the convention. If Humphrey did win the nomination, Martin believed his only chance at victory was to convince Ted Kennedy to accept the vice presidential nomination. He would not have urged the last Kennedy brother to run, however, said Martin, as "he might get killed too."[52]

As did many other Democrats who were in Chicago, Martin could not believe what he saw on the streets of the city he loved, calling the entire proceedings a disaster for his party. He noted that Johnson had been in many ways an admirable president, and Daley stood as the best mayor

Chicago had ever had, but he was appalled at the two men's behavior at the convention. "As Daley's police beat the kids in the streets, and as Johnson's political operatives smothered the convention, one could only feel that two stubborn old men were destroying any chance the Democratic Party had to keep the unspeakable Richard Nixon out of the White House," said Martin. Sitting in a room at the Chicago Club, a private social club, with actor Ralph Bellamy, who had been part of a memorial to Stevenson at the convention, Martin looked out the window onto South Michigan Avenue and saw protestors being chased down the street by the police as tear-gas bombs went off among them. Disheartened by what he had seen, Martin called Fran, who had stayed in Michigan. She told him she had just returned from the family's camp at Smith Lake, where she had seen a black fox. "Bellamy could hardly believe that anywhere in the United States one could still see a black fox in one's driveway," Martin remembered.[53]

In the chaos that was the Chicago convention, Humphrey received his party's nomination on the first ballot, winning 1,761¾ votes to 601 for McCarthy and 146½ for McGovern. Humphrey had finally gotten the presidential nomination he had long sought, but his victory was tarnished by the horrible scenes on Chicago's streets; the only bright spot appeared to be his popular selection of Edmund Muskie, U.S. senator from Maine, as his vice presidential running mate. The violence at the convention, coupled with McCarthy's renegade campaign, the Tet Offensive, and the assassinations of King and Kennedy all worked together to throw the Democratic Party into disarray as it attempted to take on Nixon and his vice presidential choice, little-known Maryland governor Spiro T. Agnew. A Gallup poll taken after the convention had 43 percent of the electorate supporting Nixon, 30 percent Humphrey, and 19 percent for a wildcard in the campaign, former Alabama governor George Wallace, famous for his stand against integration in his state. Wallace was the presidential candidate for the American Independent Party and was on the ballot in all fifty states. Assured of strong support in the South and among backlash blue-collar workers in the industrial North attracted to his "law and order" message, Wallace hoped he could win enough states to throw the election into the House of Representatives. He sought the power "to say just who *would* be the next President," said Wallace. "And I make it no secret that I would want something in return before I make my choice."[54]

The turmoil that faced the Democratic Party at the start of the presidential campaign in September made Martin forget his earlier vow to stay out of politics. Martin said he liked and respected Humphrey and still felt gratitude for the former U.S. senator standing up to defend him and Juan Bosch from attacks in Congress that they were communists. There was, however, a stronger motive: it now appeared likely that Nixon would be the country's next president. Martin did not want that to happen and said he would be able to live with himself "better during the next four years if I knew I had done everything possible to prevent his winning." During the campaign, when his liberal friends such as Schlesinger refused to help Humphrey, Martin always warned them, "All right – you can abstain if you want to, but you're going to help elect Richard Nixon." Although Schlesinger regarded Nixon as "the greatest shit in 20th century American politics," he refrained from giving any active support to Humphrey until he had separated himself from the Johnson administration's policies on Vietnam. In the end, Schlesinger came out in support of Humphrey, but it was too little and too late to help; Martin considered the last-minute endorsement as "probably worthless." Humphrey noted that with a few exceptions, "the Democratic party did not campaign for me with much enthusiasm until the very last days of the campaign."[55]

On Sunday, September 29, Martin went to Washington to begin his work with the Humphrey campaign at its headquarters off of Connecticut Avenue just behind the Mayflower Hotel. Although at first Martin believed he would be doing the editorial advance work he had pioneered, the situation had changed, and he worked as one of Humphrey's speechwriters under the administrative leadership of John Stewart, a legislative assistant for the vice president. Adlai Stevenson III had written Martin on Monday, September 23, that he had talked with the vice president and he had passed along a request that Martin give him "some desperately needed help with speech writing. Ted [Van Dyk] now knows that what Hubert really wants is rhetoric, not advance work." Stevenson said he felt "terrible" about diverting Martin from his work on his father's biography, but the situation called for him to do all he could for Humphrey. To Martin, the vice president's early campaign speeches sounded "wooden, more like position papers," not surprising because the writers were not "professional political speech writers; they were issues men, legislative assistants and others from the VP staff." After he arrived and the campaign swung into full gear, the speeches got more political. They also got that way because Humphrey had begun to feel more like a candidate instead of like the vice president. "He need not give statesmanlike addresses benefitting the high office he held," said Martin. "He could get out in the gutter and slug . . . like any other candidate."[56]

Early on the vice president seemed to have insurmountable obstacles in his path to victory. He had to endure not only chants of "Dump the Hump" and worse from antiwar protestors at appearances around the country, but he also had to deal with a paucity of donations; nobody wanted to back a hopeless cause. As of mid-September, noted Van Dyk, the Humphrey campaign had only $200,000 in cash on hand (Humphrey estimated he needed $10 million to $15 million to run a proper campaign). "You cannot raise money for a losing candidate," Martin noted, "and the polls made HHH's cause look so hopeless in September that nobody could raise a dime for him." At this point during the campaign the vice president had no time for fund raising, as he was busy trying to pull his fragmented party back together, said Van Dyk. Humphrey spent as much time in private meetings with leading Democrats as he did in public outreach with voters. "His campaign was floundering," Martin said of Humphrey. "He had little staff, few good writers, no position papers; no direction." Later Martin realized that the press's view of Humphrey having a "poor staff" had been inaccurate. Although not as brilliant as Stevenson's or John Kennedy's, the vice president's staff was sound, with Van Dyk "a very competent technician and a pretty good politician"; Stewart the same, if less experienced; and O'Brien "great," said Martin. Van Dyk considered Martin to be "an all-around good guy" and appreciated his knowledge about the country and his ability, because of his journalistic background, to produce speeches on deadline. "To be a good speechwriter in a campaign you've got to be able to turn things out quick," Van Dyk said, "and he could do that – sit down and turn it out, get it in on time, and move on to the next [speech]."[57]

Humphrey began becoming his own man again after a September 30 television broadcast from Salt Lake City, Utah, in which he had taken an independent stance from Johnson's war policies by noting, "As President I would be willing to stop the bombing of the North as an acceptable risk for peace." Contributions began trickling in and Van Dyk noticed the absence of major heckling during the vice president's campaign appearances. "It was as if someone had turned off a switch," he said. Martin watched Humphrey's speech at the Washington home of his friend, journalist John Steele. "He [Humphrey] did not go as far on Viet Nam as I wished," Martin recalled, "but he did open the door, I thought, to move away from LBJ a little at a time."[58]

The enormity of the challenge still ahead, however, hit Humphrey full force at a meeting with his advisers, Martin included, on Friday, October 4, at the vice president's apartment in Washington. As they discussed the details of a national print advertising campaign, Humphrey interrupted, saying, according to Martin, "What I want to ask you is where the hell is the campaign? I've been going around the country, for 15 days, beating my brains out, making speech after speech; and after each somebody in the crowd comes up to me and asks me for some buttons, or bumper stickers, or something, and I say I haven't got any but I'm sure my local organizer does have – then I turn to him and by God he hasn't got any either. Now where the hell is the campaign?" Finally, Larry O'Brien, in charge of the general election campaign for Humphrey, informed the candidate that while the mockups of promotional materials had been prepared, the Democratic Party did not have enough cash or credit to produce them, could not even pay for the fuel for the vice president's jet, and stood little chance in raising any funds because of the perception that Humphrey had no chance of winning in November. Humphrey sat in silence for a moment, Martin noted, before saying, "Well. All right. *I* can raise money. I'll go out and make speeches at fund-raising dinners. We've got to do it." As Martin furiously took notes for use in upcoming speeches, the vice president also set out the themes he wanted to emphasize as the campaign moved forward. Humphrey said, "I'll tell you what the issues are in this campaign. The issues don't mean a damn. Only three things matter. Number One, who can you trust? Number Two, who can get peace? Number Three, who can hold this country together?" Humphrey added that his opponent's greatest weakness was that he was untrustworthy. "I'm compassionate. I'm not very smart. But

I'm not tricky," Humphrey reminded his advisers. "Nobody ever said that. They've said I'm gabby, I talk too much, said I wobble or try to please too many people. But they don't think I'm a cheat or tricky."[59]

After his first meeting with Humphrey, whom he had not seen in person since the convention, Martin began to feel better about the rest of the campaign. All summer and fall he had been hearing from his liberal friends that Humphrey's time as Johnson's vice president had "destroyed the old Hubert," that he was a shell of his former self, and that his cause was hopeless. The cause might well be hopeless if the Democrats could not manage to raise enough campaign funds, but Martin believed that Humphrey had become "sharp and hard" for the fight ahead and he knew what issues should be emphasized – trust, the war, and holding the country together. "And if he lost, it wouldn't be because he was weak, or spiritless, or unable to lead," Martin said. "He was strong. 'The old Hubert' was not gone. I was glad."[60]

By the week of October 14, the Humphrey campaign had begun to catch fire as several things happened at once, noted Martin. Humphrey had staked out his own position on Vietnam and had begun to benefit from his underdog status, while Nixon's campaign seemed to stagnate, stuck on its message of a secret plan to end the war. "Nixon ran a campaign of avoidance – he avoided the issues, he avoided Humphrey, and he avoided the people," noted O'Brien. "We were never able to get a hand on him." Martin viewed the election as different from the ones he had previously been involved in. Ordinarily an incumbent defends his record, he said, while his opponent attacks. "In this case the incumbent, HHH, swung to the attack, while his opponent, Nixon, merely talked about the need for new leadership," Martin said.[61]

As Election Day neared, Martin believed that Humphrey had closed the gap on Nixon, helped in no small part by last-minute vital financial and logistical support from organized labor, as the American Federation of Labor and the Congress of Industrial Organizations registered 4.6 million voters, distributed 115 million pieces of literature, and spent millions of dollars in an attempt to stop traditional Democrats from bolting the party for Wallace. Before returning to Minnesota, where Humphrey would cast his ballot at a rural polling place near Waverly, Martin accomplished his final task for the campaign, writing three possible statements for election night, one if Humphrey won, another if he lost, and a third if the election were thrown into the House of Representatives. "The last was the hardest," Martin recalled, as he pondered what Nixon and Wallace might do if no candidate won a clear-cut victory. A few days earlier on the campaign plane, Martin had cornered Humphrey and said to him: "I want to say this before the election. Win lose or draw you've run a good campaign, an honorable campaign. You've said nothing you'll ever regret, and this is important for you and the country. And you've kept the liberal cause alive."[62]

As voting results started to trickle in, Martin, watching the returns at the Leamington Hotel in Minneapolis, believed his candidate just might pull off the impossible when voting in New York and Michigan looked good for Humphrey (he went on to win both states). The vice president's victory in Pennsylvania had Van Dyk believing that the Democrats could defeat Nixon. "But then it hung. And hung," Martin said. "I think I went to bed around 3 or 4 A M, with California, Illinois, and Ohio still out." Nixon won all three of those states and squeaked into office, winning 43.4 percent of the vote to 42.7 for Humphrey and 13.5 percent for Wallace. The Republican candidate enjoyed a substantial triumph in the Electoral College, with 301 electoral votes to 191 for Humphrey and 46 for Wallace. Although gracious in his concession statement, Humphrey, when he learned from O'Brien that urban precincts in New Jersey and Ohio were failing to produce their expected Democratic votes and the election was most likely lost, had said, "The American people will learn they just elected a papier-mâché president."[63]

Although some Democrats believed that if the race had lasted another week Humphrey might have managed to pull off the upset, Martin disagreed. In his opinion, the vice president's campaign reached its peak on Election Day and would have lost votes in another week. "Where we needed the time was on the other end, at the start," he said. The Republicans had their convention earlier than the Democrats, giving them a few weeks' head start. The late August date had been set earlier, when Johnson was still a viable candidate, so the Democrats could celebrate the president's sixtieth birthday on August 27. If the Chicago convention had not torn the party to pieces, Humphrey might well have been able to raise the money he needed; $10 million in September would have won the election for him, Martin said, and kept Nixon out of the White House. "What that would have saved the country!" he noted years later. Humphrey's spirited effort, however, made the election far closer than anyone would have thought possible back on Labor Day. Although frustrated by the final election results, Martin was not sorry he had become involved in either Robert Kennedy's or Humphrey's campaign. "I know I did everything I could in both," he said. "Not enough; but all I could."[64]

On Wednesday, November 20, Martin and Fran returned home to Highland Park, Illinois, and, six years after Martin had left the country to take up his post as the U.S. ambassador to the Dominican Republic, he retrieved his family's old Victorian house from the tenants who had been renting it. Once back in his office at his home, Martin renewed his work on the Stevenson biography. There would be other distractions, however, to take him away from the book, the first volume of which was finally published in 1976. Martin once again offered his writing talent to a Democratic candidate in what became his final foray into the hurly-burly of a presidential race, and he served as a sometimes reluctant mentor to a new generation of journalists yearning to break free from the strictures of journalism's past.

TEN

As Time Goes By

AS A GRADUATE STUDENT AT NORTHWESTERN UNIVERSITY'S
Medill School of Journalism in Evanston, Illinois, Jim Borg took an independent writing class in the fall of 1975 that required him to research
and write an article that might be suitable for publication in such national periodicals as *Esquire* or *The New Yorker*. A few months earlier,
Chicago newspapers had been full of reports about the death of Steven
Stawnychy, a recruit at the Great Lakes Naval Training Center who had
been abused by his instructors. On the evening of June 3, 1975, Stawnychy had committed suicide by letting himself be struck by a Chicago
and North Western train. "He walked over and laid his head down on
the tracks," said the engineer of the train that hit Stawnychy. "When
I realized what he was up to, I just went into 'emergency' and tried to
stop – but, of course, it was too short a distance." For his article, Borg
wanted to "put all the pieces together into a comprehensive story that
also looked at Stawnychy's background" in an attempt to unravel why
the recruit had taken his own life.[1]

On a gray day late that fall, Borg took an early draft of his article to
be critiqued by his professor, John Bartlow Martin, during a meeting
in the study at Martin's Victorian home in Highland Park, just a thirty-
minute drive from the Northwestern campus. "The study was modestly
furnished and obviously a place where work was done, nothing for show,"
Borg recalled. "The ashtray on his desk was nearly overflowing but I don't
remember him smoking as we worked." Martin showed Borg how to cut
and blend the story, paring down each of his sentences to ensure that
every word counted. The result was magic, said Borg, today assistant city

editor at the *Honolulu Star-Advertiser*. He described his editorial session with Martin as "the most instructive half hour of my life." Martin also assisted Borg in obtaining a grant from Medill that enabled him to travel to Stawnychy's hometown in Minnesota to complete his research. Borg completed his article, had it published as the cover story in the April 1976 issue of the *Chicago Tribune Magazine*, and won an award for it in a United Press International competition.[2]

Martin's teaching career at one of the country's top-ranked journalism schools began in 1969, when he started as a visiting lecturer at Medill. He accepted the job to help support his family while he labored to finish his Adlai E. Stevenson biography. His hiring had been part of Dean Ira William "Bill" Cole's effort to bring professional reporters and nationally known individuals in the profession to teach at Medill. In addition to Martin, others who became familiar figures at Fisk Hall were Newton Minow, former Federal Communications Commission chairman, and Sig Michelson, former CBS News president. "I was a fan of John's work," said Peter Jacobi, who began teaching at Medill in 1961, remained there for eighteen years, and served as assistant and associate dean during that time. "His magazine pieces were so carefully reported and brilliantly written. I felt he would make an excellent teacher for our students, particularly the more advanced ones." Jacobi remembered there was a "certain pride" felt at Medill for having secured Martin as a teacher, and "because he was a true gentleman, we came to like him as a colleague." After just a year at Medill, Cole promoted Martin to full professor, complete with tenure, a salary that topped out at nearly $30,000 a year, plus health insurance, which proved vital in dealing with the health woes that plagued Martin, a longtime smoker, during the ten years he remained at the university. Although Martin always told his students that writing could not be taught, he did believe that if they already had the ability to write a decent English sentence, he could perhaps "teach them to write a better one," as well as instruct them on how to do the legwork necessary to produce a decent magazine article.[3]

During his time at Medill, Martin taught two graduate-level seminars, including one on the limits of American power, similar to the course he had taught at the City University of New York. His other seminar, officially known as Journalism D26, Independent Writing Projects, focused on the how and why of producing serious nonfiction magazine articles. The class helped students improve their writing, sharpened their reporting skills, guided them in organizing their research, and showed them how to structure their material in a way suitable for magazine publication. The class met irregularly as a group, with Martin spending more time in one-on-one consultations with his students about their projects than in a formal classroom setting. He required them to read, and discussed with them, two well-known books that had often influenced his own work: *The Elements of Style* by William Strunk Jr. and E. B. White, and *A Dictionary of Modern English Usage* by Henry Watson Fowler. Martin discovered that some of his students had been previously introduced to Strunk and White either in high school or as undergraduates, but "doting fathers read *Huckleberry Finn* to small children before they are old enough to understand that *Huckleberry Finn* is a book about human freedom. Students read Strunk too soon. They need to read him while they are trying to write seriously." Gregg Easterbrook, a student of Martin's during the 1976–77 school year and today an author and contributing editor for the *Atlantic Monthly* and *Washington Monthly*, recalled that when students slipped up even verbally from the dictates of Strunk and White, they were sure to hear about it from their professor. "He didn't suffer fools gladly," Easterbrook said.[4]

From Fowler's classic tome, Martin shared articles on such issues as the that/which problem, formal words, hackneyed phrases, paragraph rhythm, pedantry, meaningless words, and others. "He was very strict about formal grammar rules," Easterbrook said, adding that Martin's lessons on the subject came during a time when proper grammar had been in decline. As a way to improve their style, Martin encouraged his students to read good writing, using as examples his own magazine stories from *Harper's* and the *Saturday Evening Post*; Edmund Wilson's *Patriotic Gore: Studies in the Literature of the American Civil War*; Lillian Hellman's *Pentimento*; and Paul Horgan's *Approaches to Writing*.[5]

Most of the fifty-four students who took Martin's advanced writing classes at Medill each year had no experience producing anything more complicated than a spot news story, but Martin still made them submit an outline for a magazine article, then report and write and rewrite a story running anywhere from fourteen to eighteen and a half pages. He allowed his students to pick their own topics, and he let them use newspaper clippings and library materials to prepare their outlines. For their rough drafts and finished article, however, they had to use only interviews, documents, and other primary sources. "The rock-bottom foundation of all journalism is reporting," said Martin. "Writing is important, editing is important. But in the end everything depends on reporting." For those unsure of what to write about, he provided a list of potential topics, using such local stories as the possibility of a third airport for Chicago, a slum fire, voting patterns in Chicago and its suburbs during presidential elections, and public housing. Martin also distributed as a guide a 1954 outline he had done for *Post* editors on a possible story about the life and death of Gus Amedeo, a Chicago burglar who had killed a policeman and had been gunned down in return (published in the *Post* in 1955 as "The Making of a Killer"). Although general interest magazines such as the *Post, Life,* and *Look* were on the decline by the time he joined the Medill faculty, hurt by television's domination of the home entertainment market, Martin maintained an abiding faith "in the ability of a good writer to make a living by simply being able to communicate facts, whether in magazines, books, TV, or elsewhere. The writer serves truth. He is needed."[6]

When he began his career at Medill, universities across the country, including Northwestern, had been beset by unrest. These were the days, Martin remembered, of the shooting by National Guard troops of students at Kent State, the radical actions of the Weather Underground, and the militancy of the Black Panthers, a time known in Chicago as the Days of Rage. Martin said that by and large he had been on the side of the students, overlooking their long hair, beads, sandals, and chains. While some of them insulted and harassed their professors, Martin said he escaped such outbursts. "It was a hard time to be a student, a hard time to be a parent, and even a rather hard time to be a teacher," said Martin. He preferred the turmoil of that period – "students were at least alive," Martin noted – to the "inertia and careerism" that infected students in the post–Vietnam War era.[7]

After a few years of unmet deadlines, broken appointments, and sloppy article drafts seemingly dashed off at the last possible moment, Martin began approaching "each new student somewhat warily." Writing for magazines proved to be beyond the capabilities of most of his students, as they tended to produce academic papers, not magazine pieces, while nearly most had great difficulty in structuring the material they collected. All too many of them simply could not "write a clean crisp English sentence," and Martin wondered if elementary schools and high schools in the United States had somehow stopped teaching basic English grammar, let alone syntax. Worst of all, students had a lackadaisical attitude about the profession they had chosen. "They do not understand," said Martin, "that writing is a serious and difficult business. They have an unspoken contempt for their material. They need to be made to take it seriously. A writer bears a heavy responsibility. They do not seem to feel it."[8]

Growing weary of marking the same errors again and again on every article draft he received, Martin, to save time, had a set of rubber stamps created that offered such straightforward criticisms as: "awkward," "loose, wordy," "not entirely clear," "says little," and "what mean?" Many years after his days at Medill, Easterbrook still remembered the corrections Martin made on one of his assignments. Martin had invited Easterbrook, whom he considered to be one of the most promising writers he had in his course, to his Highland Park home to discuss his manuscript about the Republican Party in Chicago. What struck Easterbrook, besides that his professor had been willing to invite him to his home and talk to him for a half an hour about his work, was that when Martin returned his article he had made comments on almost every sentence, with some sentences having more than one suggestion for improvement. The corrections – "dull," "sloppy," "overwritten," "bad grammar" – were stamped on his manuscript using orange, green, and red ink. "My God," Easterbrook thought to himself at the time, "this guy uses these words so often he had stamps made." Martin also dissuaded his students from erroneous usages that had slowly crept into the English language: "media" for "television," "image" for "reputation," as well as "impact" as a verb for "affect" and "input" for "suggestion." Easterbrook in particular recalled Martin's maxim that good writing had to be rigorous and that every word on the page had to be there for a reason. It was a lesson that should be learned by a writer in any style or genre, said Easterbrook.[9]

Taking a class with Martin could be an intimidating experience for Medill students, as he had no problem in telling them exactly what he thought about their writing. Niles Howard signed up for Martin's course while at Medill in the early 1970s, believing it would put his career on the fast track. He believed so even though neither he nor his fellow students were really sure what the difference was between a newspaper article and a magazine article. When Martin, whom Howard described as "a little introverted, not gregarious, not a back-slapper, but thoughtful," returned his first writing assignment to him, the professor had scrawled on it, "This isn't even an article. Why don't you try again?" A chagrined Howard, who today runs his own communications marketing company, went to Martin's office and asked for guidance on what he might do to improve his piece. The two of them talked for almost an hour on "how I might salvage my academic standing (let alone my ego)," said Howard. The memory of what he and Martin talked about has faded over time, but one point his teacher made stuck with him, and it is advice he still hears whenever he sits down at a keyboard and starts to write. "A magazine article is not a bunch of facts and quotes," Howard quoted Martin as saying. "It's a journey from point A to point B. Your job is to persuade the reader to ride along."[10]

If students took their work seriously, Martin treated them with courtesy and did all he could to help them hone their craft. An army veteran from Alabama, Mike Plemmons arrived at Medill in the late 1970s with considerable newspaper experience, having worked at two daily newspapers in the South and another newspaper in Massachusetts. Plemmons spent his first semester at Medill in Washington, D.C., reporting for the Medill News Service, which allowed students the opportunity to live in the nation's capital and report on the activities of the federal government. A professor-editor at the news service recommended to Plemmons that he study with Martin when he returned to his studies at Northwestern. The next semester, Plemmons took Martin's advanced writing class and decided to create what he called an "experimental" article on the education system, giving three points of view – a seventh-grade student's, his parents', and his teacher's – side by side. Halfway through his project, Plemmons was sorry he had ever taken it on. The interviews were easy enough, but he could not find his "lede," the opening paragraph enticing readers to go further into his twenty-page manuscript. One day, while going over a draft of the article with Martin, Plemmons remembered that Martin circled a paragraph in his story, a quote from a seventh-grade teacher, sat forward in his creaky chair, and said, looking directly at him, "This is good." Rewriting a piece that size in the days before laptop computers and digital word processing required hard, tedious work, but Plemmons decided to take Martin's advice, abandoning his previous story structure and restarting his piece with the paragraph Martin had circled. "It worked, of course," said Plemmons. "The rest of the story wrote itself." On the last page of Plemmons's finished article, Martin simply wrote, "I like this piece." Although he never published the story he wrote for Martin's class, Plemmons kept the manuscript for several years, cherishing the memory of a time when a professor took his writing seriously and treated him like a colleague.[11]

By the mid-1970s, many Medill students were drawn, thanks to the work of such reporters as Bob Woodward and Carl Bernstein of the *Washington Post,* to careers as investigative reporters. Others wanted jobs where they could practice the New Journalism that had been pioneered by such talented writers as Tom Wolfe, Hunter Thompson, Norman Mailer, Gay Talese, and Joan Didion. Journalism historian Marc Weingarten noted that in the turbulent 1960s, Wolfe and his cohorts had realized that traditional reporting was "inadequate to chronicle the tremendous cultural and social changes of the era." Martin, however, had quite a different viewpoint. He still believed in the old-fashioned advice from Strunk and White that a writer should always place himself in the background and write in a way that drew the reader's attention to the writing, rather than to the writer. In his estimation, New Journalism required a writer to give his views about every fact, to constantly perform, and to "become, indeed, virtually the principal actor in the drama." Few of his young writers, however, had anything interesting to say, Martin noted, while the elders they wrote about "have a good deal interesting to say but we cannot hear them because of the authors' noise." He also was annoyed with young writers who did not take the trouble to learn grammar or how to write a clear English sentence, or who invented dialogue or fabricated "composite characters" without first informing their readers. "To my mind, this is writing fiction, or, less politely, faking a story, lying," said Martin. "To all this, my students would reply that I am an old grouch. They would be right."[12]

The conflict between the old and new generations Martin experienced at Northwestern cropped up again when he offered his speech-writing talents to another Democratic presidential candidate. On this occasion, the candidate was an underdog, George McGovern, U.S. senator from South Dakota, who led his party in 1972 against incumbent Richard Nixon. In the early primaries leading up to the Democratic National Convention in Miami Beach, Florida, however, Martin had supported Edmund Muskie. "The thing I like about him is his thoughtfulness. He's not erratic, not impulsive," Martin said. He sometimes traveled with the senator or went to Washington, D.C., to meet with Muskie's senior advisers, including Clark Clifford, Jim Rowe, and U.S. senator Al Gore Sr. Muskie had been an effective vice presidential candidate running with Hubert Humphrey in 1968, and four years later, political pundits crowned him as the frontrunner for the nomination. Muskie piled up endorsements from a number of the nation's leading Democratic politicians, who expressed admiration for his "Lincolnesque" calm and aura of electability. The man from Maine stood, they all agreed, as the only Democratic candidate capable of defeating Nixon. The early campaign failed to excite Martin, who wrote a friend that he believed the politicians were doing their best to "bore the people to death. I've never seen a year with so many candidates, so many primaries, and so much vacuity."[13]

The Muskie presidential boom imploded, however, after the crucial New Hampshire primary in early March. Muskie won the primary, but by a smaller margin than many had predicted, seriously damaging his stature as the inevitable choice of the Democrats for the November election; by late April he had dropped out of the race. In the end, Martin said that Muskie proved to be "a surprisingly weak candidate, and he was overwhelmed by the sudden surge of revolt and fragmentation that swept the Democratic Party." The beneficiary of Muskie's fall was McGovern, the prairie populist described by Robert Kennedy as "the most decent man in the Senate," whose strong showing in New Hampshire and straightforwardness impressed even conservative members of his party. He had articulated his campaign theme, "Come Home, America" – what he called a restatement of America's treasured values – at a March 21, 1970, speech in Denver before a roomful of fellow Democrats. McGovern called upon the nation to "come home from the wilderness of needless war and excessive militarism to build a society in which we cared about one another – especially the old, the sick, the hungry, the jobless, the homeless." Such a message seemed tailor-made for the huge influx of young voters now eligible to vote because of the passage of the Twenty-sixth Amendment adopted in 1971 that had lowered the voting age from twenty-one to eighteen.[14]

With Muskie floundering, McGovern used his effective grassroots organization, drawn to his sincere commitment to end the Vietnam War, to achieve victories in such key primary states as Wisconsin, Massachusetts, Nebraska, and California. McGovern survived a bitter, last-ditch effort from Humphrey to deny him the presidential nomination at the convention in July. The GOP tried to win over the blue-collar, normally Democratic voters who had turned to George Wallace in 1968 by repeating the erroneous charge from his fellow Democrats that McGovern was the candidate of the three A's: amnesty (leniency for those who resisted being drafted to fight in Vietnam), abortion (favoring legalized abortion before the U.S. Supreme Court's 1973 *Roe vs. Wade* decision), and acid (the legalization of drugs, in particular marijuana). As the son of a Methodist minister and a decorated World War II bomber pilot, McGovern disputed the notion that he was too militant to be president, noting, "Ordinarily, we don't send wild-eyed radicals to the United States Senate from South Dakota."[15]

Just eighteen days after the Democratic convention ended on July 13, McGovern's quest to topple Nixon suffered a fatal blow when his running mate, Thomas Eagleton, a first-term, politically moderate U.S. senator from Missouri, stepped down. The McGovern team had turned to Eagleton, a Muskie supporter, after their candidate's other choices for the job, including Ted Kennedy, Humphrey, and Walter Mondale, had turned him down and after Eagleton had assured them he had no skeletons in his closet that might come back to haunt them. In the days before extensive background checks were a regular part of such decisions, McGovern and his staff were unaware that Eagleton had been hospitalized for physical and nervous exhaustion on more than one occasion and had twice received electroshock (today known as electro-convulsive) therapy. Reports about Eagleton's medical problems began circulating among the national press. "I was not plagued with haunting memories of my medical past," Eagleton later said, and he said he did not consider what had happened to him "as illegal or immoral or shameful." He said his health problems were the furthest thing from his mind when McGovern asked him to be his running mate and compared his health problems as nothing worse than "a broken leg that had healed." Gary Hart, one of McGovern's top advisers, noted that Eagleton's health issues had even escaped the scrutiny of the senator's home state newspapers, including the *Saint Louis Post-Dispatch,* well regarded for its investigative journalism. "Those who claim the McGovern staff could, or should, have uncovered this kind of information about an individual not even under serious consideration prior to the convention don't know what they're talking about," said Hart.[16]

Before all the facts about Eagleton's health had been presented to him, McGovern impulsively and unwisely told Dick Dougherty, his press secretary, to put out a statement that he was "a thousand percent behind Tom Eagleton." Later, McGovern talked to Eagleton's psychiatrists and learned specific details about his running mate's medical history that he believed "raised serious doubts about his capacity to carry the burdens and responsibility of the presidency." Calls were also coming from the editorial pages of major national newspapers, including the *Washington Post* and *New York Times,* for Eagleton to resign from the ticket. On July 31 Eagleton finally agreed to do so, and a special session of the Democratic National Committee ratified McGovern's replacement candidate, former Peace Corps director Sargent Shriver. McGovern's reputation for competence and integrity took a major hit with the Eagleton affair. The public sympathized with the Missouri senator, who had stonewalled any release of the most damaging details about his previous hospital-izations, making McGovern the villain in the affair in the eyes of the public. "I did what I had to do," McGovern noted years later, "but the Eagleton matter ended whatever chance there was to defeat Richard Nixon in 1972."[17]

The fifty-seven-year-old Martin went to Washington in early September 1972 to start working as a McGovern speechwriter. From that

point until Election Day in November, he traveled back and forth between the nation's capital and his Illinois home so he could teach his
classes at Northwestern. While in Washington, Martin stayed at the
Hay-Adams Hotel and toiled out of offices on the seventh floor at Mc-
Govern headquarters at 1910 K Street, an eight-story former apartment
building that had also once been Muskie's campaign headquarters. A
number of people asked him to assist McGovern, Martin recalled, and
he could not resist helping anyone who ran against the one man he most
despised in politics: Nixon. Headquarters had the uproarious and in-
formal atmosphere of a college dormitory, with "scores of barefoot girls
in blue jeans and boys in long hair and beards racing about mindlessly,
taping up funny signs in the corridors," said Martin. With affection,
Hart described the offices as possessing an "exquisite madness," and he
praised the "unbound enthusiasm and wry humor" of the young staff and
volunteers. Martin had a more jaundiced view of the proceedings, recalling that if he left his desk unguarded at headquarters, he found upon
his return that his pens, paper, and sometimes even his typewriter had
vanished. "The kids are rude, insensitive, heedless, discourteous," he
said. "Not all; but most." His arrival had "raised the average age of the
staff to 10 ½," Martin said in a letter to his wife, Fran. Larry O'Brien,
named chairman of the fall campaign by McGovern as a way to ease the
concerns of traditional Democrats, wondered what he might be getting
himself in for when he noticed that the sign over the door at the headquarters did not include any mention of the Democratic Party. McGovern's followers seemed to view the party as the enemy, "or at best as a
slightly repugnant means to an end," said O'Brien.[18]

Latecomers to the McGovern cause were often treated harshly by
those who had been with McGovern from the beginning. Robert Shrum,
who had written speeches for Muskie before assuming the same role for
the South Dakota senator, noted that "resentment toward those who
hadn't been with McGovern from the start were rife." According to Martin, the "cocksure young staff" jealously guarded access to the candidate.
At McGovern headquarters, however, Martin worked with two men he
knew from previous presidential contests, Ted Van Dyk, the director of
issues and speeches, and Milt Gwirtzman, who parceled out assignments
and transmitted speech material to the McGovern campaign plane by

telecopier after Van Dyk had reviewed the text. The plan was to rotate speechwriters on McGovern's Boeing 727 campaign plane, the *Dakota Queen,* named in honor of the B-24 bomber he flew in World War II, with each of them spending a week with McGovern and then returning to headquarters. The rotation might never happen, Martin told Fran, something that was fine with him as he much preferred eating lunch at the Federal City Club in Washington than at, for example, the Ypsilanti, Michigan, airport.[19]

In addition to Martin, other speechwriters on the staff included Robert Shrum, Sandy Berger, Bob Hunter, and Stephen Schlesinger, the son of Martin's good friend Arthur M. Schlesinger Jr. "We had a good crew," recalled Van Dyk. Shrum spent most of his time traveling with McGovern, assisting the candidate's main writer, John Holum, his longtime legislative assistant. It proved to be a perplexing situation for Martin. "Having started out in this business 20 years ago with Arthur and now finding myself sitting next to Arthur's son, doing what I was doing 20 years ago, I find myself wondering if there is a message I'm not getting," he wrote Fran. Martin praised Van Dyk and Gwirtzman as "able professionals," but he lamented that none of the young staffers assembled at headquarters had ever before worked on a national campaign and, because they had won the primaries against phenomenal odds (early on McGovern had support from only 4 percent of the voting public) and faced strong opposition from the party establishment, thought they could do no wrong. Theodore H. White, the famous chronicler of presidential races with his *The Making of the President* series, described the attitude of McGovern's young workers as not the politics of exclusion, but "the politics of the faithful few." They had plunged into national politics, Martin observed, without understanding that a national campaign was "a vastly different exercise from a bunch of scattered primaries." Some of the senior staff also seemed more interested in gaining publicity for themselves than working selflessly on behalf of the candidate, noisily resigning every few days and expressing their opinions freely to the traveling press corps. "The old tradition of the staff with a passion for anonymity was junked," Martin said.[20]

As nearly as he could figure, Martin believed that the McGovern campaign's strategy involved writing off the South except for Arkansas and Texas, as well as the states west of the Mississippi River except for California, Minnesota, and South Dakota. The candidate planned on concentrating on the larger states in a belt from Illinois to Massachusetts, plus Wisconsin. "As to issues, forget credibility and trust – he [McGovern] destroyed that issue himself," said Martin, referring to the Eagleton fiasco. "Instead, concentrate on the old Democratic bread and butter issues – jobs, high prices, populism, government for special interests vs. government for the people. . . . Plus Vietnam." By focusing on such tried-and-true Democratic issues, McGovern hoped to win back defecting blue-collar members of the party, as well as the still powerful figures who had opposed him at the convention, including Mayor Richard Daley of Chicago and former president Lyndon Johnson; McGovern paid courtesy calls on both men. As Van Dyk pointed out in a memorandum to key McGovern advisers in late August, traditional Democratic voters, who are primarily in the big industrial states, needed to be reminded that McGovern and the Democratic Party "are good for ordinary people. They are good for them economically. They listen to them. They believe in them." Unfortunately, Martin said, following this strategy hurt McGovern "heavily among the people who had supported him because he was anti-politician. He revealed himself as practicing the crudest kind of old politics – and doing it far more clumsily than Nixon or Daley." Martin also questioned the staff's initial decision to run what he called "a strictly TV campaign – they hit 3 cities a day in order to stage TV visual events, thus hitting the network news programs plus 3 local TV outlets." On these stops McGovern or Shriver might eat with workers at a local factory's cafeteria; visit a farm, supermarket, or bowling alley; or tour an area in need of highlighting because of a specific social problem.[21]

Animated by their opposition to the Vietnam War, the McGovern staff fought just as hard against uphill odds as the Humphrey campaign had just four years earlier, said Van Dyk. "I had great confidence in my policy and speechwriting staff," he said. The few experienced professionals at headquarters were realistic about their candidate's chances against Nixon. Only a major blunder on the president's part or some "major unforeseeable outside event" could give McGovern a chance at victory, said Martin. According to Van Dyk, possible setbacks for the Nixon administration included either a ghastly military setback in Vietnam or damaging details being uncovered from a scandal involving the June 17 break-in at the Democratic National Committee headquarters at the Watergate complex in Washington, D.C., then being seriously investigated by only a few newspapers, including the *Washington Post*. Such a miracle seemed more and more unlikely, especially given Nixon's decision to do as little campaigning for his re-election as possible. Instead, he used his position as the chief executive to garner headlines, watching his approval rating steadily climb as a result of his foreign policy successes, including normalizing relations with China and easing tensions with the Soviet Union at a Moscow summit meeting. The president sought to remain above the political fray, saying and doing as little as he pleased "without being held properly accountable" by the press, said Van Dyk. McGovern, however, faced daily scrutiny from a host of reporters as he barnstormed across the country. Late in the campaign Martin wrote a speech in which he pointed out that for the first time in American history the country had a presidential contest with only one candidate. "The whole speech elaborated that theme. It got a line or two in the paper," he said. "Why? Don't people care? Or when McGovern said it, maybe they didn't believe it."[22]

Unlike his previous experiences with Democratic presidential candidates, Martin never really got to know McGovern, possibly because, for the first time, he did not have the opportunity to travel with the candidate; he could not remember even seeing McGovern in person since the 1968 Chicago convention. "Never before had I worked for a candidate I didn't believe in," Martin said. "I am afraid I don't believe in him. He knows Vietnam and hunger; but that's all. He's not a national politician, has no national feeling." Martin compared McGovern unfavorably to the other Democratic presidential candidates he had previously worked for, faulting his leadership abilities and failure to make issues he talked about in his speeches resonate with the public. "Someone wrote that the words are fine but the tune is all wrong when he speaks," Martin said. "When he showed anger, it came through as whining, complaining; when he showed compassion, he sounded like a hick preacher. He never sounded Presidential. . . . No eloquence. Nothing to inspire. No joy. No fun. No wit or humor."[23]

In spite of all his criticisms of McGovern, Martin said there was something good and decent about the man. In October, when Henry Kissinger, Nixon's national security adviser, announced, falsely as it turned out, that "peace was at hand in Vietnam," Martin had been impressed by McGovern's reaction to the news. He remembered that McGovern had been cornered by the press and given little time to reflect on Kissinger's announcement, but he had agreed with a reporter's assertion that if Nixon ended the war it meant certain defeat for his presidential campaign. McGovern asserted, however, that losing the election would be a small price to pay for ending the bloodshed in Vietnam and finally bringing American troops safely home. "Furthermore," said Martin, "he said it with conviction and force." McGovern made many mistakes during the campaign, but also his luck had finally run out. "During the primaries," said Martin, "he got every lucky break; but at and after the convention, he got every bad break."[24]

Martin had found it hard to be effective writing from McGovern headquarters in Washington. Staff members on the plane with the candidate usually ignored what headquarters sent them and preferred to use the material they had prepared while on the campaign trail. The casual attitude displayed by some of McGovern's writers also bothered Martin. He noted that during the Stevenson and Johnson campaigns, every time the candidate made a major speech, a number of drafts were written "amid much agonizing, and the final was polished and repolished endlessly – and the result was damn good. But McGovern's writers seemed to dash off [a] major speech on the backs of old envelopes – and the results showed it." Portions of the speeches he wrote did get used, but the material was never central to the campaign, and "it never changed or sharpened" McGovern's image for the voters, Martin said. Scheduled to join the McGovern party on the plane near the end of the campaign, Martin, who had gone home so he could teach his classes at Northwestern, received a telephone call from Holum telling him there was no room for him on the plane. "So I stayed home, idle," Martin noted. On Election Day, November 7, Martin voted, something he called a gloomy formality. In the election pool at headquarters, he had guessed McGovern winning 270 electoral votes, the bare minimum needed to win. He made a more realistic guess of 85 electoral votes in the pool at his class at Northwestern.[25]

The voting results were a disaster for the McGovern campaign, as Nixon swept into a second term, winning 60.7 percent of the votes. Mc-Govern only won one state, Massachusetts, and lost in the Electoral College by a 520 to 17 margin. By dinnertime on election evening, Van Dyk and others at McGovern headquarters knew their candidate would lose in a landslide. Near the end of the campaign, McGovern also knew that defeat loomed ahead. Some of his advisers expressed worries that the candidate still harbored hopes of an upset, so Shrum decided to break the bad news to McGovern, doing so in a hotel room in an unnamed city near the campaign's end. McGovern greeted Shrum, asked him to sit down, poured each of them a vodka on the rocks, handed one to him, thanked him for coming, and said, "Bob, I know, I know. But I just need to believe for one more day." McGovern may have suffered a humiliating loss, but other Democratic candidates running for office weathered the storm, and the party held on to its majorities in the U.S. Senate and House. Martin saw the results as an indication that there was a great deal of anti-McGovern voting rather than a pro-Nixon surge. "Then, having voted for Nixon, they split their tickets and voted for Democratic candidates for Senate, Governor, House, and local," he said. Muskie or Humphrey might have managed to beat Nixon, and at least they would not have lost time in August and part of September trying to win back the support of labor unions and the Democratic organization, Martin said.[26]

The most unfortunate outcome of the election for Martin was that "one of the worst, if not the worst, Presidents in American history now has the biggest mandate, or nearly the biggest, in history." He worried that Nixon's landslide gave the president the misapprehension that he had a "license to do anything. I really fear for the country." Martin shared similar concerns with one of his classes at Northwestern, especially about where the Watergate scandal might lead. One day after class one of his students, Joe Gandelman, asked Martin in a private conversation his opinion about the Nixon administration. "He seemed truly frustrated and fearful," Gandelman recalled. Even before any evidence had been uncovered about the extent of the White House's involvement in the break-in of DNC headquarters and the cover-up that followed, Martin had been convinced that Nixon and his advisers knew about the crime. Gandelman remembered Martin softly saying something that chilled him: "We've heard there have been people going through Larry O'Brien's tax returns. This is a scary bunch. I've never seen anything like it. They're thugs." A little less than two years after the election, on August 9, 1974, Nixon resigned as the nation's thirty-seventh president after congressional and media investigations had uncovered the extent of his administration's crimes and dirty tricks, vindicating many of the charges McGovern had made in the campaign and confirming Martin's darkest suspicions.[27]

The McGovern campaign proved to be the last hurrah for Martin when it came to direct involvement in Democratic Party presidential politics. The experience proved to be "liberating" for him. When he had been on the plane with such presidential candidates as Stevenson and John F. Kennedy during an election, Martin had forgiven them when they made mistakes; after all, it was *his* candidate, sitting only a few seats away, who had made the error. "But if you're on the outside, you see him for what he is, a blunderer," he said. The malaise Martin experienced during the McGovern campaign had not all been the fault of the candidate, but it had shown that the country had changed and he had not. The increasing role of primaries in deciding presidential nominees troubled Martin, who thought it was foolish that a "few farmers in Iowa and New Hampshire should choose the leader of the Western world." Control of politics had been reformed from the rule of party bosses and handed over to the people, as had been intended, but now lay with pollsters, advertisers, and television. Martin lamented the rise of "television consultants," who instructed their candidates not only in what words and gestures to use, but concocted strategy and selected what issues to address. Television converted serious political questions into mere theater and thereby killed the notion of "serious political speeches," he added. In remembering the colleagues he had worked with on presidential campaign staffs – Carl McGowan, John Kenneth Galbraith, Arthur Schlesinger, Ted Sorensen, Kenny O'Donnell, Fred Dutton, Lawrence O'Brien, Ted Van Dyk, and Milton Gwirtzman – Martin said that none of them imagined they were molding their candidate's image, "not one talked to the press much or leaked anything to the press that harmed the candidate; not one ever imagined that he was himself the candidate." Martin viewed the well-paid poll takers and image consultants dominating campaigns as "monsters" seeking to advance their own cause instead of that of their candidates. Journalists had also grown too dependent on polls, spending far too much time in horse-race reporting, wondering who was ahead and if a candidate's campaign might be headed for trouble if he or she failed to meet expectations created by the polls. "Why don't reporters go out and report?" Martin wondered. "Reporters ought to be out in bars and union halls and places where people are and find out what they're thinking instead of just taking Gallup's word for what people think."[28]

With the end of his direct involvement in the blood sport of national presidential politics, Martin could focus his attention on a project he had first started in December 1965: the Stevenson biography. When he began his work on the book, Martin expected it to take three years to finish. It took him far longer than that because of the great volume of material he had uncovered about Stevenson. "I have to say that I came away from the whole exercise admiring him more than I had when I began," Martin said of his subject. "I always knew he had political courage – I was with him when he attacked [U.S. senator Joseph] McCarthy and President [Dwight] Eisenhower wouldn't," said Martin. "But I didn't know how miserable, how horrible his private life had been. I learned he also had private courage." Stevenson had to deal with a sometimes traumatic childhood, "a foolish father, a pretentious and suffocating mother, a domineering older sister, a disastrous marriage, and, despite all the friends and comings and goings, an essentially lonely life," Martin said. His subject never complained about these hardships, assuming, Martin noted, that a person's private life was supposed to be torture. On June 5, 1970, Martin, who averaged writing fifty pages a day, finally finished the rough draft of his manuscript, which ran more than 16,000 pages and contained some two and a half million words. "I write a long, awkward – and lousy – rough draft," Martin noted. "It's simply an attempt to get facts down in some order." For the next year and a half, he spent his time cutting and rewriting the manuscript into a semifinal draft of approximately 3,200 pages, or nearly a million words.[29]

Martin spent another three years clearing the manuscript with people he had promised to show it to in return for their cooperation (among
them George Ball, Arthur Schlesinger Jr., Theodore White, Jane Dick,
and Newton Minow) and obtaining clearances for quotations from letters other people had written to Stevenson, including such important
figures in his life as Jacob Avery, Agnes Meyer, Carl McGowan, Dore
Schary, Wilson Wyatt, Louis Kohn, John Kenneth Galbraith, and many
others. Although some biographers paraphrase letters written to their
subject in an attempt to avoid the trouble of seeking permissions, Martin wanted to include verbatim quotes from the letters, especially those
from Stevenson's female admirers, in order "to preserve the flavor of their
friendships." Final approval also had to be obtained through negotiations with Stevenson's eldest son, Adlai III, meetings that included Minow as potential arbiter and sometimes included Martin's editors from
Doubleday, Samuel S. Vaughan and Ken McCormick. There were times
when Martin lost his patience and wondered if he was in danger of writing a book by committee. "If we make this Stevenson book so that it
pleases everybody," Martin wrote his agent Dorothy Olding, "we will
not have a book worth reading."[30]

The storm passed, however, and Martin believed he had endured
the troubles for a good cause. "He [Adlai III] raised numerous objections, but we never were forced to arbitration," Martin said. Most of the
younger Stevenson's protests involved the book's explorations of his
father's relations with his female friends, some ill-timed statements Stevenson had uttered about Jews, and his feelings about African Americans. "I must say I thought young Adlai behaved well; I am not sure I
would want to read a candid biography of my own father," Martin said.
"In any case, he did not gut the book, nor did I falsify it." Martin confessed that when he wrote the rough draft, he had been too keenly aware
of his status as a Stevenson partisan, and, in an attempt to be objective,
"had been hypercritical of him," focusing too much attention on his
subject's flaws and weaknesses. This caused a reader of one of the drafts
to tell Vaughan that he believed the author did not like his subject. Adlai
III's critical comments and suggestions for changes, which were adopted
in the final draft, helped to restore balance to the book, Martin said. It
had not always been possible to unravel all the complexities of Steven-

son's life in writing the biography of this "sometimes ambiguous man," but Martin believed he had answered all of the important questions.[31]

The manuscript for the Stevenson biography proved to be too long to publish in one book, so Doubleday released the book in two volumes: *Adlai Stevenson of Illinois* (1976), covering his life from birth to his first presidential campaign in 1952, and *Adlai Stevenson and the World* (1977), exploring Stevenson's career after the 1952 campaign up until his death in 1965 and published just twenty-five years after Martin had first met him; together the books became known as *The Life of Adlai Stevenson.* No stranger to biography, Schlesinger praised the books as "superb" and complimented his former speechwriting partner for his ability to combine "affection, insight, and objectivity" into what he regarded as "one of the greatest American political biographies of the [twentieth] century." Taken in full, the more than 1,600 pages produced by Martin represented, noted Jeff Broadwater, a subsequent Stevenson biographer, one of the "most impressive pieces of detective work in the history of American biography," an opinion that was shared by many other reviewers, though some had reservations about the book's vast number of details. As Galbraith noted in his review of the first volume in the *New York Times Book Review,* Martin had been able to organize the vast amount of material on Stevenson into "a far more coherent and interesting story than anyone would think possible. Some writers take many words to say little; John Bartlow Martin takes many words, but fewer than would be supposed, to say everything." There was no malice or meanness of thought in the book, and Galbraith said Martin never allowed his friendship with Stevenson to affect his narrative. Although not always flattering to a man Martin unabashedly considered to be one of his heroes, the books represented an honest and unflinching look at one of the leading U.S. politicians and statesmen of the twentieth century. The striking and rigorously documented biography demonstrated to all who read it that Stevenson's polished speeches, his candor, and his forthrightness had worked together to elevate the tone of America's politics, according to a review in *Time* magazine. "He [Stevenson] set a standard that later presidential aspirants have yet to match," the reviewer for *Time* concluded. Martin's former hometown newspaper, the *Indianapolis Star,* gave him the highest compliment a biographer could receive when its reviewer noted, "After reading Martin's book, one can say with some degree of satisfaction that he knows Adlai Stevenson – knows him, in fact, about as well as he could have been known as a living person."[32]

Martin had started work on the Stevenson biography while still in his fifties, a time, he said, when a person is expected to earn his highest income and do his most important work. He spent this vital period of his life immersed in writing about Stevenson, and he never had any regrets about his decision. "I've heard it said that some writers who spend so long on a biography become bored with their subject, or, worse, come to resent him for taking so much of their lives to write his," said Martin. "Luckily I escaped both infections." After the dissatisfaction he had experienced during the McGovern campaign, Martin had been inspired in writing his book by the pleasant memories of his days with Stevenson during the Illinois governor's 1952 run for the presidency, marked as it was by "a sort of ebullience, a freshness, a verve" not seen since in politics. Stevenson took politics "out of the gutter," Martin said, and believed it to be "a high calling, and that showed through in the way he handled himself as a politician. I think that was the thing that attracted all of us to him in the first place." Martin's experience with the Stevenson biography had its setbacks. Both volumes were "widely and favorably reviewed," but sales were only modest, Martin noted. He also shared Fran's disappointment that neither volume won a Pulitzer Prize or a National Book Award. Martin came to believe that if he had written the biography fast and had it published in one volume shortly after Stevenson's death, it probably would have become a bestseller and won at least one major honor. "On the other hand," Martin said, "it would have been a very different book." The enormous amount of documentation he uncovered contributed to the biography's length, but it did not overwhelm him, Martin said. He always tried to remember that he alone had complete access to all of Stevenson's papers and that he owed an obligation to history to provide a complete view of the former governor's life. "Adlai Stevenson was one of the most important figures in my life," Martin said. "In life, he gave me a great deal, and I like to think I helped him."[33]

While still writing about Stevenson, Martin pondered what he would do with his own life after the project ended. For several months in the late 1960s, he wrote a regular, one-page column for *Life*. Impressed by Martin's work, the magazine's editors began negotiating a contract to make him a permanent contributor. "At that point, however, the editors were fired; my career at *Life* ended (and so, for a time, did *Life*)," Martin recalled. The magazine market no longer seemed as stable at it had been for him in the 1950s. With the Stevenson book nearing publication, Martin wrote to Olding expressing his desire to end his teaching career at Medill. Although thankful the job had given him the income he needed to finish the biography ("it pays the grocery bill and helps on the gin bill," Martin joked to a friend), Martin could not see himself "tottering into retirement with a gin bottle in one hand and in the other a sheaf of student papers." Instead, he wanted to write his way out of his financial need to teach. He shared with Olding several ideas for doing so, including a host of thousand-word columns that might catch the eye of the few national magazines then remaining on newsstands. "I'm spoiled, I know. I've always been lucky enough to do what I wanted – to write and to work in government, and even to write what I wanted to write and do what I wanted to do in government," Martin wrote Olding. "I'm now for the first time doing what nearly everyone else has to do – doing something that I don't like for the money." In spite of his ambition to quit teaching, Martin remained at Medill until the spring of 1980, when he concluded, with his sixty-fifth birthday on the horizon, that it was time for him to leave.[34]

When he began his freelance career as a young man, Martin had quickly learned the lesson of writing magazine articles only when he had a firm assignment from an editor and books only when he had a signed contract from a publisher. "When you write for a living," he said, "you cannot afford to write on speculation." With his steady income from Medill, and later from Social Security during his retirement, Martin decided to write on speculation, and he found the experience to be cathartic. Now he could write on whatever subject pleased him, always keeping in the back of his mind the danger that his writing could become "undisciplined and even self-indulgent." Chance permitting, he intended to "write till I drop." In addition to producing numerous book reviews and articles on issues of the day for newspapers, including the *Chicago Tribune, Chicago Sun-Times, Washington Post, Philadelphia Enquirer,* and *USA Today,* Martin spent much of his time on a project close to his heart: a first-person account about Smith Lake in Michigan's Upper Peninsula. He called his manuscript "Sometimes in the Summer," borrowing the title from a line out of a book by his writer friend John Voelker that Martin said was one of the most exquisite sentences he had ever read in English: "Sometimes in the Summer in the nighttime, when there was a moon there was a mist, so that the fields looked like a lake." (He later retitled the manuscript "Ten Summers," which, as he told Voelker, was "probably not an improvement.") Martin wrote and rewrote the Smith Lake book, changing and rewording each sentence and sometimes altering the manuscript's concept. "Having nearly always avoided writing in the first person, I found doing so extremely difficult, the hardest writing I ever did," he said. Martin loved the book when he finished it, considering it one of the best pieces of writing he had ever done. Unfortunately, publishers failed to share his enthusiasm for its qualities, and the manuscript languished, unpublished. "It was frustrating to him that he could not make clear to others – editors, his agent – what was so special about this place," said Martin's son, Fred. "The woods, the clear dry air, the animals and fish, the difficult circumstances of living in the wilderness, the solitude: it all meant so much to him." Ever since he had taken on the subject of the Upper Peninsula in 1944 for his first book, *Call It North Country,* Martin had grown accustomed to having difficulty convincing anyone to read about the region he cherished. "In that respect," he noted, "it resembles the old saying about Latin America – the people of the United States will do anything for Latin America except read about it."[35]

All of his life, influenced as he had been by such authors as Ernest Hemingway and John Dos Passos, Martin secretly desired to try his hand at a new genre: fiction. He set out to write a novel on a subject he knew well, politics, and two of the disturbing influences he had noticed creeping into the field, poll taking and television. To feel comfortable tackling such a new form of writing, Martin tried to make it as close as possible to the heavy-fact work he had done before, producing an elaborate outline of his plot and constructing detailed biographies for his characters. The main cast included U.S. senator James T. Heller of Illinois, described by one reviewer as "one part Paul Douglas, two parts Adlai Stevenson III"; Joe Mackey, Heller's top aide and popular with party insiders; Cathy Crothers, a television reporter Mackey has an affair with; and Richard Cutler, an East Coast media consultant and the book's villain, brought in to resurrect Heller's failing re-election campaign. Cutler takes $200,000 from the Heller campaign and bribes the leading television poll taker to falsify his results and predict a landslide victory for Heller so contributors will stop giving money to his Republican opponent, congressman Roy M. Andrews, only to have his unscrupulous behavior exposed. "I constructed a detailed campaign schedule and wrote notes about places – the uproarious campaign headquarters, rallies, a TV studio, the campaign plane, and so on," Martin recalled. "Only then did I start writing the rough draft." The book ends on a positive note, with Heller keeping his integrity intact by resigning and warning a Senate committee of the dangers posed by polls and television. In a statement Martin no doubt supported wholeheartedly, Heller tells the committee that television and pollsters had too much power over the American political system: "The power is there. The temptation is there. As we all know, power corrupts. . . . We must take care."[36]

Martin had known during his career that magazines consumed vast amounts of material trying to fill each issue. For example, the *Post* had published an average of eight heavy-fact articles per issue for fifty-two weeks a year. Television consumed even more. In writing his novel, published in 1980 as *The Televising of Heller,* Martin discovered that fiction chewed up material faster than magazines or television. He put into the book's 279 pages scores of people he had known as well as his experiences from a dozen political campaigns. "When I finished, I thought I could never write another novel – I'd put into this one everything I knew," said Martin. Galbraith and Schlesinger, veterans, like Martin, of many campaigns, liked the book and contributed glowing blurbs for use by its publisher, Doubleday, as did John Houseman, Newton Minow, and Bill Moyers. Schlesinger later called the book "one of the best fictional accounts of what a modern political campaign is like," and some reviewers termed Martin's plot as far more entertaining than many real campaigns they remembered.[37]

There were mixed responses from television people to the issues Martin addressed in *Heller.* A reviewer for a magazine closely tied to the broadcast industry, *TV Guide,* had nothing but scorn for Martin's inaugural novel. Among the forty thousand books published annually in the United States, the review noted, there have to be many that "no sensible person would read beyond the dust jackets. This is one." Martin's wife, children, and devoted friends may read the book with pleasure, but the reviewer believed nobody else would as the author had created "what may be the most boring political novel ever written." But actor and producer John Houseman, who had used Martin's Centralia coal mine disaster article for a made-for-television production in the late 1950s, believed *Heller* could be turned into a television movie, and the CBS network concurred. Houseman bought the screen rights and prepared to go into production. According to Martin, at that time CBS had potential scripts analyzed by a computer, and if the computer decided that a show might receive poor ratings, the network turned it down. "The computer hated *Heller*; CBS dropped it," said Martin. "The final irony – a computer bars from TV a novel denouncing poll taking and TV."[38]

Inspired by his first taste of writing and publishing fiction, Martin began work on an autobiographical novel based heavily on his grim memories of growing up in a dysfunctional family in Indiana and his unhappy marriage to his first wife, Barbara, which he titled "Farewell to Indianapolis." He put that work aside, however, after deciding it read too much like Eugene O'Neill's *Long Day's Journey into Night* and Thomas Wolfe's *Look Homeward, Angel*. A subsequent novel about an American ambassador to a small Caribbean country, called "Your Excellency," failed to find a publisher. Undaunted by these letdowns, Martin proposed to Olding in December 1980 that for the next two years he should concentrate on writing his memoirs, in which he would explore his career as a reporter, writer, diplomat, and political insider. "I can omit or include anything I choose," Martin noted. "The yardstick should be: If it's a good story, include it; if not, omit." For inspiration, he turned to the autobiography of liberal U.S. Supreme Court justice William O. Douglas, noting it had been compelling reading because Douglas "reflected on his life and wrung some meaning out of it. I hope to do the same." Martin also learned from Houseman, who in his memoirs played the leading role in the book. It also contained a large supporting cast, including the actors, writers, directors, and others Houseman had worked with on his dramatic productions. "But writing is solitary (which is one reason it's both so hard and so rewarding)," said Martin. "So my supporting cast will be, in the main, those ordinary people that I interviewed – those from below."[39]

Two publishers turned down Martin's memoir before a third, William Morrow and Company, agreed to release the book. "Not a lot of money but enough and the main thing is, it'll be published," Martin wrote a friend. Released in 1986 and dedicated to Martin's children, Cindy, Dan, and Fred, the memoir, titled *It Seems Like Only Yesterday: Memoirs of Writing, Presidential Politics, and the Diplomatic Life*, received some of the best reviews of any of Martin's works, and reminded many in the publishing world just how fine a writer he had been during his long career. As one of the extinct breeds of journalists from the heyday of the "big slick" magazines of the 1950s, Martin, said a reviewer in the *New York Times*, had produced with "candor, modesty, and a fine reportorial gift for detail and anecdote," a "disarmingly unstuffy" memoir offering rewards for aspiring journalists or those already in the profession and offering examples on "how a superb professional goes about his job." Herman Kogan, a fellow journalist and a friend for fifty years, enjoyed Martin's stories about giving advice to a variety of Democratic politicians over the years, "all of it wise and sensible, and drafted along the lines of his liberalism, love of country and sympathy for the underdog." But while reading the book, Kogan achieved his greatest satisfaction in discovering just how Martin had created the "tremendous output" of articles as a freelancer. "Martin has, in the best sense of the word, been a creative writer," said Kogan. "Hard work and . . . talent enabled Martin to create in his scores of stories an American panorama of the times in which he flourished." Another reviewer said that in his memoirs, Martin gave valuable lessons about the business of writing almost subconsciously, and certainly in an unobjectionable way, "because writing is his trade."[40]

Martin savored his good notices for only a few months before illness struck. The late 1970s and 1980s had been a period of health problems for both Martin and Fran, who suffered an aneurysm of her abdominal aorta but survived, a time in his life Martin remembered as "a consuming, paralyzing nightmare." In December 1976 Martin was hospitalized for congestive heart failure. Martin had smoked two and a half packs of cigarettes a day for most of his life, but after this incident he gave up cigarettes, instead smoking eight La Corona Belvedere cigars a day and also abstaining from hard liquor. On January 4, 1979, Martin had surgery to remove a benign tumor from his right lung, a procedure that "scared the hell out of me," he admitted to a friend. After years of trying to seek relief from snowy Illinois in the winter months by traveling to warmer climates such as Puerto Rico and the Dominican Republic, the Martins decided to ride out the cold weather in their Highland Park home, perhaps because they would have better access to medical care. "The climate bothered us little; we simply stayed in the house, arguing with the cat [named Miss Prettyface] and watching old movies on television, especially W. C. Fields, Laurel and Hardy, and *Casablanca*," Martin recalled. His parents left their house so seldom, said Fred, that they could go nine months before they had to refuel their car, a Mercedes 240 diesel. Every spring, Martin and Fran packed up their car with the essentials, including manuscripts, books, and a few clothes, and drove to their camp at Smith Lake on the same tank of gas they had used to drive home the previous fall. They stayed at Smith Lake for three or four months enjoying the solitude and wildlife. They could watch a moose swim the length of the lake, observe a fierce mink chasing Miss Prettyface, and encounter a bear wandering up to their porch. Martin remembered Fran telling him that if she sat on their porch and stared at the lake and trees long enough, she might see an eagle perched on top of the tallest pine tree near their camp; one day, she did.[41]

Medical problems intruded on Martin's beloved sanctuary. In March 1983 he wrote Voelker that Fran had to drive them to the Upper Peninsula, as his vision had become so bad he could no longer drive. By the next spring, the Martins between them had "too many unresolved medical problems for both of us to go to such a remote place," so for the first time in forty-four years (except years when they were out of the country), he and Fran could not spend their summer in the Upper Peninsula. By June 1985 they were well enough to spend a month at Smith Lake, thanks to their sons, Fred and Dan, who arranged their vacations so they could drive their parents to their camp and stay with them. Diagnosed with throat cancer in 1986, Martin received the grim news with the same straightforward manner he used to thoroughly document his medical history for his physicians. "He described to me in detail what path the cancer would take that was unstoppably killing him and how he would die," Fred remembered, "in the same matter-of-fact tone that he had used with me before when, say, giving driving directions to Upper Michigan." Martin died at Highland Park Hospital on January 3, 1987, at the age of seventy-one, and his body was buried in an Elmhurst, Illinois, cemetery next to Fran's parents and his aunt, Verl Garrison. Ill health forced Fran to give up the family's house on Maple Avenue and move to Washington, D.C., to be cared for by her sons. Fran died on February 26, 1994. That spring, the bodies of Fran and John Bartlow Martin were buried side-by-side at the Herman Cemetery in Herman, Michigan, located just a few miles from their camp at Smith Lake.[42]

Before his death, Martin had seen his work recognized with honorary degrees from Knox College in Galesburg, Illinois, and Indiana University in Bloomington. He also had the "great satisfaction" of seeing his children settled in life and making concrete contributions to society, with Cindy a trained social worker assisting refugees from Southeast Asia; Dan working as an advance man for several Illinois politicians and for Ted Kennedy before starting a career with the Inter-American Development Bank; and Fred as a historian, writer, and political adviser for such Democrats as Walter Mondale, Geraldine Ferraro, and Mario Cuomo. "They avoided the shattering disasters I'd done so much writing about – no violence, no prisons, no real problems," said Martin. He added that he and Fran were relieved they avoided the fate of some of their friends whose children had dropped out of view, never to be heard of again, during the turbulent 1960s. His children agree that their father did not try to dictate their choice of career, but provided for them a sound example on how to live their lives, never losing his fundamental faith in American democracy and belief in the individual's importance. Without ever directly saying so, Martin, said Fred, made it clear to his children "that he thought the calling of public service was a higher calling; and we as kids thought our parents were involved in something more important and worthy than could be had by people in ordinary jobs in business or law. We lived in a house where the bar was set very high for the choice of career; or better put, we set it high ourselves living in that house."[43]

In the end, Martin, posthumously inducted into the Indiana Journalism Hall of Fame in 1999, believed he had made a difference with his writing. He felt satisfaction about what he had accomplished and thankful that he had been fortunate enough to be active as a writer during a time when he could produce serious journalism about significant subjects for the enjoyment and edification of a national audience. Shortly after his memoirs had been published, and just a few weeks before his death, Martin received a visitor at his Highland Park home: Schlesinger, his friend since 1952 and fellow liberal Democratic Party stalwart and author. Although Martin could no longer speak because of his throat cancer, he could communicate by scrawling notes on a yellow legal pad. "He was very brave, drank a couple of martinis, smoked a cigar, was stoical about his fate," Schlesinger recalled. The two men shared stories about their times together in politics with the likes of Stevenson and the Kennedy brothers. Before Schlesinger departed, Martin scribbled a valedictory note on his pad that read, "We had the best of it."[44]

Notes

1. The Responsible Reporter

1. John Bartlow Martin, "The Blast in Centralia No. 5: A Mine Disaster No One Stopped," *Harper's*, March 1948, 193–220.

2. Jim Suhr, "Man Recalls 1947 Illinois Mine Disaster that Killed Father, Three Other Relatives," Associated Press, January 6, 2006; Martin, "The Blast in Centralia No. 5."

3. "Coming next month in . . . Harper's Magazine," *Harper's*, February 1948; "Contents," *Harper's*, March 1948; Martin, "The Blast in Centralia No. 5," 220. DeWitt Wallace, the founder of *Reader's Digest,* began commissioning articles for other magazines and later using them himself in the mid-1930s. Among the magazines to accept such articles, in addition to *Harper's*, were *American Mercury, Scribner's, North American Review, Atlantic, Nation,* and *New Republic.* Critics referred to the system as "planted articles," while the *Digest* preferred the phrase "cooperatively planned." Theodore Peterson, *Magazines in the Twentieth Century* (Urbana: University of Illinois Press, 1964), 231.

4. John Bartlow Martin, *It Seems Like Only Yesterday: Memoirs of Writing, Presidential Politics, and the Diplomatic Life* (New York: William Morrow and Company, 1986), 54, 57.

5. Ibid., 57–58.

6. Martin, "The Blast in Centralia No. 5," 205; Anthony Fleege, "The 1947 Centralia Mine Disaster," *Journal of the Illinois State Historical Society* 102 (Summer 2009): 170.

7. Martin, *It Seems Like Only Yesterday,* 59.

8. Ibid., 58–61.

9. Ibid., 62–65.

10. Ibid., 65.

11. Ibid., 65–66.

12. Ibid., 67–68; Howard Greenfeld, *Ben Shahn: An Artist's Life* (New York: Random House, 1998), 224–25; John D. Voelker to John Bartlow Martin, March 9, 1948, John D. Voelker Papers, Central Upper Michigan Peninsula and Northern Michigan University Archives, Marquette, Michigan.

13. "Notes on Crime Writing," in John Bartlow Martin, *Butcher's Dozen, and Other Murders* (New York: Harper and Brothers, 1950), 222–23, 1; Sherley Uhl, "John Martin, Former Reporter for the Times, Neck-Deep in New Book about Hoosier Land," *Indianapolis Times,* July 31, 1946; "The Press: The Free-Lancers," *Time,* May 30, 1955; Martin, *It Seems Like Only Yesterday,* 38.

14. John Frederick Martin, "John Bartlow Martin," *The American Scholar* 59

(Winter 1990): 95–100; "The Best Reporter," *Newsweek*, May 27, 1957; "The Press: The Free-Lancers"; John Kuenster, "John Bartlow Martin: The Responsible Reporter," *The Voice of Saint Jude: A National Catholic Monthly* 28 (April 1960): 35.

15. Uhl, "John Martin, Former Reporter for *The Times*, Neck-Deep in New Book about Hoosier Land"; Martin, "John Bartlow Martin," 95; Martin, *It Seems Like Only* Yesterday, 43; Fred Martin, memorandum to author, October 8, 2013.

16. Susan Drake and Sharron Karrow, "Writing the Wrongs: Stevenson's Biographer Makes People the Issue," *Byline: Northwestern's Journalism Magazine* 11 (Spring 1976): 8; "Preliminary Remarks" for Advanced Reporting Class, John Bartlow Martin Papers, 1960–1987, Northwestern University Archives, Evanston, Illinois; Martin, *Butcher's Dozen*, 218; Martin, *It Seemed Like Only Yesterday*, 55–56, 137; Allen Borden, "John Bartlow Martin," *Wilson Library Bulletin* 30 (January 1956): 364.

17. "Preliminary Remarks"; Martin memo to Elizabeth Yamashita, December 7, 1977, Martin Papers, Northwestern University Archives; "NU Professor Recalls Events Leading to Writing Biography of Adlai Stevenson," *Northwestern News*, April 23, 1976, Martin Papers, Northwestern University Archives; Martin, "John Bartlow Martin," 97.

18. Martin, *It Seems Like Only Yesterday*, 56–57, 67, 76; Cindy Martin Coleman, interview with author, September 19, 2013; Fred Martin, memorandum to author, October 8, 2013.

19. Martin, *It Seems Like Only Yesterday*, 67.

20. Martin, *It Seems Like Only Yesterday*, 50–51, 66, 137; "Memo on Memoirs," December 5, 1980, John Bartlow Martin

Papers, Manuscripts Division, Library of Congress, Washington, D.C. (hereafter cited as Martin Papers, Library of Congress).

21. "Memo on Memoirs," December 5, 1980, Martin Papers, Library of Congress; John Bartlow Martin, "Backstage at the Statehouse: What Those Politicians Do to You!" *Saturday Evening Post*, December 19, 1953, 81.

22. Martin, *Butcher's Dozen*, 223; Martin, *It Seems Like Only Yesterday*, 92, 134.

23. "Writer John Bartlow Martin, Former Envoy, Journalism Prof," *Chicago Tribune*, January 5, 1987; "John Bartlow Martin: The Responsible Reporter," 35–37, 39; Russell Lynes to John Bartlow Martin, October 16, 1952, Martin Papers, Library of Congress; "The Best Reporter"; and "Memo on Memoirs," December 5, 1980, Martin Papers, Library of Congress.

24. Kuenster, "John Bartlow Martin: The Responsible Reporter," 35–37; Martin, *It Seems Like Only Yesterday*, 317.

25. Martin, *It Seems Like Only Yesterday*, 69.

26. Ibid., 24, and untitled 1982 interview, Martin Papers, Library of Congress.

27. Martin, *It Seems Like Only Yesterday*, 148; Roger O. Boorstin, "John Bartlow Martin, 71, Author and Envoy, Dies," *New York Times*, January 5, 1987; Newton Minow, telephone interview with the author, June 26, 2013; John Fischer, "A Footnote on Adlai Stevenson," *Harper's*, November 1965, 23; John Bartlow Martin, RFK [Robert F. Kennedy] Notes, June 28, 1968, Martin Papers, Library of Congress.

28. John Bartlow Martin, RFK Notes, June 29, 1968, Martin Papers, Library of Congress; Robert G. Schultz, "Envoy Has Boss Now, His First in 25 Years," *Indianapolis Times*, March 4, 1962; Arthur M. Schlesinger Jr., "John Bartlow

Martin, 1915–1987," in *The Century Year-book, 1987* (New York: The Century Association, 1987), 265; Martin, "Memo on Memoirs."

29. Martin, *It Seems Like Only Yesterday*, 202–203, and Minow, interview.

30. Martin, "John Bartlow Martin," 98; Lorraine Bannon, "Kennedy Teacher Recalls When . . . ," *The Record* (Yorkville, Ill.), November 22, 1973.

31. Martin, "Memo on Memoirs."

32. Martin, *It Seems Like Only Yesterday*, 299, 323; Martin, "John Bartlow Martin," 98.

33. Martin, *It Seems Like Only Yesterday*, 318–19.

34. Ibid., 299, 316–18, 343.

35. Martin, memo to Elizabeth Yamashita About Teaching Writing, May 31, 1974, Martin Papers, Northwestern University Archives; undated Martin memo to Eric Norment; Peter Jacobi, e-mail to author, August 15, 2013; announcement for the First Annual John Bartlow Martin Award for Public Interest Magazine Journalism, Martin Papers, Northwestern University Archives.

36. Martin, *It Seems Like Only Yesterday*, 237; Martin, "John Bartlow Martin," 99; Dan Martin, e-mail to author, September 20, 2013.

37. John Bartlow Martin, "The Heartland's Backyard Frontier: Upper Michigan," *Chicago Tribune*, July 31, 1983.

38. Martin, "John Bartlow Martin," 97; John L. Perry, "Journalist Who Never Stopped Writing or Caring," *Rome (Ga.) News-Tribune*, January 11, 1987.

2. A Mean Street in a Mean City

1. See Edward A. Leary, *Indianapolis: The Story of a City* (Indianapolis: Bobbs-Merrill Company, 1971), 154–56; "The Indianapolis News Souvenir: Dedication Ceremonies and History, Indiana Sol-diers' and Sailors' Monument," *Indianapolis News*, May 15, 1902.

2. John Bartlow Martin, *It Seems Like Only Yesterday: Memoirs of Writing, Presidential Politics, and the Diplomatic Life* (New York: William and Morrow Company, 1986), 18; John Bartlow Martin, "Beauty and the Beast: The Downfall of D. C. Stephenson, Grand Dragon of the Indiana K.K.K.," *Harper's*, September 1944, 319, 322; John Bartlow Martin, "For Personal and Otherwise," John Bartlow Martin Papers, Manuscripts Division, Library of Congress, Washington, D.C. (hereafter cited as Martin Papers, Library of Congress).

3. Martin, *It Seems Like Only Yesterday*, 17.

4. John Bartlow Martin, "The History of Me," April 26, 1928, 1–3, Martin Papers, Library of Congress.

5. "Big Powder Plant Opened," *New York Times*, June 2, 1918; *"Old Hickory": The World's Greatest Powder Plant, the Building of Which Broke All Speed Records for War-Time Construction* (Wilmington, Del.: Du Pont Engineering Company, n.d.); Martin, "The History of Me," 4.

6. Martin, "The History of Me," 5; Martin, "For Personal and Otherwise," Martin Papers, Library of Congress.

7. Martin, "The History of Me," 9, 18.

8. Ibid., 18–19. In 1926 the Indianapolis City Council, a Klan-dominated legislative body, approved an ordinance making it illegal for whites to live in an area that had a majority African American population, or for African Americans to do so in a white neighborhood without the written consent of the dominant race. Mayor John Duvall signed the measure into law. In a case later brought by the Indianapolis National Association for the Advancement of Colored People, a Marion County Circuit Court ruled that the

law violated the Fourteenth Amendment. See Emma Lou Thornbrough, *Indiana Blacks in the Twentieth Century* (Bloomington: Indiana University Press, 2000), 52–53.

9. Martin, *It Seems Like Only Yesterday*, 17; Bess Watson, "John Martin Retired Building Firm Head," *Indianapolis News*, July 8, 1960; Martin, "For Personal and Otherwise."

10. Martin, *It Seems Like Only Yesterday*, 17–18.

11. Ibid., 18–19, 52–53, 188–89; Martin, "For Personal and Otherwise."

12. Martin, *It Seems Like Only Yesterday*, 19–20. Unknown at the time of Martin's youth in Indianapolis, the Rh factor incompatibility occurs during pregnancy when a mother has Rh-negative blood and her baby has Rh-positive blood. Rh antibodies can attack the baby's red blood cells, impairing the flow of oxygen and resulting in deformities and sometimes even death. First babies for a mother usually escape harm. "What is Rh Incompatibility?" National Heart, Lung, and Blood Institute, http://www.nhlbi.nih.gov /health/health-topics/topics/rh/.

13. Martin, *It Seems Like Only Yesterday*, 19–20.

14. Ibid., 20–21.

15. Ted Stahly, "Arsenal Technical High School," in David J. Bodenhamer and Robert G. Barrows, eds., *The Encyclopedia of Indianapolis*, 265–66 (Bloomington: Indiana University Press, 1994); Marjorie Lagemann Snodgrass, *The First Fifty Years: 1912–1962, An Oral History* (Indianapolis, Ind.: Arsenal Technical High School, [1994]), 44–45.

16. Snodgrass, *The First Fifty Years*, 48; Martin, *It Seems Like Only Yesterday*, 21.

17. John Bartlow Martin, "The Difference," *The Arsenal Cannon* 36 (January 1931): 43; John Bartlow Martin, "Content-

ment," *The Arsenal Cannon* 38 (January 1932): 22.

18. Martin, *It Seems Like Only Yesterday*, 21–22; Martin, "For Personal and Otherwise."

19. Deborah B. Markisohn, "Great Depression," in David J. Bodenhamer and Robert G. Barrows, eds., *The Encyclopedia of Indianapolis*, 636–39 (Bloomington: Indiana University Press, 1994); James H. Madison, *Indiana through Tradition and Change: A History of the Hoosier State and its People, 1920–1945* (Indianapolis: Indiana Historical Society, 1982), 105; Martin, *It Seems Like Only Yesterday*, 22.

20. "Senior Jottings," *The Arsenal Cannon* 39 (June 1932): 30; Martin, *It Seems Like Only Yesterday*, 22.

21. Martin, *It Seems Like Only Yesterday*, 23; Rough draft of memoir, Martin Papers, Library of Congress.

22. Owen R. Davison, letter to editor, *DePauw Magazine*, Spring 2002, http:// www.depauw.edu/pa/magazine/spring 2002/letters.asp; Martin, "For Personal and Otherwise."

23. Martin, *It Seems Like Only Yesterday*, 23–24; William Manchester, *The Glory and the Dream: A Narrative History of America, 1932–1972* (New York: Bantam Books, 1975), 76–77.

24. Martin, *It Seems Like Only Yesterday*, 24; John Bartlow Martin, "One Nation, Indomitable," *Chicago Tribune*, April 27, 1975.

25. Martin, *It Seems Like Only Yesterday*, 24; John Lewis Niblack, *The Life and Times of a Hoosier Judge* (Indianapolis, Ind.?: 1973), 147–48.

26. Martin, *It Seems Like Only Yesterday*, 25; Natalie Seibert, "Paper's Independence from University Evolves over Time," *The DePauw*, April 5, 2002.

27. Barbara Felicihin and Pam Munch, "From Hot Lead to Macs, A Changing

Production" and "Reflections on The De-
Pauw Experience through the Years," *The
DePauw*, April 5, 2002.

28. Davison, letter to editor.

29. "The Dog Watch," *The DePauw*,
March 17, 1935.

30. "The Dog Watch," *The DePauw*,
May 29, 1935.

31. "The Dog Watch," *The DePauw*,
June 3, 1935; "The Dog Watch," *The De-
Pauw*, December 14, 1935.

32. "The Adventures of John Bartlow
Martin '37"; James S. Sweet letter to editor,
DePauw Magazine, Winter 2001, 12; Davi-
son, letter to editor.

33. Martin, *It Seems Like Only Yesterday*, 12–13, 32; Sweet, letter.

34. Martin, *It Seems Like Only Yesterday*, 13; undated correspondence
between John Bartlow Martin and
[Robert] Baker, Martin Papers, Library
of Congress.

35. Editor's Note in "The Pinch Hitter,"
The DePauw, April 26, 1937.

36. Martin, *It Seemed Like Only Yester-
day*, 13–14; John Sherman, "Indianapolis
Times," in David J. Bodenhamer and
Robert G. Barrows, *The Encyclopedia
of Indianapolis*, 811 (Bloomington: Indiana
University Press, 1994); "The Times Cru-
saded for the Public," *Indianapolis Times*,
October 11, 1965.

37. Jack Schreibman and Andy Olof-
son, "Heze Clark Dies, Times' Legendary
Police Reporter," Ted Knap, "Mueller, 4
Ex-Chiefs Join in Mourning," and Irving
Leibowitz, "Dunked in Ink as a Boy of 5,
Heze Had Newspapering in Blood," all in
Indianapolis Times, August 31, 1956.

38. Martin, *It Seems Like Only Yester-
day*, 14–15; John Bartlow Martin memo to
Elizabeth Yamashita, December 7, 1977,
John Bartlow Martin Papers, 1960–1987,
Northwestern University Archives, Evan-
ston, Illinois.

39. John Bartlow Martin, "Dominican
Republic, 1939," unpublished travelogue,
Martin Papers, Library of Congress.

40. Ibid.; Martin, *It Seems Like Only
Yesterday*, 14.

41. John Bartlow Martin, *Overtaken by
Events: The Dominican Crisis from the Fall
of Trujillo to the Civil War* (Garden City,
N.Y.: Doubleday and Company, 1966),
16–18, 33–35; Martin, "For Personal and
Otherwise""; Martin, *It Seems Like Only
Yesterday*, 15.

42. Martin, "For Personal and Otherwise"; Martin, *It Seems Like Only Yesterday*, 11.

43. Martin, "For Personal and Otherwise"; Martin, *It Seems Like Only Yesterday*, 12.

44. Martin, "For Personal and Otherwise"; Martin, *It Seems Like Only Yesterday*,
15; Rough draft of memoir, Martin Papers,
Library of Congress.

45. John Bartlow Martin, "To Chicago,
With Love," *Saturday Evening Post*, October 15, 1960, 19–20.

46. Martin, *It Seems Like Only Yesterday*, 16.

47. Ibid., 16–17, 36.

48. Martin, Rough draft of memoir.

49. Martin, *It Seems Like Only Yester-
day*, 26; John Bartlow Martin, "To a Boy
Growing Up . . . ," *Chicago Tribune*, Febru-
ary 4, 1968; Thomas Dyja, *The Third Coast:
When Chicago Built the American Dream*
(New York: The Penguin Press, 2013), xxv.

3. Two Cents a Word

1. "Hotel Chain Enters Chicago; Has
Leased Bradley for 10 Years," *Chicago
Daily Tribune*, June 5, 1938; George J. Tan-
ber, "Hotel Shakes Off Decades of De-
cline," *Toledo Blade*, February 1, 2006;
John Bartlow Martin, "To Chicago, With
Love," *Saturday Evening Post*, October 15,
1960.

2. Martin, "To Chicago, With Love"; John Bartlow Martin, *It Seems Like Only Yesterday: Memoirs of Writing, Presidential Politics, and the Diplomatic Life* (New York: William Morrow and Company, 1986), 27.

3. Martin, "To Chicago, With Love"; Anita O'Day with George Eells, *High Times, Hard Times* (New York: Limelight Editions, 2007), 63.

4. Martin, *It Seems Like Only Yesterday*, 31.

5. Robert Polito, *Savage Art: A Biography of Jim Thompson* (New York: Vintage Books, 1996), 190–191; John Bartlow Martin, Rough draft of memoir, John Bartlow Martin Papers, Manuscript Division, Library of Congress, Washington, D.C. (hereafter cited as Martin Papers, Library of Congress).

6. Martin, *It Seems Like Only Yesterday*, 28–29.

7. Martin, "To Chicago, With Love."

8. "Notes on Crime Writing," in John Bartlow Martin, *Butcher's Dozen, and Other Murders* (New York: Harper and Brothers, 1950), 221.

9. John Cooney, *The Annenbergs: The Salvaging of a Tainted Dynasty* (New York: Simon & Schuster, 1982), 18–22; Martin, *It Seems Like Only Yesterday*, 30–31.

10. Martin, *It Seems Like Only Yesterday*, 29, 32; John Bartlow Martin, "Personal and Otherwise," undated memo, Martin Papers, Library of Congress.

11. Martin, Rough draft of memoir; Martin, *It Seems Like Only Yesterday*, 29.

12. Martin, Rough draft of memoir.

13. Martin, Rough draft of memoir; Martin, *It Seems Like Only Yesterday*, 34–35.

14. John Bartlow Martin, *Call It North Country: The Story of Upper Michigan* (1944; reprint, Detroit, Mich.: Wayne State University Press, 1986), 257; John

Bartlow Martin, "Wilderness North of Chicago," *Harper's*, May 1954, 71; Martin, *It Seems Like Only Yesterday*, 36.

15. Martin, Rough draft of memoir; Martin, *Call It North Country*, 260; John Martin, "Don't Go Trout Fishing," *Outdoor Life*, May 1943, 25.

16. John Bartlow Martin, "Boy Hunt," *Harper's*, December 1944, 39–40; Martin, *Call It North Country*, viii, 263; Martin, "Wilderness North of Chicago," 74.

17. Fran Martin to John Martin, July 16, 1941, Martin Papers, Library of Congress; Martin, *It Seems Like Only Yesterday*, 36–37.

18. John Bartlow Martin to Fran Martin, July 28, 1944, and John Martin to Red [?], May 23, 1941, Martin Papers, Library of Congress; Martin, *It Seems Like Only Yesterday*, 53.

19. Martin, *It Seems Like Only Yesterday*, 37; Darwin Payne, *The Man of Only Yesterday: Frederick Lewis Allen* (New York: Harper and Row, 1975), 83, 154, 222–23.

20. See Joseph E. Persico, *Roosevelt's Secret War: FDR and World War II Espionage* (New York: Random House, 2001), 199–205; "George John Dasch and the Nazi Saboteurs," Federal Bureau of Investigation, http://www.fbi.gov/about-us/history/famous-cases/nazi-saboteurs.

21. Michael Dobbs, *Saboteurs: The Nazi Raid on America* (New York: Alfred A. Knopf, 2004), 130–31; John Martin, "The Making of a Nazi Saboteur," *Harper's*, April 1943, 532–40.

22. John Martin to editor, *Harper's*, December 8, 1942, and Frederick Lewis Allen to John Martin, December 16, 1942, Martin Papers, Library of Congress.

23. Martin, Rough draft of memoir.

24. Frederick Lewis Allen to John Martin, February 9, 1943, and Martin to

Allen, February 11, 1943, Martin Papers, Library of Congress.

25. Martin, *It Seems Like Only Yesterday*, 38, 43–44.

26. Ibid., 41–43.

27. Ibid.

28. John Bartlow Martin, "Is Muncie Still Middletown?" *Harper's*, July 1944, 97–109; Martin, *It Seems Like Only Yesterday*, 44–45.

29. Martin, Rough draft of memoir; Martin, *It Seems Like Only Yesterday*, 38–39; Harry Keller to John Martin, January 14, 1944, Martin Papers, Library of Congress.

30. Herbert Mitgang, "Alfred A. Knopf, 91, is Dead; Founder of Publishing House," *New York Times*, August 12, 1984; Martin, *It Seems Like Only Yesterday*, 39; Ben Abramson to Alfred Knopf, February 22, 1943, John Martin to Alfred Knopf, March 19, 1943, and Alfred Knopf to John Martin, March 23, 1943, Martin Papers, Library of Congress.

31. Martin, *Call It North Country*, vii; John Martin to Harry Keller, August 24, 1943, Martin Papers, Library of Congress.

32. Francis Nipp to John Martin, 1943, and John Martin to Harry Keller, August 24, 1943, Martin Papers, Library of Congress; Martin, *It Seems Like Only Yesterday*, 40–41.

33. Martin, *Call It North Country*, 192, 197–98, 211.

34. Martin, *It Seems Like Only Yesterday*, 41; James Gray, "Michigan Peninsula," *New York Times*, May 21, 1944; August Derleth, "Life in the Upper Michigan Country," *Chicago Sun*, May 28, 1944; John D. Voelker to John Martin, June 3, 1944, Martin Papers, Library of Congress; Martin, *Call It North Country*, viii.

35. John Bartlow Martin to Alfred Knopf, August 26, 1944, and Alfred Knopf to John Bartlow Martin, August 28, 1944, Martin Papers, Library of Congress.

36. John Bartlow Martin to Francis Nipp, September 1, 1944, Martin Papers, Library of Congress.

37. Order to Report for Induction, October 26, 1944; John Bartlow Martin to Alfred Knopf, March 31, 1944, and John Bartlow Martin to Harry Keller, April 21, 1944, Martin Papers, Library of Congress.

38. Martin, *It Seems Like Only Yesterday*, 46, 52; John Bartlow Martin to Fran Martin, November 17, 1944, Martin Papers, Library of Congress.

39. John Bartlow Martin to Fran Martin, November 18, 1944, Martin Papers, Library of Congress.

40. Martin, *It Seems Like Only Yesterday*, 46; John Bartlow Martin to Fran Martin, December 2, 1944, Martin Papers, Library of Congress.

41. Martin, *It Seems Like Only Yesterday*, 46–47; John Bartlow Martin to J. W. and Laura Martin, March 25, 1945, Martin Papers, Library of Congress.

42. John Bartlow Martin, "Anything Bothering You, Soldier?" *Harper's*, November 1945, 457; Martin, *It Seems Like Only Yesterday*, 47.

43. Martin, "Anything Bothering You, Soldier?" 456; John Bartlow Martin to J. W. and Laura Martin, July 5, 1945, Martin Papers, Library of Congress.

44. Martin, *It Seems Like Only Yesterday*, 47–48; Martin, "Anything Bothering You, Soldier?" 455–57.

45. Martin, "Anything Bothering You, Soldier?" 455–57.

46. J. W. Martin to John Bartlow Martin, December 6, 1945, John Bartlow Martin to Fran Martin, January 19, 1946, and John Bartlow Martin to Fran Martin, November 30, 1945, Martin Papers, Library of Congress.

4. The Big Slicks

1. John Bartlow Martin, Military Diaries, February 17, 1946, John Bartlow Martin Papers, Manuscript Division, Library of Congress, Washington, D.C. (hereafter cited as Martin Papers, Library of Congress), and Cindy Martin Coleman, interview with the author, September 19, 2013.

2. John Bartlow Martin to Fran Martin, February 2, 1946, Martin Papers, Library of Congress.

3. John Bartlow Martin to Francis Nipp, January 25, 1946, Martin Papers, Library of Congress.

4. John Bartlow Martin to Alfred A. Knopf, March 14, 1946, Martin Papers, Library of Congress.

5. Alfred A. Knopf to John Bartlow Martin, May 22, 1946, Martin Papers, Library of Congress; John Bartlow Martin, *It Seems Like Only Yesterday: Memoirs of Writing, Presidential Politics, and the Diplomatic Life* (New York: William Morrow and Company, 1986), 48. Many years after doing the work for *Life,* Martin learned through a friend at the magazine, John Steele, that both *Life* and *Time* still consulted Martin's notes on the Midwest. Martin, *It Seems Like Only Yesterday,* 49.

6. John Bartlow Martin to J. W. and Laura Martin, June 19, 1946, Martin Papers, Library of Congress; Martin, *It Seems Like Only Yesterday,* 49.

7. John Bartlow Martin to George [?], August 20, 1946, Martin Papers, Library of Congress; John Bartlow Martin, *Indiana: An Interpretation* (New York: Alfred A. Knopf, 1947), 108.

8. John Bartlow Martin to Ralph F. Gates, April 29, 1947, and Ben H. Riker to Alfred Knopf, April 22, 1947, Martin Papers, Library of Congress.

9. Alfred A. Knopf to John Bartlow Martin, April 14, 1947, Alfred A. Knopf Jr.

to John Bartlow Martin, April 28, 1947, and Irving P. Hotchkiss to John Bartlow Martin, August 15, 1947, Martin Papers, Library of Congress.

10. Martin, *Indiana: An Interpretation,* vii, viii, 122, 269, and 270–73.

11. Martin, *It Seems Like Only Yesterday,* 49; Martin, *Indiana: An Interpretation,* 140, 156.

12. Martin, *It Seems Like Only Yesterday,* 49; Review of *Indiana: An Interpretation, Indiana Magazine of History* (September 1948): 308–309; Eugene Pulliam Jr. review of *Indiana: An Interpretation, Indianapolis Star,* November 9, 1947; Henry Butler, "History, Biography and Traveling Mingled in Interesting New Book on Hoosierland," *Indianapolis Times,* November 15, 1947.

13. Gilbert Bailey, "Hoosier History," *New York Times,* December 7, 1947; Elrick B. Davis, "Here are Real Hoosiers," *New York Herald-Tribune,* December 7, 1947; Arthur M. Schlesinger Jr., *Robert Kennedy and His Times* (Boston: Houghton Mifflin Company, 1978), 880; James H. Madison, "Introduction," in John Bartlow Martin, *Indiana: An Interpretation* (1947; reprint, Bloomington and Indianapolis: Indiana University Press, 1992), vii, xv.

14. Martin, *It Seems Like Only Yesterday,* 50–51.

15. Marc Rose, "Why That Manuscript is Rejected," *The Quill: A Magazine for Journalists,* May 1952, 9.

16. John Houseman, *Unfinished Business: Memoirs: 1902–1988* (New York: Applause Theatre Book Publishers, 1989), 364–65; Martin, *It Seems Like Only Yesterday,* 127–28.

17. Houseman, *Unfinished Business,* 378; Martin, *It Seems Like Only Yesterday,* 129.

18. "Centralia Blast Documented Graphically," *New York Times,* January 27,

1958; Houseman, *Unfinished Business*, 378; Martin, *It Seems Like Only Yesterday*, 129.

19. Martin, *It Seems Like Only Yesterday*, 49, 82; "About John Bartlow Martin," in John Bartlow Martin, *Why Did They Kill?* (New York: Ballantine Books, 1953).

20. Martin, *It Seems Like Only Yesterday*, 83–84; "Gunnar Myrdal, Analyst of Race Crisis, Dies," *New York Times*, May 18, 1987.

21. John Bartlow Martin, "The Hickman Story," *Harper's*, August 1948, 40–41.

22. Martin, "The Hickman Story," 42; Joe Allen, "The Fight to Save James Hickman in Post-wwII Chicago," *Dissident Voice*, http://dissidentvoice.org/2009/07/the-fight-to-save-james-hickman-in-post-wwii-chicago/.

23. Martin, "The Hickman Story," 39–40.

24. Ibid.

25. Martin, "The Hickman Story," 49; Allen, "The Fight to Save James Hickman in Post-wwII Chicago."

26. Martin, "The Hickman Story," 50–51.

27. Ibid., 51–52.

28. Martin, *It Seems Like Only Yesterday*, 84–85, and Howard Greenfeld, *Ben Shahn: An Artist's Life* (New York: Random House, 1998), 226–27.

29. Martin, *It Seems Like Only Yesterday*, 85–86.

30. Frederick Lewis Allen to John Bartlow Martin, July 2, 1946, Martin Papers, Library of Congress.

31. John Bartlow Martin to Frederick Lewis Allen, August 7, 1946, Martin Papers, Library of Congress.

32. "Harold Ober, 78, Book Agent, Dies," *New York Times*, November 1, 1959; John Bartlow Martin to Dorothy Olding, May 12, 1960, Martin Papers, Library of Congress; Martin, *It Seems Like Only Yesterday*, 74–76.

33. John Bartlow Martin to Harold Ober, October 24, 1951, Martin Papers, Library of Congress.

34. Theodore Peterson, *Magazines in the Twentieth Century* (Urbana: University of Illinois Press, 1964), 12–13, 188; Martin, *It Seems Like Only Yesterday*, 77.

35. Martin, *It Seems Like Only Yesterday*, 73, 105.

36. John Bartlow Martin, "Why Did They Kill?" *Saturday Evening Post*, June 14, 1951, 19–20.

37. John Bartlow Martin biography for *Why Did They Kill?*, 1952, Martin Papers, Library of Congress.

38. Ibid. In a letter to his parents in Indianapolis, Martin explained how he came to name his second child Daniel. "The Daniel for nobody in either family. We think it is a good name," Martin wrote. "To some people it'll sound biblical, to others Irish, to others Jewish, to others midwestern (as in Dan'l Boone – the initials D. B. are the same), and to us just Danny Martin. Maybe if he can please all the churchgoers, Irish, Jews, and Midwesterners he can be president! Not to mention the Martins." John Bartlow Martin to J. W. and Laura Martin, April 20, 1951, Martin Papers, Library of Congress.

39. Martin, *It Seems Like Only Yesterday*, 81; Martin, "Why Did They Kill?" *Saturday Evening Post*, June 14, 1952, 20.

40. Martin, *It Seems Like Only Yesterday*, 82; Martin, "Why Did They Kill?" *Saturday Evening Post*, July 5, 1952, 100–102.

41. Martin, *It Seems Like Only Yesterday*, 82; Martin, "Why Did They Kill?"

42. Martin biography for *Why Did They Kill?*; Croswell Bowen, "One Boy Took the Dare," *New York Times*, March 15, 1953; George Plimpton, *Truman Capote: In Which His Friends, Enemies, Acquaintances, and Detractors Recall His Turbulent Career* (New York: Nan A. Talese, 1997), 197.

43. Ben Yagoda, *About Town: The New Yorker and the World It Made* (New York: Scribner, 2000), 347–48; Plimpton, *Truman Capote*, 215–17; Stanley Kauffmann, "Capote in Kansas," *The New Republic*, January 22 1966; http://www.newrepublic .com/article/film/capote-kansas; Joseph Haas, "Best of the Paperbacks," *Chicago Daily News*, July 23, 1966.

44. John Bartlow Martin, "Prison: The Enemy of Society," *Harper's*, April 1954, 29–38; Martin, *It Seems Like Only Yesterday*, 91–92; John Kuenster, "John Bartlow Martin: The Responsible Reporter," *The Voice of Saint Jude: A National Catholic Monthly* 28 (April 1960): 35.

45. Martin, *It Seems Like Only Yesterday*, 69; John Bartlow Martin, "Murder on His Conscience: Nathan Leopold's Thirty Desperate Years," *Saturday Evening Post*, April 2, 1955, 17–18.

46. Martin, *It Seems Like Only Yesterday*, 115–16; John Bartlow Martin, memo to Stuart Rose on Nathan Leopold, May 24, 1954, Martin Papers, Library of Congress (hereafter cited as Leopold memo).

47. Martin, Leopold memo; Hal Higdon, *The Crime of the Century: The Leopold and Loeb Case* (New York: G. P. Putnam's Sons, 1975), 315–16. Leopold's representatives approached Levin about collaborating on Leopold's autobiography, and the novelist met with him at Stateville. "To my surprise and even discomfiture," Levin said, "Leopold kept our talk revolving entirely around the business side of publication. Whenever I tried to turn to anything related to the crime, he smoothly changed back to questions about percentages, film rights, and syndication." See Meyer Levin, *The Obsession* (New York: Simon & Schuster, 1973), 109.

48. Martin, *It Seems Like Only Yesterday*, 116.

49. "Keeping Posted: The Leopold Interviews," *Saturday Evening Post*, April 23, 1955, 140; John Bartlow Martin to Ralph [?], January 19, 1955, and February 13, 1955, Martin Papers, Library of Congress.

50. Martin, *It Seems Like Only Yesterday*, 116; Nathan Leopold to John Bartlow Martin, November 27, 1954, Martin Papers, Library of Congress.

51. Martin, "Murder on His Conscience," *Saturday Evening Post*, April 23, 1955, 138.

52. John Bartlow Martin to Governor William G. Stratton, June 18, 1957, Martin Papers, Library of Congress; Martin, *It Seems Like Only Yesterday*, 117–18.

53. Martin, *It Seems Like Only Yesterday*, 76.

54. Ibid., 77–78.

55. Ibid., 92–93.

56. Ibid., 87–88, 162.

57. Ibid., 87.

58. "The Press: The Fact Finder," *Time*, May 12, 1958, http://content-time.com/time/subscriber/print-out/0,8816,8634422,00.html; "The Best Reporter," *Newsweek*, May 27, 1957.

59. Ben Hibbs to John Bartlow Martin, February 27, 1958, and John Bartlow Martin to Ben Hibbs, March 5, 1958, Martin Papers, Library of Congress.

60. Ben Hibbs to John Bartlow Martin, March 7, 1958, Martin Papers, Library of Congress.

61. Martin, *It Seems Like Only Yesterday*, 148.

5. All the Way with Adlai

1. John Bartlow Martin, *It Seems Like Only Yesterday: Memoirs of Writing, Presidential Politics, and the Diplomatic Life* (New York: William Morrow and Company, 1986), 141–42.

2. Cindy Martin Coleman, e-mail to author, October 15, 2013.

3. David McCullough, *Truman* (New York: Simon & Schuster, 1992), 890–91; Jeff Broadwater, *Adlai Stevenson and American Politics: The Odyssey of a Cold War Liberal* (New York: Twayne Publishers, 1994), 110; Martin, *It Seems Like Only Yesterday*, 142.

4. Martin, *It Seems Like Only Yesterday*, 142; and John Bartlow Martin, 1952 Presidential Campaign Journal (hereafter cited as Martin 1952 Campaign Journal), John Bartlow Martin Papers, Manuscript Division, Library of Congress, Washington, D.C. (hereafter cited as Martin Papers, Library of Congress).

5. John Bartlow Martin, *Adlai Stevenson* (New York: Harper and Brothers Publishers, 1952), 59–79.

6. Martin, *It Seems Like Only Yesterday*, 142–43.

7. John Bartlow Martin, *Adlai Stevenson of Illinois: The Life of Adlai Stevenson* (Garden City, N.Y.: Doubleday and Company, 1976), 532, 561; Martin, *It Seems Like Only Yesterday*, 142–44.

8. Martin, *It Seems Like Only Yesterday*, 145–46; Martin, *Adlai Stevenson of Illinois*, 585–86.

9. Sidney Warren, *The Battle for the Presidency* (Philadelphia: J. B. Lippincott Company, 1968), 272; Kevin Mattson, *Just Plain Dick: Richard Nixon's Checkers Speech and the "Rocking, Socking" Election of 1952* (New York: Bloomsbury, 2012), 9, 51; Martin, *It Seems Like Only Yesterday*, 145–46.

10. John Kenneth Galbraith, *A Life in Our Times: Memoirs* (Boston: Houghton Mifflin Company, 1981), 292; Carl McGowan oral history, July 27, 1960, Washington, D.C., Harry Truman Library and Museum, Independence, Missouri.

11. Martin, *It Seems Like Only Yesterday*, 185; Kenneth S. Davis, *The Politics of Honor: A Biography of Adlai E. Stevenson*

(New York: G. P. Putnam's Sons, 1967), 279; Martin, *Adlai Stevenson of Illinois*, 613–14; Martin, Martin 1952 Campaign Journal.

12. Martin, Martin 1952 Campaign Journal; Martin, *Adlai Stevenson of Illinois*, 620.

13. Martin, Martin 1952 Campaign Journal; Martin, *It Seems Like Only Yesterday*, 148.

14. "Stevenson Staff Young and Homey," *New York Times*, September 1, 1952; John Fischer, "A Footnote on Adlai Stevenson," *Harper's Magazine*, November 1965, 20.

15. Martin, *Adlai Stevenson of Illinois*, 631–32; David C. Bell oral history, October 16, 1968, Harry Truman Library and Museum, Independence, Missouri; McGowan oral history; Fischer, "A Footnote on Adlai Stevenson," 28.

16. Martin, *Adlai Stevenson of Illinois*, 632; Bell oral history; Fischer, "A Footnote on Adlai Stevenson," 20, 27.

17. Martin, Martin 1952 Campaign Journal.

18. Martin, *It Seems Like Only Yesterday*, 147–48, 154.

19. Arthur M. Schlesinger Jr., *Journals: 1952–2000* (New York: Penguin Books, 2008), 13; Martin, *Adlai Stevenson of Illinois*, 631, 640, 655; Martin, Martin 1952 Campaign Journal.

20. Martin, *Adlai Stevenson of Illinois*, 641–42; Martin 1952 Campaign Journal; John Bartlow Martin, *Adlai Stevenson and the World: A Life of Adlai Stevenson* (Garden City, N.Y.: Doubleday and Company, 1977), 294; Scott Farris, *Almost President: The Men Who Lost the Race But Changed the Nation* (Guilford, Conn.: Lyons Press, 2012), 152.

21. Martin, *It Seems Like Only Yesterday*, 155, 157; Arthur Schlesinger Jr., "John Bartlow Martin, 1915–1987," in *The Century*

Yearbook, 1987 (New York: The Century Association, 1987), 264.

22. McGowan oral history; Martin, Martin 1952 Campaign Journal; Martin, *Adlai Stevenson of Illinois*, 635.

23. Martin, *Adlai Stevenson of Illinois*, 634–35; Martin, Martin 1952 Campaign Journal.

24. Martin, Martin 1952 Campaign Journal; Martin, *It Seems Like Only Yesterday*, 157. Martin said that during the campaign he had a strange attitude about his book on Stevenson. He wanted it to sell well to publicize the governor, but he "would just as soon not have benefitted [financially] therefrom." Martin, Martin 1952 Campaign Journal.

25. Martin, Martin 1952 Campaign Journal; Martin, *Adlai Stevenson of Illinois*, 636.

26. Martin, Martin 1952 Campaign Journal; Martin, *It Seems Like Only Yesterday*, 155.

27. Martin, Martin 1952 Campaign Journal; Galbraith, *A Life in Our Times*, 294; Martin, *Adlai Stevenson of Illinois*, 637.

28. Martin, Martin 1952 Campaign Journal; Martin, *Adlai Stevenson of Illinois*, 639.

29. John Bartlow Martin, memo to Newton Minow, October 9, 1952, Martin Papers, Library of Congress; Martin, Martin 1952 Campaign Journal.

30. Martin, *Adlai Stevenson of Illinois*, 776–77.

31. Ibid., 777–78. In his memoirs, Ted Sorensen said that in his acceptance speech at the Democratic National Convention, John F. Kennedy wished to include "a vivid phrase" to reflect his emphasis on the challenges facing America as well as "invoking the courage and achievements of the past." They decided the phrase "the New Frontier" best fit their goals. "To the best of my recollection," said Sorensen, "neither the senator nor I had read or heard the phrase elsewhere." He did note it was no coincidence that his grandparents were pioneers on the Nebraska frontier. Later, Sorensen read an article in the *New York Herald-Tribune* claiming the phrase had originated with Max Freedman and Walt Rostow, and Bill Safire, a fellow presidential speechwriter, told him that presidential candidates Alf Landon and Henry Wallace had used a similar phrase years earlier. See Ted Sorensen, *Counselor: A Life at the Edge of History* (New York: HarperCollins Publishers, 2008), 218–19.

32. Martin, *Adlai Stevenson of Illinois*, 778–79.

33. Ibid., 640 and 780.

34. Martin, Martin 1952 Campaign Journal.

35. Martin, *Adlai Stevenson of Illinois*, 664.

36. Martin, 1952 Martin Campaign Journal.

37. Martin, *Adlai Stevenson of Illinois*, 641, 707; Martin, *It Seems Like Only Yesterday*, 156.

38. Martin, *It Seems Like Only Yesterday*, 156–57.

39. Barton J. Bernstein, "Election of 1952," in Arthur M. Schlesinger Jr., ed., *History of American Presidential Elections, 1789–2001*, vol. 8, 1944–1956, 3248 (Philadelphia: Chelsea House Publishers, 2002); Martin, *It Seems Like Only Yesterday*, 157; Martin, Martin 1952 Campaign Journal; Jean Edward Smith, *Eisenhower in War and Peace* (New York: Random House, 2012), 544.

40. Bernstein, "Election of 1952," 3243–45; Mattson, *Just Plain Dick*, 146–47; Lee Huebner, "The Checkers Speech after 60 Years," *The Atlantic*, http://www.the atlantic.com/politics/print/2012/09/the

-checkers-speech-after-60-years/262172/; Jim Newton, *Eisenhower: The White House Years* (New York: Doubleday, 2011), 69.

41. Jeffrey Frank, *Ike and Dick: Portrait of a Strange Political Marriage* (New York: Simon & Schuster, 2013), 47; Mattson, *Just Plain Dick*, 144–47. In addition to buttressing salaries for top administration officials (Flanagan had received $7,900 and Mc-Gowan $3,000), the Stevenson fund also paid for Christmas presents to household staff at the governor's mansion, a party for Springfield children, sending flowers to Stevenson's ailing friends, and even to buy uniforms for the governor's male and female bowling teams. See Martin, *Adlai Stevenson of Illinois*, 696, 702–703.

42. Martin, Martin 1952 Campaign Journal; Huebner, "The Checkers Speech after 60 Years"; Smith, *Eisenhower in War and Peace*, 541; Frank, *Ike and Dick*, 56.

43. Martin, *Adlai Stevenson of Illinois*, 705; McCullough, *Truman*, 912; McGowan oral history; Smith, *Eisenhower in War and Peace*, 547.

44. Martin, Martin 1952 Campaign Journal; Martin, *Adlai Stevenson of Illinois*, 751, 756.

45. Martin, *Adlai Stevenson of Illinois*, 751–53; Martin, *It Seems Like Only Yesterday*, 158.

46. Martin, Martin 1952 Campaign Journal; Martin, *Adlai Stevenson of Illinois*, 759.

47. Bernstein, "Election of 1952," 3258–59; McGowan oral history; Martin, Martin 1952 Campaign Journal.

48. Martin, *It Seems Like Only Yesterday*, 159–60; Martin, Martin 1952 Campaign Journal.

49. Martin, Martin 1952 Campaign Journal; Martin, *Adlai Stevenson of Illinois*, 709.

50. Martin, Martin 1952 Campaign Journal.

6. The New America

1. John Bartlow Martin, *It Seems Like Only Yesterday: Memoirs of Writing, Presidential Politics, and the Diplomatic Life* (New York: William Morrow and Company, 1986), 160–61; John Bartlow Martin, 1952 Presidential Campaign Journal, John Bartlow Martin Papers, Manuscript Division, Library of Congress, Washington, D.C. (hereafter cited as Martin Papers, Library of Congress).

2. Martin, *It Seems Like Only Yesterday*, 162; John Bartlow Martin, *Adlai Stevenson and the World: The Life of Adlai E. Stevenson* (Garden City, N.Y.: Doubleday and Company, 1977), 20–21.

3. Martin, *Adlai Stevenson and the World*, 146–47; John Bartlow Martin, "Adlai Girds for Battle," *Saturday Evening Post*, October 22, 1955, 115; Martin, *It Seems Like Only Yesterday*, 162–63.

4. Martin, *It Seems Like Only Yesterday*, 162–63.

5. John Bartlow Martin, "Who Really Runs Chicago?" *Saturday Evening Post*, November 19, 1955, 39, 79; Martin, *It Seems Like Only Yesterday*, 107–108.

6. Martin, *Adlai Stevenson and the World*, 163; Martin, "Who Really Runs Chicago?" 79–80; Martin, *It Seems Like Only Yesterday*, 113.

7. John Bartlow Martin to Bob [?], October 28, 1955, Martin Papers, Library of Congress.

8. Martin, *It Seems Like Only Yesterday*, 111–12; Adam Cohen and Elizabeth Taylor, *American Pharaoh: Mayor Richard J. Daley: His Battle for Chicago and the Nation* (Boston: Little, Brown and Company, 2000), 121; John Bartlow Martin, "Who Really Runs Chicago?" *Saturday Evening Post*, November 26, 1955, 30.

9. Martin, "Who Really Runs Chicago?" November 26, 1955, 30, 145–46; Martin, *It Seems Like Only Yesterday*,

112–13; Cohen and Taylor, *American Pharaoh,* 121, 130.

10. Martin, "Who Really Runs Chicago?" November 26, 1955, 146; Martin, *It Seems Like Only Yesterday,* 113.

11. Martin, *Adlai Stevenson and the World,* 282; Jeff Broadwater, *Adlai Stevenson and American Politics: The Odyssey of a Cold War Liberal* (New York: Twayne Publishers, 1994), 157–58; Gary A. Donaldson, *The First Modern Campaign: Kennedy, Nixon, and the Election of 1960* (Lanham, Md.: Rowman & Littlefield Publishers, 2007), 13; Jean Edward Smith, *Eisenhower in War and Peace* (New York: Random House, 2012), 683.

12. Martin, *It Seems Like Only Yesterday,* 163–64.

13. Martin, *Adlai Stevenson and the World,* 279–80; John Bartlow Martin to Bob [?], April 1, 1956, Martin Papers, Library of Congress; Broadwater, *Adlai Stevenson and American Politics,* 157–58; Martin, *It Seems Like Only Yesterday,* 165.

14. Martin, *Adlai Stevenson and the World,* 288–89, 317.

15. Martin, *It Seems Like Only Yesterday,* 167–68.

16. Martin, *Adlai Stevenson and the World,* 292–93; Martin, *It Seems Like Only Yesterday,* 168.

17. Martin, *Adlai Stevenson and the World,* 318; Martin, *It Seems Like Only Yesterday,* 168; John Bartlow Martin, memo on speech group to Robert F. Kennedy, June 13, 1960, Martin Papers, Library of Congress.

18. Martin, *Adlai Stevenson and the World,* 319–20; Martin, *It Seems Like Only Yesterday,* 169; "The Care and Feeding of the Baby," *Time,* July 16, 1956, http://cgi.cnn.com/ALLPOLITICS/1996/analysis/back.time/9607/17/.

19. Martin, *Adlai Stevenson and the World,* 337.

20. Martin, *Adlai Stevenson and the World,* 337–38; Martin, *It Seems Like Only Yesterday,* 170.

21. Martin, *Adlai Stevenson and the World,* 349–50; Arthur M. Schlesinger Jr., *A Thousand Days: John F. Kennedy in the White House* (New York: Fawcett Premier, 1971), 16–17. In addition to Kennedy's Catholicism, Democratic Party leaders were put off by his youth and inexperience. If Stevenson had to have a Catholic as a running mate, Congressman Sam Rayburn told Stevenson that he far and away preferred veteran congressman John McCormack instead of "that little piss-ant Kennedy." See Broadwater, *Adlai Stevenson and American Politics,* 162.

22. Martin, *Adlai Stevenson and the World,* 234, 351–52.

23. Martin, *Adlai Stevenson and the World,* 235, 341, 345, 358; John Kenneth Galbraith, *A Life in Our Times: Memoirs* (Boston: Houghton Mifflin Company, 1981), 344.

24. Broadwater, *Adlai Stevenson and American Politics,* 171; Jim Newton, *Eisenhower: The White House Years* (New York: Doubleday, 2011), 215; Martin, *Adlai Stevenson and the World,* 391–92.

25. John Bartlow Martin, memo to Arthur Schlesinger, October 19, 1975, Martin Papers, Library of Congress; Martin, *It Seems Like Only Yesterday,* 172, 176; Evan Thomas, *Robert Kennedy: His Life* (New York: Simon & Schuster, 2000), 74.

26. Pierre Salinger, *With Kennedy* (Garden City, N.Y.: Doubleday and Company, 1966), 13–14, 17–18; Clark R. Mollenhoff, *Tentacles of Power: The Story of Jimmy Hoffa* (Cleveland, Ohio: World Publishing Company, 1965), 124.

27. Martin, *Adlai Stevenson and the World,* 234; Martin memo to Schlesinger; Martin, *It Seems Like Only Yesterday,* 172.

28. "Keeping Posted: How One Reporter Works," *Saturday Evening Post,* June 27, 1959, 112; John Bartlow Martin, "The Struggle to Get Hoffa: Part One: Kennedy Sets a Snare," *Saturday Evening Post,* June 27, 1959, 19–21, 94; Robert F. Kennedy, *The Enemy Within* (New York: Harper and Brothers, 1960), 162.

29. Martin, memo to Schlesinger; Martin, *It Seems Like Only Yesterday,* 173–74; Arthur M. Schlesinger Jr., *Robert Kennedy and His Times* (Boston: Houghton Mifflin Company, 1978) 145; Chris Matthews, *Jack Kennedy: Elusive Hero* (New York: Simon & Schuster, 2011), 234. Although O'Donnell served as Robert Kennedy's "right-hand man" while investigating the Teamsters, he had joined the staff, noted Walter Sheridan, at the instigation of John F. Kennedy, to make sure "Bob didn't mess everything up politically." Robert Kennedy believed, however, that if he did the right thing, everything would turn out right in the end. Walter Sheridan oral history by Roberta Greene, March 23, 1970, John F. Kennedy Presidential Library, Boston.

30. Martin, *It Seems Like Only Yesterday,* 174, 186; Walter Sheridan, interview in Jean Stein and George Plimpton, *American Journey: The Times of Robert Kennedy* (New York: Harcourt Brace Jovanovich, 1970), 56.

31. Martin, *It Seems Like Only Yesterday,* 174; Martin, memo to Schlesinger; Martin, "The Struggle to Get Hoffa: Part One," 92; John Bartlow Martin, "The Struggle to Get Hoffa: Part Five: Hoffa Confounds His Enemies," *Saturday Evening Post,* July 25, 1959, 86; Sheridan, interview, March 23, 1970.

32. John Bartlow Martin, "The Struggle to Get Hoffa: Part Three: The Labor Boss Leaves a Baffling Trail," *Saturday Evening Post,* July 11, 1959, 80; Martin, *It Seems Like Only Yesterday,* 176; Sheridan oral history.

33. Edwin Guthman, *We Band of Brothers* (New York: Harper and Row Publishers, 1971), 57–58; Martin, memo to Schlesinger; Thomas, *Robert Kennedy,* 88.

34. Martin, *It Seems Like Only Yesterday,* 175.

35. John Bartlow Martin, "The Struggle to Get Hoffa: Part Two: The Making of a Labor Boss," *Saturday Evening Post,* July 4, 1959, 27, 54–55; Martin, *It Seems Like Only Yesterday,* 178–80.

36. John Bartlow Martin, "The Struggle to Get Hoffa: Conclusion: How Long Will He Last?" *Saturday Evening Post,* August 8, 1959, 63–64; Martin, *It Seems Like Only Yesterday,* 182.

37. Martin, *It Seems Like Only Yesterday,* 182; Martin, memo to Schlesinger.

38. Martin, memo to Schlesinger.

39. Martin, *It Seems Like Only Yesterday,* 183; Martin, *Adlai Stevenson and the World,* 493; Theodore H. White, *The Making of the President, 1960* (New York: Book-of-the-Month Club, Inc., 1988), 47.

40. John Bartlow Martin, memo on speech group to Robert Kennedy, June 13, 1960, Martin Papers, Library of Congress.

41. John Bartlow Martin, memo on speech group, and Robert F. Kennedy to John Bartlow Martin, June 16, 1960, Martin Papers, Library of Congress.

42. Martin, *It Seems Like Only Yesterday,* 188, 190.

43. Ibid., 191.

44. W. J. Rorabaugh, *The Real Making of the President: Kennedy, Nixon, and the 1960 Election* (Lawrence: University Press of Kansas, 2009), 70–72; Donaldson, *The First Modern Campaign,* 75–76; Martin, *Adlai Stevenson and the World,* 525.

45. Martin, memo to Schlesinger.

46. Archibald Cox oral history, June 19 and 20, 2000, Columbia University Librar-

ies Oral History Research Office, http://
columbia.edu/cu/lweb/digital/collections
/oral_hist/cox/interview.html; Joseph
Kraft oral history by John F. Stewart, January 9, 1967, Kennedy Library; Myer Feldman oral history by Charles T. Morrissey,
February 27, 1966, Kennedy Library; Ken
Gormley, *Archibald Cox: Conscience of a
Nation* (Reading, Mass.: Addison-Wesley,
1997), 127–28; "JFK's 'Caroline' Plane
Made History," Yahoo Voices, http://
voices.yahoo.com/jfks-caroline-plane
-made-history-8889083.html/

47. Martin, *It Seems Like Only Yesterday*, 192–93.

48. Theodore C. Sorensen, *Kennedy*
(New York: Harper and Row Publishers,
1965), 179; John Bartlow Martin to William Blair, March 29, 1961, Martin Papers,
Library of Congress; "Democrats: Whistle
While You Work," *Time*, September 19,
1960, http://content.time.com/time
/magazine/article/0,9171,826610,00.html/.

49. Kraft, oral history.

50. Martin, *It Seems Like Only Yesterday*, 194–95, 197; Sorensen, *Kennedy*, 177.

51. Martin, *It Seems Like Only Yesterday*, 195; Sorensen, *Kennedy*, 187; Theodore
Sorensen, memorandum for speechwriters, July 23, 1960, Martin Papers, Library
of Congress.

52. Martin, *It Seems Like Only Yesterday*, 196; Schlesinger, *Journals: 1952–2000*
(New York: Penguin Books, 2008), 85–86;
Kraft oral history; Cox oral history;
Gormley, *Archibald Cox*, 134. Schlesinger
and Kennedy discussed the speechwriting
problem, and the candidate indicated he
did not want to bring Schlesinger and Galbraith directly into the campaign and have
the press write stories about "the Kennedy
team collapsing and Stevenson's writers
taking over." Kennedy told Schlesinger
that if he had anything he wanted to get to
him, to go through his wife, Jacqueline, a

"channel designed," said Schlesinger, "to
simplify his relations with his immediate staff." Schlesinger, *A Thousand Days*,
72–73.

53. Gormley, *Archibald Cox*, 131; Ted
Sorensen, *Counselor: A Life at the Edge
of History* (New York: Harper Collins
Publishers, 2008), 135; Salinger, *With Kennedy*, 163.

54. Donaldson, *The First Modern
Campaign*, 113–18; Kayla Webley, "How
the Nixon-Kennedy Debate Changed
the World," *Time*, September 23, 2010,
http://content.time.come/time/nation/
article/0,8599,2021078,00.html/.

55. Kenneth P. O'Donnell and David
F. Powers, with Joe McCarthy, *"Johnny, We
Hardly Knew Ye": Memories of John Fitzger-
ald Kennedy* (Boston: Little, Brown and
Company, 1972), 222, 224; Rorabaugh, *The
Real Making of the President*, 178–79; Rob-
ert A. Caro, *The Years of Lyndon Johnson:
The Passage of Power* (New York: Alfred A.
Knopf, 2012), 155–56.

56. Martin, *It Seems Like Only Yesterday*, 199–200.

7. The Honorable Ambassador

1. "Mob of Dominicans Attack U.S.
Office," *Chicago Tribune*, March 9, 1962;
John Bartlow Martin, *Overtaken by Events:
The Dominican Crisis from the Fall of Tru-
jillo to the Civil War* (Garden City, N.Y.:
Doubleday and Company, 1966), 85.

2. Martin, *Overtaken by Events*, 4–5.

3. John Bartlow Martin, *It Seems
Like Only Yesterday: Memoirs of Writing,
Presidential Politics, and the Diplomatic Life*
(New York: William Morrow and Com-
pany, 1986), 199.

4. Ibid., 201.

5. Ibid.

6. Ibid., 202.

7. Newton Minow, telephone interview with author, June 27, 2013; John

Bartlow Martin, "Television USA: The Big Squeeze," *Saturday Evening Post,* November 11, 1961, 62–63; Mary Ann Watson, *The Expanding Vista: American Television in the Kennedy Years* (New York: Oxford University Press, 1990), 19.

8. Minow, interview; Martin, *It Seems Like Only Yesterday,* 202–203; John Bartlow Martin to Newton Minow, March 20, 1961, Newton Minow to John Bartlow Martin, March 22, 1961, and undated statement by John Bartlow Martin, John Bartlow Martin Papers, Manuscripts Division, Library of Congress, Washington, D.C. (hereafter cited as Martin Papers, Library of Congress).

9. John Bartlow Martin, "Television USA: Wasteland or Wonderland? A Famous Writer's Close-up Report on the Controversial State of TV," *Saturday Evening Post,* October 21, 1961, 20–21.

10. Ibid.; James L. Baughman, "Minow's Viewers: Understanding the Response to the 'Vast Wasteland' Address," *Federal Communications Law Journal* 55, issue 3 (2003): 452.

11. John Bartlow Martin to Newt Minow, April 8, 1961, John Bartlow Martin to Arthur M. Schlesinger Jr., April 8, 1961, and Newt Minow to John Bartlow Martin, April 17, 1961, Martin Papers, Library of Congress.

12. Watson, *The Expanding Vista,* 22; Minow, interview; Martin, *It Seems Like Only Yesterday,* 203.

13. Newton Minow, "Television," *Vital Speeches of the Day* 57, issue 18 (July 1, 1991): 556; Newton Minow, interview, Archive of American Television, http://www.emmytvlegends.org/interviews/people/newton-n-minow#.

14. Martin, "Television USA: The Big Squeeze," 65; Watson, *The Expanding Vista,* 27; Martin, *It Seems Like Only Yesterday,* 203.

15. G. Pope Atkins and Larman C. Wilson, *The Dominican Republic and the United States: From Imperialism to Transnationalism* (Athens: University of Georgia Press, 1998), 119.

16. Martin, *It Seems Like Only Yesterday,* 203–204; Arthur M. Schlesinger Jr., *A Thousand Days: John F. Kennedy in the White House* (New York: Fawcett Premier, 1971), 193; Stephen G. Rabe, *The Most Dangerous Area in the World: John F. Kennedy Confronts Communist Revolution in Latin America* (Chapel Hill: University of North Carolina Press, 1999), 9, 19; Jeffrey F. Taffet, *Foreign Aid as Foreign Policy: The Alliance for Progress in Latin America* (New York: Routledge, 2007), Kindle book, chap. 6.

17. John Bartlow Martin to Arthur M. Schlesinger Jr., June 1, 1961, and John Bartlow Martin to Fran Martin, June 21, 1961, Martin Papers, Library of Congress.

18. Chester Bowles to Arthur M. Schlesinger Jr., June 27, 1961, Arthur M. Schlesinger to John Bartlow Martin, July 7, 1961, Robert F. Kennedy to John Bartlow Martin, July 19, 1961, Adlai Stevenson to Dean Rusk, August 26, 1961, and Dean Rusk to Adlai Stevenson, September 7, 1961, Martin Papers, Library of Congress.

19. Martin, *It Seems Like Only Yesterday,* 204–206.

20. Ibid.; Martin, *Overtaken by Events,* 64–69, 74–75, 80.

21. John Bartlow Martin, notes dictated November 16, 1963, New York, Martin Papers, Library of Congress; Taffet, *Foreign Aid as Foreign Policy,* chap. 6.

22. Martin, *Overtaken by Events,* 82; Dominican Republic, Martin Report, Papers of John F. Kennedy, John F. Kennedy Presidential Library and Museum, Boston, Mass.; Martin, *It Seems Like Only Yesterday,* 208.

23. Martin, *It Seems Like Only Yester-day*, 208–209; Schlesinger, *A Thousand Days*, 705; Martin, *Overtaken by Events*, 82.

24. Martin, *Overtaken by Events*, 82–83; Martin, *It Seems Like Only Yesterday*, 209; Atkins and Wilson, *The Dominican Republic and the United States*, 125–27; Eric Thomas Chester, *Rag-Tags, Scum, Riff-Raff and Commies: The U.S. Intervention in the Dominican Republic, 1965–66* (New York: Monthly Review Press, 2001), 25–27.

25. John Bartlow Martin, memoran-dum, Political Reconstruction of the Dominican Republic, January 30, 1962, Martin Papers, Library of Congress.

26. Martin, *It Seems Like Only Yester-day*, 205–206, 210; Robert G. Schultz, "En-voy Has Boss Now, His First in 25 Years," *Indianapolis Times*, March 4, 1962.

27. Martin, *It Seems Like Only Yester-day*, 211–12.

28. Martin, *Overtaken by Events*, 86, 147.

29. Fred Martin, memo to author, Oc-tober 8, 2013; Fran Martin to Marion and Jerry Goldwach, July 25, 1962, and Fran Martin to Francis Nipp, May 2, 1963, Mar-tin Papers, Library of Congress; Martin, *Overtaken by Events*, 355; Martin, *It Seems Like Only Yesterday*, 223.

30. Martin, *It Seems Like Only Yes-terday*, 218–20; John Bartlow Martin, memorandum dictated November 16, 1963, Martin Papers, Library of Congress.

31. Martin, *It Seems Like Only Yester-day*, 217, 220–21.

32. Martin, *Overtaken by Events*, 86–91.

33. Chester, *Rag-Tags, Scum, Riff-Raff and Commies*, 18; Juan Bosch, *The Unfinished Experiment: Democracy in the Dominican Republic* (New York: Frederick A. Praeger, 1965), 16–17; Martin, *It Seems Like Only Yesterday*, 218; John Bartlow, memorandum dictated November 29, 1962, Martin Papers, Library of Congress.

34. Martin, *Overtaken by Events*, 98; Fran Martin to Marion and Jerry Gold-wach, July 25, 1963, Martin Papers, Library of Congress.

35. Martin, *Overtaken by Events*, 100, 122; Martin, *It Seems Like Only Yesterday*, 218–19.

36. John Bartlow Martin, memoranda dictated October 27, 1962, and Novem-ber 16, 1963, Martin Papers, Library of Congress.

37. Fran Martin to Marion and Jerry Goldwach, July 25, 1963, Martin Papers, Library of Congress; Martin, *Overtaken by Events*, 101; Martin, *It Seems Like Only Yesterday*, 224.

38. Martin, *Overtaken by Events*, 142–44; Martin, notes dictated November 16, 1963.

39. Martin, *It Seems Like Only Yester-day*, 225; Dan Kurzman, *Santo Domingo: Portrait of the Damned* (New York: G. P. Putnam's Sons, 1965), 118.

40. Martin, *Overtaken by Events*, 376–77.

41. Martin, *It Seems Like Only Yes-terday*, 226–27; Fran Martin to Newton Minow, March 5, 1963, and Fran Martin to Robert R. Hurt, April 29, 1963, Martin Papers, Library of Congress.

42. Fran Martin to Monica Bayley, March 25, 1963, Martin Papers, Library of Congress; Martin, *Overtaken by Events*, 377; Martin, *It Seems Like Only Yesterday*, 228.

43. Atkins and Wilson, *The Dominican Republic and the United States*, 129; Charles H. Weston Jr., "The Failure of the Demo-cratic Left in the Dominican Republic: A Case Study of the Overthrow of the Juan Bosch Government," Discussion Paper Number 65, June 1, 1979, Department of Political Science, Western Illinois Uni-versity; John Bartlow Martin, Dominican Republic journal, and notes for personal

file, December 20, 1962, Martin Papers, Library of Congress.

44. Juan Bosch, recorded interview with Lloyd N. Cutler, June 9, 1964, John F. Kennedy Library Oral History Program; notes for personal file, December 20, 1962.

45. Notes for personal file, December 20, 1962; Bosch, *The Unfinished Experiment*, 115–16; Martin, *Overtaken by Events*, 344.

46. Bosch, *The Unfinished Experiment*, 131–32; Notes for personal file, February 23, 1963; Martin, *Overtaken by Events*, 329–30; Martin, *It Seems Like Only Yesterday*, 233.

47. Martin, *Overtaken by Events*, 351.

48. Martin, *Overtaken by Events*, 716; Martin, *It Seems Like Only Yesterday*, 236; John Bartlow Martin, *U.S. Policy in the Caribbean* (Boulder, Colo.: Westview Press, 1978), 77–78; notes for personal file, March 22, 1963, and July 31, 1963, Martin Papers, Library of Congress.

49. Notes for personal file, March 22, 1963, and July 31, 1963. For Hendrix's opinion about Martin, see "Diplomatic Talent Wasted," *Miami News*, June 1, 1962, and "Our Weak Link Diplomats," *Miami News*, August 1, 1962.

50. Martin, *Overtaken by Events*, 389, 395 448, 450; Abraham F. Lowenthal, *The Dominican Intervention* (Baltimore: Johns Hopkins University Press, 1994), 14; Sam Halper, "After Trujillo," *The New Republic* December 24, 1966, p. 25.

51. Bosch, *The Unfinished Experiment*, 162–63; Harry W. Shlaudeman, interview with William E. Knight, May 24, 1993, the Association for Diplomatic Studies and Training Foreign Affairs Oral History Project, Library of Congress, Washington, D.C.

52. Martin, *It Seems Like Only Yesterday*, 237–39.

53. Martin, *Overtaken by Events*, 470–78.

54. Martin, *Overtaken by Events*, 519, 521–23; Martin, *It Seems Like Only Yesterday*, 239.

55. Martin, *Overtaken by Events*, 565–66, 583; Foreign Service of the United States telegram for ambassador, September 24, 1963, Martin Papers, Library of Congress; Martin, *It Seems Like Only Yesterday*, 240.

56. Martin, *Overtaken by Events*, 610; Martin, *It Seems Like Only Yesterday*, 240.

57. Martin, *Overtaken by Events*, 601–602; Martin, *It Seems Like Only Yesterday*, 241.

58. *Overtaken by Events*, 616.

59. Ibid., 621–22; Martin, *U.S. Policy in the Caribbean*, 80.

60. Martin, *Overtaken by Events*, 631–33.

61. Ibid., 634, 742; Martin, *It Seems Like Only Yesterday*, 246.

8. LBJ and Adlai

1. John Bartlow Martin, *It Seems Like Only Yesterday: Memoirs of Writing, Presidential Politics, and the Diplomatic Life* (New York: William Morrow and Company, 1986), 247–48, 250–51.

2. John Bartlow Martin, *Overtaken by Events: The Dominican Crisis from the Fall of Trujillo to the Civil War* (Garden City, N.Y.: Doubleday and Company, 1966), 639–40; John Bartlow Martin to Paul Horgan, April 26, 1965, John Bartlow Martin Papers, Manuscripts Division, Library of Congress, Washington, D.C. (hereafter cited as Martin Papers, Library of Congress).

3. Martin, *It Seems Like Only Yesterday*, 250; Paul Horgan, *Tracings: A Book of Partial Portraits* (New York: Farrar, Straus and Giroux, 1993), 216, 226; Edmund Wilson, *The Sixties: The Last Journal, 1960–1972* (New York: Farrar, Straus and Giroux, 1993), 452, 466.

4. Horgan, *Tracings*, 226–27. In his journals, Wilson recalled that Stafford was also at the dinner. He described the evening as "quite jolly – a good deal of liquor was drunk" by the adults. Wilson, *The Sixties*, 466.

5. Martin, *It Seems Like Only Yesterday*, 275; Dan Martin, e-mail to author, September 20, 2013.

6. Martin, *It Seems Like Only Yesterday*, 275–76; John Bartlow Martin, "The Heartland's Backyard Frontier," *Chicago Tribune*, July 31, 1983.

7. Martin, *It Seems Like Only Yesterday*, 276–77; Dan Martin, e-mail, March 11, 2014; Fred Martin, memo to author, October 8, 2013.

8. Martin, *It Seems Like Only Yesterday*, 277.

9. Robert A. Caro, *The Years of Lyndon Johnson: The Passage of Power* (New York: Alfred A. Knopf, 2012), 410–11, 588–93; Gary Donaldson, *Liberalism's Last Hurrah: The Presidential Campaign of 1964* (Armonk, N.Y.: M. E. Sharpe, 2003), 49; Martin, *Overtaken by Events*, 335.

10. Martin, *It Seems Like Only Yesterday*, 232; John Bartlow Martin, "Election of 1964," in Arthur M. Schlesinger Jr., ed., *History of American Presidential Elections, 1789–2001: 1960–1968*, vol. 9, 3565 (1971; reprint, Philadelphia: Chelsea House Publishers, 2002).

11. Martin, *It Seems Like Only Yesterday*, 265–66; John Bartlow Martin oral history interview with Paige Mulholland, January 30, 1971, Lyndon Baines Johnson Presidential Library, Austin, Tex.; Martin, "Election of 1964," 3567.

12. Martin, "Election of 1964," 3591; Donaldson, *Liberalism's Last Hurrah*, 235, 243, 246; Vaughn Davis Bornet, *The Presidency of Lyndon B. Johnson* (Lawrence: University Press of Kansas, 1983), 104–105.

13. Donaldson, *Liberalism's Last Hurrah*, 247–48.

14. Martin, *It Seems Like Only Yesterday*, 266–67.

15. Martin oral history; Martin, *It Seems Like Only Yesterday*, 266; Robert D. Johnson, *All the Way with LBJ: The 1964 Presidential Election* (New York: Cambridge University Press, 2009), 242–43; Martin, "Election of 1964," 3591.

16. Donaldson, *Liberalism's Last Hurrah*, 269; John Bartlow Martin, memorandum to Bill Moyers, October 2, 1964, Martin Papers, Library of Congress.

17. Martin, "Election of 1964," 3594; Martin, *It Seems Like Only Yesterday*, 267.

18. Tad Szulc, "When the Marines Stormed Ashore in Santo Domingo," *Saturday Evening Post*, July 31, 1965, 36; Martin oral history; Tad Szulc, *Dominican Diary* (New York: Delacorte Press, 1965), 21.

19. Robert Dallek, *Lyndon B. Johnson: Portrait of a President* (New York: Oxford University Press, 2004), 214; Martin, *Overtaken by Events*, 638; Dan Kurzman, *Santo Domingo: Revolt of the Damned* (New York: G. P. Putnam's Sons, 1965), 118–19; Szulc, "When the Marines Stormed Ashore," 37–38.

20. Kurzman, *Santo Domingo*, 129; Pope Atkins and Larman C. Wilson, *The Dominican Republic and the United States: From Imperialism to Transnationalism* (Athens: University of Georgia Press, 1998), 134–36; Abraham F. Lowenthal, *The Dominican Intervention* (Baltimore, Md.: Johns Hopkins University Press, 1994), 92–94.

21. Szulc, *Dominican Diary*, 37–38.

22. Charles Roberts, *LBJ's Inner Circle* (New York: Delacorte Press, 1965), 205; Randall B. Woods, *LBJ: Architect of American Ambition* (New York: Free Press, 2006), 628–29, 632.

23. Martin, *It Seems Like Only Yesterday*, 252; Martin oral history.

24. Roberts, *LBJ's Inner Circle*, 201; Martin oral history; Woods, *LBJ: Architect of American Ambition*, 626–28; McGeorge Bundy oral history interview III, by Paige E. Mulholland, March 19, 1969, Johnson Presidential Library.

25. Martin, *Overtaken by Events*, 660–61.

26. Ibid.; Marguerite Higgins, "Johnson's Diplomacy," *Charleston News and Courier*, May 11, 1965; Martin, interview.

27. Martin, *Overtaken by Events*, 662–63; Martin, *It Seems Like Only Yesterday*, 253.

28. Eric Thomas Chester, *Rag-Tags, Scum, Riff-Raff, and Commies: The U.S. Intervention in the Dominican Republic, 1965–66* (New York: Monthly Review Press, 2001), 91; John Bartlow Martin, "The Dominican Upheaval," *Life*, May 28, 1965, 29–30; Martin, *Overtaken by Events*, 663.

29. Martin, *Overtaken by Events*, 665; Martin, "The Dominican Upheaval," 30.

30. Martin, *It Seems Like Only Yesterday*, 253–54; Martin, *Overtaken by Events*, 667–68; Martin, "The Dominican Upheaval," 30.

31. Martin, *It Seems Like Only Yesterday*, 253.

32. Szulc, *Dominican Diary*, 84; Martin, *Overtaken by Events*, 668–70, 676; Martin, interview.

33. Martin, "The Dominican Upheaval," 68; Martin, *Overtaken by Events*, 672.

34. Martin, *Overtaken by Events*, 676; Alan McPherson, "Misled by Himself: What the Johnson Tapes Reveal about the Dominican Intervention of 1965," *Latin American Research Review* 38, no. 2: 142; Kurzman, *Santo Domingo*, 189, 193, and 199; Tad Szulc, "U.S. Troops Split Dominican Rebels," *New York Times*, May 4, 1965.

35. Kurzman, *Santo Domingo*, 189–92; Szulc, *Dominican Diary*, 106; Martin, *Overtaken by Events*, 673.

36. Martin, "The Dominican Upheaval," 70C; Martin, *Overtaken by Events*, 678–79; Martin oral history.

37. Martin, *Overtaken by Events*, 680–81; Martin, "The Dominican Upheaval," 70D; Martin oral history.

38. Martin, *Overtaken by Events*, 695–96; Martin, interview; Szulc, "When the Marines Stormed Ashore in Santo Domingo," 47.

39. Martin, *It Seems Like Only Yesterday*, 254–55; Martin, *Overtaken by Events*, 698–99.

40. Atkins and Wilson, *The Dominican Republic and the United States*, 139–42; Harry W. Shlaudeman, interview with William E. Knight, May 24, 1993, the Foreign Affairs Oral History Collection of the Association for Diplomatic Studies and Training, Library of Congress, Washington, D.C.; Martin, *It Seems Like Only Yesterday*, 256.

41. Martin, *It Seems Like Only Yesterday*, 249.

42. John Bartow Martin, *Adlai Stevenson and the World: The Life of Adlai E. Stevenson* (Garden City, N.Y.: Doubleday and Company, 1977), 844; Robert G. Spivak, "'Intellectual Myopia' on Viet Nam Protests," *Beaver County (Pa.) Times*, August 6, 1965; Martin, *It Seems Like Only Yesterday*, 256.

43. Martin, *Adlai Stevenson and the World*, 862–63; Jeff Broadwater, *Adlai Stevenson and American Politics: The Odyssey of a Cold War Liberal* (New York: Twayne Publishers, 1994), 227.

44. John Bartlow Martin to Cindy (Martin) and Tony Campbell, July 17, 1965, Cindy Martin Coleman personal papers; Martin, *It Seems Like Only Yesterday*, 262.

45. Steve Neal, "Stevenson Was Truly One for the Books," *Chicago Tribune*, July 14, 1985.

46. John Bartlow Martin to Ivan von Auw Jr., October 25, 1965, and John Bartlow Martin to Dorothy Olding, August 2, 1967, Martin Papers, Library of Congress.

47. Martin, *It Seems Like Only Yesterday*, 263–64; John Bartlow Martin, *Adlai Stevenson of Illinois: The Life of Adlai Stevenson* (Garden City, N.Y.: Doubleday and Company, 1976), 606; Susan Drake and Sharron Karrow, "Writing the Wrongs: Stevenson's Biographer Makes People the Issue," *Byline: Northwestern's Journalism Magazine* 11 (Spring 1976): 8; Dorothy Olding to John Bartlow Martin, September 19, 1967, Martin Papers, Library of Congress.

48. Martin, *Adlai Stevenson of Illinois*, vi.

49. Martin, *It Seems Like Only Yesterday*, 263–64; "Martin's 'Stevenson' Published to Critical Acclaim," *Medilletter,* March 29, 1976, John Bartlow Martin Papers, 1960–1987, Northwestern University Archives, Evanston, Illinois; Paul McGrath, "'Fact-finder' Martin Still Hunts for History," *Chicago Sun-Times,* March 21, 1976.

50. Martin, *It Seems Like Only Yesterday*, 264–65; John Bartlow Martin to Dorothy Olding, August 2, 1967, Martin Papers, Library of Congress.

51. Martin, *It Seems Like Only Yesterday,* 265.

9. The Return of the Native

1. Greta E. Shankle, "Marott Hotel," in David J. Bodenhamer and Robert G. Barrows, eds., *Encyclopedia of Indianapolis,* 974–75 (Bloomington and Indianapolis: Indiana University Press, 1994); John Bartlow Martin, RFK Notes, June 28, 1968, John Bartlow Martin Papers, Manuscripts Division, Library of Congress, Washington, D.C. (hereafter cited as Martin Papers, Library of Congress).

2. John Bartlow Martin, *It Seems Like Only Yesterday: Memoirs of Writing, Presidential Politics, and the Diplomatic Life* (New York: William Morrow and Company, 1986), 282–83.

3. Martin, *It Seems Like Only Yesterday*, 283; Edwin O. Guthman and C. Richard Allen, eds., *RFK: Collected Speeches* (New York: Viking, 1993), 357. For a complete review of Robert F. Kennedy's campaign in the Hoosier State, see Ray E. Boomhower, *Robert F. Kennedy and the 1968 Indiana Primary* (Bloomington: Indiana University Press, 2008). See also Thurston Clarke, *The Last Campaign: Robert F. Kennedy and 82 Days That Inspired America* (New York: Henry Holt and Company, 2008).

4. Martin, *It Seems Like Only Yesterday*, 277.

5. Ibid., 278.

6. Martin, *It Seems Like Only Yesterday*, 248–49; Guthman and Allen, *RFK,* xvi and 405.

7. Guthman and Allen, *RFK,* 405–407, 414–15; Arthur M. Schlesinger Jr., *Robert Kennedy and His Times* (Boston: Houghton Mifflin Company, 1978), 650, 653, and 662.

8. Evan Thomas, *Robert Kennedy: His Life* (New York: Simon & Schuster, 2000,) 348, 354; Martin, *It Seems Like Only Yesterday,* 274; John Bartlow Martin to Robert F. Kennedy, February 25, 1968, Martin Papers, Library of Congress; Jules Witcover, *The Year the Dream Died: Revisiting 1968 in America* (New York: Warner Books, 1997), 104.

9. Arthur Herzog, *McCarthy for President* (New York: The Viking Press, 1969), 30; Walter LaFeber, *The Deadly Bet: LBJ, Vietnam, and the 1968 Election* (Lanham, Md.: Rowman & Littlefield Publishers, 2005), 38.

10. Don Oberdorfer, *Tet! The Turning Point in the Vietnam War* (Baltimore: Johns Hopkins University Press, 2001), 158; Albert Eisele, *Almost to the Presidency: A Biography of Two American Politicians* (Blue Earth, Minn.: The Piper Company, 1972), 300.

11. Martin, RFK Notes; "Kennedy's Statement and Excerpts from News Conference," *New York Times*, March 17, 1968.

12. Jules Witcover, *85 Days: The Last Campaign of Robert Kennedy* (New York: Quill, 1988), 124; Dennis Wainstock, *The Turning Point: The 1968 United States Presidential Campaign* (Jefferson, N.C.: McFarland and Company, 1988), 59; Martin, *It Seems Like Only Yesterday*, 285–86.

13. Martin, RFK Notes; John Bartlow Martin to Robert F. Kennedy, March 29, 1968, and John Bartlow Martin memorandum to Robert F. Kennedy, Ted Sorensen, and Indiana schedulers, writers and television men, April 1968, Martin Papers, Library of Congress; William Haddad oral history interview, by Larry J. Hackman, February 27, 1969, New York, John F. Kennedy Presidential Library, Boston, Mass.

14. Lyndon Baines Johnson, *The Vantage Point: Perspectives of the Presidency, 1963–1969* (New York: Holt, Rinehart, and Winston, 1971), 427, 435; Doris Kearns, *Lyndon Johnson and the American Dream* (New York: Harper and Row, 1976), 343.

15. Lewis L. Gould, *1968: The Election That Changed America* (Chicago: Ivan R. Dee, 1993), 52; Martin, *It Seems Like Only Yesterday*, 280; Donald Janson, "Branigin to Stay in Race in Indiana," *New York Times*, April 2, 1968; Stan Evans, "Branigin for Vice-President?" *Indianapolis News*, April 19, 1968; Martin, RFK Notes.

16. Martin, RFK Notes; Martin, *It Seems Like Only Yesterday*, 280–82.

17. Martin, RFK Notes.

18. Martin, *It Seems Like Only Yesterday*, 284–85; Guthman and Allen, eds., *RFK*, 358–61.

19. Charles Kaiser, *1968 in America: Music, Politics, Chaos, Counterculture, and the Shaping of a Generation* (New York: Grove Press, 1988), 145; Martin, *It Seems Like Only Yesterday*, 284.

20. Martin, RFK Notes; Martin, *It Seems Like Only Yesterday*, 285.

21. Martin, RFK Notes; John Douglas oral history interview by Larry J. Hackman, June 24, 1969, Washington, D.C., Kennedy Library.

22. Martin, *It Seems Like Only Yesterday*, 287.

23. John Bartlow Martin to Ted Sorenson, April 14, 1968, Martin Papers, Library of Congress; RFK Notes.

24. Douglas oral history.

25. Martin, RFK Notes; Martin, *It Seems Like Only Yesterday*, 288.

26. Martin, *It Seems Like Only Yesterday*, 288–89; Milton Gwirtzman oral history interview by Roberta Greene, April 4, 1972, Washington, D.C., Kennedy Library; Martin, RFK Notes.

27. Martin, *It Seems Like Only Yesterday*, 292–93; Warren Weaver Jr., "Kennedy: Meet the Conservative," *New York Times*, April 28, 1968; Douglas Oral History.

28. Martin, RFK Notes; Martin, *It Seems Like Only Yesterday*, 290.

29. Martin, RFK Notes; Schlesinger, *Robert Kennedy and His Times*, 901; Clarke, *The Last Campaign*, 118–19; Martin, *It Seems Like Only Yesterday*, 298.

30. Douglas oral history; RFK Notes; Martin, *It Seems Like Only Yesterday*, 296–97.

31. Jack Newfield, *Robert Kennedy: A Memoir* (New York: E. P. Dutton, 1969), 263–64; Pierre Salinger, memo to Ted

Sorenson, Tom Johnston, Dun Gifford, May 8, 1968, Robert F. Kennedy 1968 Presidential Campaign Papers, Kennedy Library; Witcover, *85 Days*, 180–81.

32. Martin, RFK Notes.

33. Ibid.

34. Martin, *It Seems Like Only Yesterday*, 299; Martin, RFK Notes; Eugene McCarthy, *The Year of the People* (Garden City, N.Y.: Doubleday and Company, 1969), 143, 149; William Vanden Heuvel and Milton Gwirtzman, *On His Own: Robert F. Kennedy, 1964–1968* (Garden City, N.Y.: Doubleday and Company, 1970), 367; Witcover, *85 Days*, 202, 206.

35. Martin, RFK Notes; Martin, *It Seems Like Only Yesterday*, 299–300.

36. Martin, RFK Notes.

37. Joseph A. Palermo, *In His Own Right: The Political Odyssey of Senator Robert F. Kennedy* (New York: Columbia University Press, 2001), 238; Martin, RFK Notes; Schlesinger, *Robert Kennedy and His Times*, 908; Martin, *It Seems Like Only Yesterday*, 300.

38. Martin, RFK Notes.

39. Kaiser, *1968 in America*, 179; Jean Stein and George Plimpton, *American Journey: The Times of Robert Kennedy* (New York: Harcourt Brace Jovanovich, 1970), 311–12; Martin, RFK Notes.

40. John Bartlow Martin, memo to Robert F. Kennedy, June 3, 1968, Martin Papers, Library of Congress.

41. Martin, *It Seems Like Only Yesterday*, 303–304.

42. Martin, RFK Notes.

43. Wallace Turner, "The Shooting: A Victory Celebration that Ended with Shots, Screams and Curses," *New York Times*, June 6, 1968; Gladwin Hill, "Kennedy is Dead, Victim of Assassin," *New York Times*, June 6, 1968.

44. Martin, RFK Notes; Martin, *It Seems Like Only Yesterday*, 304–305.

45. Ibid.

46. Martin, *It Seems Like Only Yesterday*, 305–306; "Thousands in Last Tribute to Kennedy," *New York Times*; Senator Edward M. Kennedy, Eulogy, June 8, 1968, in Pierre Salinger, Edwin Guthman, Frank Mankiewicz, and John Seigenthaler, eds. *"An Honorable Profession": A Tribute to Robert F. Kennedy*, 3 (Garden City, N.Y.: Doubleday and Company, 1968).

47. Martin, *It Seems Like Only Yesterday*, 306; John Herbers, "Many in Capital Throng Had Cheered Kennedy," *New York Times*, June 9, 1968; "Robert F. Kennedy Memorial," Arlington National Cemetery website, http://www.arlingtoncemetery.org/visitor_information/Robert_F_Kennedy.html/.

48. Martin, *It Seems Like Only Yesterday*, 307; Martin, RFK Notes.

49. Gould, *1968: The Election That Changed America*, 127–29; Lewis Chester, Godfrey Hodgson, and Bruce Page, *An American Melodrama: The Presidential Campaign of 1968* (New York: Viking Press, 1969), 521; Tom Wicker, "Humphrey Nominated on the First Ballot After His Plank on Vietnam is Approved," *New York Times*, August 30, 1968.

50. John Bartlow Martin to George Ball, July 10, 1968, and John Bartlow Martin to Adlai Stevenson III, July 24, 1968, Martin Papers, Library of Congress.

51. John Bartlow Martin, memo to the vice president, August 9, 1968, Martin Papers, Library of Congress.

52. John Bartlow Martin, memorandum on the Hubert Humphrey presidential campaign of 1968, December 14, 1968, Martin Papers, Library of Congress (hereafter cited as Humphrey Memo); Arthur M. Schlesinger Jr., *Journals: 1952–2000* (New York: Penguin Books, 2008), 297; Martin, *It Seems Like Only Yesterday*, 308.

53. Martin, *It Seems Like Only Yesterday*, 298, 307–308.

54. Eisele, *Almost to the Presidency*, 332–33; Gould, *1968: The Election That Changed America*, 65–66, 135.

55. Martin, Humphrey Memo; Martin, *It Seems Like Only Yesterday*, 309; Schlesinger, *Journals*, 299–301; Hubert H. Humphrey, *The Education of a Public Man: My Life and Politics* (Garden City, N.Y.: Doubleday and Company, 1976), 397.

56. Adlai Stevenson III to John Bartlow Martin, September 23, 1968, Martin Papers, Library of Congress.

57. Carol Solbert, *Hubert Humphrey: A Biography* (New York: W. W. Norton and Company, 1984), 373; Ted Van Dyk, *Heroes, Hacks, and Fools: Memoirs from the Political Inside* (Seattle: University of Washington Press, 2007), 84–85; Ted Van Dyk, telephone interview with the author, September 13, 2013.

58. Solbert, *Hubert Humphrey*, 383–84; Van Dyk, *Heroes, Hacks, and Fools*, 88; Martin, Humphrey Memo; Martin, *It Seems Like Only Yesterday*, 308–309.

59. Martin, Humphrey Memo.

60. Ibid.

61. Lawrence O'Brien, *No Final Victories: A Life in Politics – From John F. Kennedy to Watergate* (Garden City, N.Y.: Doubleday and Company, 1974), 262; Martin, Humphrey Memo.

62. Martin, Humphrey Memo.

63. Kaiser, *1968 in America*, 252; Gould, *1968: The Election That Changed America*, 161–62; Van Dyk, *Heroes, Hacks, and Fools*, 95–96.

64. Martin, Humphrey Memo; Martin, *It Seems Like Only Yesterday*, 310.

10. As Time Goes By

1. Jim Borg, e-mail to author, July 22, 2013. See also, Jim Borg, "Steven Stawnychy, 1957–1975," *Chicago Tribune*, April 11, 1976; and "Guard Accused of 'Drop-Kicking' Sailor into Bunk," *Miami News*, August 11, 1975.

2. Jim Borg, e-mail; John Bartlow Martin to Elizabeth Yamashita, November 12, 1975, John Bartlow Martin Papers, 1960–1987, Northwestern University Archives, Evanston, Illinois (hereafter cited as Martin Papers, Northwestern Archives).

3. John Bartlow Martin, *It Seems Like Only Yesterday: Memoirs of Writing, Presidential Politics, and the Diplomatic Life* (New York: William Morrow and Company, 1986), 313–14; Alice W. Snyder, *Inventing Medill: A History of the Medill School of Journalism, Northwestern University, 1921–1996* (Evanston, Ill.: Northwestern University Press, 1996), 149–50; Peter Jacobi, e-mail to author, August 15, 2013.

4. Syllabus for Journalism D26, Independent Writing Projects, Winter Quarter, 1973; John Bartlow Martin to Elizabeth Yamashita, May 31, 1974, Martin Papers, Northwestern Archives; Gregg Easterbrook, telephone interview with the author, July 16, 2013.

5. Easterbrook, interview; Syllabus for Journalism D26.

6. Syllabus for Journalism D26; Martin to Yamashita, May 31, 1974, Martin Papers, Northwestern Archives; and John Bartlow Martin, "The Making of a Killer," *Saturday Evening Post*, March 26, 1955.

7. Martin, *It Seems Like Only Yesterday*, 315–16.

8. Martin, *It Seems Like Only Yesterday*, 314–15, and Martin to Yamashita, May 31, 1974, Martin Papers, Northwestern Archives.

9. Martin, *It Seems Like Only Yesterday*, 314; John Bartlow Martin to Gregg Easterbrook, November 20 and December 28, 1976, Martin Papers, Northwestern Archives; Easterbrook, interview.

10. Niles Howard, telephone interview with the author, February 21, 2014; Niles Howard, "My First Hard Lesson in Journalism," Wall and Main Media Blog, http://wallandmainmedia.com/magazine-article/.

11. Mike Plemmons, e-mail to author, July 24, 2013; Snyder, *Inventing Medill*, 117. In an article on Martin he wrote while working for the *Milwaukee Sentinel*, Plemmons was effusive in praising his mentor, saying of him, "He is the one for whom these fledgling writers stay up nights, the one whose penciled criticisms are treasured like autographs." See Mike Plemmons, "Adlai Biographer is Writers' Mentor," *Milwaukee Sentinel*, November 29, 1977.

12. Martin, *It Seems Like Only Yesterday*, 315, 317; Marc Weingarten, *The Gang That Couldn't Write Straight: Wolfe, Thompson, Didion, and the New Journalism Revolution* (New York: Crown Books, 2006), 6.

13. Martin, *It Seems Like Only Yesterday*, 322; Diana Diamond, "Political Bug: Aide to President, Speech Writer and Biographer of Candidates, Highland Park's Martin was Bitten Early," *Lerner-Life Newspapers*, April 27, 1972; John Bartlow Martin to John Voelker, February 24, 1972, John D. Voelker Papers, Central Upper Michigan Peninsula and Northern Michigan University Archives, Marquette, Michigan (hereafter cited as Voelker Papers).

14. Martin, *It Seems Like Only Yesterday*, 322; George McGovern, *Grassroots: The Autobiography of George McGovern* (New York: Random House, 1977), 169.

15. Bruce Miroff, *The Liberals' Moment: The McGovern Insurgency and the Identity Crisis of the Democratic Party* (Lawrence: University Press of Kansas, 2007), 52–68; Ted Van Dyk, *Heroes, Hacks,*

and Fools: Memoirs from the Political Inside (Seattle: University of Washington Press, 2007), 134; Scott Farris, *Almost President: The Men Who Lost the Race But Changed the Nation* (Guilford, Conn.: Lyons Press, 2011), 213. In an April 1972 article, conservative columnist Robert Novak had quoted an unnamed Democratic senator saying about McGovern, "The people don't know McGovern is for amnesty, abortion, and legalization of pot. Once middle America–Catholic middle America, in particular–finds this out, he's dead." This was the source for the charge that McGovern was the candidate of "amnesty, abortion, and acid." Ironically, Novak asserted in July 2007 that the quote came from Eagleton, who had died on March 4, 2007. See Terry Ganey, "A Slice of History," *Columbia (Mo.) Daily Tribune*, August 19, 2007.

16. Theodore H. White, *The Making of the President 1972* (New York: Atheneum Publishers, 1973), 199; Ganey, "A Slice of History"; Gary Hart, *Right from the Start: A Chronicle of the McGovern Campaign* (New York: Quadrangle/The New York Times Book Company, 1973), 264–65.

17. Miroff, *The Liberal's Moment*, 89–96; McGovern, *Grassroots*, 215.

18. Martin, *It Seems Like Only Yesterday*, 323; Hart, *Right from the Start*, 281; John Bartlow Martin to Fran Martin, September 13, 1972, Martin Papers, Manuscripts Division, Library of Congress, Washington, D.C. (hereafter cited as Martin Papers, Library of Congress); Lawrence O'Brien, *No Final Victories: A Life in Politics – From John F. Kennedy to Watergate* (Garden City, N.Y.: Doubleday and Company, 1974), 324–25.

19. Robert Shrum, *No Excuses: Concessions of a Serial Campaigner* (New York: Simon & Schuster, 2007), 37; Martin, *It Seems Like Only Yesterday*, 322.

20. John Bartlow Martin, memorandums on McGovern campaign, October 19 and 26 and November 7, 1972, Martin Papers, Library of Congress; Ted Van Dyk, telephone interview with the author, September 13, 2013; White, *The Making of the President, 1972*, 316.

21. Martin, memorandums of October 19 and 26; Ted Van Dyk, memorandum to George McGovern, August 23, 1972, Martin Papers, Library of Congress; Hart, *Right from the Start*, 289.

22. Gil Troy, *See How They Ran: The Changing Role of the Presidential Candidates* (Cambridge, Mass.: Harvard University Press, 1996), 227; Van Dyk, *Heroes, Hacks, and Fools*, 141, 145; John Bartlow Martin, memorandum on McGovern campaign, October 30, 1972, Martin Papers, Library of Congress.

23. Martin, memorandums of October 19 and November 7.

24. Ibid.

25. Martin, November 7 memorandum.

26. Van Dyk, *Heroes, Hacks, and Fools*, 147; Shrum, *No Excuses*, 52; and Martin, November 7 memorandum.

27. Martin, November 7 memorandum; Joe Gandelman, "My Personal Watergate Memories," The Moderate Voice website, http://themoderatevoice.com/3039/my-personal-watergate-memories/.

28. Martin, *It Seems Like Only Yesterday*, 325–31; and Paul McGrath, "'Factfinder' Martin Still Hunts for History," *Chicago Sun-Times*, March 21, 1976.

29. Susan Drake and Sharron Karrow, "Writing the Wrongs: Stevenson's Biographer Makes People the Issue," *Byline: Northwestern's Journalism Magazine* 11 (Spring 1976): 7; Martin, *It Seems Like Only Yesterday*, 313; "NU Professor Recalls Events Leading to Writing Biography of Adlai Stevenson," Northwestern University news release, April 23,

1976, Martin Papers, Northwestern Archives.

30. John Bartlow Martin to Dorothy Olding, March 6, 1975, Martin Papers, Library of Congress.

31. Martin, *It Seems Like Only Yesterday*, 311; Samuel S. Vaughan to John Bartlow Martin, March 27, 1975, Martin Papers, Library of Congress; John Bartlow Martin, *Adlai Stevenson of Illinois: The Life of Adlai E. Stevenson* (Garden City, N.Y.: Doubleday and Company, 1976), vii.

32. Arthur M. Schlesinger Jr., "John Bartlow Martin, 1915–1987," in *The Century Yearbook* (New York: The Century Association, 1987), 266; Jeff Broadwater, *Adlai Stevenson and American Politics: The Odyssey of a Cold War Liberal* (New York: Twayne Publishers, 1994), 272; John Kenneth Galbraith, "Adlai Stevenson of Illinois," *New York Times Book Review*, March 7, 1976; Edwin Warner, "Living for Two," *Time*, March 22, 1976, http://content.time.com/timemagazine/article/0,9171,911796,00.html/; Ben Cole, "Adlai Stevenson of Illinois Combines Vividness, Candor," *Indianapolis Star*, May 16, 1976.

33. Martin, *It Seems Like Only Yesterday*, 263, 312–13; Elaine Snyderman, "Biographer Martin Explores Stevenson Mystique," May 6, 1976, article in unnamed newspaper, Martin Papers, Library of Congress.

34. Martin, *It Seems Like Only Yesterday*, 320; John Bartlow Martin to John Voelker, January 11, 1973, Voelker Papers; John Bartlow Martin to Dorothy Olding, December 6, 1975, Martin Papers, Library of Congress.

35. Martin, *It Seems Like Only Yesterday*, 343–44; John Bartlow Martin to John Voelker, April 26, 1977, Voelker Papers.

36. John Bartlow Martin to Dorothy Olding, December 5, 1980, Memo on

Memoirs, Martin Papers, Library of Congress; Martin, *It Seems Like Only Yesterday,* 344; William Brashler, "A Fast-Paced Political Melodrama," *Chicago Tribune,* February 17, 1980; John Bartlow Martin, *The Televising of Heller* (Garden City, N.Y.: Doubleday and Company, 1980), 278.

37. Martin, *It Seems Like Only Yesterday,* 344; Schlesinger, "John Bartlow Martin, 1915–1987," 266.

38. Elen Torgerson Shaw, "TV Bookshelf," *TV Guide,* July 12, 1980; Martin, *It Seems Like Only Yesterday,* 345.

39. Martin, *It Seems Like Only Yesterday,* 345; Memo on Memoirs.

40. John Bartlow Martin to John Voelker, August 25, 1985, Voelker Papers; Lester Bernstein, "Two Cents a Word," *New York Times,* October 12, 1986; Herman Kogan, "Stories from a Life at the Typewriter," *Chicago Sun-Times,* September 28, 1986; Robert A. Lincoln, "Author's Memoirs Yield Guidebook to Good Writing," *Richmond (Va.) Times-Dispatch,* October 5, 1986.

41. John Bartlow Martin to Arthur Schlesinger Jr., January 15, 1978, John Bartlow Martin, memorandum on medical history to Doctor Saul A. Mackler, January 1, 1979, and John Bartlow Martin, memorandum on recent medical history, March 25, 1979, Martin Papers, Library of Congress; Martin, *It Seems Like Only Yesterday,* 342–43.

42. John Bartlow Martin to John Voelker, March 6, 1983, June 24, 1984, and May 20, 1985, Voelker Papers; Dan Martin, e-mail to author, March 24, 2014.

43. Martin, *It Seems Like Only Yesterday,* 320, 341; Fred Martin, memorandum to author, October 8, 2013.

44. Schlesinger, "John Bartlow Martin, 1915–1987," 267. In his private journal, Schlesinger lamented the damage inflicted on his friends by cigarettes. In addition to Martin, other friends whose lives had been cut short because of "Lady Nicotine" included Steve Smith, Mary McCarthy, Joe Alsop, John Huston, Ed Murrow, Humphrey Bogart, Yul Brynner, Alan Lerner, and Jimmy Wechsler. "So many good people might still be alive had they never succumbed," Schlesinger noted. See Arthur M. Schlesinger Jr., *Journals: 1952–2000* (New York: Penguin Books, 2008), 695.

Selected Bibliography

MAJOR WORKS BY JOHN
BARTLOW MARTIN

Author's Note: These works are arranged in chronological, instead of alphabetical, order to showcase Martin's growth as a writer.

Books

Call It North Country: The Story of Upper Michigan. New York: Alfred A. Knopf, 1944. Reprint, Detroit, Mich.: Wayne State University Press, 1986.

Indiana: An Intepretation. New York: Alfred A. Knopf, 1947.

Butcher's Dozen, and Other Murders. New York: Harper and Brothers, 1950.

Adlai Stevenson. New York: Harper and Brothers, 1952.

My Life in Crime: The Autobiography of a Professional Criminal. New York: Harper and Row, 1952.

Why Did They Kill? New York: Ballantine Books, 1953.

Break Down the Walls: American Prisons: Present, Past, and Future. New York: Ballantine Books, 1954.

The Deep South Says "Never." New York: Ballantine Books, 1957.

Jimmy Hoffa's Hot. Greenwich, Conn.: Fawcett Publications, 1959.

The Pane of Glass. New York: Harper and Brothers, 1959.

Overtaken by Events: The Dominican Crisis from the Fall of Trujillo to the Civil War. New York: Doubleday and Company, 1966.

Presidential Television. With Lee Miller and Newton Minow. New York: Basic Books, 1973.

Adlai Stevenson of Illinois: The Life of Adlai E. Stevenson. Garden City, N.Y.: Doubleday and Company, 1976.

Adlai Stevenson and the World: The Life of Adlai E. Stevenson. Garden City, N.Y.: Doubleday and Company, 1977.

U.S. Policy in the Caribbean. Boulder, Colo.: Westview Press, 1978.

The Televising of Heller. Garden City, N.Y.: Doubleday and Company, 1980.

It Seems Like Only Yesterday: Memoirs of Writing, Presidential Politics, and the Diplomatic Life. New York: William Morrow and Company, 1986.

Articles

"The Return from Manila." Ken, May 18, 1939.

"Don't Call My Boy a Murderer." Actual Detective Stories, November 1939.

"Blasting the Mollies Reign of Terror." Official Detective Stories, February 1940–November 1941.

"The Cards They Say Love – and Death." *Actual Detective Stories,* July 1940.

"This Was My Boy Johnnie." *Official Detective Stories,* February 1941 (as H. L. Spade).

"Heroes of the Crime Laboratory." *Official Detective Stories,* March 1942.

"They Sent a Woman to Catch a Woman." *Actual Detective Stories,* June 1942.

"The Making of a Nazi Saboteur." *Harper's,* April 1943.

"Don't Go Trout Fishing." *Outdoor Life,* May 1943.

"Rocky Road to Smallmouths." *Outdoor Life,* July 1943.

"The Polkadot Gang." *Harper's,* September 1943.

"Master of the Murder Castle." *Harper's,* December 1943.

"The Great Gold Conspiracy." *Harper's,* April 1944.

"Heroes of the Inland Seas." *Esquire,* April 1944.

"A New Attack on Delinquency." *Harper's,* May 1944.

"Who Killed Estelle Carey?" *Harper's,* June 1944.

"Is Muncie Still Middletown?" *Harper's,* July 1944.

"Beauty and the Beast." *Harper's,* September 1944.

"Colonel McCormick of the *Tribune.*" *Harper's,* October 1944.

"$5,000 to Break a $1,000,000 Ring." *Official Detective Stories,* November 1944 (as H. L. Spade).

"Boy Hunt." *Harper's,* December 1944.

"Today We Take Up Your Ally, Russia." *Harper's,* August 1945.

"A Rabbit Running." *Outdoor Life,* October 1945.

"Anything Bothering You, Soldier?" *Harper's,* November 1945.

"Peekaboo Pennington, Private Eye." *Harper's,* May 1946.

"Middletown Revisited." *Harper's,* August 1946.

"Murder of a Journalist." *Harper's,* September 1946.

"Catch Me Before I Kill More." *Official Detective Stories,* November 1946–April 1947.

"A Gentleman from Indiana." *Harper's,* January 1947.

"The McNear Murder." *Harper's,* July 1947.

"There Goes Upper Michigan." *Harper's,* December 1947.

"The Blast in Centralia No. 5." *Harper's,* March 1948.

"End of a Boy's Life." *McCall's,* July 1948.

"The Hickman Story." *Harper's,* August 1948.

"What the Miners Say about John L. Lewis." *Saturday Evening Post,* January 15, 1949.

"Certain Wise Men." *McCall's,* March 1949.

"The Trials of Axis Sally." *McCall's,* June 1949.

"Incident at Fernwood." *Harper's,* October 1949.

"Have You Seen Orja Corns?" *Saturday Evening Post,* March 4, 1950.

"The Sheltons: America's Bloodiest Gang." *Saturday Evening Post,* March 18, 1950.

"Criminal at Large." *Saturday Evening Post,* May 27, 1950.

"South Pacific." *Cosmopolitan,* May 1950.

"A Burglar's Advice." *McCall's,* June 1950.

"The Big Uranium Rush of 1950." *Saturday Evening Post,* November 18, 1950.

"The Strangest Place in Chicago." *Harper's,* December 1950.

"The Kirsten Flagstad Story." *Cosmopolitan,* December 1950.

"Train Ride in Guatemala." *Cosmopolitan,* January 1951.

"He Was a Stool Pigeon!" *Saturday Evening Post,* March 24, 1951.

"How Corrupt Is Chicago?" *Saturday Evening Post*, March 31, 1951.

"The Case of Anne Milton, Ex-Convict." *Saturday Evening Post*, July 7, 1951.

"America's Toughest Prison." *Saturday Evening Post*, October 20–November 3, 1951.

"North to Find Iron." *Harper's*, December 1951, January 1952.

"Life and Death in Coaltown." *New York Times Magazine*, January 13, 1952.

"The Northlake Outrage." *Saturday Evening Post*, January 19, 1952.

"The Treasure Pits of Upper Michigan." *Saturday Evening Post*, February 16, 1952.

"Death on M-24." *Saturday Evening Post*, April 5, 1952.

"Why Did They Kill?" *Saturday Evening Post*, June 14–July 5, 1952.

"The Drafting of Adlai Stevenson." With Eric Larrabee. *Harper's*, October 1952.

"The Moretti Case." *Saturday Evening Post*, December 6–20, 1952.

"How Lincoln Came Alive for Us." *Saturday Evening Post*, April 18, 1952.

"Why Did It Happen: The Riot at Jackson Prison." *Saturday Evening Post*, June 6–27, 1953.

"Backstage at the Statehouse: What Those Politicians Do To You!" *Saturday Evening Post*, December 12–26, 1953.

"Prison: The Enemy of Society." *Harper's*, April 1954.

"Wilderness North of Chicago." *Harper's*, May 1954.

"Crisis in Coaltown." *Saturday Evening Post*, September 18, 1954.

"The Making of a Killer." *Saturday Evening Post*, March 26, 1955.

"Murder on His Conscience." *Saturday Evening Post*, April 2–23, 1955.

"The Town That Reformed," *Saturday Evening Post*, October 1, 1955.

"Adlai Girds for Battle." *Saturday Evening Post*, October 22, 1955.

"Who Really Runs Chicago?" *Saturday Evening Post*, November 19–26, 1955.

"Inside the Asylum." *Saturday Evening Post*, October 6–November 10, 1956.

"The Deep South Says 'Never!'" *Saturday Evening Post*, June 15–July 13, 1957.

"The Mother Who Lived a Miracle." *McCall's*, November 1957.

"Robert Traver." *Book-of-the-Month-Club News*, December 1957.

"The Changing Midwest." *Saturday Evening Post*, January 11–February 1, 1958.

"The Strange Boy." *Look*, August 5, 1958.

"Divorce." *Saturday Evening Post*, November 1–22, 1958.

"A Better Break for the Mentally Ill." *Harper's*, February 1959.

"The Struggle to Get Hoffa." *Saturday Evening Post*, June 27–August 8, 1959.

"The Innocent and the Guilty." *Saturday Evening Post*, July 30–August 27, 1960.

"To Chicago, With Love." *Saturday Evening Post*, October 15, 1960.

"Crime Without Reason." *Saturday Evening Post*, November 5, 1960.

"Abortion." *Saturday Evening Post*, May 20–June 3, 1961.

"Television U.S.A.: Wasteland or Wonderland? A Famous Writer's Close-up Report on the Controversial State of T v." *Saturday Evening Post*, October 21, 1961.

"The Dominican Upheaval." *Life*, May 28, 1965.

"My Chicago." *Holiday*, March 1967.

"The Criminal Mentality." *Playboy*, January 1968.

"In the House That Adlai Loved." *Life*, March 28, 1969.

"Seashells from East and West." *Life*, May 2, 1969.

"Strange Journey to Finland." *Holiday*, October 1969.

"Election of 1964." In Arthur M. Schlesinger Jr., editor, *History of American Presidential Elections, 1789–2001:*

1960–1968. Volume 9. 1971. Reprint, Philadelphia: Chelsea House Publishers, 2002.

"One Nation, Indomitable." *Chicago Tribune Magazine*, April 27, 1975.

"A Commonwealth's Choice." *Harper's*, December 1977.

"The Heartland's Backyard Frontier: Upper Michigan." *Chicago Tribune*, July 31, 1983.

MANUSCRIPT COLLECTIONS

Benjamin Franklin Magazine Awards File, 1953–1958. University of Illinois at Urbana-Champaign Archives, Urbana-Champaign, Ill.

John Bartlow Martin Papers. Manuscript Division, Library of Congress, Washington, D.C.

John Bartlow Martin Papers, 1960–1987. Northwestern University Archives, Evanston, Ill.

John D. Voelker Papers. Central Upper Michigan Peninsula and Northern Michigan University Archives, Marquette, Mich.

ORAL HISTORY INTERVIEWS

Harry Truman Library and Museum, Independence, Mo.
David C. Bell, October 16, 1968
Carl McGowan, July 27, 1960

John F. Kennedy Presidential Library, Boston, Mass.
John Douglas, June 24, 1969
Myer Feldman, February 27, 1966
Milton Gwirtzman, April 4, 1972
William Haddad, February 27, 1969
Joseph Kraft, January 9, 1967
Walter Sheridan, March 23, 1970

Lyndon Baines Johnson Presidential Library, Austin, Tex.
John Bartlow Martin, January 30, 1971
McGeorge Bundy, March 19, 1969

ARTICLES

Baughman, James L. "Minow's Viewers: Understanding the Response to the 'Vast Wasteland' Address." *Federal Communications Law Journal* 55, issue 3 (2003): 449–58.

Bernstein, Barton J. "Election of 1952." In *History of American Presidential Elections, 1789–2001*, edited by Arthur M. Schlesinger Jr. Volume 8. Philadelphia: Chelsea House Publishers, 2002.

Boomhower, Ray E. "A Voice for Those from Below: John Bartlow Martin, Reporter." *Traces of Indiana and Midwestern History* 10 (Spring 1997): 4–13.

Drake, Susan, and Sharron Karrow. "Writing the Wrongs: Stevenson's Biographer Makes People the Issue." *Byline: Northwestern's Journalism Magazine* 11 (Spring 1976): 7–8.

Fischer, John. "A Footnote on Adlai Stevenson." *Harper's*, November 1965, 18–29.

Fleege, Anthony. "The 1947 Centralia Mine Disaster." *Journal of the Illinois State Historical Society* 102 (Summer 2009): 163–76.

Kauffmann, Stanley. "Capote in Kansas." *New Republic*, January 22, 1966, 19–23.

Kuenster, John. "John Bartlow Martin: The Responsible Reporter." *The Voice of Saint Jude: A National Catholic Monthly* 28 (April 1960): 34–39.

Markisohn, Deborah B. "Great Depression." In *Encyclopedia of Indianapolis*, edited by David J. Bodenhamer and Robert G. Barrows. Bloomington: Indiana University Press, 1994.

Martin, John Frederick. "John Bartlow Martin." *The American Scholar* 59 (Winter 1990): 95–100.

McPherson, Alan. "Misled by Himself: What the Johnson Tapes Reveal about the Dominican Intervention of 1965." *Latin American Research Review* 38, no. 2: 127–46.

Schlesinger, Arthur M. Jr. "John Bartlow Martin, 1915–1987." In *The Century Yearbook*. New York: Century Association, 1987.

Shankle, Greta E. "Marott Hotel." In *Encyclopedia of Indianapolis*, edited by David J. Bodenhamer and Robert G. Barrows. Bloomington: Indiana University Press, 1994.

Sherman, John. *"Indianapolis Times."* In *Encyclopedia of Indianapolis*, edited by David J. Bodenhamer and Robert G. Barrows. Bloomington: Indiana University Press, 1994.

Stahly, Ted. "Arsenal Technical High School." In *Encyclopedia of Indianapolis*, edited by David J. Bodenhamer and Robert G. Barrows. Bloomington: Indiana University Press, 1994.

Szulc, Tad. "When the Marines Stormed Ashore in Santo Domingo." *Saturday Evening Post*, July 31, 1965.

BOOKS

Atkins, G. Pope, and Larman C. Wilson. *The Dominican Republic and the United States: From Imperialism to Transnationalism.* Athens: University of Georgia Press, 1998.

Boomhower, Ray E. *Robert F. Kennedy and the 1968 Indiana Primary.* Bloomington: Indiana University Press, 2008.

Bornet, Vaughn Davis. *The Presidency of Lyndon B. Johnson.* Lawrence: University Press of Kansas, 1983.

Bosch, Juan. *The Unfinished Experiment: Democracy in the Dominican Republic.* New York: Frederick A. Praeger, 1965.

Broadwater, Jeff. *Adlai Stevenson and American Politics: The Odyssey of a Cold War Liberal.* New York: Twayne Publishers, 1994.

Caro, Robert A. *The Years of Lyndon Johnson: The Passage of Power.* New York: Alfred A. Knopf, 2012.

Chester, Eric Thomas. *Rag-Tags, Scum, Riff-Raff, and Commies: The U.S. Intervention in the Dominican Republic, 1965–66.* New York: Monthly Review Press, 2001.

Chester, Lewis, Godfrey Hodgson, and Bruce Page. *An American Melodrama: The Presidential Campaign of 1968.* New York: Viking Press, 1969.

Clarke, Thurston. *The Last Campaign: Robert F. Kennedy and 82 Days That Inspired America.* New York: Henry Holt and Company, 2008.

Cohen, Adam, and Elizabeth Taylor. *American Pharaoh: Mayor Richard J. Daley: His Battle for Chicago and the Nation.* Boston: Little, Brown and Company, 2000.

Cooney, John. *The Annenbergs: The Salvaging of a Tainted Dynasty.* New York: Simon & Schuster, 1982.

Dallek, Robert. *Lyndon B. Johnson: Portrait of a President.* New York: Oxford University Press, 2004.

Davis, Kenneth S. *The Politics of Honor: A Biography of Adlai E. Stevenson.* New York: G. P. Putnam's Sons, 1967.

Dobbs, Michael. *Saboteurs: The Nazi Raid on America.* New York: Alfred A. Knopf, 2004.

Donaldson, Gary A. *The First Modern Campaign: Kennedy, Nixon, and the Election of 1960.* Lanham, Md.: Rowman & Littlefield Publishers, 2007.

———. *Liberalism's Last Hurrah: The Presidential Campaign of 1964.* Armonk, N.Y.: M. E. Sharpe, 2003.

Dyja, Thomas L. *The Third Coast: When Chicago Built the American Dream*. New York: The Penguin Press, 2013.

Eisele, Albert. *Almost to the Presidency: A Biography of Two American Politicians*. Blue Earth, Minn.: The Piper Company, 1972.

Farris, Scott. *Almost President: The Men Who Lost the Race but Changed the Nation*. Guilford, Conn.: Lyons Press, 2012.

Frank, Jeffrey. *Ike and Dick: Portrait of a Strange Political Marriage*. New York: Simon & Schuster, 2013.

Galbraith, John Kenneth. *A Life in Our Times: Memoirs*. Boston: Houghton Mifflin Company, 1981.

Goodwin, Richard N. *Remembering America: A Voice from the Sixties*. Boston: Little, Brown and Company, 1988.

Gould, Lewis L. *1968: The Election That Changed America*. Chicago: Ivan R. Dee, 1993.

Gormley, Ken. *Archibald Cox: Conscience of a Nation*. Reading, Mass.: Addison-Wesley, 1997.

Greenfeld, Howard. *Ben Shahn: An Artist's Life*. New York: Random House, 1998.

Guthman, Edwin. *We Band of Brothers*. New York: Harper and Row Publishers, 1971.

Guthman, Edwin, and C. Richard Allen, eds. *RFK: Collected Speeches*. New York: Viking, 1993.

Hart, Gary. *Right from the Start: A Chronicle of the McGovern Campaign*. New York: Quadrangle/New York Times Book Company, 1973.

Henggeler, Paul R. *In His Steps: Lyndon Johnson and the Kennedy Mystique*. Chicago: Ivan R. Dee, 1991.

Herzog, Arthur. *McCarthy for President*. New York: Viking Press, 1969.

Heuvel, William Vanden, and Milton Gwirtzman. *On His Own: Robert F. Kennedy, 1964–1968*. Garden City, N.Y.: Doubleday and Company, 1970.

Higdon, Hal. *The Crime of the Century: The Leopold and Loeb Case*. New York: G. P. Putnam's Sons, 1975.

Horgan, Paul. *Tracings: A Book of Partial Portraits*. New York: Farrar, Straus and Giroux, 1993.

Houseman, John. *Unfinished Business: Memoirs: 1902–1988*. New York: Applause Theatre Book Publishers, 1989.

Humphrey, Hubert H. *The Education of a Public Man: My Life and Politics*. Garden City, N.Y.: Doubleday and Company, 1976.

Johnson, Lyndon Baines. *The Vantage Point: Perspectives of the Presidency, 1963–1969*. New York: Holt, Rinehart, and Winston, 1971.

Johnson, Robert David. *All the Way with LBJ: The 1964 Presidential Election*. New York: Cambridge University Press, 2009.

Kaiser, Charles. *1968 in America: Music, Politics, Chaos, Counterculture, and the Shaping of a Generation*. New York: Grove Press, 1988.

Kearns, Doris. *Lyndon Johnson and the American Dream*. New York: Harper and Row, 1976.

Kennedy, Robert F. *The Enemy Within*. New York: Harper and Brothers, 1960.

Kurzman, Dan. *Santo Domingo: Revolt of the Damned*. New York: G. P. Putnam's Sons, 1965.

LaFeber, Walter. *The Deadly Bet: LBJ, Vietnam, and the 1968 Election*. Lanham, Md.: Rowman & Littlefield Publishers, 2005.

Lagemann Snodgrass, Marjorie. *The First Fifty Years: 1912–1962: An Oral History*. Indianapolis, Ind.: Arsenal Technical High School [1994].

Leary, Edward A. *Indianapolis: The Story of a City*. Indianapolis, Ind.: Bobbs-Merrill Company, 1971.

Levin, Meyer. *The Obsession*. New York: Simon & Schuster, 1973.

Lowenthal, Abraham F. *The Dominican Intervention*. Baltimore, Md.: Johns Hopkins University Press, 1994.

Madison, James H. *Indiana through Tradition and Change: A History of the Hoosier State and Its People, 1920–1945*. Indianapolis: Indiana Historical Society, 1982.

Manchester, William. *The Glory and the Dream: A Narrative History of America, 1932–1972*. New York: Bantam Books, 1975.

Margolis, Jon. *The Last Innocent Year: America in 1964: The Beginning of the 'Sixties.'* New York: William and Morrow Company, 1999.

Matthews, Chris. *Jack Kennedy: Elusive Hero*. New York: Simon & Schuster, 2011.

Mattson, Kevin. *Just Plain Dick: Richard Nixon's Checkers Speech and the "Rocking, Socking" Election of 1952*. New York: Bloomsbury, 2012.

McCarthy, Eugene. *The Year of the People*. Garden City, N.Y.: Doubleday and Company, 1969.

McCullough, David. *Truman*. New York: Simon & Schuster, 1992.

McGovern, George. *Grassroots: The Autobiography of George McGovern*. New York: Random House, 1977.

Miroff, Bruce. *The Liberals' Moment: The McGovern Insurgency and the Identity Crisis of the Democratic Party*. Lawrence: University Press of Kansas, 2007.

Mollenhoff, Clark R. *Tentacles of Power: The Story of Jimmy Hoffa*. Cleveland, Ohio: World Publishing Company, 1965.

Moskin, J. Robert. *American Statecraft: The Story of the U.S. Foreign Service*. New York: Thomas Dunne Books, 2013.

Newfield, Jack. *Robert Kennedy: A Memoir*. New York: E. P. Dutton, 1969.

Newton, Jim. *Eisenhower: The White House Years*. New York: Doubleday, 2011.

Niblack, John Lewis. *The Life and Times of a Hoosier Judge*. [Indianapolis, Ind.: privately printed, 1973].

Oberdorfer, Don. *Tet! The Turning Point in the Vietnam War*. Baltimore: Johns Hopkins University Press, 2001.

O'Brien, Lawrence. *No Final Victories: A Life in Politics – From John F. Kennedy to Watergate*. Garden City, N.Y.: Doubleday and Company, 1974.

O'Day, Anita. *High Times, Hard Times*. With George Eells. New York: Limelight Editions, 2007.

O'Donnell, Kenneth P., and David F. Powers. *"Johnny, We Hardly Knew Ye": Memories of John Fitzgerald Kennedy*. With Joe McCarthy. Boston: Little, Brown and Company, 1972.

Palermo, Joseph A. *In His Own Right: The Political Odyssey of Senator Robert F. Kennedy*. New York: Columbia University Press, 2001.

Palmer, Bruce Jr. *Intervention in the Caribbean: The Dominican Crisis of 1965*. Lexington: University Press of Kentucky, 1989.

Payne, Darwin. *The Man of Only Yesterday: Frederick Lewis Allen*. New York: Harper and Row, 1975.

Persico, Joseph E. *Roosevelt's Secret War: FDR and World War II Espionage*. New York: Random House, 2001.

Peters, Charles. *Lyndon B. Johnson*. The American Presidents Series. New York: Times Books, 2010.

Peterson, Theodore. *Magazines in the Twentieth Century.* Urbana: University of Illinois Press, 1964.

Plimpton, George. *Truman Capote: In Which His Friends, Enemies, Acquaintances, and Detractors Recall His Turbulent Career.* New York: Nan A. Talese, 1997.

Pohl, Frances K. *Ben Shahn: New Deal Artist in a Cold War Climate, 1947–1954.* Austin: University of Texas Press, 1989.

Polito, Robert. *Savage Art: A Biography of Jim Thompson.* New York: Vintage Books, 1996.

Rabe, Stephen G. *The Most Dangerous Area in the World: John F. Kennedy Confronts Communist Revolution in Latin America.* Chapel Hill: University of North Carolina Press, 1999.

Richardson, Elmo. *The Presidency of Dwight D. Eisenhower.* Lawrence: Regents Press of Kansas, 1979.

Roberts, Charles. *LBJ's Inner Circle.* New York: Delacorte Press, 1965.

Rorabaugh, W. J. *The Real Making of the President: Kennedy, Nixon, and the 1960 Election.* Lawrence: University Press of Kansas, 2009.

Salinger, Pierre. *With Kennedy.* Garden City, N.Y.: Doubleday and Company, 1966.

Salinger, Pierre, Edwin Guthman, Frank Mankiewicz, and John Seigenthaler, eds. *"An Honorable Profession": A Tribute to Robert F. Kennedy.* Garden City, N.Y.: Doubleday and Company, 1968.

Schlesinger, Andrew, and Stephen Schlesinger, eds. *The Letters of Arthur Schlesinger Jr.* New York: Random House, 2013.

Schlesinger, Arthur M. Jr. *Journals: 1952–2000.* New York: Penguin Books, 2008.

——. *Robert Kennedy and His Times.* Boston: Houghton Mifflin Company, 1978.

——. *A Thousand Days: John F. Kennedy in the White House.* New York: Fawcett Premier, 1971.

Shrum, Robert. *No Excuses: Concessions of a Serial Campaigner.* New York: Simon & Schuster, 2007.

Smith, Jean Edward. *Eisenhower in War and Peace.* New York: Random House, 2012.

Snyder, Alice W. *Inventing Medill: A History of the Medill School of Journalism, Northwestern University, 1921–1996.* Evanston, Ill.: Northwestern University, 1996.

Solbert, Carol. *Hubert Humphrey: A Biography.* New York: W. W. Norton and Company, 1984.

Sorensen, Ted. *Counselor: A Life at the Edge of History.* New York: HarperCollins Publishers, 2008.

——. *Kennedy.* New York: Harper and Row Publishers, 1965.

Stein, Jean, and George Plimpton. *American Journey: The Times of Robert Kennedy.* New York: Harcourt Brace Jovanovich, 1970.

Szulc, Tad. *Dominican Diary.* New York: Delacorte Press, 1965.

Taffet, Jeffrey F. *Foreign Aid as Foreign Policy: The Alliance for Progress in Latin America.* New York: Routledge, 2007.

Thomas, Evan. *Robert Kennedy: His Life.* New York: Simon & Schuster, 2000.

Thornbrough, Emma Lou. *Indiana Blacks in the Twentieth Century.* Bloomington: Indiana University Press, 2000.

Troy, Gil. *See How They Ran: The Changing Role of the Presidential Candidates.* Cambridge, Mass.: Harvard University Press, 1996.

Updegrove, Mark K. *Indomitable Will: LBJ in the Presidency.* New York: Crown Publishers, 2012.

Van Dyk, Ted. *Heroes, Hacks, and Fools: Memoirs from the Political Inside.* Seattle: University of Washington Press, 2007.

Wainstock, Dennis. *The Turning Point: The 1968 United States Presidential Campaign.* Jefferson, N.C.: McFarland and Company, 1988.

Warren, Sidney. *The Battle for the Presidency.* Philadelphia: J. B. Lippincott Company, 1968.

Watson, Mary Ann. *The Expanding Vista: American Television in the Kennedy Years.* New York: Oxford University Press, 1990.

Weber, Ronald. *Hired Pens: Professional Writers in America's Golden Age of Print.* Athens: Ohio University Press, 1997.

Weil, Gordon L. *The Long Shot: George McGovern Runs for President.* New York: W. W. Norton and Company, 1973.

Weingarten, Marc. *The Gang That Couldn't Write Straight: Wolfe, Thompson, Didion, and the New Journalism Revolution.* New York: Crown Books, 2006.

White, Theodore H. *The Making of the President, 1960.* New York: Book-of-the-Month Club, 1988.

———. *The Making of the President 1972.* New York: Atheneum Publishers, 1973.

Witcover, Jules. *85 Days: The Last Campaign of Robert Kennedy.* New York: Quill, 1988.

———. *The Year the Dream Died: Revisiting 1968 in America.* New York: Warner Books, 1997.

Wilson, Edmund. *The Sixties: The Last Journal, 1960–1972.* New York: Farrar, Straus and Giroux, 1993.

Woods, Randall B. *LBJ: Architect of American Ambition.* New York: Free Press, 2006.

Yagoda, Ben. *About Town: The New Yorker and the World It Made.* New York: Scribner, 2000.

Index

RAY E. BOOMHOWER is the author of numerous books and articles on Indiana history, including *Robert F. Kennedy and the 1968 Indiana Primary* (IUP, 2008) and *The People's Choice: Congressman Jim Jontz of Indiana* (2012). In addition, he is the author of biographies on such notable figures as Gus Grissom, Ernie Pyle, and Lew Wallace. Boomhower is the senior editor for *Traces of Indiana and Midwestern History*, the quarterly magazine of the Indiana Historical Society. In 2010 he received the Regional Author Award in the annual Eugene and Marilyn Glick Indiana Authors Awards.